THREE BY ANNIE DILLARD

Encounters with Chinese Writers

Teaching a Stone to Talk

Living by Fiction

Holy the Firm

Tickets for a Prayer Wheel

THREE BY
ANNIE DILLARD

ANNIE DILLARD

HarperPerennial
A Division of HarperCollins*Publishers*

Grateful acknowledgment is made to the following for permission to reprint excerpts from these books:

Dodd, Mead & Company, Inc., for selections from *The Insect World of J. Henri Fabre,* selected and edited by Edwin Way Teale; *Days Without Time* by Edwin Way Teale; *The Strange Lives of Familiar Insects* by Edwin Way Teale.

Methuen & Co. Ltd. for selections from *Space and Sight* by Marius von Senden.

Portions of *Pilgrim at Tinker Creek* previously appeared in the following publications: *The Atlantic, Harper's Magazine, Travel and Leisure, Sports Illustrated, Prose, The Christian Science Monitor, The Carolina Quarterly, The Living Wilderness, Cosmopolitan.*

Parts of *An American Childhood* have appeared, in different form, in the *New York Times Magazine, American Heritage Magazine,* and the *New York Times Book Review.*

Excerpts from *The Writing Life* appeared in *Black Warrior Review, Esquire,* the *New York Times Book Review, Tikkun,* and *TriQuarterly.*

The Writing Life was originally published in 1989 by Harper & Row, Publishers. *An American Childhood* was originally published in 1987 by Harper & Row, Publishers. *Pilgrim at Tinker Creek* was originally published in 1974 by Harper's Magazine Press in association with Harper & Row, Publishers.

First HarperPerennial edition published 1990.

LIBRARY OF CONGRESS CATALOG CARD NUMBER 90-55495

ISBN 0-06-092064-5

90 91 92 93 94 CC/FG 10 9 8 7 6 5 4 3 2 1

CONTENTS

PILGRIM AT
TINKER CREEK

for Richard

It ever was, and is, and shall be,
ever-living Fire, in measures being
kindled and in measures going out.

HERACLITUS

CONTENTS

CHAPTER 1

Heaven and Earth in Jest

I USED TO HAVE a cat, an old fighting tom, who would jump through the open window by my bed in the middle of the night and land on my chest. I'd half-awaken. He'd stick his skull under my nose and purr, stinking of urine and blood. Some nights he kneaded my bare chest with his front paws, powerfully, arching his back, as if sharpening his claws, or pummeling a mother for milk. And some mornings I'd wake in daylight to find my body covered with paw prints in blood; I looked as though I'd been painted with roses.

It was hot, so hot the mirror felt warm. I washed before the mirror in a daze, my twisted summer sleep still hung about me like sea kelp. What blood was this, and what roses? It could have been the rose of union, the blood of murder, or the rose of beauty bare and the blood of some unspeakable sacrifice or birth. The sign on my body could have been an emblem or a stain, the keys to the kingdom or the mark of Cain. I never knew. I never knew as I washed, and the blood streaked, faded, and finally disappeared, whether I'd purified myself or ruined the blood sign of the passover. We wake, if we

ever wake at all, to mystery, rumors of death, beauty, violence. . . . "Seem like we're just set down here," a woman said
to me recently, "and don't nobody know why."

These are morning matters, pictures you dream as the final
wave heaves you up on the sand to the bright light and drying
air. You remember pressure, and a curved sleep you rested
against, soft, like a scallop in its shell. But the air hardens your
skin; you stand; you leave the lighted shore to explore some
dim headland, and soon you're lost in the leafy interior, intent,
remembering nothing.

I still think of that old tomcat, mornings, when I wake.
Things are tamer now; I sleep with the window shut. The cat
and our rites are gone and my life is changed, but the memory
remains of something powerful playing over me. I wake expectant, hoping to see a new thing. If I'm lucky I might be
jogged awake by a strange birdcall. I dress in a hurry, imagining the yard flapping with auks, or flamingos. This morning it
was a wood duck, down at the creek. It flew away.

I live by a creek, Tinker Creek, in a valley in Virginia's Blue
Ridge. An anchorite's hermitage is called an anchor-hold;
some anchor-holds were simple sheds clamped to the side of
a church like a barnacle to a rock. I think of this house clamped
to the side of Tinker Creek as an anchor-hold. It holds me at
anchor to the rock bottom of the creek itself and it keeps me
steadied in the current, as a sea anchor does, facing the stream
of light pouring down. It's a good place to live; there's a lot
to think about. The creeks—Tinker and Carvin's—are an active mystery, fresh every minute. Theirs is the mystery of the
continuous creation and all that providence implies: the uncertainty of vision, the horror of the fixed, the dissolution of the
present, the intricacy of beauty, the pressure of fecundity, the
elusiveness of the free, and the flawed nature of perfection.
The mountains—Tinker and Brushy, McAfee's Knob and
Dead Man—are a passive mystery, the oldest of all. Theirs is

the one simple mystery of creation from nothing, of matter itself, anything at all, the given. Mountains are giant, restful, absorbent. You can heave your spirit into a mountain and the mountain will keep it, folded, and not throw it back as some creeks will. The creeks are the world with all its stimulus and beauty; I live there. But the mountains are home.

The wood duck flew away. I caught only a glimpse of something like a bright torpedo that blasted the leaves where it flew. Back at the house I ate a bowl of oatmeal; much later in the day came the long slant of light that means good walking.

If the day is fine, any walk will do; it all looks good. Water in particular looks its best, reflecting blue sky in the flat, and chopping it into graveled shallows and white chute and foam in the riffles. On a dark day, or a hazy one, everything's washed-out and lackluster but the water. It carries its own lights. I set out for the railroad tracks, for the hill the flocks fly over, for the woods where the white mare lives. But I go to the water.

Today is one of those excellent January partly cloudies in which light chooses an unexpected part of the landscape to trick out in gilt, and then shadow sweeps it away. You know you're alive. You take huge steps, trying to feel the planet's roundness arc between your feet. Kazantzakis says that when he was young he had a canary and a globe. When he freed the canary, it would perch on the globe and sing. All his life, wandering the earth, he felt as though he had a canary on top of his mind, singing.

West of the house, Tinker Creek makes a sharp loop, so that the creek is both in back of the house, south of me, and also on the other side of the road, north of me. I like to go north. There the afternoon sun hits the creek just right, deepening the reflected blue and lighting the sides of trees on the banks. Steers from the pasture across the creek come down to drink; I always flush a rabbit or two there; I sit on a fallen trunk in the shade and watch the squirrels in the sun. There are two

separated wooden fences suspended from cables that cross the
creek just upstream from my tree-trunk bench. They keep the
steers from escaping up or down the creek when they come
to drink. Squirrels, the neighborhood children, and I use the
downstream fence as a swaying bridge across the creek. But
the steers are there today.

I sit on the downed tree and watch the black steers slip on
the creek bottom. They are all bred beef: beef heart, beef
hide, beef hocks. They're a human product like rayon.
They're like a field of shoes. They have cast-iron shanks and
tongues like foam insoles. You can't see through to their
brains as you can with other animals; they have beef fat behind
their eyes, beef stew.

I cross the fence six feet above the water, walking my hands
down the rusty cable and tightroping my feet along the narrow
edge of the planks. When I hit the other bank and terra firma,
some steers are bunched in a knot between me and the barbed-
wire fence I want to cross. So I suddenly rush at them in an
enthusiastic sprint, flailing my arms and hollering, "Lightning!
Copperhead! Swedish meatballs!" They flee, still in a knot,
stumbling across the flat pasture. I stand with the wind on my
face.

When I slide under a barbed-wire fence, cross a field, and
run over a sycamore trunk felled across the water, I'm on a
little island shaped like a tear in the middle of Tinker Creek.
On one side of the creek is a steep forested bank; the water
is swift and deep on that side of the island. On the other side
is the level field I walked through next to the steers' pasture;
the water between the field and the island is shallow and
sluggish. In summer's low water, flags and bulrushes grow
along a series of shallow pools cooled by the lazy current.
Water striders patrol the surface film, crayfish hump along the
silt bottom eating filth, frogs shout and glare, and shiners and
small bream hide among roots from the sulky green heron's
eye. I come to this island every month of the year. I walk
around it, stopping and staring, or I straddle the sycamore log

over the creek, curling my legs out of the water in winter, trying to read. Today I sit on dry grass at the end of the island by the slower side of the creek. I'm drawn to this spot. I come to it as to an oracle; I return to it as a man years later will seek out the battlefield where he lost a leg or an arm.

A couple of summers ago I was walking along the edge of the island to see what I could see in the water, and mainly to scare frogs. Frogs have an inelegant way of taking off from invisible positions on the bank just ahead of your feet, in dire panic, emitting a froggy "Yike!" and splashing into the water. Incredibly, this amused me, and, incredibly, it amuses me still. As I walked along the grassy edge of the island, I got better and better at seeing frogs both in and out of the water. I learned to recognize, slowing down, the difference in texture of the light reflected from mudbank, water, grass, or frog. Frogs were flying all around me. At the end of the island I noticed a small green frog. He was exactly half in and half out of the water, looking like a schematic diagram of an amphibian, and he didn't jump.

He didn't jump; I crept closer. At last I knelt on the island's winterkilled grass, lost, dumbstruck, staring at the frog in the creek just four feet away. He was a very small frog with wide, dull eyes. And just as I looked at him, he slowly crumpled and began to sag. The spirit vanished from his eyes as if snuffed. His skin emptied and drooped; his very skull seemed to collapse and settle like a kicked tent. He was shrinking before my eyes like a deflating football. I watched the taut, glistening skin on his shoulders ruck, and rumple, and fall. Soon, part of his skin, formless as a pricked balloon, lay in floating folds like bright scum on top of the water: it was a monstrous and terrifying thing. I gaped bewildered, appalled. An oval shadow hung in the water behind the drained frog; then the shadow glided away. The frog skin bag started to sink.

I had read about the giant water bug, but never seen one. "Giant water bug" is really the name of the creature, which is an enormous, heavy-bodied brown beetle. It eats insects, tadpoles, fish, and frogs. Its grasping forelegs are mighty and hooked inward. It seizes a victim with these legs, hugs it tight, and paralyzes it with enzymes injected during a vicious bite. That one bite is the only bite it ever takes. Through the puncture shoot the poisons that dissolve the victim's muscles and bones and organs—all but the skin—and through it the giant water bug sucks out the victim's body, reduced to a juice. This event is quite common in warm fresh water. The frog I saw was being sucked by a giant water bug. I had been kneeling on the island grass; when the unrecognizable flap of frog skin settled on the creek bottom, swaying, I stood up and brushed the knees of my pants. I couldn't catch my breath.

Of course, many carnivorous animals devour their prey alive. The usual method seems to be to subdue the victim by drowning or grasping it so it can't flee, then eating it whole or in a series of bloody bites. Frogs eat everything whole, stuffing prey into their mouths with their thumbs. People have seen frogs with their wide jaws so full of live dragonflies they couldn't close them. Ants don't even have to catch their prey: in the spring they swarm over newly hatched, featherless birds in the nest and eat them tiny bite by bite.

That it's rough out there and chancy is no surprise. Every live thing is a survivor on a kind of extended emergency bivouac. But at the same time we are also created. In the Koran, Allah asks, "The heaven and the earth and all in between, thinkest thou I made them *in jest?*" It's a good question. What do we think of the created universe, spanning an unthinkable void with an unthinkable profusion of forms? Or what do we think of nothingness, those sickening reaches of time in either direction? If the giant water bug was not made in jest, was it then made in earnest? Pascal uses a nice term to describe the notion of the creator's, once having called for the universe, turning his back to it: *Deus Absconditus.* Is this what we think happened? Was the sense of it there, and God absconded with it, ate it, like a wolf who disappears round the edge of the house with the Thanksgiving turkey? "God is subtle," Einstein said, "but not malicious." Again, Einstein said that "nature conceals her mystery by means of her essential grandeur, not by her cunning." It could be that God has not absconded but spread, as our vision and understanding of the universe have spread, to a fabric of spirit and sense so grand and subtle, so powerful in a new way, that we can only feel blindly of its hem. In making the thick darkness a swaddling band for the sea, God "set bars and doors" and said, "Hitherto shalt thou come, but no further." But have we come even that far? Have we rowed out to the thick darkness, or are we all playing pinochle in the bottom of the boat?

Cruelty is a mystery, and the waste of pain. But if we describe a world to compass these things, a world that is a long, brute game, then we bump against another mystery: the inrush of power and light, the canary that sings on the skull. Unless all ages and races of men have been deluded by the same mass hypnotist (who?), there seems to be such a thing as beauty, a grace wholly gratuitous. About five years ago I saw a mockingbird make a straight vertical descent from the roof gutter of a four-story building. It was an act as careless and spontaneous as the curl of a stem or the kindling of a star.

The mockingbird took a single step into the air and dropped. His wings were still folded against his sides as though he were singing from a limb and not falling, accelerating thirty-two feet per second per second, through empty air. Just a breath before he would have been dashed to the ground, he unfurled his wings with exact, deliberate care, revealing the broad bars of white, spread his elegant, white-banded tail, and so floated onto the grass. I had just rounded a corner when his insouciant step caught my eye; there was no one else in sight. The fact of his free fall was like the old philosophical conundrum about the tree that falls in the forest. The answer must be, I think, that beauty and grace are performed whether or not we will or sense them. The least we can do is try to be there.

20   Another time I saw another wonder: sharks off the Atlantic
coast of Florida. There is a way a wave rises above the ocean
horizon, a triangular wedge against the sky. If you stand where
the ocean breaks on a shallow beach, you see the raised water
in a wave is translucent, shot with lights. One late afternoon
at low tide a hundred big sharks passed the beach near the
mouth of a tidal river in a feeding frenzy. As each green wave
rose from the churning water, it illuminated within itself the
six- or eight-foot-long bodies of twisting sharks. The sharks
disappeared as each wave rolled toward me; then a new wave
would swell above the horizon, containing in it, like scorpions
in amber, sharks that roiled and heaved. The sight held awesome wonders: power and beauty, grace tangled in a rapture
with violence.

21   We don't know what's going on here. If these tremendous
events are random combinations of matter run amok, the yield
of millions of monkeys at millions of typewriters, then what
is it in us, hammered out of those same typewriters, that they
ignite? We don't know. Our life is a faint tracing on the
surface of mystery, like the idle, curved tunnels of leaf miners
on the face of a leaf. We must somehow take a wider view,
look at the whole landscape, really see it, and describe what's
going on here. Then we can at least wail the right question
into the swaddling band of darkness, or, if it comes to that,
choir the proper praise.

22   At the time of Lewis and Clark, setting the prairies on fire
was a well-known signal that meant, "Come down to the
water." It was an extravagant gesture, but we can't do less. If
the landscape reveals one certainty, it is that the extravagant
gesture is the very stuff of creation. After the one extravagant
gesture of creation in the first place, the universe has continued to deal exclusively in extravagances, flinging intricacies
and colossi down aeons of emptiness, heaping profusions on
profligacies with ever-fresh vigor. The whole show has been
on fire from the word go. I come down to the water to cool

my eyes. But everywhere I look I see fire; that which isn't flint is tinder, and the whole world sparks and flames.

I have come to the grassy island late in the day. The creek is up; icy water sweeps under the sycamore log bridge. The frog skin, of course, is utterly gone. I have stared at that one spot on the creek bottom for so long, focusing past the rush of water, that when I stand, the opposite bank seems to stretch before my eyes and flow grassily upstream. When the bank settles down I cross the sycamore log and enter again the big plowed field next to the steers' pasture.

The wind is terrific out of the west; the sun comes and goes. I can see the shadow on the field before me deepen uniformly and spread like a plague. Everything seems so dull I am amazed I can even distinguish objects. And suddenly the light runs across the land like a comber, and up the trees, and goes again in a wink: I think I've gone blind or died. When it comes again, the light, you hold your breath, and if it stays you forget about it until it goes again.

It's the most beautiful day of the year. At four o'clock the eastern sky is a dead stratus black flecked with low white clouds. The sun in the west illuminates the ground, the mountains, and especially the bare branches of trees, so that everywhere silver trees cut into the black sky like a photographer's negative of a landscape. The air and the ground are dry; the mountains are going on and off like neon signs. Clouds slide east as if pulled from the horizon, like a tablecloth whipped off a table. The hemlocks by the barbed-wire fence are flinging themselves east as though their backs would break. Purple shadows are racing east; the wind makes me face east, and again I feel the dizzying, drawn sensation I felt when the creek bank reeled.

At four-thirty the sky in the east is clear; how could that big blackness be blown? Fifteen minutes later another darkness is coming overhead from the northwest; and it's here. Everything is drained of its light as if sucked. Only at the horizon do inky black mountains give way to distant, lighted mountains—lighted not by direct illumination but rather paled by glowing sheets of mist hung before them. Now the blackness is in the east; everything is half in shadow, half in sun, every clod, tree, mountain, and hedge. I can't see Tinker Mountain through the line of hemlock, till it comes on like a streetlight, ping, *ex nihilo.* Its sandstone cliffs pink and swell. Suddenly the light goes; the cliffs recede as if pushed. The sun hits a clump of sycamores between me and the mountains; the sycamore arms light up, and *I can't see the cliffs.* They're gone. The pale network of sycamore arms, which a second ago was transparent as a screen, is suddenly opaque, glowing with light. Now the sycamore arms snuff out, the mountains come on, and there are the cliffs again.

I walk home. By five-thirty the show has pulled out. Nothing is left but an unreal blue and a few banked clouds low in the north. Some sort of carnival magician has been here, some fast-talking worker of wonders who has the act backwards. "Something in this hand," he says, "something in this hand, something up my sleeve, something behind my back . . ." and abracadabra, he snaps his fingers, and it's all gone. Only the bland, blank-faced magician remains, in his unruffled coat, barehanded, acknowledging a smattering of baffled applause. When you look again the whole show has pulled up stakes and moved on down the road. It never stops. New shows roll in from over the mountains and the magician reappears unannounced from a fold in the curtain you never dreamed was an opening. Scarves of clouds, rabbits in plain view, disappear into the black hat forever. Presto chango. The audience, if there is an audience at all, is dizzy from head-turning, dazed.

Like the bear who went over the mountain, I went out to see what I could see. And, I might as well warn you, like the bear, all that I could see was the other side of the mountain: more of same. On a good day I might catch a glimpse of another wooded ridge rolling under the sun like water, another bivouac. I propose to keep here what Thoreau called "a meteorological journal of the mind," telling some tales and describing some of the sights of this rather tamed valley, and exploring, in fear and trembling, some of the unmapped dim reaches and unholy fastnesses to which those tales and sights so dizzyingly lead.

I am no scientist. I explore the neighborhood. An infant who has just learned to hold his head up has a frank and forthright way of gazing about him in bewilderment. He hasn't the faintest clue where he is, and he aims to learn. In a couple of years, what he will have learned instead is how to fake it: he'll have the cocksure air of a squatter who has come to feel he owns the place. Some unwonted, taught pride diverts us from our original intent, which is to explore the neighborhood, view the landscape, to discover at least *where* it is that we have been so startlingly set down, if we can't learn why.

So I think about the valley. It is my leisure as well as my work, a game. It is a fierce game I have joined because it is being played anyway, a game of both skill and chance, played against an unseen adversary—the conditions of time—in which the payoffs, which may suddenly arrive in a blast of light at any moment, might as well come to me as anyone else. I stake the time I'm grateful to have, the energies I'm glad to direct. I risk getting stuck on the board, so to speak, unable to move in any direction, which happens enough, God knows; and I risk the searing, exhausting nightmares that plunder rest and force me face down all night long in some muddy ditch seething with hatching insects and crustaceans.

But if I can bear the nights, the days are a pleasure. I walk out; I see something, some event that would otherwise have been utterly missed and lost; or something sees me, some enormous power brushes me with its clean wing, and I resound like a beaten bell.

I am an explorer, then, and I am also a stalker, or the instrument of the hunt itself. Certain Indians used to carve long grooves along the wooden shafts of their arrows. They called the grooves "lightning marks," because they resembled the curved fissure lightning slices down the trunks of trees. The function of lightning marks is this: if the arrow fails to kill the game, blood from a deep wound will channel along the lightning mark, streak down the arrow shaft, and spatter to the ground, laying a trail dripped on broad-leaves, on stones, that the barefoot and trembling archer can follow into whatever deep or rare wilderness it leads. I am the arrow shaft, carved along my length by unexpected lights and gashes from the very sky, and this book is the straying trail of blood.

Something pummels us, something barely sheathed. Power broods and lights. We're played on like a pipe; our breath is not our own. James Houston describes two young Eskimo girls sitting cross-legged on the ground, mouth on mouth, blowing by turns each other's throat cords, making a low, unearthly music. When I cross again the bridge that is really the steers' fence, the wind has thinned to the delicate air of twilight; it crumples the water's skin. I watch the running sheets of light raised on the creek's surface. The sight has the appeal of the purely passive, like the racing of light under clouds on a field, the beautiful dream at the moment of being dreamed. The breeze is the merest puff, but you yourself sail headlong and breathless under the gale force of the spirit.

CHAPTER 2

Seeing

WHEN I WAS SIX or seven years old, growing up in Pittsburgh, I used to take a precious penny of my own and hide it for someone else to find. It was a curious compulsion; sadly, I've never been seized by it since. For some reason I always "hid" the penny along the same stretch of sidewalk up the street. I would cradle it at the roots of a sycamore, say, or in a hole left by a chipped-off piece of sidewalk. Then I would take a piece of chalk, and, starting at either end of the block, draw huge arrows leading up to the penny from both directions. After I learned to write I labeled the arrows: SURPRISE AHEAD or MONEY THIS WAY. I was greatly excited, during all this arrow-drawing, at the thought of the first lucky passer-by who would receive in this way, regardless of merit, a free gift from the universe. But I never lurked about. I would go straight home and not give the matter another thought, until, some months later, I would be gripped again by the impulse to hide another penny.

It is still the first week in January, and I've got great plans. I've been thinking about seeing. There are lots of things to see, unwrapped gifts and free surprises. The world is fairly studded and strewn with pennies cast broadside from a generous hand. But—and this is the point—who gets excited by a mere penny? If you follow one arrow, if you crouch motionless on a bank to watch a tremulous ripple thrill on the water and are rewarded by the sight of a muskrat kit paddling from its den, will you count that sight a chip of copper only, and go your rueful way? It is dire poverty indeed when a man is so malnourished and fatigued that he won't stoop to pick up a penny. But if you cultivate a healthy poverty and simplicity, so that finding a penny will literally make your day, then, since the world is in fact planted in pennies, you have with your poverty bought a lifetime of days. It is that simple. What you see is what you get.

I used to be able to see flying insects in the air. I'd look ahead and see, not the row of hemlocks across the road, but the air in front of it. My eyes would focus along that column of air, picking out flying insects. But I lost interest, I guess, for I dropped the habit. Now I can see birds. Probably some people can look at the grass at their feet and discover all the crawling creatures. I would like to know grasses and sedges—and care. Then my least journey into the world would be a field trip, a series of happy recognitions. Thoreau, in an expansive mood, exulted, "What a rich book might be made about buds, including, perhaps, sprouts!" It would be nice to think so. I cherish mental images I have of three perfectly happy people. One collects stones. Another—an Englishman, say—watches clouds. The third lives on a coast and collects drops of seawater which he examines microscopically and mounts. But I don't see what the specialist sees, and so I cut myself off, not only from the total picture, but from the various forms of happiness.

Unfortunately, nature is very much a now-you-see-it, now-you-don't affair. A fish flashes, then dissolves in the water before my eyes like so much salt. Deer apparently ascend bodily into heaven; the brightest oriole fades into leaves.

These disappearances stun me into stillness and concentration; they say of nature that it conceals with a grand nonchalance, and they say of vision that it is a deliberate gift, the revelation of a dancer who for my eyes only flings away her seven veils. For nature does reveal as well as conceal: now-you-don't-see-it, now-you-do. For a week last September migrating red-winged blackbirds were feeding heavily down by the creek at the back of the house. One day I went out to investigate the racket; I walked up to a tree, an Osage orange, and a hundred birds flew away. They simply materialized out of the tree. I saw a tree, then a whisk of color, then a tree again. I walked closer and another hundred blackbirds took flight. Not a branch, not a twig budged: the birds were apparently weight-less as well as invisible. Or, it was as if the leaves of the Osage orange had been freed from a spell in the form of red-winged blackbirds; they flew from the tree, caught my eye in the sky, and vanished. When I looked again at the tree the leaves had reassembled as if nothing had happened. Finally I walked directly to the trunk of the tree and a final hundred, the real diehards, appeared, spread, and vanished. How could so many hide in the tree without my seeing them? The Osage orange, unruffled, looked just as it had looked from the house, when three hundred red-winged blackbirds cried from its crown. I looked downstream where they flew, and they were gone. Searching, I couldn't spot one. I wandered downstream to force them to play their hand, but they'd crossed the creek and scattered. One show to a customer. These appearances catch at my throat; they are the free gifts, the bright coppers at the roots of trees.

It's all a matter of keeping my eyes open. Nature is like one of those line drawings of a tree that are puzzles for children: Can you find hidden in the leaves a duck, a house, a boy, a bucket, a zebra, and a boot? Specialists can find the most incredibly well-hidden things. A book I read when I was young recommended an easy way to find caterpillars to rear: you simply find some fresh caterpillar droppings, look up, and there's your caterpillar. More recently an author advised me to set my mind at ease about those piles of cut stems on the ground in grassy fields. Field mice make them; they cut the grass down by degrees to reach the seeds at the head. It seems that when the grass is tightly packed, as in a field of ripe grain, the blade won't topple at a single cut through the stem; instead, the cut stem simply drops vertically, held in the crush of grain. The mouse severs the bottom again and again, the stem keeps dropping an inch at a time, and finally the head is low enough for the mouse to reach the seeds. Meanwhile, the mouse is positively littering the field with its little piles of cut stems into which, presumably, the author of the book is constantly stumbling.

If I can't see these minutiae, I still try to keep my eyes open. I'm always on the lookout for antlion traps in sandy soil, monarch pupae near milkweed, skipper larvae in locust leaves. These things are utterly common, and I've not seen one. I bang on hollow trees near water, but so far no flying squirrels have appeared. In flat country I watch every sunset in hopes of seeing the green ray. The green ray is a seldom-seen streak of light that rises from the sun like a spurting fountain at the moment of sunset; it throbs into the sky for two seconds and disappears. One more reason to keep my eyes open. A photography professor at the University of Florida just happened to see a bird die in midflight; it jerked, died, dropped, and smashed on the ground. I squint at the wind because I read Stewart Edward White: "I have always maintained that if you looked closely enough you could *see* the wind—the dim, hardly-made-out, fine débris fleeing high in the air." White was an excellent observer, and devoted an entire chapter of *The Mountains* to the subject of seeing deer: "As soon as you can forget the naturally obvious and construct an artificial obvious, then you too will see deer."

But the artificial obvious is hard to see. My eyes account for less than one percent of the weight of my head; I'm bony and dense; I see what I expect. I once spent a full three minutes looking at a bullfrog that was so unexpectedly large I couldn't see it even though a dozen enthusiastic campers were shouting directions. Finally I asked, "What color am I looking for?" and a fellow said, "Green." When at last I picked out the frog, I saw what painters are up against: the thing wasn't green at all, but the color of wet hickory bark.

The lover can see, and the knowledgeable. I visited an aunt and uncle at a quarter-horse ranch in Cody, Wyoming. I couldn't do much of anything useful, but I could, I thought, draw. So, as we all sat around the kitchen table after supper, I produced a sheet of paper and drew a horse. "That's one lame horse," my aunt volunteered. The rest of the family joined in: "Only place to saddle that one is his neck"; "Looks like we better shoot the poor thing, on account of those terrible growths." Meekly, I slid the pencil and paper down the table. Everyone in that family, including my three young cousins, could draw a horse. Beautifully. When the paper came back it looked as though five shining, real quarter horses had been corraled by mistake with a papier-mâché moose; the real horses seemed to gaze at the monster with a steady, puzzled air. I stay away from horses now, but I can do a creditable goldfish. The point is that I just don't know what the lover knows; I just can't see the artificial obvious that those in the know construct. The herpetologist asks the native, "Are there snakes in that ravine?" "Nosir." And the herpetologist comes home with, yessir, three bags full. Are there butterflies on that mountain? Are the bluets in bloom, are there arrowheads here, or fossil shells in the shale?

Peeping through my keyhole I see within the range of only about thirty percent of the light that comes from the sun; the rest is infrared and some little ultraviolet, perfectly apparent to many animals, but invisible to me. A nightmare network of ganglia, charged and firing without my knowledge, cuts and splices what I do see, editing it for my brain. Donald E. Carr points out that the sense impressions of one-celled animals are *not* edited for the brain: "This is philosophically interesting in a rather mournful way, since it means that only the simplest animals perceive the universe as it is."

A fog that won't burn away drifts and flows across my field of vision. When you see fog move against a backdrop of deep pines, you don't see the fog itself, but streaks of clearness floating across the air in dark shreds. So I see only tatters of clearness through a pervading obscurity. I can't distinguish the fog from the overcast sky; I can't be sure if the light is direct or reflected. Everywhere darkness and the presence of the unseen appalls. We estimate now that only one atom dances alone in every cubic meter of intergalactic space. I blink and squint. What planet or power yanks Halley's Comet out of orbit? We haven't seen that force yet; it's a question of distance, density, and the pallor of reflected light. We rock, cradled in the swaddling band of darkness. Even the simple darkness of night whispers suggestions to the mind. Last summer, in August, I stayed at the creek too late.

Where Tinker Creek flows under the sycamore log bridge to the tear-shaped island, it is slow and shallow, fringed thinly in cattail marsh. At this spot an astonishing bloom of life supports vast breeding populations of insects, fish, reptiles, birds, and mammals. On windless summer evenings I stalk along the creek bank or straddle the sycamore log in absolute stillness, watching for muskrats. The night I stayed too late I was hunched on the log staring spellbound at spreading, reflected stains of lilac on the water. A cloud in the sky suddenly lighted as if turned on by a switch; its reflection just as suddenly materialized on the water upstream, flat and floating, so that I couldn't see the creek bottom, or life in the water under the cloud. Downstream, away from the cloud on the water, water turtles smooth as beans were gliding down with the current in a series of easy, weightless push-offs, as men bound on the moon. I didn't know whether to trace the progress of one turtle I was sure of, risking sticking my face in one of the bridge's spider webs made invisible by the gathering dark, or take a chance on seeing the carp, or scan the mudbank in hope of seeing a muskrat, or follow the last of the swallows who caught at my heart and trailed it after them like streamers as they appeared from directly below, under the log, flying upstream with their tails forked, so fast.

But shadows spread, and deepened, and stayed. After thousands of years we're still strangers to darkness, fearful aliens in an enemy camp with our arms crossed over our chests. I stirred. A land turtle on the bank, startled, hissed the air from its lungs and withdrew into its shell. An uneasy pink here, an unfathomable blue there, gave great suggestion of lurking beings. Things were going on. I couldn't see whether that sere rustle I heard was a distant rattlesnake, slit-eyed, or a nearby sparrow kicking in the dry flood debris slung at the foot of a willow. Tremendous action roiled the water everywhere I looked, big action, inexplicable. A tremor welled up beside a gaping muskrat burrow in the bank and I caught my breath, but no muskrat appeared. The ripples continued to fan upstream with a steady, powerful thrust. Night was knitting over my face an eyeless mask, and I still sat transfixed. A distant airplane, a delta wing out of nightmare, made a gliding shadow on the creek's bottom that looked like a stingray cruising upstream. At once a black fin slit the pink cloud on the water, shearing it in two. The two halves merged together and seemed to dissolve before my eyes. Darkness pooled in the cleft of the creek and rose, as water collects in a well. Untamed, dreaming lights flickered over the sky. I saw hints of hulking underwater shadows, two pale splashes out of the water, and round ripples rolling close together from a blackened center.

At last I stared upstream where only the deepest violet remained of the cloud, a cloud so high its underbelly still glowed feeble color reflected from a hidden sky lighted in turn by a sun halfway to China. And out of that violet, a sudden enormous black body arced over the water. I saw only a cylindrical sleekness. Head and tail, if there was a head and tail, were both submerged in cloud. I saw only one ebony fling, a headlong dive to darkness; then the waters closed, and the lights went out.

14   I walked home in a shivering daze, up hill and down. Later I lay open-mouthed in bed, my arms flung wide at my sides to steady the whirling darkness. At this latitude I'm spinning 836 miles an hour round the earth's axis; I often fancy I feel my sweeping fall as a breakneck arc like the dive of dolphins, and the hollow rushing of wind raises hair on my neck and the side of my face. In orbit around the sun I'm moving 64,800 miles an hour. The solar system as a whole, like a merry-go-round unhinged, spins, bobs, and blinks at the speed of 43,200 miles an hour along a course set east of Hercules. Someone has piped, and we are dancing a tarantella until the sweat pours. I open my eyes and I see dark, muscled forms curl out of water, with flapping gills and flattened eyes. I close my eyes and I see stars, deep stars giving way to deeper stars, deeper stars bowing to deepest stars at the crown of an infinite cone.

15   "Still," wrote van Gogh in a letter, "a great deal of light falls on everything." If we are blinded by darkness, we are also blinded by light. When too much light falls on everything, a special terror results. Peter Freuchen describes the notorious kayak sickness to which Greenland Eskimos are prone. "The Greenland fjords are peculiar for the spells of completely quiet weather, when there is not enough wind to blow out a match and the water is like a sheet of glass. The kayak hunter must sit in his boat without stirring a finger so as not to scare the shy seals away. . . . The sun, low in the sky, sends a glare into his eyes, and the landscape around moves into the realm of the unreal. The reflex from the mirror-like water hypnotizes him, he seems to be unable to move, and all of a sudden it is as if he were floating in a bottomless void, sinking, sinking, and sinking. . . . Horror-stricken, he tries to stir, to cry out, but he cannot, he is completely paralyzed, he just falls and falls." Some hunters are especially cursed with this panic, and bring ruin and sometimes starvation to their families.

16   Sometimes here in Virginia at sunset low clouds on the southern or northern horizon are completely invisible in the lighted sky. I only know one is there because I can see its reflection in still water. The first time I discovered this mystery I looked from cloud to no-cloud in bewilderment, checking my bearings over and over, thinking maybe the ark of the covenant was just passing by south of Dead Man Mountain. Only much later did I read the explanation: polarized light from the sky is very much weakened by reflection, but the light in clouds isn't polarized. So invisible clouds pass among visible clouds, till all slide over the mountains; so a greater light extinguishes a lesser as though it didn't exist.

17   In the great meteor shower of August, the Perseid, I wail all day for the shooting stars I miss. They're out there showering down, committing hara-kiri in a flame of fatal attraction, and hissing perhaps at last into the ocean. But at dawn what looks like a blue dome clamps down over me like a lid on a pot. The stars and planets could smash and I'd never know. Only a piece of ashen moon occasionally climbs up or down the inside of the dome, and our local star without surcease explodes on our heads. We have really only that one light, one source for all power, and yet we must turn away from it by universal decree. Nobody here on the planet seems aware of this strange, powerful taboo, that we all walk about carefully averting our faces, this way and that, lest our eyes be blasted forever.

18   Darkness appalls and light dazzles; the scrap of visible light that doesn't hurt my eyes hurts my brain. What I see sets me swaying. Size and distance and the sudden swelling of meanings confuse me, bowl me over. I straddle the sycamore log bridge over Tinker Creek in the summer. I look at the lighted creek bottom: snail tracks tunnel the mud in quavering curves. A crayfish jerks, but by the time I absorb what has happened, he's gone in a billowing smokescreen of silt. I look at the water: minnows and shiners. If I'm thinking minnows, a carp will fill my brain till I scream. I look at the water's surface:

skaters, bubbles, and leaves sliding down. Suddenly, my own face, reflected, startles me witless. Those snails have been tracking my face! Finally, with a shuddering wrench of the will, I see clouds, cirrus clouds. I'm dizzy, I fall in. This looking business is risky.

Once I stood on a humped rock on nearby Purgatory Mountain, watching through binoculars the great autumn hawk migration below, until I discovered that I was in danger of joining the hawks on a vertical migration of my own. I was used to binoculars, but not, apparently, to balancing on humped rocks while looking through them. I staggered. Everything advanced and receded by turns; the world was full of unexplained foreshortenings and depths. A distant huge tan object, a hawk the size of an elephant, turned out to be the browned bough of a nearby loblolly pine. I followed a sharp-shinned hawk against a featureless sky, rotating my head unawares as it flew, and when I lowered the glass a glimpse of my own looming shoulder sent me staggering. What prevents the men on Palomar from falling, voiceless and blinded, from their tiny, vaulted chairs?

I reel in confusion; I don't understand what I see. With the naked eye I can see two million light-years to the Andromeda galaxy. Often I slop some creek water in a jar and when I get home I dump it in a white china bowl. After the silt settles I return and see tracings of minute snails on the bottom, a planarian or two winding round the rim of water, roundworms shimmying frantically, and finally, when my eyes have adjusted to these dimensions, amoebae. At first the amoebae look like muscae volitantes, those curled moving spots you seem to see in your eyes when you stare at a distant wall. Then I see the amoebae as drops of water congealed, bluish, translucent, like chips of sky in the bowl. At length I choose one individual and give myself over to its idea of an evening. I see it dribble a grainy foot before it on its wet, unfathomable way. Do its unedited sense impressions include the fierce focus of my eyes? Shall I take it outside and show it Andromeda, and

blow its little endoplasm? I stir the water with a finger, in case
it's running out of oxygen. Maybe I should get a tropical
aquarium with motorized bubblers and lights, and keep this
one for a pet. Yes, it would tell its fissioned descendants, the
universe is two feet by five, and if you listen closely you can
hear the buzzing music of the spheres.

Oh, it's mysterious lamplit evenings, here in the galaxy, one
after the other. It's one of those nights when I wander from
window to window, looking for a sign. But I can't see. Terror
and a beauty insoluble are a ribband of blue woven into the
fringes of garments of things both great and small. No culture
explains, no bivouac offers real haven or rest. But it could be
that we are not seeing something. Galileo thought comets
were an optical illusion. This is fertile ground: since we are
certain that they're not, we can look at what our scientists have
been saying with fresh hope. What if there are *really* gleaming,
castellated cities hung upside-down over the desert sand?
What limpid lakes and cool date palms have our caravans
always passed untried? Until, one by one, by the blindest of
leaps, we light on the road to these places, we must stumble
in darkness and hunger. I turn from the window. I'm blind as
a bat, sensing only from every direction the echo of my own
thin cries.

I chanced on a wonderful book by Marius von Senden,
called *Space and Sight*. When Western surgeons discovered
how to perform safe cataract operations, they ranged across
Europe and America operating on dozens of men and women
of all ages who had been blinded by cataracts since birth. Von
Senden collected accounts of such cases; the histories are fascinating. Many doctors had tested their patients' sense percep-
tions and ideas of space both before and after the operations.
The vast majority of patients, of both sexes and all ages, had,
in von Senden's opinion, no idea of space whatsoever. Form,
distance, and size were so many meaningless syllables. A patient "had no idea of depth, confusing it with roundness."

Before the operation a doctor would give a blind patient a cube and a sphere; the patient would tongue it or feel it with his hands, and name it correctly. After the operation the doctor would show the same objects to the patient without letting him touch them; now he had no clue whatsoever what he was seeing. One patient called lemonade "square" because it pricked on his tongue as a square shape pricked on the touch of his hands. Of another postoperative patient, the doctor writes, "I have found in her no notion of size, for example, not even within the narrow limits which she might have encompassed with the aid of touch. Thus when I asked her to show me how big her mother was, she did not stretch out her hands, but set her two index-fingers a few inches apart." Other doctors reported their patients' own statements to similar effect. "The room he was in . . . he knew to be but part of the house, yet he could not conceive that the whole house could look bigger"; "Those who are blind from birth . . . have no real conception of height or distance. A house that is a mile away is thought of as nearby, but requiring the taking of a lot of steps. . . . The elevator that whizzes him up and down gives no more sense of vertical distance than does the train of horizontal."

For the newly sighted, vision is pure sensation unencumbered by meaning: "The girl went through the experience that we all go through and forget, the moment we are born. She saw, but it did not mean anything but a lot of different kinds of brightness." Again, "I asked the patient what he could see; he answered that he saw an extensive field of light, in which everything appeared dull, confused, and in motion. He could not distinguish objects." Another patient saw "nothing but a confusion of forms and colours." When a newly sighted girl saw photographs and paintings, she asked, " 'Why do they put those dark marks all over them?' 'Those aren't dark marks,' her mother explained, 'those are shadows. That is one of the ways the eye knows that things have shape. If it were not for shadows many things would look flat.' 'Well, that's how things do look,' Joan answered. 'Everything looks flat with dark patches.' "

But it is the patients' concepts of space that are most revealing. One patient, according to his doctor, "practiced his vision in a strange fashion; thus he takes off one of his boots, throws it some way off in front of him, and then attempts to gauge the distance at which it lies; he takes a few steps towards the boot and tries to grasp it; on failing to reach it, he moves on a step or two and gropes for the boot until he finally gets hold of it." "But even at this stage, after three weeks' experience of seeing," von Senden goes on, " 'space,' as he conceives it, ends with visual space, i.e. with colour-patches that happen to bound his view. He does not yet have the notion that a larger object (a chair) can mask a smaller one (a dog), or that the latter can still be present even though it is not directly seen."

In general the newly sighted see the world as a dazzle of color-patches. They are pleased by the sensation of color, and learn quickly to name the colors, but the rest of seeing is tormentingly difficult. Soon after his operation a patient "generally bumps into one of these colour-patches and observes them to be substantial, since they resist him as tactual objects do. In walking about it also strikes him—or can if he pays attention—that he is continually passing in between the colours he sees, that he can go past a visual object, that a part of it then steadily disappears from view; and that in spite of this, however he twists and turns—whether entering the room from the door, for example, or returning back to it—he always has a visual space in front of him. Thus he gradually comes to realize that there is also a space behind him, which he does not see."

The mental effort involved in these reasonings proves overwhelming for many patients. It oppresses them to realize, if they ever do at all, the tremendous size of the world, which they had previously conceived of as something touchingly manageable. It oppresses them to realize that they have been visible to people all along, perhaps unattractively so, without their knowledge or consent. A disheartening number of them refuse to use their new vision, continuing to go over objects with their tongues, and lapsing into apathy and despair. "The child can see, but will not make use of his sight. Only when pressed can he with difficulty be brought to look at objects in his neighbourhood; but more than a foot away it is impossible to bestir him to the necessary effort." Of a twenty-one-year-old girl, the doctor relates, "Her unfortunate father, who had hoped for so much from this operation, wrote that his daughter carefully shuts her eyes whenever she wishes to go about the house, especially when she comes to a staircase, and that she is never happier or more at ease than when, by closing her eyelids, she relapses into her former state of total blindness." A fifteen-year-old boy, who was also in love with a girl at the asylum for the blind, finally blurted out, "No, really, I can't stand it any more; I want to be sent back to the asylum again. If things aren't altered, I'll tear my eyes out."

Some do learn to see, especially the young ones. But it changes their lives. One doctor comments on "the rapid and complete loss of that striking and wonderful serenity which is characteristic only of those who have never yet seen." A blind man who learns to see is ashamed of his old habits. He dresses up, grooms himself, and tries to make a good impression. While he was blind he was indifferent to objects unless they were edible; now, "a sifting of values sets in . . . his thoughts and wishes are mightily stirred and some few of the patients are thereby led into dissimulation, envy, theft and fraud."

On the other hand, many newly sighted people speak well of the world, and teach us how dull is our own vision. To one patient, a human hand, unrecognized, is "something bright and then holes." Shown a bunch of grapes, a boy calls out, "It is dark, blue and shiny. . . . It isn't smooth, it has bumps and hollows." A little girl visits a garden. "She is greatly astonished, and can scarcely be persuaded to answer, stands speechless in front of the tree, which she only names on taking hold of it, and then as 'the tree with the lights in it.' " Some delight in their sight and give themselves over to the visual world. Of a patient just after her bandages were removed, her doctor writes, "The first things to attract her attention were her own hands; she looked at them very closely, moved them repeatedly to and fro, bent and stretched the fingers, and seemed greatly astonished at the sight." One girl was eager to tell her blind friend that "men do not really look like trees at all," and astounded to discover that her every visitor had an utterly different face. Finally, a twenty-two-year-old girl was dazzled by the world's brightness and kept her eyes shut for two weeks. When at the end of that time she opened her eyes again, she did not recognize any objects, but, "the more she now directed her gaze upon everything about her, the more it could be seen how an expression of gratification and astonishment overspread her features; she repeatedly exclaimed: 'Oh God! How beautiful!' "

I saw color-patches for weeks after I read this wonderful book. It was summer; the peaches were ripe in the valley orchards. When I woke in the morning, color-patches wrapped round my eyes, intricately, leaving not one unfilled spot. All day long I walked among shifting color-patches that parted before me like the Red Sea and closed again in silence, transfigured, wherever I looked back. Some patches swelled and loomed, while others vanished utterly, and dark marks flitted at random over the whole dazzling sweep. But I couldn't sustain the illusion of flatness. I've been around for too long. Form is condemned to an eternal danse macabre with meaning: I couldn't unpeach the peaches. Nor can I remember ever having seen without understanding; the color-patches of infancy are lost. My brain then must have been smooth as any balloon. I'm told I reached for the moon; many babies do. But the color-patches of infancy swelled as meaning filled them; they arrayed themselves in solemn ranks down distance which unrolled and stretched before me like a plain. The moon rocketed away. I live now in a world of shadows that shape and distance color, a world where space makes a kind of terrible sense. What gnosticism is this, and what physics? The fluttering patch I saw in my nursery window—silver and green and shape-shifting blue—is gone; a row of Lombardy poplars takes its place, mute, across the distant lawn. That humming oblong creature pale as light that stole along the walls of my room at night, stretching exhilaratingly around the corners, is gone, too, gone the night I ate of the bittersweet fruit, put two and two together and puckered forever my brain. Martin Buber tells this tale: "Rabbi Mendel once boasted to his teacher Rabbi Elimelekh that evenings he saw the angel who rolls away the light before the darkness, and mornings the angel who rolls away the darkness before the light. 'Yes,' said Rabbi Elimelekh, 'in my youth I saw that too. Later on you don't see these things any more.' "

Why didn't someone hand those newly sighted people paints and brushes from the start, when they still didn't know what anything was? Then maybe we all could see color-patches too, the world unraveled from reason, Eden before Adam gave names. The scales would drop from my eyes; I'd see trees like men walking; I'd run down the road against all orders, hallooing and leaping.

Seeing is of course very much a matter of verbalization. Unless I call my attention to what passes before my eyes, I simply won't see it. It is, as Ruskin says, "not merely unnoticed, but in the full, clear sense of the word, unseen." My eyes alone can't solve analogy tests using figures, the ones which show, with increasing elaborations, a big square, then a small square in a big square, then a big triangle, and expect me to find a small triangle in a big triangle. I have to say the words, describe what I'm seeing. If Tinker Mountain erupted, I'd be likely to notice. But if I want to notice the lesser cataclysms of valley life, I have to maintain in my head a running description of the present. It's not that I'm observant; it's just that I talk too much. Otherwise, especially in a strange place, I'll never know what's happening. Like a blind man at the ball game, I need a radio.

32   When I see this way I analyze and pry. I hurl over logs and roll away stones; I study the bank a square foot at a time, probing and tilting my head. Some days when a mist covers the mountains, when the muskrats won't show and the microscope's mirror shatters, I want to climb up the blank blue dome as a man would storm the inside of a circus tent, wildly, dangling, and with a steel knife claw a rent in the top, peep, and, if I must, fall.

33   But there is another kind of seeing that involves a letting go. When I see this way I sway transfixed and emptied. The difference between the two ways of seeing is the difference between walking with and without a camera. When I walk with a camera I walk from shot to shot, reading the light on a calibrated meter. When I walk without a camera, my own shutter opens, and the moment's light prints on my own silver gut. When I see this second way I am above all an unscrupulous observer.

34   It was sunny one evening last summer at Tinker Creek; the sun was low in the sky, upstream. I was sitting on the sycamore log bridge with the sunset at my back, watching the shiners the size of minnows who were feeding over the muddy sand in skittery schools. Again and again, one fish, then another, turned for a split second across the current and flash! the sun shot out from its silver side. I couldn't watch for it. It was always just happening somewhere else, and it drew my vision just as it disappeared: flash, like a sudden dazzle of the thinnest blade, a sparking over a dun and olive ground at chance intervals from every direction. Then I noticed white specks, some sort of pale petals, small, floating from under my feet on the creek's surface, very slow and steady. So I blurred my eyes and gazed towards the brim of my hat and saw a new world. I saw the pale white circles roll up, roll up, like the world's

turning, mute and perfect, and I saw the linear flashes, gleaming silver, like stars being born at random down a rolling scroll of time. Something broke and something opened. I filled up like a new wineskin. I breathed an air like light; I saw a light like water. I was the lip of a fountain the creek filled forever; I was ether, the leaf in the zephyr; I was flesh-flake, feather, bone.

When I see this way I see truly. As Thoreau says, I return to my senses. I am the man who watches the baseball game in silence in an empty stadium. I see the game purely; I'm abstracted and dazed. When it's all over and the white-suited players lope off the green field to their shadowed dugouts, I leap to my feet; I cheer and cheer.

But I can't go out and try to see this way. I'll fail, I'll go mad. All I can do is try to gag the commentator, to hush the noise of useless interior babble that keeps me from seeing just as surely as a newspaper dangled before my eyes. The effort is really a discipline requiring a lifetime of dedicated struggle; it marks the literature of saints and monks of every order East and West, under every rule and no rule, discalced and shod. The world's spiritual geniuses seem to discover universally that the mind's muddy river, this ceaseless flow of trivia and trash, cannot be dammed, and that trying to dam it is a waste of effort that might lead to madness. Instead you must allow the muddy river to flow unheeded in the dim channels of consciousness; you raise your sights; you look along it, mildly, acknowledging its presence without interest and gazing beyond it into the realm of the real where subjects and objects act and rest purely, without utterance. "Launch into the deep," says Jacques Ellul, "and you shall see."

The secret of seeing is, then, the pearl of great price. If I thought he could teach me to find it and keep it forever I would stagger barefoot across a hundred deserts after any lunatic at all. But although the pearl may be found, it may not be sought. The literature of illumination reveals this above all:

although it comes to those who wait for it, it is always, even to the most practiced and adept, a gift and a total surprise. I return from one walk knowing where the killdeer nests in the field by the creek and the hour the laurel blooms. I return from the same walk a day later scarcely knowing my own name. Litanies hum in my ears; my tongue flaps in my mouth Ailinon, alleluia! I cannot cause light; the most I can do is try to put myself in the path of its beam. It is possible, in deep space, to sail on solar wind. Light, be it particle or wave, has force: you rig a giant sail and go. The secret of seeing is to sail on solar wind. Hone and spread your spirit till you yourself are a sail, whetted, translucent, broadside to the merest puff.

When her doctor took her bandages off and led her into the garden, the girl who was no longer blind saw "the tree with the lights in it." It was for this tree I searched through the peach orchards of summer, in the forests of fall and down winter and spring for years. Then one day I was walking along Tinker Creek thinking of nothing at all and I saw the tree with the lights in it. I saw the backyard cedar where the mourning doves roost charged and transfigured, each cell buzzing with flame. I stood on the grass with the lights in it, grass that was wholly fire, utterly focused and utterly dreamed. It was less like seeing than like being for the first time seen, knocked breathless by a powerful glance. The flood of fire abated, but I'm still spending the power. Gradually the lights went out in the cedar, the colors died, the cells unflamed and disappeared. I was still ringing. I had been my whole life a bell, and never knew it until at that moment I was lifted and struck. I have since only very rarely seen the tree with the lights in it. The vision comes and goes, mostly goes, but I live for it, for the moment when the mountains open and a new light roars in spate through the crack, and the mountains slam.

CHAPTER 3

Winter

I

IT IS THE FIRST OF FEBRUARY, and everyone is talking about starlings. Starlings came to this country on a passenger liner from Europe. One hundred of them were deliberately released in Central Park, and from those hundred descended all of our countless millions of starlings today. According to Edwin Way Teale, "Their coming was the result of one man's fancy. That man was Eugene Schieffelin, a wealthy New York drug manufacturer. His curious hobby was the introduction into America of all the birds mentioned in William Shakespeare." The birds adapted to their new country splendidly.

When John Cowper Powys lived in the United States, he wrote about chickadees stealing crumbs from his favorite flock of starlings. Around here they're not so popular. Instead of quietly curling for sleep, one by one, here and there in dense shrubbery, as many birds do, starlings roost all together in vast hordes and droves. They have favorite roosting sites to which they return winter after winter; apparently southwest Virginia

is their idea of Miami Beach. In Waynesboro, where the starlings roost in the woods near the Coyner Springs area, residents can't go outside for any length of time, or even just to
hang laundry, because of the stink—"will knock you over"—
the droppings, and the lice.

Starlings are notoriously difficult to "control." The story is
told of a man who was bothered by starlings roosting in a large
sycamore near his house. He said he tried everything to get
rid of them and finally took a shotgun to three of them and
killed them. When asked if that discouraged the birds, he
reflected a minute, leaned forward, and said confidentially,
"Those three it did."

Radford, Virginia, had a little stink of its own a few years
ago. Radford had starlings the way a horse has flies, and in
similarly unapproachable spots. Wildlife biologists estimated
the Radford figure at one hundred fifty thousand starlings.
The people complained of the noise, the stench, the inevitable
whitewash effect, and the possibility of an epidemic of an
exotic, dust-borne virus disease. Finally, in January, 1972,
various officials and biologists got together and decided that
something needed to be done. After studying the feasibility of
various methods, they decided to kill the starlings with foam.
The idea was to shoot a special detergent foam through hoses
at the roosting starlings on a night when weathermen predicted a sudden drop in temperature. The foam would penetrate the birds' waterproof feathers and soak their skins. Then
when the temperature dropped, the birds would drop too,
having quietly died of exposure.

Meanwhile, before anything actually happened, the papers
were having a field day. Every crazy up and down every mountain had his shrill say. The local bird societies screamed for
blood—the starlings' blood. Starlings, after all, compete with
native birds for food and nesting sites. Other people chal-
lenged the mayor of Radford, the Virginia Tech Wildlife
Bureau, the newspaper's editors and all its readers in Radford

and everywhere else, to tell how THEY would like to freeze to death inside a bunch of bubbles.

The Wildlife Bureau went ahead with its plan. The needed equipment was expensive, and no one was quite sure if it would work. Sure enough, on the night they sprayed the roosts the temperature didn't drop far enough. Out of the hundred and fifty thousand starlings they hoped to exterminate, they got only three thousand. Somebody figured out that the whole show had cost citizens two dollars per dead starling.

That is, in effect, the story of the Radford starlings. The people didn't give up at once, however. They mulled and fussed, giving the starlings a brief reprieve, and then came up with a new plan. Soon, one day when the birds returned at sunset to their roost, the wildlife managers were ready for them. They fired shotguns loaded with multiple, high-powered explosives into the air. BANG, went the guns; the birds settled down to sleep. The experts went back to their desks and fretted and fumed some more. At last they brought out the ultimate weapon: recordings of starling distress calls. Failure. YIKE OUCH HELP went the recordings; snore went the birds. That, *in toto,* is the story of the Radford starlings. They still thrive.

Our valley starlings thrive, too. They plod morosely around the grass under the feeder. Other people apparently go to great lengths to avoid feeding them. Starlings are early to bed and late to rise, so people sneak out with grain and suet before dawn, for early rising birds, and whisk it away at the first whiff of a starling; after sunset, when the starlings are safely to roost bothering somebody else, they spread out the suet and grain once again. I don't care what eats the stuff.

It is winter proper; the cold weather, such as it is, has come to stay. I bloom indoors in the winter like a forced forsythia; I come in to come out. At night I read and write, and things I have never understood become clear; I reap the harvest of the rest of the year's planting.

Outside, everything has opened up. Winter clear-cuts and reseeds the easy way. Everywhere paths unclog; in late fall and winter, and only then, can I scale the cliffs to the Lucas orchard, circle the forested quarry pond, or follow the left-hand bank of Tinker Creek downstream. The woods are acres of sticks; I could walk to the Gulf of Mexico in a straight line. When the leaves fall the striptease is over; things stand mute and revealed. Everywhere skies extend, vistas deepen, walls become windows, doors open. Now I can see the house where the Whites and the Garretts lived on the hill under oaks. The thickly grown banks of Carvin's Creek where it edges the road have long since thinned to a twiggy haze, and I can see Maren and Sandy in blue jackets out running the dogs. The mountains' bones poke through, all shoulder and knob and shin. All that summer conceals, winter reveals. Here are the birds' nests hid in the hedge, and squirrels' nests splotched all over the walnuts and elms.

Today a gibbous moon marked the eastern sky like a smudge of chalk. The shadows of its features had the same blue tone and light value as the sky itself, so it looked transparent in its depths, or softly frayed, like the heel of a sock. Not too long ago, according to Edwin Way Teale, the people of Europe believed that geese and swans wintered there, on the moon's pale seas. Now it is sunset. The mountains warm in tone as the day chills, and a hot blush deepens over the land. "Observe," said da Vinci, "observe in the streets at twilight, when the day is cloudy, the loveliness and tenderness spread on the faces of men and women." I have seen those faces, when the day is cloudy, and I have seen at sunset on a clear winter day houses, ordinary houses, whose bricks were coals and windows flame.

At dusk every evening an extended flock of starlings appears out of the northern sky and winds toward the setting sun. It is the winter day's major event. Late yesterday, I climbed across the creek, through the steers' pasture, beyond the grassy island where I had seen the giant water bug sip a frog, and up a high hill. Curiously, the best vantage point on the hill was occupied by a pile of burnt books. I opened some of them carefully: they were good cloth- and leather-bound novels, a complete, charred set of encyclopedias decades old, and old, watercolor-illustrated children's books. They flaked in my hands like pieces of pie. Today I learned that the owners of the house behind the books had suffered a fire. But I didn't know that then; I thought they'd suffered a terrible fit of pique. I crouched beside the books and looked over the valley.

On my right a woods thickly overgrown with creeper descended the hill's slope to Tinker Creek. On my left was a planting of large shade trees on the ridge of the hill. Before me the grassy hill pitched abruptly and gave way to a large, level field fringed in trees where it bordered the creek. Beyond the creek I could see with effort the vertical sliced rock where men had long ago quarried the mountain under the forest. Beyond that I saw Hollins Pond and all its woods and pastures; then I saw in a blue haze all the world poured flat and pale between the mountains.

Out of the dimming sky a speck appeared, then another, and another. It was the starlings going to roost. They gathered deep in the distance, flock sifting into flock, and strayed towards me, transparent and whirling, like smoke. They seemed to unravel as they flew, lengthening in curves, like a loosened skein. I didn't move; they flew directly over my head for half an hour. The flight extended like a fluttering banner, an unfurled oriflamme, in either direction as far as I could see. Each individual bird bobbed and knitted up and down in the flight at apparent random, for no known reason except that that's how starlings fly, yet all remained perfectly spaced. The flocks each tapered at either end from a rounded middle, like an eye. Over my head I heard a sound of beaten air, like a million shook rugs, a muffled whuff. Into the woods they sifted without shifting a twig, right through the crowns of trees, intricate and rushing, like wind.

After half an hour, the last of the stragglers had vanished into the trees. I stood with difficulty, bashed by the unexpectedness of this beauty, and my spread lungs roared. My eyes pricked from the effort of trying to trace a feathered dot's passage through a weft of limbs. Could tiny birds be sifting through me right now, birds winging through the gaps between my cells, touching nothing, but quickening in my tissues, fleet?

Some weather's coming; you can taste on the sides of your tongue a quince tang in the air. This fall everyone looked to the bands on a woolly bear caterpillar, and predicted as usual the direst of dire winters. This routine always calls to mind the Angiers' story about the trappers in the far north. They approached an Indian whose ancestors had dwelled from time immemorial in those fir forests, and asked him about the severity of the coming winter. The Indian cast a canny eye over the landscape and pronounced, "Bad winter." The others asked him how he knew. The Indian replied unhesitatingly, "The white man makes a big woodpile." Here the woodpile is an exercise doggedly, exhaustedly maintained despite what must be great temptation. The other day I saw a store displaying a neatly stacked quarter-cord of fireplace logs manufactured of rolled, pressed paper. On the wrapper of each "log" was printed in huge letters the beguiling slogan, "The ROMANCE Without The HEARTACHE."

I lay a cherry log fire and settle in. I'm getting used to this planet and this curious human culture which is as cheerfully enthusiastic as it is cheerfully cruel. I never cease to marvel at the newspapers. In my life I've seen one million pictures of a duck that has adopted a kitten, or a cat that has adopted a duckling, or a sow and a puppy, a mare and a muskrat. And for the one millionth time I'm fascinated. I wish I lived near them, in Corpus Christi or Damariscotta; I wish I had the wonderful pair before me, mooning about the yard. It's all beginning to smack of home. The winter pictures that come

Contrast of
her own internal
camera

Sentimentality

in over the wire from every spot on the continent are getting
to be as familiar as my own hearth. I wait for the annual aerial
photograph of an enterprising fellow who has stamped in
the snow a giant Valentine for his girl. Here's the annual
chickadee-trying-to-drink-from-a-frozen-birdbath picture, cap-
tioned, "Sorry, Wait Till Spring," and the shot of an utterly
bundled child crying piteously on a sled at the top of a snowy
hill, labeled, "Needs a Push." How can an old world be so
innocent?

18

Finally I see tonight a picture of a friendly member of the
Forest Service in Wisconsin, who is freeing a duck frozen onto
the ice by chopping out its feet with a hand ax. It calls to mind
the spare, cruel story Thomas McGonigle told me about herring gulls frozen on ice off Long Island. When his father was
young, he used to walk out on Great South Bay, which had
frozen over, and frozen the gulls to it. Some of the gulls were
already dead. He would take a hunk of driftwood and brain
the living gulls; then, with a steel knife he hacked them free
below the body and rammed them into a burlap sack. The
family ate herring gull all winter, close around a lighted table
in a steamy room. And out on the Bay, the ice was studded
with paired, red stumps.

19

Winter knives. With their broad snow knives, Eskimos used
to cut blocks of snow to spiral into domed igloos for tempo-
rary shelter. They sharpened their flensing knives by licking
a thin coat of ice on the blade. Sometimes an Eskimo would
catch a wolf with a knife. He slathered the knife with blubber
and buried the hilt in snow or ice. A hungry wolf would scent
the blubber, find the knife, and lick it compulsively with
numbed tongue, until he sliced his tongue to ribbons, and
bled to death.

20

This is the sort of stuff I read all winter. The books I read
are like the stone men built by the Eskimos of the great desolate tundras west of Hudson's Bay. They still build them
today, according to Farley Mowat. An Eskimo traveling alone

in flat barrens will heap round stones to the height of a man,
travel till he can no longer see the beacon, and build another.
So I travel mute among these books, these eyeless men and
women that people the empty plain. I wake up thinking: What
am I reading? What will I read next? I'm terrified that I'll run
out, that I will read through all I want to, and be forced to
learn wildflowers at last, to keep awake. In the meantime I lose
myself in a liturgy of names. The names of the men are Knud
Rasmussen, Sir John Franklin, Peter Freuchen, Scott, Peary,
and Byrd; Jedediah Smith, Peter Skene Ogden, and Milton
Sublette; or Daniel Boone singing on his blanket in the Green
River country. The names of waters are Baffin Bay, Repulse
Bay, Coronation Gulf, and the Ross Sea; the Coppermine
River, the Judith, the Snake, and the Musselshell; the Pelly,
the Dease, the Tanana, and Telegraph Creek. Beaver plews,
zero degrees latitude, and gold. I like the clean urgency of
these tales, the sense of being set out in a wilderness with a
jackknife and a length of twine. If I can get up a pinochle
game, a little three-hand cutthroat for half a penny a point
and a bottle of wine, fine; if not I'll spend these southern
nights caught in the pack off Franz Josef Land, or casting for
arctic char.

II

It snowed. It snowed all yesterday and never emptied the
sky, although the clouds looked so low and heavy they might
drop all at once with a thud. The light is diffuse and hueless,
like the light on paper inside a pewter bowl. The snow looks
light and the sky dark, but in fact the sky is lighter than the
snow. Obviously the thing illuminated cannot be lighter than
its illuminator. The classical demonstration of this point involves simply laying a mirror flat on the snow so that it reflects
in its surface the sky, and comparing by sight this value to that
of the snow. This is all very well, even conclusive, but the

illusion persists. The dark is overhead and the light at my feet; I'm walking upside-down in the sky.

Yesterday I watched a curious nightfall. The cloud ceiling took on a warm tone, deepened, and departed as if drawn on a leash. I could no longer see the fat snow flying against the sky; I could see it only as it fell before dark objects. Any object at a distance—like the dead, ivy-covered walnut I see from the bay window—looked like a black-and-white frontispiece seen through the sheet of white tissue. It was like dying, this watching the world recede into deeper and deeper blues while the snow piled; silence swelled and extended, distance dissolved, and soon only concentration at the largest shadows let me make out the movement of falling snow, and that too failed. The snow on the yard was blue as ink, faintly luminous; the sky violet. The bay window betrayed me, and started giving me back the room's lamps. It was like dying, that growing dimmer and deeper and then going out.

Today I went out for a look around. The snow had stopped, and a couple of inches lay on the ground. I walked through the yard to the creek; everything was slate-blue and gunmetal and white, except for the hemlocks and cedars, which showed a brittle, secret green if I looked for it under the snow. Lo and behold, here in the creek was a silly-looking coot. It looked like a black and gray duck, but its head was smaller; its clunky white bill sloped straight from the curve of its skull like a cone from its base. I had read somewhere that coots were shy. They were liable to take umbrage at a footfall, skitter terrified along the water, and take to the air. But I wanted a good look. So when the coot tipped tail and dove, I raced towards it across the snow and hid behind a cedar trunk. As it popped up again its neck was as rigid and eyes as blank as a rubber duck's in the bathtub. It paddled downstream, away from me. I waited until it submerged again, then made a break for the trunk of the Osage orange. But up it came all at once, as though the child in the tub had held the rubber duck under the water with both hands, and suddenly released it. I froze stock-still, thinking that after all I really was, actually and at bottom, a tree, a dead tree perhaps, even a wobbly one, but a treeish creature nonetheless. The coot wouldn't notice that a tree hadn't grown in that spot the moment before; what did it know? It was new to the area, a mere dude. As tree I allowed myself only the luxury of keeping a wary eye on the coot's eye. Nothing; it didn't suspect a thing—unless, of course, it was just leading me on, beguiling me into scratching my nose, when the jig would be up once and for all, and I'd be left unmasked, untreed, with no itch and an empty creek. So.

At its next dive I made the Osage orange and looked around from its trunk while the coot fed from the pool behind the riffles. From there I ran downstream to the sycamore, getting treed in open ground again—and so forth for forty minutes, until it gradually began to light in my leafy brain that maybe the coot wasn't shy after all. That all this subterfuge was unnecessary, that the bird was singularly stupid, or at least not of an analytical turn of mind, and that in fact I'd been making a perfect idiot of myself all alone in the snow. So from behind the trunk of a black walnut, which was my present blind, I stepped boldly into the open. Nothing. The coot floated just across the creek from me, absolutely serene. Could it possibly be that I'd been flirting all afternoon with a *decoy?* No, decoys don't dive. I walked back to the sycamore, actually moving in plain sight not ten yards from the creature, which gave no sign of alarm or flight. I stopped; I raised my arm and waved. Nothing. In its beak hung a long, wet strand of some shore plant; it sucked it at length down its throat and dove again. I'll kill it. I'll hit the thing with a snowball, I really will; I'll make a mud-hen hash.

But I didn't even make a snowball. I wandered upstream, along smooth banks under trees. I had gotten, after all, a very good look at the coot. Now here were its tracks in the snow,

three-toed and very close together. The wide, slow place in
the creek by the road bridge was frozen over. From this bank
at this spot in summer I can always see tadpoles, fat-bodied,
scraping brown algae from a sort of shallow underwater ledge.
Now I couldn't see the ledge under the ice. Most of the
tadpoles were now frogs, and the frogs were buried alive in
the mud at the bottom of the creek. They went to all that
trouble to get out of the water and breathe air, only to hop
back in before the first killing frost. The frogs of Tinker Creek
are slathered in mud, mud at their eyes and mud at their
nostrils; their damp skins absorb a muddy oxygen, and so they
pass the dreaming winter.

Also from this bank at this spot in summer I can often see
turtles by crouching low to catch the triangular poke of their
heads out of water. Now snow smothered the ice; if it stays
cold, I thought, and the neighborhood kids get busy with
brooms, they can skate. Meanwhile, a turtle in the creek under
the ice is getting oxygen by an almost incredible arrangement.
It sucks water posteriorly into its large cloacal opening, where
sensitive tissues filter the oxygen directly into the blood, as a
gill does. Then the turtle discharges the water and gives another suck. The neighborhood kids can skate right over this
curious rush of small waters.

Under the ice the bluegills and carp are still alive; this far
south the ice never stays on the water long enough that fish
metabolize all the oxygen and die. Farther north, fish sometimes die in this way and float up to the ice, which thickens
around their bodies and holds them fast, open-eyed, until the
thaw. Some worms are still burrowing in the silt, dragonfly
larvae are active on the bottom, some algae carry on a dim
photosynthesis, and that's about it. Everything else is dead,
killed by the cold, or mutely alive in any of various still forms:
egg, seed, pupa, spore. Water snakes are hibernating as dense
balls, water striders hibernate as adults along the bank, and
mourning cloak butterflies secret themselves in the bark of
trees: all of these emerge groggily in winter thaws, to slink,

skitter, and flit about in one afternoon's sunshine, and then at
dusk to seek shelter, chill, fold, and forget.

The muskrats are out: they can feed under the ice, where
the silver trail of bubbles that rises from their fur catches and
freezes in streaming, glittering globes. What else? The birds,
of course, are fine. Cold is no problem for warm-blooded
animals, so long as they have food for fuel. Birds migrate for
food, not for warmth as such. That is why, when so many
people all over the country started feeding stations, southern
birds like the mockingbird easily extended their ranges north.
Some of our local birds go south, like the female robin; other
birds, like the coot, consider *this* south. Mountain birds come
down to the valley in a vertical migration; some of them, like
the chickadees, eat not only seeds but such tiny fare as aphid
eggs hid near winter buds and the ends of twigs. This afternoon I watched a chickadee swooping and dangling high in a
tulip tree. It seemed astonishingly heated and congealed, as
though a giant pair of hands had scooped a skyful of molecules
and squeezed it like a snowball to produce this fireball, this
feeding, flying, warm solid bit.

Other interesting things are going on wherever there is
shelter. Slugs, of all creatures, hibernate, inside a waterproof
sac. All the bumblebees and paper wasps are dead except the
queens, who sleep a fat, numbed sleep, unless a mouse finds
one and eats her alive. Honeybees have their own honey for
fuel, so they can overwinter as adults, according to Edwin Way
Teale, by buzzing together in a tightly packed, living sphere.
Their shimmying activity heats the hive; they switch positions
from time to time so that each bee gets its chance in the cozy
middle and its turn on the cold outside. Ants hibernate en
masse; the woolly bear hibernates alone in a bristling ball.
Ladybugs hibernate under shelter in huge orange clusters
sometimes the size of basketballs. Out West, people hunt for
these overwintering masses in the mountains. They take them
down to warehouses in the valleys, which pay handsomely.
Then, according to Will Barker, the mail-order houses ship

them to people who want them to eat garden aphids. They're
mailed in the cool of night in boxes of old pine cones. It's a
clever device: How do you pack a hundred living ladybugs?
The insects naturally crawl deep into the depths of the pine
cones; the sturdy "branches" of the opened cones protect
them through all the bumpings of transit.

I crossed the bridge invigorated and came to a favorite spot.
It is the spit of land enclosed in the oxbow of Tinker Creek.
A few years ago I called these few acres the weed-field; they
grew mostly sassafras, ivy, and poke. Now I call it the woods
by the creek; young tulip grows there, and locust and oak. The
snow on the wide path through the woods was unbroken. I
stood in a little clearing beside the dry ditch that the creek
cuts, bisecting the land, in high water. Here I ate a late lunch
of ham sandwiches and wished I'd brought water and left
more fat on the ham.

There was something new in the woods today—a bunch of
sodden, hand-lettered signs tied to the trees all along the
winding path. They said "SLOW," "Slippery When Wet,"
"Stop," "PIT ROW," "ESSO," and "BUMP!!" These signs indicated an awful lot of excitement over a little snow. When I saw
the first one, "SLOW," I thought, sure, I'll go slow; I won't
screech around on the unbroken path in the woods by the
creek under snow. What was going on here? The other signs
made it clear. Under "BUMP!!" lay, sure enough, a bump. I
scraped away the smooth snow. Hand-fashioned of red clay,
and now frozen, the bump was about six inches high and
eighteen inches across. The slope, such as it was, was gentle;
tread marks stitched the clay. On the way out I saw that I'd
missed the key sign, which had fallen: "Welcome to the Martinsville Speedway." So my "woods by the creek" was a motorbike trail to the local boys, their "Martinsville Speedway."
I had always wondered why they bothered to take a tractor-
mower to these woods all summer long, keeping the many
paths open; it was a great convenience to me.

Now the speedway was a stillnessway. Next to me in a

sapling, a bird's nest cradled aloft a newborn burden of snow. From a crab apple tree hung a single frozen apple with blistered and shiny skin; it was heavy and hard as a stone. Everywhere through the trees I saw the creek run blue under the ledge of ice from the banks; it made a thin, metallic sound like foil beating foil.

When I left the woods I stepped into a yellow light. The sun behind a uniform layer of gray had the diffuse shine of a very much rubbed and burnished metal boss. On the mountains the wan light slanted over the snow and gouged out shallow depressions and intricacies in the mountains' sides I never knew were there. I walked home. No school today. The motorbike boys were nowhere in sight; they were probably skidding on sleds down the very steep hill and out onto the road. Here my neighbor's small children were rolling a snowman. The noon sun had dampened the snow; it caught in slabs, leaving green, irregular tracks on the yard. I just now discovered the most extraordinary essay, a treatise on making a snowman. ". . . By all means use what is ready to hand. In a fuel-oil burning area, for instance, it is inconceivable that fathers should sacrifice their days hunting downtown for lumps of coal for their children's snowmen's eyes. Charcoal briquettes from the barbecue are an unwieldy substitute, and fuel-oil itself is of course out of the question. Use pieces of rock, brick, or dark sticks; use bits of tire tread or even dark fallen leaves rolled tightly, cigarwise, and deeply inserted into sockets formed by a finger." Why, why in the blue-green world write this sort of thing? Funny written culture, I guess; we pass things on.

There are seven or eight categories of phenomena in the world that are worth talking about, and one of them is the weather. Any time you care to get in your car and drive across the country and over the mountains, come into our valley, cross Tinker Creek, drive up the road to the house, walk across the yard, knock on the door and ask to come in and talk about the weather, you'd be welcome. If you came tonight from up north, you'd have a terrific tailwind; between Tinker and Dead Man you'd chute through the orchardy pass like an iceboat. When I let you in, we might not be able to close the door. The wind shrieks and hisses down the valley, sonant and surd, drying the puddles and dismantling the nests from the trees.

Inside the house, my single goldfish, Ellery Channing, whips around and around the sides of his bowl. Can he feel a glassy vibration, a ripple out of the north that urges him to swim for deeper, warmer waters? Saint-Exupéry says that when flocks of wild geese migrate high over a barnyard, the cocks and even the dim, fatted chickens fling themselves a foot or so into the air and flap for the south. Eskimo sled dogs feed all summer on famished salmon flung to them from creeks. I have often wondered if those dogs feel a wistful downhill drift in the fall, or an upstream yank, an urge to leap ladders, in the spring. To what hail do you hark, Ellery?—what sunny bottom under chill waters, what Chinese emperor's petaled pond? Even the spiders are restless under this wind, roving about alert-eyed over their fluff in every corner.

I allow the spiders the run of the house. I figure that any predator that hopes to make a living on whatever smaller creatures might blunder into a four-inch square bit of space in the corner of the bathroom where the tub meets the floor, needs every bit of my support. They catch flies and even field crickets in those webs. Large spiders in barns have been known to trap, wrap, and suck hummingbirds, but there's no danger of that here. I tolerate the webs, only occasionally sweeping away the very dirtiest of them after the spider itself has scrambled to safety. I'm always leaving a bath towel draped over the tub so that the big, haired spiders, who are constantly getting trapped by the tub's smooth sides, can use its rough surface as an exit ramp. Inside the house the spiders have only given me one mild surprise. I washed some dishes and set them to dry over a plastic drainer. Then I wanted a cup of coffee, so I picked from the drainer my mug, which was still warm from the hot rinse water, and across the rim of the mug, strand after strand, was a spider web.

Outside in summer I watch the orb-weavers, the spiders at their wheels. Last summer I watched one spin her web, which was especially interesting because the light just happened to be such that I couldn't see the web at all. I had read that spiders lay their major straight lines with fluid that isn't sticky, and then lay a nonsticky spiral. Then they walk along that safe road and lay a sticky spiral going the other way. It seems to be very much a matter of concentration. The spider I watched was a matter of mystery: she seemed to be scrambling up, down, and across the air. There was a small white mass of silk visible at the center of the orb, and she returned to this hub after each frenzied foray between air and air. It was a sort of Tinker Creek to her, from which she bore lightly in every direction an invisible news. She had a nice ability to make hairpin turns at the most acute angles in the air, all at topmost speed. I understand that you can lure an orb-weaver spider, if you want one, by vibrating or twirling a blade of grass against the web, as a flying insect would struggle if caught. This little ruse has never worked for me; I need a tuning fork; I leave the webs on the bushes bristling with grass.

Things are well in their place. Last week I found a brown, cocoonlike object, light and dry, and pocketed it in an outside, unlined pocket where it wouldn't warm and come alive. Then I saw on the ground another one, slightly torn open, so I split it further with my fingers, and saw a pale froth. I held it closer; the froth took on intricacy. I held it next to my eye and saw a tiny spider, yellowish but so infinitesimal it was translucent, waving each of its eight legs in what was clearly threat behavior. It was one of hundreds of spiders, already alive, all squirming in a tangled orgy of legs. Not on me they won't; I emptied that pocket fast. Things out of place are ill. Tonight I hear outside a sound of going in the tops of the mulberry trees; I stay in to do battle with—what? Once I looked into a little

wooden birdhouse hung from a tree; it had a pointed roof like
an Alpine cottage, a peg perch, and a neat round door. Inside,
watching me, was a coiled snake. I used to kill insects with
carbon tetrachloride—cleaning fluid vapor—and pin them in
cigar boxes, labeled, in neat rows. That was many years ago:
I quit when one day I opened a cigar-box lid and saw a carrion
beetle, staked down high between its wing covers, trying to
crawl, swimming on its pin. It was dancing with its own
shadow, untouching, and had been for days. If I go downstairs
now will I see a possum just rounding a corner, trailing its
scaled pink tail? I know that one night, in just this sort of
rattling wind, I will go to the kitchen for milk and find on the
back of the stove a sudden stew I never fixed, bubbling, with
a deer leg sticking out.

In a dry wind like this, snow and ice can pass directly into
the air as a gas without having first melted to water. This
process is called sublimation; tonight the snow in the yard and
the ice in the creek sublime. A breeze buffets my palm held
a foot from the wall. A wind like this does my breathing for
me; it engenders something quick and kicking in my lungs.
Pliny believed the mares of the Portuguese used to raise their
tails to the wind, "and turn them full against it, and so conceive that genital air instead of natural seed: in such sort, as
they become great withal, and quicken in their time, and bring
forth foals as swift as the wind, but they live not above three
years." Does the white mare Itch in the dell in the Adams'
woods up the road turn tail to this wind with white-lashed,
lidded eyes? A single cell quivers at a windy embrace; it swells
and splits, it bubbles into a raspberry; a dark clot starts to
throb. Soon something perfect is born. Something wholly new
rides the wind, something fleet and fleeting I'm likely to miss.

To sleep, spiders and fish; the wind won't stop, but the
house will hold. To shelter, starlings and coot; bow to the
wind.

CHAPTER 4

The Fixed

I

I HAVE JUST LEARNED to see praying mantis egg cases. Suddenly I see them everywhere; a tan oval of light catches my eye, or I notice a blob of thickness in a patch of slender weeds. As I write I can see the one I tied to the mock orange hedge outside my study window. It is over an inch long and shaped like a bell, or like the northern hemisphere of an egg cut through its equator. The full length of one of its long sides is affixed to a twig; the side that catches the light is perfectly flat. It has a dead straw, deadweed color, and a curious brittle texture, hard as varnish, but pitted minutely, like frozen foam. I carried it home this afternoon, holding it carefully by the twig, along with several others—they were light as air. I dropped one without missing it until I got home and made a count.

Within the week I've seen thirty or so of these egg cases in a rose-grown field on Tinker Mountain, and another thirty in weeds along Carvin's Creek. One was on a twig of tiny dog-

wood on the mud lawn of a newly built house. I think the
mail-order houses sell them to gardeners at a dollar apiece. It
beats spraying, because each case contains between one hundred twenty-five to three hundred fifty eggs. If the eggs survive ants, woodpeckers, and mice—and most do—then you
get the fun of seeing the new mantises hatch, and the smug
feeling of knowing, all summer long, that they're out there in
your garden devouring gruesome numbers of fellow insects
all nice and organically. When a mantis has crunched up the
last shred of its victim, it cleans its smooth green face like a
cat.

In late summer I often see a winged adult stalking the
insects that swarm about my porch light. Its body is a clear,
warm green; its naked, triangular head can revolve uncannily,
so that I often see one twist its head to gaze at me as it were
over its shoulder. When it strikes, it jerks so suddenly and with
such a fearful clatter of raised wings, that even a hardened
entomologist like J. Henri Fabre confessed to being startled
witless every time.

Adult mantises eat more or less everything that breathes and
is small enough to capture. They eat honeybees and butterflies, including monarch butterflies. People have actually seen
them seize and devour garter snakes, mice, and even *hummingbirds*. Newly hatched mantises, on the other hand, eat small
creatures like aphids and each other. When I was in elementary school, one of the teachers brought in a mantis egg case
in a Mason jar. I watched the newly hatched mantises emerge
and shed their skins; they were spidery and translucent, all
over joints. They trailed from the egg case to the base of the
Mason jar in a living bridge that looked like Arabic calligra-
phy, some baffling text from the Koran inscribed down the air
by a fine hand. Over a period of several hours, during which
time the teacher never summoned the nerve or the sense to
release them, they ate each other until only two were left. Tiny
legs were still kicking from the mouths of both. The two
survivors grappled and sawed in the Mason jar; finally both

died of injuries. I felt as though I myself should swallow the corpses, shutting my eyes and washing them down like jagged pills, so all that life wouldn't be lost.

When mantises hatch in the wild, however, they straggle about prettily, dodging ants, till all are lost in the grass. So it was in hopes of seeing an eventual hatch that I pocketed my jackknife this afternoon before I set out to walk. Now that I can see the egg cases, I'm embarrassed to realize how many I must have missed all along. I walked east through the Adams' woods to the cornfield, cutting three undamaged egg cases I found at the edge of the field. It was a clear, picturesque day, a February day without clouds, without emotion or spirit, like a beautiful woman with an empty face. In my fingers I carried the thorny stems from which the egg cases hung like roses; I switched the bouquet from hand to hand, warming the free hand in a pocket. Passing the house again, deciding not to fetch gloves, I walked north to the hill by the place where the steers come to drink from Tinker Creek. There in the weeds on the hill I found another eight egg cases. I was stunned—I cross this hill several times a week, and I always look for egg cases here, because it was here that I had once seen a mantis laying her eggs.

It was several years ago that I witnessed this extraordinary procedure, but I remember, and confess, an inescapable feeling that I was watching something not real and present, but a horrible nature movie, a "secrets-of-nature" short, beautifully photographed in full color, that I had to sit through unable to look anywhere else but at the dimly lighted EXIT signs along the walls, and that behind the scenes some amateur moviemaker was congratulating himself on having stumbled across this little wonder, or even on having contrived so natural a setting, as though the whole scene had been shot very carefully in a terrarium in someone's greenhouse.

I was ambling across this hill that day when I noticed a speck of pure white. The hill is eroded; the slope is a rutted wreck of red clay broken by grassy hillocks and low wild roses whose roots clasp a pittance of topsoil. I leaned to examine the white thing and saw a mass of bubbles like spittle. Then I saw something dark like an engorged leech rummaging over the spittle, and then I saw the praying mantis.

She was upside-down, clinging to a horizontal stem of wild rose by her feet which pointed to heaven. Her head was deep in dried grass. Her abdomen was swollen like a smashed finger; it tapered to a fleshy tip out of which bubbled a wet, whipped froth. I couldn't believe my eyes. I lay on the hill this way and that, my knees in thorns and my cheeks in clay, trying to see as well as I could. I poked near the female's head with a grass; she was clearly undisturbed, so I settled my nose an inch from that pulsing abdomen. It puffed like a concertina, it throbbed like a bellows; it roved, pumping, over the glistening, clabbered surface of the egg case testing and patting, thrusting and smoothing. It seemed to act so independently that I forgot the panting brown stick at the other end. The bubble creature seemed to have two eyes, a frantic little brain, and two busy, soft hands. It looked like a hideous, harried mother slicking up a fat daughter for a beauty pageant, touching her up, slobbering over her, patting and hemming and brushing and stroking.

The male was nowhere in sight. The female had probably eaten him. Fabre says that, at least in captivity, the female will mate with and devour up to seven males, whether she has laid her egg cases or not. The mating rites of mantises are well known: a chemical produced in the head of the male insect says, in effect, "No, don't go near her, you fool, she'll eat you alive." At the same time a chemical in his abdomen says, "Yes, by all means, now and forever yes."

While the male is making up what passes for his mind, the female tips the balance in her favor by eating his head. He mounts her. Fabre describes the mating, which sometimes lasts six hours, as follows: "The male, absorbed in the performance of his vital functions, holds the female in a tight embrace. But the wretch has no head; he has no neck; he has hardly a body. The other, with her muzzle turned over her shoulder continues very placidly to gnaw what remains of the gentle swain. And, all the time, that masculine stump, holding on firmly, goes on with the business! . . . I have seen it done with my own eyes and have not yet recovered from my astonishment."

I watched the egg-laying for over an hour. When I returned the next day, the mantis was gone. The white foam had hardened and browned to a dirty suds; then, and on subsequent days, I had trouble pinpointing the case, which was only an inch or so off the ground. I checked on it every week all winter long. In the spring the ants discovered it; every week I saw dozens of ants scrambling over the sides, unable to chew a way in. Later in the spring I climbed the hill every day, hoping to catch the hatch. The leaves of the trees had long since unfolded, the butterflies were out, and the robins' first broods were fledged; still the egg case hung silent and full on the stem. I read that I should wait for June, but still I visited the case every day. One morning at the beginning of June everything was gone. I couldn't find the lower thorn in the clump of three to which the egg case was fixed. I couldn't find the clump of three. Tracks ridged the clay, and I saw the lopped stems: somehow my neighbor had contrived to run a tractor-mower over that steep clay hill on which there grew nothing to mow but a few stubby thorns.

So. Today from this same hill I cut another three undamaged cases and carried them home with the others by their twigs. I also collected a suspiciously light cynthia moth cocoon. My fingers were stiff and red with cold, and my nose ran. I had forgotten the Law of the Wild, which is, "Carry Kleenex." At home I tied the twigs with their egg cases to various sunny bushes and trees in the yard. They're easy to find because I used white string; at any rate, I'm unlikely to mow my own trees. I hope the woodpeckers that come to the feeder don't find them, but I don't see how they'd get a purchase on them if they did.

Night is rising in the valley; the creek has been extinguished for an hour, and now only the naked tips of trees fire tapers into the sky like trails of sparks. The scene that was in the back of my brain all afternoon, obscurely, is beginning to rise from night's lagoon. It really has nothing to do with praying mantises. But this afternoon I threw tiny string lashings and hitches with frozen hands, gingerly, fearing to touch the egg cases even for a minute because I remembered the Polyphemus moth.

I have no intention of inflicting all my childhood memories on anyone. Far less do I want to excoriate my old teachers who, in their bungling, unforgettable way, exposed me to the natural world, a world covered in chitin, where implacable realities hold sway. The Polyphemus moth never made it to the past; it crawls in that crowded, pellucid pool at the lip of the great waterfall. It is as present as this blue desk and brazen lamp, as this blackened window before me in which I can no longer see even the white string that binds the egg case to the hedge, but only my own pale, astonished face.

Once, when I was ten or eleven years old, my friend Judy brought in a Polyphemus moth cocoon. It was January; there were doily snowflakes taped to the schoolroom panes. The teacher kept the cocoon in her desk all morning and brought it out when we were getting restless before recess. In a book we found what the adult moth would look like; it would be beautiful. With a wingspread of up to six inches, the Polyphemus is one of the few huge American silk moths, much larger than, say, a giant or tiger swallowtail butterfly. The moth's enormous wings are velveted in a rich, warm brown, and edged in bands of blue and pink delicate as a watercolor wash. A startling "eyespot," immense, and deep blue melding to an almost translucent yellow, luxuriates in the center of each hind wing. The effect is one of a masculine splendor foreign to the butterflies, a fragility unfurled to strength. The Polyphemus moth in the picture looked like a mighty wraith, a beating essence of the hardwood forest, alien-skinned and brown, with spread, blind eyes. This was the giant moth packed in the faded cocoon. We closed the book and turned to the cocoon. It was an oak leaf sewn into a plump oval bundle; Judy had found it loose in a pile of frozen leaves.

We passed the cocoon around; it was heavy. As we held it in our hands, the creature within warmed and squirmed. We were delighted, and wrapped it tighter in our fists. The pupa began to jerk violently, in heart-stopping knocks. Who's there? I can still feel those thumps, urgent through a muffling of spun silk and leaf, urgent through the swaddling of many years, against the curve of my palm. We kept passing it around. When it came to me again it was hot as a bun; it jumped half out of my hand. The teacher intervened. She put it, still heaving and banging, in the ubiquitous Mason jar.

It was coming. There was no stopping it now, January or not. One end of the cocoon dampened and gradually frayed in a furious battle. The whole cocoon twisted and slapped around in the bottom of the jar. The teacher fades, the classmates fade, I fade: I don't remember anything but that thing's struggle to be a moth or die trying. It emerged at last, a sodden crumple. It was a male; his long antennae were thickly plumed, as wide as his fat abdomen. His body was very thick, over an inch long, and deeply furred. A gray, furlike plush covered his head; a long, tan furlike hair hung from his wide thorax over his brown-furred, segmented abdomen. His multijointed legs, pale and powerful, were shaggy as a bear's. He stood still, but he breathed.

He couldn't spread his wings. There was no room. The chemical that coated his wings like varnish, stiffening them permanently, dried, and hardened his wings as they were. He was a monster in a Mason jar. Those huge wings stuck on his back in a torture of random pleats and folds, wrinkled as a dirty tissue, rigid as leather. They made a single nightmare clump still wracked with useless, frantic convulsions.

The next thing I remember, it was recess. The school was

in Shadyside, a busy residential part of Pittsburgh. Everyone was playing dodgeball in the fenced playground or racing around the concrete schoolyard by the swings. Next to the playground a long delivery drive sloped downhill to the sidewalk and street. Someone—it must have been the teacher—had let the moth out. I was standing in the driveway, alone, stock-still, but shivering. Someone had given the Polyphemus moth his freedom, and he was walking away.

He heaved himself down the asphalt driveway by infinite degrees, unwavering. His hideous crumpled wings lay glued and rucked on his back, perfectly still now, like a collapsed tent. The bell rang twice; I had to go. The moth was receding down the driveway, dragging on. I went; I ran inside. The Polyphemus moth is still crawling down the driveway, crawling down the driveway hunched, crawling down the driveway on six furred feet, forever.

Shading the glass with a hand, I can see how shadow has pooled in the valley. It washes up the sandstone cliffs on Tinker Mountain and obliterates them in a deluge; freshets of shadow leak into the sky. I am exhausted. In Pliny I read about the invention of clay modeling. A Sicyonian potter came to Corinth. There his daughter fell in love with a young man who had to make frequent long journeys away from the city. When he sat with her at home, she used to trace the outline of his shadow that a candle's light cast on the wall. Then, in his absence she worked over the profile, deepening it, so that she might enjoy his face, and remember. One day the father slapped some potter's clay over the gouged plaster; when the clay hardened he removed it, baked it, and "showed it abroad." The story ends here. Did the boy come back? What did the girl think of her father's dragging her lover all over town by the hair? What I really want to know is this: Is the shadow still there? If I went back and found the shadow of that face there on the wall by the fireplace, I'd rip down the house with my hands for that hunk.

The shadow's the thing. Outside shadows are blue, I read,

because they are lighted by the blue sky and not the yellow sun. Their blueness bespeaks infinitesimal particles scattered down inestimable distance. Muslims, whose religion bans representational art as idolatrous, don't observe the rule strictly; but they do forbid sculpture, because it casts a shadow. So shadows define the real. If I no longer see shadows as "dark marks," as do the newly sighted, then I see them as making some sort of sense of the light. They give the light distance; they put it in its place. They inform my eyes of my location here, here O Israel, here in the world's flawed sculpture, here in the flickering shade of the nothingness between me and the light.

Now that shadow has dissolved the heavens' blue dome, I can see Andromeda again; I stand pressed to the window, rapt and shrunk in the galaxy's chill glare. "Nostalgia of the Infinite," di Chirico: cast shadows stream across the sunlit courtyard, gouging canyons. There is a sense in which shadows are actually cast, hurled with a power, cast as Ishmael was cast, *out,* with a flinging force. This is the blue strip running through creation, the icy road side stream on whose banks the mantis mates, in whose unweighed waters the giant water bug sips frogs. Shadow Creek is the blue subterranean stream that chills Carvin's Creek and Tinker Creek; it cuts like ice under the ribs of the mountains, Tinker and Dead Man. Shadow Creek storms through limestone vaults under forests, or surfaces anywhere, damp, on the underside of a leaf. I wring it from rocks; it seeps into my cup. Chasms open at the glance of an eye; the ground parts like a wind-rent cloud over stars. Shadow Creek: on my least walk to the mailbox I may find myself kneedeep in its sucking, frigid pools. I must either wear rubber boots, or dance to keep warm.

II

Fish gotta swim and bird gotta fly; insects, it seems, gotta do one horrible thing after another. I never ask why of a vulture or shark, but I ask why of almost every insect I see. More than one insect—the possibility of fertile reproduction—is an assault on all human value, all hope of a reasonable god. Even that devout Frenchman, J. Henri Fabre, who devoted his entire life to the study of insects, cannot restrain a feeling of unholy revulsion. He describes a bee-eating wasp, the Philanthus, who has killed a honeybee. If the bee is heavy with honey, the wasp squeezes its crop "so as to make her disgorge the delicious syrup, which she drinks by licking the tongue which her unfortunate victim, in her death-agony, sticks out of her mouth at full length. . . . At the moment of some such horrible banquet, I have seen the Wasp, with her prey, seized by the Mantis: the bandit was rifled by another bandit. And here is an awful detail: while the Mantis held her transfixed under the points of the double saw and was already munching her belly, the Wasp continued to lick the honey of her Bee, unable to relinquish the delicious food even amid the terrors of death. Let us hasten to cast a veil over these horrors."

The remarkable thing about the world of insects, however, is precisely that there is no veil cast over these horrors. These are mysteries performed in broad daylight before our very eyes; we can see every detail, and yet they are still mysteries. If, as Heraclitus suggests, god, like an oracle, neither "declares nor hides, but sets forth by signs," then clearly I had better be scrying the signs. The earth devotes an overwhelming proportion of its energy to these buzzings and leaps in the grass, to these brittle gnawings and crawlings about. Theirs is the biggest wedge of the pie: Why? I ought to keep a giant water bug in an aquarium on my dresser, so I can think about it. We have brass candlesticks in our houses now; we ought to display praying mantises in our churches. Why do we turn from the insects in loathing? Our competitors are not only cold-blooded, and green- and yellow-blooded, but are also cased in a clacking horn. They lack the grace to go about as we do, softside-out to the wind and thorns. They have rigid eyes and brains strung down their backs. But they make up the bulk of our comrades-at-life, so I look to them for a glimmer of companionship.

When a grasshopper landed on my study window last summer, I looked at it for a long time. Its hard wing covers were short; its body was a dead waxen yellow, with black-green, indecipherable marks. Like all large insects, it gave me pause, plenty pause, with its hideous horizontal, multijointed mouthparts and intricate, mechanical-looking feet, all cups and spikes. I looked at its tapered, chitin-covered abdomen, plated and barred as a tank tread, and was about to turn away when I saw it breathe, puff puff, and I grew sympathetic. Yeah, I said, puff puff, isn't it? It jerked away with a buzz like a rasping file, audible through the pane, and continued to puff in the grass. So puff it is, and that's all there is; though I'm partial to honey myself.

Nature is, above all, profligate. Don't believe them when they tell you how economical and thrifty nature is, whose leaves return to the soil. Wouldn't it be cheaper to leave them on the tree in the first place? This deciduous business alone is a radical scheme, the brainchild of a deranged manic-depressive with limitless capital. Extravagance! Nature will try anything once. This is what the sign of the insects says. No form is too gruesome, no behavior too grotesque. If you're dealing with organic compounds, then let them combine. If it works, if it quickens, set it clacking in the grass; there's always room for one more; you ain't so handsome yourself. This is a spendthrift economy; though nothing is lost, all is spent.

That the insects have adapted is obvious. Their failures to adapt, however, are dazzling. It is hard to believe that nature is partial to such dim-wittedness. Howard Ensign Evans tells of dragonflies trying to lay eggs on the shining hoods of cars.

Other dragonflies seem to test a surface, to learn if it's really water, by dipping the tips of their abdomens in it. At the Los Angeles La Brea tar pits, they dip their abdomens into the reeking tar and get stuck. If by tremendous effort a dragonfly frees itself, Evans reports, it is apt to repeat the maneuver. Sometimes the tar pits glitter with the dry bodies of dead dragonflies.

J. Henri Fabre's pine processionaries speak to the same point. Although the new studies show that some insects can on occasion strike out into new territory, leaving instinct behind, still a blindered and blinkered enslavement to instinct is the rule, as the pine processionaries show. Pine processionaries are moth caterpillars with shiny black heads, who travel about at night in pine trees along a silken road of their own making. They straddle the road in a tight file, head to rear touching, and each caterpillar adds its thread to the original track first laid by the one who happens to lead the procession. Fabre interferes; he catches them on a daytime exploration approaching a circular track, the rim of a wide palm vase in his greenhouse. When the leader of the insect train completes a full circle, Fabre removes the caterpillars still climbing the vase and brushes away all extraneous silken tracks. Now he has a closed circuit of caterpillars, leaderless, trudging round his vase on a never-ending track. He wants to see how long it will take them to catch on. To his horror, they march not just an hour or so, but all day. When Fabre leaves the greenhouse at night, they are still tracing that wearying circle, although night is the time they usually feed.

In the chill of the next morning they are deadly still; when they rouse themselves, however, they resume what Fabre calls their "imbecility." They slog along all day, head to tail. The next night is bitterly cold; in the morning Fabre finds them slumped on the vase rim in two distinct clumps. When they line up again, they have two leaders, and the leaders in nature often explore to the sides of an already laid track. But the two ranks meet, and the entranced circle winds on. Fabre can't believe his eyes. The creatures have had neither water nor food nor rest; they are shelterless all day and all night long. Again the next night a hard frost numbs the caterpillars, who huddle in heaps. By chance the first one to wake is off the track; it strikes out in a new direction, and encounters the soil in the pot. Six others follow his track. Now the ones on the vase have a leader, because there is a gap in the rim. But they drag on stubbornly around their circle of hell. Soon the seven rebels, unable to eat the palm in the vase, follow their trail back to the rim of the pot and join the doomed march. The circle often breaks as starved or exhausted caterpillars stagger to a halt; but they soon breach the gap they leave, and no leaders emerge.

The next day a heat spell hits. The caterpillars lean far over the rim of the vase, exploring. At last one veers from the track. Followed by four others, it explores down the long side of the vase; there, next to the vase, Fabre has placed some pine needles for them to feed on. They ramble within nine inches of the pine needles, but, incredibly, wander upward to the rim and rejoin the dismal parade. For two more days the processionaries stagger on; at last they try the path laid down the vase by the last group. They venture out to new ground; they straggle at last to their nest. It has been seven days. Fabre himself, "already familiar with the abysmal stupidity of insects as a class whenever the least accident occurs," is nevertheless clearly oppressed by this new confirmation that the caterpillars lack "any gleam of intelligence in their benighted minds." "The caterpillars in distress," he concludes, "starved, shelterless, chilled with cold at night, cling obstinately to the silk ribbon covered hundreds of times, because they lack the rudimentary glimmers of reason which would advise them to abandon it."

I want out of this still air. What street-corner vendor wound the key on the backs of tin soldiers and abandoned them to the sidewalk, and crashings over the curb? Elijah mocked the

prophets of Baal, who lay a bullock on a woodpile and begged
Baal to consume it: "Cry aloud: for he is a god; either he is
talking, or he is pursuing, or he is in a journey, or peradven-
ture he sleepeth, and must be awaked." Cry aloud. It is the
fixed that horrifies us, the fixed that assails us with the tremendous force of its mindlessness. The fixed is a Mason jar, and
we can't beat it open. The prophets of Baal gashed themselves
with knives and lancets, and the wood stayed wood. The fixed
is the world without fire—dead flint, dead tinder, and nowhere a spark. It is motion without direction, force without
power, the aimless procession of caterpillars round the rim of
a vase, and I hate it because at any moment I myself might step
to that charmed and glistening thread. Last spring in the flood
I saw a brown cattail bob in the high muddy water of Carvin's
Creek, up and down, side to side, a jerk a second. I went back
the next day and nothing had changed; that empty twitching
beat on in an endless, sickening tattoo. What geomancy reads
what the windblown sand writes on the desert rock? I read
there that all things live by a generous power and dance to a
mighty tune; or I read there that all things are scattered and
hurled, that our every arabesque and grand jeté is a frantic
variation on our one free fall.

Two weeks ago, in the dark of night, I bundled up and quit
the house for Tinker Creek. Long before I could actually see
the creek, I heard it shooting the sandstone riffles with a
chilled rush and splash. It has always been a happy thought to
me that the creek runs on all night, new every minute,
whether I wish it or know it or care, as a closed book on a shelf
continues to whisper to itself its own inexhaustible tale. So
many things have been shown me on these banks, so much
light has illumined me by reflection here where the water
comes down, that I can hardly believe that this grace never
flags, that the pouring from ever-renewable sources is endless,
impartial, and free. But that night Tinker Creek had vanished,
usurped, and Shadow Creek blocked its banks. The night-cold

pulsed in my bones. I stood on the frozen grass under the Osage orange. The night was moonless; the mountains loomed over the stars. By half looking away I could barely make out the gray line of foam at the riffles; the skin tightened over the corners of my mouth, and I blinked in the cold. That night the fact of the creek's running on in the dark—from high on the unseen side of Tinker Mountain, miles away—smacked sinister. Where was the old exhilaration? This dumb dead drop over rocks was a hideous parody of real natural life, warm and willful. It was senseless and horrifying; I turned away. The damned thing was flowing because it was *pushed*.

That was two weeks ago; tonight I don't know. Tonight the moon is full, and I wonder. I'm pleased with my day's "work," with the cocoon and egg cases hung on the hedge. Van Gogh found nerve to call this world "a study that didn't come off," but I'm not so sure. Where do I get my standards that I fancy the fixed world of insects doesn't meet? I'm tired of reading; I pick up a book and learn that "pieces of the leech's body can also swim." Take a deep breath, Elijah: light your pile. Van Gogh is utterly dead; the world may be fixed, but it never was broken. And shadow itself may resolve into beauty.

Once, when Tinker Creek had frozen inches thick at a wide part near the bridge, I found a pileated woodpecker in the sky by its giant shadow flapping blue on the white ice below. It flew under the neighborhood children's skates; it soared whole and wholly wild though they sliced its wings. I'd like a chunk of that shadow, a pane of freshwater ice to lug with me everywhere, fluttering huge under my arm, to use as the Eskimos did for a window on the world. Shadow is the blue patch where the light doesn't hit. It is mystery itself, and mystery is the ancients' ultima Thule, the modern explorers' Point of Relative Inaccessibility, that boreal point most distant from all known lands. There the twin oceans of beauty and horror meet. The great glaciers are calving. Ice that sifted to earth as snow in the time of Christ shears from the pack with a roar and crumbles to water. It could be that our instruments have not looked deeply enough. The RNA deep in the mantis's jaw is a beautiful ribbon. Did the crawling Polyphemus have in its watery heart one cell, and in that cell one special molecule, and in that molecule one hydrogen atom, and round that atom's nucleus one wild, distant electron that split showed a forest, swaying?

In lieu of a pinochle game, I'll walk a step before bed. No hesitation about gloves now; I swath myself in wool and down from head to foot, and step into the night.

The air bites my nose like pepper. I walk down the road, leap a ditch, and mount the hill where today I clipped the egg cases, where years ago I watched the female mantis frothing out foam. The rutted clay is frozen tonight in shards; its scarps loom in the slanting light like pressure ridges in ice under aurora. The light from the moon is awesome, full and wan. It's not the lustre of noonday it gives, but the lustre of elf-light, utterly lambent and utterly dreamed. I crash over clumps of brittle, hand-blown grass—and I stop still. The frozen twigs of the huge tulip poplar next to the hill clack in the cold like tinsnips.

I look to the sky. What do I know of deep space with its red giants and white dwarfs? I think of our own solar system, of the five mute moons of Uranus—Ariel, Umbriel, Titania, Oberon, Miranda—spinning in their fixed sleep of thralldom. These our actors, as I foretold you, were all spirits. At last I look to the moon; it hangs fixed and full in the east, enormously scrubbed and simple. Our own hometown ultima moon. It must have been a wonderful sight from there, when the olive continents cracked and spread, and the white ice rolled down and up like a window blind. My eyes feel cold when I blink; this is enough of a walk tonight. I lack the apparatus to feel a warmth that few have felt—but it's there. According to Arthur Koestler, Kepler felt the focused warmth when he was experimenting on something entirely different, using concave mirrors. Kepler wrote, "I was engaged in other experiments with mirrors, without thinking of the warmth; I involuntarily turned around to see whether somebody was breathing on my hand." It was warmth from the moon.

CHAPTER 5

Untying the Knot

YESTERDAY I SET OUT to catch the new season, and instead I found an old snakeskin. I was in the sunny February woods by the quarry; the snakeskin was lying in a heap of leaves right next to an aquarium someone had thrown away. I don't know why that someone hauled the aquarium deep into the woods to get rid of it; it had only one broken glass side. The snake found it handy, I imagine; snakes like to rub against something rigid to help them out of their skins, and the broken aquarium looked like the nearest likely object. Together the snakeskin and the aquarium made an interesting scene on the forest floor. It looked like an exhibit at a trial—circumstantial evidence—of a wild scene, as though a snake had burst through the broken side of the aquarium, burst through his ugly old skin, and disappeared, perhaps straight up in the air, in a rush of freedom and beauty.

The snakeskin had unkeeled scales, so it belonged to a nonpoisonous snake. It was roughly five feet long by the yardstick, but I'm not sure because it was very wrinkled and dry, and every time I tried to stretch it flat it broke. I ended up with

seven or eight pieces of it all over the kitchen table in a fine
film of forest dust.

The point I want to make about the snakeskin is that, when
I found it, it was whole and tied in a knot. Now there have
been stories told, even by reputable scientists, of snakes that
have deliberately tied themselves in a knot to prevent larger
snakes from trying to swallow them—but I couldn't imagine
any way that throwing itself into a half hitch would help a
snake trying to escape its skin. Still, ever cautious, I figured
that one of the neighborhood boys could possibly have tied it
in a knot in the fall, for some whimsical boyish reason, and left
it there, where it dried and gathered dust. So I carried the skin
along thoughtlessly as I walked, snagging it sure enough on
a low branch and ripping it in two for the first of many times.
I saw that thick ice still lay on the quarry pond and that the
skunk cabbage was already out in the clearings, and then I
came home and looked at the skin and its knot.

The knot had no beginning. Idly I turned it around in my
hand, searching for a place to untie; I came to with a start when
I realized I must have turned the thing around fully ten times.
Intently, then, I traced the knot's lump around with a finger:
it was continuous. I couldn't untie it any more than I could
untie a doughnut; it was a loop without beginning or end.
These snakes *are* magic, I thought for a second, and then of
course I reasoned what must have happened. The skin had
been pulled inside-out like a peeled sock for several inches;
then an inch or so of the inside-out part—a piece whose length
was coincidentally equal to the diameter of the skin—had
somehow been turned right-side out again, making a thick
lump whose edges were lost in wrinkles, looking exactly like
a knot.

So. I have been thinking about the change of seasons. I
don't want to miss spring this year. I want to distinguish the
last winter frost from the out-of-season one, the frost of spring.
I want to be there on the spot the moment the grass turns
green. I always miss this radical revolution; I see it the next

day from a window, the yard so suddenly green and lush I could envy Nebuchadnezzar down on all fours eating grass. This year I want to stick a net into time and say "now," as men plant flags on the ice and snow and say, "here." But it occurred to me that I could no more catch spring by the tip of the tail than I could untie the apparent knot in the snakeskin; there are no edges to grasp. Both are continuous loops.

I wonder how long it would take you to notice the regular recurrence of the seasons if you were the first man on earth. What would it be like to live in open-ended time broken only by days and nights? You could say, "it's cold again; it was cold before," but you couldn't make the key connection and say, "it was cold this time last year," because the notion of "year" is precisely the one you lack. Assuming that you hadn't yet noticed any orderly progression of heavenly bodies, how long would you have to live on earth before you could feel with any assurance that any one particular long period of cold would, in fact, end? "While the earth remaineth, seedtime and harvest, and cold and heat, and summer and winter, and day and night shall not cease": God makes this guarantee very early in Genesis to a people whose fears on this point had perhaps not been completely allayed.

It must have been fantastically important, at the real beginnings of human culture, to conserve and relay this vital seasonal information, so that the people could anticipate dry or cold seasons, and not huddle on some November rock hoping pathetically that spring was just around the corner. We still very much stress the simple fact of four seasons to schoolchildren; even the most modern of modern new teachers, who don't seem to care if their charges can read or write or name two products of Peru, will still muster some seasonal chitchat and set the kids to making paper pumpkins, or tulips, for the walls. "The people," wrote Van Gogh in a letter, "are very sensitive to the changing seasons." That we are "very sensitive to the changing seasons" is, incidentally, one of the few good reasons to shun travel. If I stay at home I preserve the illusion that what is happening on Tinker Creek is the very newest thing, that I'm at the very vanguard and cutting edge of each new season. I don't want the same season twice in a row; I don't want to know I'm getting last week's weather, used weather, weather broadcast up and down the coast, old-hat weather.

But there's always unseasonable weather. What we think of the weather and behavior of life on the planet at any given season is really all a matter of statistical probabilities; at any given point, anything might happen. There is a bit of every season in each season. Green plants—deciduous green leaves—grow everywhere, all winter long, and small shoots come up pale and new in every season. Leaves die on the tree in May, turn brown, and fall into the creek. The calendar, the weather, and the behavior of wild creatures have the slimmest of connections. Everything overlaps smoothly for only a few weeks each season, and then it all tangles up again. The temperature, of course, lags far behind the calendar seasons, since the earth absorbs and releases heat slowly, like a leviathan breathing. Migrating birds head south in what appears to be dire panic, leaving mild weather and fields full of insects and seeds; they reappear as if in all eagerness in January, and poke about morosely in the snow. Several years ago our October woods would have made a dismal colored photograph for a sadist's calendar: a killing frost came before the leaves had even begun to brown; they drooped from every tree like crepe, blackened and limp. It's all a chancy, jumbled affair at best, as things seem to be below the stars.

Time is the continuous loop, the snakeskin with scales endlessly overlapping without beginning or end, or time is an ascending spiral if you will, like a child's toy Slinky. Of course we have no idea which arc on the loop is our time, let alone where the loop itself is, so to speak, or down whose lofty flight of stairs the Slinky so uncannily walks.

The power we seek, too, seems to be a continuous loop. I

have always been sympathetic with the early notion of a divine power that exists in a particular place, or that travels about over the face of the earth as a man might wander—and when he is "there" he is surely not here. You can shake the hand of a man you meet in the woods; but the spirit seems to roll along like the mythical hoop snake with its tail in its mouth. There are no hands to shake or edges to untie. It rolls along the mountain ridges like a fireball, shooting off a spray of sparks at random, and will not be trapped, slowed, grasped, fetched, peeled, or aimed. "As for the wheels, it was cried unto them in my hearing, O wheel." This is the hoop of flame that shoots the rapids in the creek or spins across the dizzy meadows; this is the arsonist of the sunny woods: catch it if you can.

CHAPTER 6

The Present

I

CATCH IT IF YOU CAN.

It is early March. I am dazed from a long day of interstate driving homeward; I pull in at a gas station in Nowhere, Virginia, north of Lexington. The young boy in charge ("Chick 'at oll?") is offering a free cup of coffee with every gas purchase. We talk in the glass-walled office while my coffee cools enough to drink. He tells me, among other things, that the rival gas station down the road, whose FREE COFFEE sign is visible from the interstate, charges you fifteen cents if you want your coffee in a Styrofoam cup, as opposed, I guess, to your bare hands.

All the time we talk, the boy's new beagle puppy is skidding around the office, sniffing impartially at my shoes and at the wire rack of folded maps. The cheerful human conversation wakes me, recalls me, not to a normal consciousness, but to a kind of energetic readiness. I step outside, followed by the puppy.

I am absolutely alone. There are no other customers. The road is vacant, the interstate is out of sight and earshot. I have hazarded into a new corner of the world, an unknown spot, a Brigadoon. Before me extends a low hill trembling in yellow brome, and behind the hill, filling the sky, rises an enormous mountain ridge, forested, alive and awesome with brilliant blown lights. I have never seen anything so tremulous and live. Overhead, great strips and chunks of cloud dash to the northwest in a gold rush. At my back the sun is setting—how can I not have noticed before that the sun is setting? My mind has been a blank slab of black asphalt for hours, but that doesn't stop the sun's wild wheel. I set my coffee beside me on the curb; I smell loam on the wind; I pat the puppy; I watch the mountain.

My hand works automatically over the puppy's fur, following the line of hair under his ears, down his neck, inside his forelegs, along his hot-skinned belly.

Shadows lope along the mountain's rumpled flanks; they elongate like root tips, like lobes of spilling water, faster and faster. A warm purple pigment pools in each ruck and tuck of the rock; it deepens and spreads, boring crevasses, canyons. As the purple vaults and slides, it tricks out the unleafed forest and rumpled rock in gilt, in shape-shifting patches of glow. These gold lights veer and retract, shatter and glide in a series of dazzling splashes, shrinking, leaking, exploding. The ridge's bosses and hummocks sprout bulging from its side; the whole mountain looms miles closer; the light warms and reddens; the bare forest folds and pleats itself like living protoplasm before my eyes, like a running chart, a wildly scrawling oscillograph on the present moment. The air cools; the puppy's skin is hot. I am more alive than all the world.

This is it, I think, this is it, right now, the present, this empty gas station, here, this western wind, this tang of coffee on the tongue, and I am patting the puppy, I am watching the mountain. And the second I verbalize this awareness in my brain, I cease to see the mountain or feel the puppy. I am opaque, so much black asphalt. But at the same second, the second I know I've lost it, I also realize that the puppy is still squirming on his back under my hand. Nothing has changed for him. He draws his legs down to stretch the skin taut so he feels every fingertip's stroke along his furred and arching side, his flank, his flung-back throat.

I sip my coffee. I look at the mountain, which is still doing its tricks, as you look at a still-beautiful face belonging to a person who was once your lover in another country years ago: with fond nostalgia, and recognition, but no real feeling save a secret astonishment that you are now strangers. Thanks. For the memories. It is ironic that the one thing that all religions recognize as separating us from our creator—our very self-consciousness—is also the one thing that divides us from our fellow creatures. It was a bitter birthday present from evolution, cutting us off at both ends. I get in the car and drive home.

Catch it if you can. The present is an invisible electron; its lightning path traced faintly on a blackened screen is fleet, and fleeing, and gone.

That I ended this experience prematurely for myself—that I drew scales over my eyes between me and the mountain and gloved my hand between me and the puppy—is not the only point. After all, it would have ended anyway. I've never seen a sunset or felt a wind that didn't. The levitating saints came down at last, and their two feet bore real weight. No, the point is that not only does time fly and do we die, but that in these reckless conditions we live at all, and are vouchsafed, for the duration of certain inexplicable moments, to know it.

Stephen Graham startled me by describing this same gift in his antique and elegant book, *The Gentle Art of Tramping.* He wrote, "And as you sit on the hillside, or lie prone under the trees of the forest, or sprawl wet-legged on the shingly beach of a mountain stream, the great door, that does not look like a door, opens." That great door opens on the present, illuminates it as with a multitude of flashing torches.

I had thought, because I had seen the tree with the lights in it, that the great door, by definition, opens on eternity. Now that I have "patted the puppy"—now that I have experienced the present purely through my senses—I discover that, although the door to the tree with the lights in it was opened *from* eternity, as it were, and shone on that tree eternal lights, it nevertheless opened on the real and present cedar. It opened on time: Where else? That Christ's incarnation occurred improbably, ridiculously, at such-and-such a time, into such-and-such a place, is referred to—with great sincerity even among believers—as "the scandal of particularity." Well, the "scandal of particularity" is the only world that I, in particular, know. What use has eternity for light? We're all up to our necks in this particular scandal. Why, we might as well ask, not a plane tree, instead of a bo? I never saw a tree that was no tree in particular; I never met a man, not the greatest theologian, who filled infinity, or even whose hand, say, was undifferentiated, fingerless, like a griddlecake, and not lobed and split just so with the incursions of time.

I don't want to stress this too much. Seeing the tree with the lights in it was an experience vastly different in quality as well as in import from patting the puppy. On that cedar tree shone, however briefly, the steady, inward flames of eternity; across the mountain by the gas station raced the familiar flames of the falling sun. But on both occasions I thought, with rising exultation, this is it, this is it; praise the lord; praise the land. Experiencing the present purely is being emptied and hollow; you catch grace as a man fills his cup under a waterfall.

Consciousness itself does not hinder living in the present. In fact, it is only to a heightened awareness that the great door to the present opens at all. Even a certain amount of interior verbalization is helpful to enforce the memory of whatever it is that is taking place. The gas station beagle puppy, after all, may have experienced those same moments more purely than I did, but he brought fewer instruments to bear on the same material, he had no data for comparison, and he profited only in the grossest of ways, by having an assortment of itches scratched.

*Self-*consciousness, however, does hinder the experience of the present. It is the one instrument that unplugs all the rest. So long as I lose myself in a tree, say, I can scent its leafy breath or estimate its board feet of lumber, I can draw its fruits or boil tea on its branches, and the tree stays tree. But the second I become aware of myself at any of these activities—looking over my own shoulder, as it were—the tree vanishes, uprooted from the spot and flung out of sight as if it had never grown. And time, which had flowed down into the tree bearing new revelations like floating leaves at every moment, ceases. It dams, stills, stagnates.

Self-consciousness is the curse of the city and all that sophistication implies. It is the glimpse of oneself in a storefront window, the unbidden awareness of reactions on the faces of other people—the novelist's world, not the poet's. I've lived there. I remember what the city has to offer: human companionship, major-league baseball, and a clatter of quickening stimulus like a rush from strong drugs that leaves you drained. I remember how you bide your time in the city, and think, if you stop to think, "next year . . . I'll start living; next year . . . I'll start my life." Innocence is a better world.

Innocence sees that this is it, and finds it world enough, and time. Innocence is not the prerogative of infants and puppies, and far less of mountains and fixed stars, which have no prerogatives at all. It is not lost to us; the world is a better place than that. Like any other of the spirit's good gifts, it is there if you want it, free for the asking, as has been stressed by stronger words than mine. It is possible to pursue innocence as hounds pursue hares: singlemindedly, driven by a kind of love, crashing over creeks, keening and lost in fields and forests, circling, vaulting over hedges and hills wide-eyed, giving loud tongue all unawares to the deepest, most incomprehensible longing, a root-flame in the heart, and that warbling chorus resounding back from the mountains, hurling itself from ridge to ridge over the valley, now faint, now clear, ringing the air through which the hounds tear, open-mouthed, the echoes of their own wails dimly knocking in their lungs.

What I call innocence is the spirit's unself-conscious state at any moment of pure devotion to any object. It is at once a receptiveness and total concentration. One needn't be, shouldn't be, reduced to a puppy. If you wish to tell me that the city offers galleries, I'll pour you a drink and enjoy your company while it lasts; but I'll bear with me to my grave those pure moments at the Tate (was it the Tate?) where I stood planted, open-mouthed, born, before that one particular canvas, that river, up to my neck, gasping, lost, receding into watercolor depth and depth to the vanishing point, buoyant, awed, and had to be literally hauled away. These are our few live seasons. Let us live them as purely as we can, in the present.

The color-patches of vision part, shift, and reform as I move through space in time. The present is the object of vision, and what I see before me at any given second is a full field of color-patches scattered just so. The configuration will never be repeated. Living is moving; time is a live creek bearing changing lights. As I move, or as the world moves around me, the fullness of what I see shatters. This second of shattering is an *augenblick,* a particular configuration, a slant of light shot in the open eye. Goethe's Faust risks all if he should cry to the moment, the *augenblick, "Verweile doch!"* "Last forever!" Who hasn't prayed that prayer? But the *augenblick* isn't going to *verweile.* You were lucky to get it in the first place. The present is a freely given canvas. That it is constantly being ripped apart and washed downstream goes without saying; it is a canvas, nevertheless.

I like the slants of light; I'm a collector. That's a good one, I say, that bit of bank there, the snakeskin and the aquarium, that patch of light from the creek on bark. Sometimes I spread my fingers into a viewfinder; more often I peek through a tiny square or rectangle—a frame of shadow—formed by the tips of index fingers and thumbs held directly before my eye. Speaking of the development of *papier collé* in late Cubism, Picasso said, "We tried to get rid of *trompe-l'oeil* to find a *trompe-l'esprit.*" Trompe-l'esprit! I don't know why the world didn't latch on to the phrase. Our whole life is a stroll—or a forced march—through a gallery hung in trompes-l'esprit.

Once I visited a great university and wandered, a stranger, into the subterranean halls of its famous biology department. I saw a sign on a door: ichthyology department. The door was open a crack, and as I walked past I glanced in. I saw just a flash. There were two white-coated men seated opposite each other on high lab stools at a hard-surfaced table. They bent over identical white enamel trays. On one side, one man, with a lancet, was just cutting into an enormous preserved fish he'd taken from a jar. On the other side, the other man, with a silver spoon, was eating a grapefruit. I laughed all the way back to Virginia.

Michael Goldman wrote in a poem, "When the Muse comes She doesn't tell you to write;/ She says get up for a minute, I've something to show you, stand here." What made me look up at that roadside tree?

The road to Grundy, Virginia, is, as you might expect, a narrow scrawl scribbled all over the most improbably peaked and hunched mountains you ever saw. The few people who live along the road also seem peaked and hunched. But what on earth—? It was hot, sunny summer. The road was just bending off sharply to the right. I hadn't seen a house in miles, and none was in sight. At the apogee of the road's curve grew an enormous oak, a massive bur oak two hundred years old, one hundred and fifty feet high, an oak whose lowest limb was beyond the span of the highest ladder. I looked up: there were clothes spread all over the tree. Red shirts, blue trousers, black pants, little baby smocks—they weren't hung from branches. They were outside, carefully spread, splayed as if to dry, on

the outer leaves of the great oak's crown. Were there pillowcases, blankets? I can't remember. There was a gay assortment
of cotton underwear, yellow dresses, children's green sweaters, plaid skirts. . . . You know roads. A bend comes and you
take it, thoughtlessly, moving on. I looked behind me for
another split second, astonished; both sides of the tree's canopy, clear to the top, bore clothes. Trompe!

But there is more to the present than a series of snapshots.
We are not merely sensitized film; we have feelings, a memory
for information and an eidetic memory for the imagery of our
own pasts.

Our layered consciousness is a tiered track for an unmatched assortment of concentrically wound reels. Each one
plays out for all of life its dazzle and blur of translucent
shadow-pictures; each one hums at every moment its own
secret melody in its own unique key. We tune in and out. But
moments are not lost. Time out of mind is time nevertheless,
cumulative, informing the present. From even the deepest
slumber you wake with a jolt—older, closer to death, and
wiser, grateful for breath. You quit your seat in a darkened
movie theatre, walk past the empty lobby, out the double glass
doors, and step like Orpheus into the street. And the cumulative force of the present you've forgotten sets you reeling,
staggering, as if you'd been struck broadside by a plank. It all
floods back to you. Yes, you say, as if you'd been asleep a
hundred years, this is it, this is the real weather, the lavender
light fading, the full moisture in your lungs, the heat from the
pavement on your lips and palms—not the dry orange dust
from horses' hooves, the salt sea, the sour Coke—but this solid
air, the blood pumping up your thighs again, your fingers
alive. And on the way home you drive exhilarated, energized,
under scented, silhouetted trees.

II

I am sitting under a sycamore by Tinker Creek. It is early spring, the day after I patted the puppy. I have come to the creek—the backyard stretch of the creek—in the middle of the day, to feel the delicate gathering of heat, real sun's heat, in the air, and to watch new water come down the creek. Don't expect more than this, and a mental ramble. I'm in the market for some present tense; I'm on the lookout, shopping around, more so every year. It's a seller's market—do you think I won't sell all that I have to buy it? Thomas Merton wrote, in a light passage in one of his Gethsemane journals: "Suggested emendation in the Lord's Prayer: Take out 'Thy Kingdom come' and substitute 'Give us time!' " But time is the one thing we have been given, and we have been given to time. Time gives us a whirl. We keep waking from a dream we can't recall, looking around in surprise, and lapsing back, for years on end. All I want to do is stay awake, keep my head up, prop my eyes open, with toothpicks, with trees.

Before me the creek is seventeen feet wide, splashing over random sandstone outcroppings and scattered rocks. I'm lucky; the creek is loud here, because of the rocks, and wild. In the low water of summer and fall I can cross to the opposite bank by leaping from stone to stone. Upstream is a wall of light split into planks by smooth sandstone ledges that cross the creek evenly, like steps. Downstream the live water before me stills, dies suddenly as if extinguished, and vanishes around a bend shaded summer and winter by overarching tulips, locusts, and Osage orange. Everywhere I look are creekside trees whose ascending boles against water and grass accent the vertical thrust of the land in this spot. The creek rests the eye, a haven, a breast; the two steep banks vault from the creek like wings. Not even the sycamore's crown can peek over the land in any direction.

My friend Rosanne Coggeshall, the poet, says that "sycamore" is the most intrinsically beautiful word in English. This sycamore is old; its lower bark is always dusty from years of floodwaters lapping up its trunk. Like many sycamores, too, it is quirky, given to flights and excursions. Its trunk lists over the creek at a dizzying angle, and from that trunk extends a long, skinny limb that spurts high over the opposite bank without branching. The creek reflects the speckled surface of this limb, pale even against the highest clouds, and that image pales whiter and thins as it crosses the creek, shatters in the riffles and melds together, quivering and mottled, like some enormous primeval reptile under the water.

I want to think about trees. Trees have a curious relationship to the subject of the present moment. There are many created things in the universe that outlive us, that outlive the sun, even, but I can't think about them. I live with trees. There are creatures under our feet, creatures that live over our heads, but trees live quite convincingly in the same filament of air we inhabit, and, in addition, they extend impressively in both directions, up and down, shearing rock and fanning air, doing their real business just out of reach. A blind man's idea of hugeness is a tree. They have their sturdy bodies and special skills; they garner fresh water; they abide. This sycamore above me, below me, by Tinker Creek, is a case in point; the sight of it crowds my brain with an assortment of diverting thoughts, all as present to me as these slivers of pressure from grass on my elbow's skin. I want to come at the subject of the present by showing how consciousness dashes and ambles around the labyrinthine tracks of the mind, returning again and again, however briefly, to the senses: "If there were but one erect and solid standing tree in the woods, all creatures would go to rub against it and make sure of their footing." But so long as I stay in my thoughts, my foot slides under trees; I fall, or I dance.

Sycamores are among the last trees to go into leaf; in the fall, they are the first to shed. They make sweet food in green broadleaves for a while—leaves wide as plates—and then go wild and wave their long white arms. In ancient Rome men honored the sycamore—in the form of its cousin, the Oriental plane—by watering its roots with wine. Xerxes, I read, "halted his unwieldly army for days that he might contemplate to his satisfaction" the beauty of a single sycamore.

You are Xerxes in Persia. Your army spreads on a vast and arid peneplain . . . you call to you all your sad captains, and give the order to halt. You have seen the tree with the lights in it, haven't you? You must have. Xerxes buffeted on a plain, ambition drained in a puff. That fusillade halts any army in its tracks. Your men are bewildered; they lean on their spears, sucking the rinds of gourds. There is nothing to catch the eye in this flatness, nothing but a hollow, hammering sky, a waste of sedge in the lee of windblown rocks, a meagre ribbon of scrub willow tracing a slumbering watercourse . . . and that sycamore. You saw it; you still stand rapt and mute, exalted, remembering or not remembering over a period of days to shade your head with your robe.

"He had its form wrought upon a medal of gold to help him remember it the rest of his life." Your teeth are chattering; it is just before dawn and you have started briefly from your daze. "Goldsmith!" The goldsmith is sodden with sleep, surly. He lights his forge, he unrolls the dusty cotton wrapping from his half-forgotten stylus and tongs, he waits for the sun. We all ought to have a goldsmith following us around. But it goes without saying, doesn't it, Xerxes, that no gold medal worn around your neck will bring back the glad hour, keep those lights kindled so long as you live, forever present? Pascal saw it. He grabbed pen and paper; he managed to scrawl the one word, FEU; he wore that scrap of paper sewn in his shirt the rest of his life. I don't know what Pascal saw. I saw a cedar. Xerxes saw a sycamore.

These trees stir me. The past inserts a finger into a slit in the skin of the present, and pulls. I remember how sycamores grew—and presumably still grow—in the city, in Pittsburgh, even along the busiest streets. I used to spend hours in the backyard, thinking God knows what, and peeling the mottled bark of a sycamore, idly, littering the grass with dried lappets and strips, leaving the tree's trunk at eye level moist, thin-skinned and yellow—until someone would catch me at it from the kitchen window, and I would awake, and look at my work in astonishment, and think oh no, this time I've killed the sycamore for sure.

Here in Virginia the trees reach enormous proportions, especially in the lowlands on banksides. It is hard to understand how the same tree could thrive both choking along Pittsburgh's Penn Avenue and slogging knee-deep in Tinker Creek. Of course, come to think of it, I've done the same thing myself. Because a sycamore's primitive bark is not elastic but frangible, it sheds continuously as it grows; seen from a distance, a sycamore seems to grow in pallor and vulnerability as it grows in height; the bare uppermost branches are white against the sky.

The sky is deep and distant, laced with sycamore limbs like a hatching of crossed swords. I can scarcely see it; I'm not looking. I don't come to the creek for sky unmediated, but for shelter. My back rests on a steep bank under the sycamore; before me shines the creek—the creek which is about all the light I can stand—and beyond it rises the other bank, also steep, and planted in trees.

I have never understood why so many mystics of all creeds experience the presence of God on mountaintops. Aren't they afraid of being blown away? God said to Moses on Sinai that even the priests, who have access to the Lord, must hallow themselves, for fear that the Lord may break out against them. This is *the* fear. It often feels best to lay low, inconspicuous, instead of waving your spirit around from high places like a lightning rod. For if God is in one sense the igniter, a fireball that spins over the ground of continents, God is also in another sense the destroyer, lightning, blind power, impartial as the atmosphere. Or God is one "G." You get a comforting sense, in a curved, hollow place, of being vulnerable to only a relatively narrow column of God as air.

In the open, anything might happen. Dorothy Dunnett, the great medievalist, states categorically: "There is no reply, in clear terrain, to an archer in cover." Any copperhead anywhere is an archer in cover; how much more so is God! Invisibility is the all-time great "cover"; and that the one infinite power deals so extravagantly and unfathomably in death—death morning, noon, and night, all manner of death—makes that power an archer, there is no getting around it. And we the people are so vulnerable. Our bodies are shot with mortality. Our legs are fear and our arms are time. These chill humors seep through our capillaries, weighting each cell with an icy dab of nonbeing, and that dab grows and swells and sucks the cell dry. That is why physical courage is so important—it fills, as it were, the holes—and why it is so invigorating. The least brave act, chance taken and passage won, makes you feel loud as a child.

But it gets harder. The courage of children and beasts is a function of innocence. We let our bodies go the way of our fears. A teen-aged boy, king of the world, will spend weeks in front of a mirror perfecting some difficult trick with a lighter, a muscle, a tennis ball, a coin. Why do we lose interest in physical mastery? If I feel like turning cartwheels—and I do—why don't I learn to turn cartwheels, instead of regretting that I never learned as a child? We could all be aerialists like squirrels, divers like seals; we could be purely patient, perfectly fleet, walking on our hands even, if our living or stature required it. We can't even sit straight, or support our weary heads.

When we lose our innocence—when we start feeling the weight of the atmosphere and learn that there's death in the pot—we take leave of our senses. Only children can hear the song of the male house mouse. Only children keep their eyes open. The only thing they *have* got is sense; they have highly developed "input systems," admitting all data indiscriminately. Matt Spireng has collected thousands of arrowheads and spearheads; he says that if you really want to find arrowheads, you must walk with a child—a child will pick up *everything.* All my adult life I have wished to see the cemented case of a caddisfly larva. It took Sally Moore, the young daughter of friends, to find one on the pebbled bottom of a shallow stream on whose bank we sat side by side. "What's this?" she asked. That, I wanted to say as I recognized the prize she held, is a memento mori for people who read too much.

We found other caddisfly cases that day, Sally and I, after I had learned to focus so fine, and I saved one. It is a hollow cylinder three quarters of an inch long, a little masterpiece of masonry consisting entirely of cemented grains of coarse sand only one layer thick. Some of the sand grains are red, and it was by searching for this red that I learned to spot the cases. The caddisfly larva will use any bits it can find to fashion its house; in fact, entomologists have amused themselves by placing a naked larva in an aquarium furnished only with, say, red sand. When the larva has laid around its body several rows of red sand, the entomologist transfers it to another aquarium in which only white bits are available. The larva busily adds rows of white to the red wall, and then here comes the entomologist again, with a third and final aquarium full of blue sand. At any rate, the point I want to make is that this tiny immature creature responds to an instinct to put something between its flesh and a jagged world. If you give a "masonry mosaic" kind of caddisfly larva only large decayed leaves, that larva, confronted by something utterly novel, will nevertheless bite the leaves into shreds and rig those shreds into a case.

The general rule in nature is that live things are soft within and rigid without. We vertebrates are living dangerously, and we vertebrates are positively piteous, like so many peeled trees. This oft was thought, but ne'er so well expressed as by Pliny, who writes of nature, "To all the rest, given she hath sufficient to clad them everyone according to their kind: as namely, shells, cods, hard hides, pricks, shags, bristles, hair, down feathers, quills, scales, and fleeces of wool. The very trunks and stems of trees and plants, she hath defended with bark and rind, yea and the same sometimes double, against the injuries both of heat and cold: man alone, poor wretch, she hath laid all naked upon the bare earth, even on his birthday, to cry and wraule presently from the very first hour that he is born into the world."

I am sitting under a sycamore tree: I am soft-shell and peeled to the least puff of wind or smack of grit. The present of our life looks different under trees. Trees have dominion. I never killed that backyard sycamore; even its frailest inner bark was a shield. Trees do not accumulate life, but deadwood, like a thickening coat of mail. Their odds actually improve as they age. Some trees, like giant sequoias, are, practically speaking, immortal, vulnerable only to another ice age. They are not even susceptible to fire. Sequoia wood barely burns, and the bark is "nearly as fireproof as asbestos. The top of one sequoia, struck by lightning a few years ago during a July thunderstorm, smoldered quietly, without apparently damaging the tree, until it was put out by a snowstorm in October." Some trees sink taproots to rock; some spread wide mats of roots clutching at acres. They will not be blown. We run around under these obelisk-creatures, teetering on our soft, small feet. We are out on a jaunt, picnicking, fattening like puppies for our deaths. Shall I carve a name on this trunk? What if *I* fell in a forest: Would a tree hear?

I am sitting under a bankside sycamore; my mind is a slope. Arthur Koestler wrote, "In his review of the literature on the psychological present, Woodrow found that its maximum span is estimated to lie between 2.3 and 12 seconds." How did anyone measure that slide? As soon as you are conscious of it, it is gone. I repeat a phrase: the thin tops of mountains. Soon the thin tops of mountains erupt, as if volcanically, from my brain's core. I can see them; they are, surprisingly, serrate—

scallopped like the blade of a kitchen knife—and brown as
leaves. The serrated edges are so thin they are translucent;
through the top of one side of the brown ridge I can see, in
silhouette, a circling sharp-shinned hawk; through another,
deep tenuous veins of metallic ore. This isn't Tinker Creek.
Where do I live, anyway? I lose myself, I float. . . . I am in
Persia, trying to order a watermelon in German. It's insane.
The engineer has abandoned the control room, and an idiot
is splicing the reels. What could I contribute to the "literature
on the psychological present?" If I could remember to press
the knob on the stopwatch, I wouldn't be in Persia. Before
they invented the unit of the second, people used to time the
lapse of short events on their pulses. Oh, but what about that
heave in the wrist when I saw the tree with the lights in it, and
my heart ceased, but I am still there?

Scenes drift across the screen from nowhere. I can never
discover the connection between any one scene and what I am
more consciously thinking, nor can I ever conjure the scene
back in full vividness. It is like a ghost, in full-dress regalia,
that wafts across the stage set unnoticed by the principle characters. It appears complete, in full color, wordless, though
already receding: the tennis courts on Fifth Avenue in Pittsburgh, an equestrian statue in a Washington park, a basement
dress shop in New York city—scenes that I thought meant
nothing to me. These aren't still shots; the camera is always
moving. And the scene is always just slipping out of sight, as
if in spite of myself I were always just descending a hill,
rounding a corner, stepping into the street with a companion
who urges me on, while I look back over my shoulder at the
sight which recedes, vanishes. The present of my consciousness is itself a mystery which is also always just rounding a
bend like a floating branch borne by a flood. Where am I? But
I'm not. "I will overturn, overturn, overturn, it: and it shall
be no more. . . ."

*   *   *

All right then. Pull yourself together. Is this where I'm
spending my life, in the "reptile brain," this lamp at the top
of the spine like a lighthouse flipping mad beams indiscriminately into the darkness, into the furred thoraxes of moths,
onto the backs of leaping fishes and the wrecks of schooners?
Come up a level; surface.

I am sitting under a sycamore by Tinker Creek. I am really
here, alive on the intricate earth under trees. But under me,
directly under the weight of my body on the grass, are other
creatures, just as real, for whom also this moment, this tree,
is "it." Take just the top inch of soil, the world squirming right
under my palms. In the top inch of forest soil, biologists found
"an average of 1,356 living creatures present in each square
foot, including 865 mites, 265 springtails, 22 millipedes, 19
adult beetles and various numbers of 12 other forms. . . . Had
an estimate also been made of the microscopic population, it
might have ranged up to two billion bacteria and many millions of fungi, protozoa and algae—in a mere *teaspoonful* of
soil." The chrysalids of butterflies linger here too, folded,
rigid, and dreamless. I might as well include these creatures
in this moment, as best I can. My ignoring them won't strip
them of their reality, and admitting them, one by one, into my
consciousness might heighten mine, might add their dim
awareness to my human consciousness, such as it is, and set up
a buzz, a vibration like the beating ripples a submerged muskrat makes on the water, from this particular moment, this tree.
Hasidism has a tradition that one of man's purposes is to assist
God in the work of redemption by "hallowing" the things of
creation. By a tremendous heave of his spirit, the devout man
frees the divine sparks trapped in the mute things of time; he
uplifts the forms and moments of creation, bearing them aloft
into that rare air and hallowing fire in which all clays must
shatter and burst. Keeping the subsoil world under trees in
mind, in intelligence, is the *least* I can do.
Earthworms in staggering processions lurch through the

grit underfoot, gobbling downed leaves and spewing forth castings by the ton. Moles mine intricate tunnels in networks; there are often so many of these mole tunnels here by the creek that when I walk, every step is a letdown. A mole is almost entirely loose inside its skin, and enormously mighty. If you can catch a mole, it will, in addition to biting you memorably, leap from your hand in a single convulsive contraction and be gone as soon as you have it. You are never really able to see it; you only feel its surge and thrust against your palm, as if you held a beating heart in a paper bag. What could I not do if I had the power and will of a mole! But the mole churns earth.

Last summer some muskrats had a den under this tree's roots on the bank; I think they are still there now. Muskrats' wet fur rounds the domed clay walls of the den and slicks them smooth as any igloo. They strew the floor with plant husks and seeds, rut in repeated bursts, and sleep humped and soaking, huddled in balls. These, too, are part of what Buber calls "the infinite ethos of the moment."

I am not here yet; I can't shake that day on the interstate. My mind branches and shoots like a tree.

Under my spine, the sycamore roots suck watery salts. Root tips thrust and squirm between particles of soil, probing minutely; from their roving, burgeoning tissues spring infinitesimal root hairs, transparent and hollow, which affix themselves to specks of grit and sip. These runnels run silent and deep; the whole earth trembles, rent and fissured, hurled and drained. I wonder what happens to root systems when trees die. Do those spread blind networks starve, starve in the midst of plenty, and desiccate, clawing at specks?

Under the world's conifers—under the creekside cedar behind where I sit—a mantle of fungus wraps the soil in a weft, shooting out blind thread after frail thread of palest dissolved white. From root tip to root tip, root hair to root hair, these filaments loop and wind; the thought of them always reminds me of Rimbaud's "I have stretched cords from steeple to steeple, garlands from window to window, chains of gold from star to star, and I dance." King David leaped and danced naked before the ark of the Lord in a barren desert. Here the very looped soil is an intricate throng of praise. Make connections; let rip; and dance where you can.

The insects and earthworms, moles, muskrats, roots and fungal strands are not all. An even frailer, dimmer movement, a pavane, is being performed deep under me now. The nymphs of cicadas are alive. You see their split skins, an inch long, brown, and translucent, curved and segmented like shrimp, stuck arching on the trunks of trees. And you see the adults occasionally, large and sturdy, with glittering black and green bodies, veined transparent wings folded over their backs, and artificial-looking, bright red eyes. But you never see the living nymphs. They are underground, clasping roots and sucking the sweet sap of trees.

In the South, the periodical cicada has a breeding cycle of thirteen years, instead of seventeen years as in the North. That a live creature spends thirteen consecutive years scrabbling around in the root systems of trees in the dark and damp— thirteen years!—is amply boggling for me. Four more years— or four less—wouldn't alter the picture a jot. In the dark of an April night the nymphs emerge, all at once, as many as eighty-four of them digging into the air from every square foot of ground. They inch up trees and bushes, shed their skins, and begin that hollow, shrill grind that lasts all summer. I guess as nymphs they never see the sun. Adults lay eggs in slits along twig bark; the hatched nymphs drop to the ground and burrow, vanish from the face of the earth, biding their time, for thirteen years. How many are under me now, wishing what? What would I think about for thirteen years? They curl, crawl, clutch at roots and suck, suck blinded, suck trees, rain or shine, heat or frost, year after groping year.

And under the cicadas, deeper down than the longest taproot, between and beneath the rounded black rocks and slanting slabs of sandstone in the earth, ground water is creeping.

Ground water seeps and slides, across and down, across and down, leaking from here to there minutely, at the rate of a mile a year. What a tug of waters goes on! There are flings and pulls in every direction at every moment. The world is a wild wrestle under the grass: earth shall be moved.

What else is going on right this minute while ground water creeps under my feet? The galaxy is careening in a slow, muffled widening. If a million solar systems are born every hour, then surely hundreds burst into being as I shift my weight to the other elbow. The sun's surface is now exploding; other stars implode and vanish, heavy and black, out of sight. Meteorites are arcing to earth invisibly all day long. On the planet the winds are blowing: the polar easterlies, the westerlies, the northeast and southeast trades. Somewhere, someone under full sail is becalmed, in the horse latitudes, in the doldrums; in the northland, a trapper is maddened, crazed, by the eerie scent of the chinook, the snoweater, a wind that can melt two feet of snow in a day. The pampero blows, and the tramontane, and the Boro, sirocco, levanter, mistral. Lick a finger: feel the now.

Spring is seeping north, towards me and away from me, at sixteen miles a day. Caribou straggle across the tundra from the spruce-fir forests of the south, first the pregnant does, hurried, then the old and unmated does, then suddenly a massing of bucks, and finally the diseased and injured, one by one. Somewhere, people in airplanes are watching the sun set and peering down at clustered houselights, stricken. In the montana in Peru, on the rain-forested slopes of the Andes, a woman kneels in a dust clearing before a dark shelter of overlapping broadleaves; between her breasts hangs a cross of smooth sticks she peeled with her teeth and lashed with twistings of vine. Along estuary banks of tidal rivers all over the world, snails in black clusters like currants are gliding up and down the stems of reed and sedge, migrating every moment with the dip and swing of tides. Behind me, Tinker Mountain, and to my left, Dead Man Mountain, are eroding one thousandth of an inch a year.

The tomcat that used to wake me is dead; he was long since grist for an earthworm's casting, and is now the clear sap of a Pittsburgh sycamore, or the honeydew of aphids sucked from that sycamore's high twigs and sprayed in sticky drops on a stranger's car. A steer across the road stumbles into the creek to drink; he blinks; he laps; a floating leaf in the current catches against his hock and wrenches away. The giant water bug I saw is dead, long dead, and its moist gut and rigid casing are both, like the empty skin of the frog it sucked, dissolved, spread, still spreading right now, in the steer's capillaries, in the wind-blown smatter of clouds overhead, in the Sargasso Sea. The mockingbird that dropped furled from a roof . . . but this is no time to count my dead. That is nightwork. The dead are staring, underground, their sleeping heels in the air.

The sharks I saw are roving up and down the coast. If the sharks cease roving, if they still their twist and rest for a moment, they die. They need new water pushed into their gills; they need dance. Somewhere east of me, on another continent, it is sunset, and starlings in breathtaking bands are winding high in the sky to their evening roost. Under the water just around the bend downstream, the coot feels with its foot in the creek, rolling its round red eyes. In the house a spider slumbers at her wheel like a spinster curled in a corner all day long. The mantis egg cases are tied to the mock-orange hedge; within each case, within each egg, cells elongate, narrow, and split; cells bubble and curve inward, align, harden or hollow or stretch. The Polyphemus moth, its wings crushed to its back, crawls down the driveway, crawls down the driveway, crawls. . . . The snake whose skin I tossed away, whose home-made, personal skin is now tangled at the county dump—that snake in the woods by the quarry stirs now, quickens now, prodded under the leafmold by sunlight, by the probing root of May apple, the bud of bloodroot. And where are you now?

* * *

I stand. All the blood in my body crashes to my feet and instantly heaves to my head, so I blind and blush, as a tree blasts into leaf spouting water hurled up from roots. What happens to me? I stand before the sycamore dazed; I gaze at its giant trunk.

Big trees stir memories. You stand in their dimness, where the very light is blue, staring unfocused at the thickest part of the trunk as though it were a long, dim tunnel—: the Squirrel Hill tunnel. You're gone. The egg-shaped patch of light at the end of the blackened tunnel swells and looms; the sing of tire tread over brick reaches an ear-splitting crescendo; the light breaks over the hood, smack, and full on your face. You have achieved the past.

Eskimo shamans bound with sealskin thongs on the igloo floor used to leave their bodies, their skins, and swim "muscle-naked" like a flensed seal through the rock of continents, in order to placate an old woman who lived on the sea floor and sent or withheld game. When he fulfilled this excruciating mission, the Eskimo shaman would awake, returned to his skin exhausted from the dark ardors of flailing peeled through rock, and find himself in a lighted igloo, at a sort of party, among dear faces.

In the same way, having bored through a sycamore trunk and tunneled beneath a Pennsylvania mountain, I blink, awed by the yellow light, and find myself in a shady side of town, in a stripped dining room, dancing, years ago. There is a din of trumpets, upbeat and indistinct, like some movie score for a love scene played on a city balcony; there is an immeasurably distant light glowing from half-remembered faces. . . . I stir. The heave of my shoulders returns me to the present, to the tree, the sycamore, and I yank myself away, shove off and moving, seeking live water.

III

Live water heals memories. I look up the creek and here it comes, the future, being borne aloft as on a winding succession of laden trays. You may wake and look from the window and breathe the real air, and say, with satisfaction or with longing, "This is it." But if you look up the creek, if you look up the creek in any weather, your spirit fills, and you are saying, with an exulting rise of the lungs, "Here it comes!"

Here it comes. In the far distance I can see the concrete bridge where the road crosses the creek. Under that bridge and beyond it the water is flat and silent, blued by distance and stilled by depth. It is so much sky, a fallen shred caught in the cleft of banks. But it pours. The channel here is straight as an arrow; grace itself is an archer. Between the dangling wands of bankside willows, beneath the overarching limbs of tulip, walnut, and Osage orange, I see the creek pour down. It spills toward me streaming over a series of sandstone tiers, down, and down, and down. I feel as though I stand at the foot of an infinitely high staircase, down which some exuberant spirit is flinging tennis ball after tennis ball, eternally, and the one thing I want in the world is a tennis ball.

There must be something wrong with a creekside person who, all things being equal, chooses to face downstream. It's like fouling your own nest. For this and a leather couch they pay fifty dollars an hour? Tinker Creek doesn't back up, pushed up its own craw, from the Roanoke River; it flows down, easing, from the northern, unseen side of Tinker Mountain. "Gravity, to Copernicus, is the nostalgia of things to become spheres." This is a curious, tugged version of the great chain of being. Ease is the way of perfection, letting fall. But, as in the classic version of the great chain, the pure trickle that leaks from the unfathomable heart of Tinker Mountain, this Tinker Creek, widens, taking shape and cleaving banks, weighted with the live and intricate impurities of time, as it descends to me, to where I happen to find myself, in this

intermediate spot, halfway between here and there. Look upstream. Just simply turn around; have you no will? The future
is a spirit, or a distillation of *the* spirit, heading my way. It is
north. The future is the light on the water; it comes, mediated,
only on the skin of the real and present creek. My eyes can
stand no brighter light than this; nor can they see without it,
if only the undersides of leaves.

Trees are tough. They last, taproot and bark, and we soften
at their feet. "For we are strangers before thee, and sojourn-
ers, as were all our fathers: our days on the earth are as a
shadow, and there is none abiding." We can't take the lightning, the scourge of high places and rare airs. But we can take
the light, the reflected light that shines up the valleys on
creeks. Trees stir memories; live waters heal them. The creek
is the mediator, benevolent, impartial, subsuming my shabbi-
est evils and dissolving them, transforming them into live
moles, and shiners, and sycamore leaves. It is a place even my
faithlessness hasn't offended; it still flashes for me, now and
tomorrow, that intricate, innocent face. It waters an undeserv-
ing world, saturating cells with lodes of light. I stand by the
creek over rock under trees.

It is sheer coincidence that my hunk of the creek is strewn
with boulders. I never merited this grace, that when I face
upstream I scent the virgin breath of mountains, I feel a spray
of mist on my cheeks and lips, I hear a ceaseless splash and
susurrus, a sound of water not merely poured smoothly down
air to fill a steady pool, but tumbling live about, over, under,
around, between, through an intricate speckling of rock. It is
sheer coincidence that upstream from me the creek's bed is
ridged in horizontal croppings of sandstone. I never merited
this grace, that when I face upstream I see the light on the
water careening towards me, inevitably, freely, down a graded
series of terraces like the balanced winged platforms on an
infinite, inexhaustible font. "Ho, if you are thirsty, come
down to the water; ho, if you are hungry, come and sit and
eat." This is the present, at last. I can pat the puppy any time

I want. This is the now, this flickering, broken light, this air that the wind of the future presses down my throat, pumping me buoyant and giddy with praise.

My God, I look at the creek. It is the answer to Merton's prayer, "Give us time!" It never stops. If I seek the senses and skill of children, the information of a thousand books, the innocence of puppies, even the insights of my own city past, I do so only, solely, and entirely that I might look well at the creek. You don't run down the present, pursue it with baited hooks and nets. You wait for it, empty-handed, and you are filled. You'll have fish left over. The creek is the one great giver. It is, by definition, Christmas, the incarnation. This old rock planet gets the present for a present on its birthday every day.

Here is the word from a subatomic physicist: "Everything that has already happened is particles, everything in the future is waves." Let me twist his meaning. Here it comes. The particles are broken; the waves are translucent, laving, roiling with beauty like sharks. The present is the wave that explodes over my head, flinging the air with particles at the height of its breathless unroll; it is the live water and light that bears from undisclosed sources the freshest news, renewed and renewing, world without end.

CHAPTER 7

Spring

I

WHEN I WAS QUITE YOUNG I fondly imagined that all foreign languages were codes for English. I thought that "hat," say, was the real and actual name of the thing, but that people in other countries, who obstinately persisted in speaking the code of their forefathers, might use the word "ibu," say, to designate not merely the concept hat, but the English *word* "hat." I knew only one foreign word, "oui," and since it had three letters as did the word for which it was a code, it seemed, touchingly enough, to confirm my theory. Each foreign language was a different code, I figured, and at school I would eventually be given the keys to unlock some of the most important codes' systems. Of course I knew that it might take years before I became so fluent in another language that I could code and decode easily in my head, and make of gibberish a nimble sense. On the first day of my first French course, however, things rapidly took on an entirely unexpected shape. I realized that I was going to have to learn speech all over again, word by word, one word at a time—and my dismay knew no bounds.

The birds have started singing in the valley. Their February squawks and naked chirps are fully fledged now, and long lyrics fly in the air. Birdsong catches in the mountains' rim and pools in the valley; it threads through forests, it slides down creeks. At the house a wonderful thing happens. The mockingbird that nests each year in the front-yard spruce strikes up his chant in high places, and one of those high places is my chimney. When he sings there, the hollow chimney acts as a soundbox, like the careful emptiness inside a cello or violin, and the notes of the song gather fullness and reverberate through the house. He sings a phrase and repeats it exactly; then he sings another and repeats that, then another. The mockingbird's invention is limitless; he strews newness about as casually as a god. He is tireless, too; toward June he will begin his daily marathon at two in the morning and scarcely pause for breath until eleven at night. I don't know when he sleeps.

When I lose interest in a given bird, I try to renew it by looking at the bird in either of two ways. I imagine neutrinos passing through its feathers and into its heart and lungs, or I reverse its evolution and imagine it as a lizard. I see its scaled legs and that naked ring around a shiny eye; I shrink and deplume its feathers to lizard scales, unhorn its lipless mouth, and set it stalking dragonflies, cool-eyed, under a palmetto. Then I reverse the process once again, quickly; its forelegs unfurl, its scales hatch feathers and soften. It takes to the air seeking cool forests; it sings songs. This is what I have on my chimney; it might as well keep me awake out of wonder as rage.

Some reputable scientists, even today, are not wholly satisfied with the notion that the song of birds is strictly and solely a territorial claim. It's an important point. We've been on earth all these years and we still don't know for certain why birds sing. We need someone to unlock the code to this foreign language and give us the key; we need a new Rosetta stone. Or should we learn, as I had to, each new word one by one? It could be that a bird sings I am sparrow, sparrow, sparrow, as Gerard Manley Hopkins suggests: "myself it speaks and spells, Crying *What I do is me: for that I came.*" Sometimes birdsong seems just like the garbled speech of infants. There is a certain age at which a child looks at you in all earnestness and delivers a long, pleased speech in all the true inflections of spoken English, but with not one recognizable syllable. There is no way you can tell the child that if language had been a melody, he had mastered it and done well, but that since it was in fact a sense, he had botched it utterly.

Today I watched and heard a wren, a sparrow, and the mockingbird singing. My brain started to trill why why why, what is the meaning meaning meaning? It's not that they know something we don't; we know much more than they do, and surely they don't even know why they sing. No; we have been as usual asking the wrong question. It does not matter a hoot what the mockingbird on the chimney is singing. If the mockingbird were chirping to give us the long-sought formula for a unified field theory, the point would be only slightly less irrelevant. The real and proper question is: Why is it beautiful? I hesitate to use the word so baldly, but the question is there. The question is there since I take it as given, as I have said, the beauty is something objectively performed—the tree that falls in the forest—having being externally, stumbled across or missed, as real and present as both sides of the moon. This modified lizard's song welling out of the fireplace has a wild, utterly foreign music; it becomes more and more beautiful as it becomes more and more familiar. If the lyric is simply "mine mine mine," then why the extravagance of the score? It has the liquid, intricate sound of every creek's tumble over every configuration of rock creek-bottom in the country. Who, telegraphing a message, would trouble to transmit a five-act play, or Coleridge's "Kubla Khan," and who, receiving the message, could understand it? Beauty itself is the language to which we have no key; it is the mute cipher, the cryptogram, the uncracked, unbroken code. And it could be that for beauty, as it turned out to be for French, that there is no key, that "oui" will never make sense in our language but only in its own, and that we need to start all over again, on a new continent, learning the strange syllables one by one.

It is spring. I plan to try to control myself this year, to watch the progress of the season in a calm and orderly fashion. In spring I am prone to wretched excess. I abandon myself to flights and compulsions; I veer into various states of physical disarray. For the duration of one entire spring I played pinochle; another spring I played second base. One spring I missed because I had lobar pneumonia; one softball season I missed with bursitis; and every spring at just about the time the leaves first blur on the willows, I stop eating and pale, like a silver eel about to migrate. My mind wanders. Second base is a Broadway, a Hollywood and Vine; but oh, if I'm out in right field they can kiss me goodbye. As the sun sets, sundogs, which are mock suns—chunks of rainbow on either side of the sun but often very distant from it—appear over the pasture by Carvin's Creek. Wes Hillman is up in his biplane; the little Waco lords it over the stillness, cutting a fine silhouette. It might rain tomorrow, if those ice crystals find business. I have no idea how many outs there are; I luck through the left-handers, staring at rainbows. The field looks to me as it must look to Wes Hillman up in the biplane: everyone is running, and I can't hear a sound. The players look so thin on the green, and the shadows so long, and the ball a mystic thing, pale to invisibility. . . . I'm better off in the infield.

In April I walked to the Adams' woods. The grass had greened one morning when I blinked; I missed it again. As I left the house I checked the praying mantis egg case. I had given all but one of the cases to friends for their gardens; now I saw that small black ants had discovered the one that was left, the one tied to the mock-orange hedge by my study window. One side of the case was chewed away, either by the ants or by something else, revealing a rigid froth slit by narrow cells. Over this protective layer the ants scrambled in a frenzy, unable to eat; the actual mantis eggs lay secure and unseen, waiting, deeper in.

The morning woods were utterly new. A strong yellow light pooled between the trees; my shadow appeared and vanished on the path, since a third of the trees I walked under were still bare, a third spread a luminous haze wherever they grew, and another third blocked the sun with new, whole leaves. The snakes were out—I saw a bright, smashed one on the path— and the butterflies were vaulting and furling about; the phlox was at its peak, and even the evergreens looked greener, newly created and washed.

Long racemes of white flowers hung from the locust trees. Last summer I heard a Cherokee legend about the locust tree and the moon. The moon goddess starts out with a big ball, the full moon, and she hurls it across the sky. She spends all day retrieving it; then she shaves a slice from it and hurls it again, retrieving, shaving, hurling, and so on. She uses up a moon a month, all year. Then, the way Park Service geologist Bill Wellman tells it, "'long about spring of course she's knee- deep in moon-shavings," so she finds her favorite tree, the locust, and hangs the slender shavings from its boughs. And there they were, the locust flowers, pale and clustered in cres- cents.

The newts were back. In the small forest pond they swam bright and quivering, or hung alertly near the water's surface. I discovered that if I poked my finger into the water and wagged it slowly, a newt would investigate; then if I held my finger still, it would nibble at my skin, softly, the way my goldfish does—and, also like my goldfish, it would swim off as if in disgust at a bad job. This is salamander metropolis. If you want to find a species wholly new to science and have your name inscribed Latinly in some secular version of an eternal rollbook, then your best bet is to come to the southern Appalachians, climb some obscure and snakey mountain where, as the saying goes, "the hand of man has never set foot," and start turning over rocks. The mountains act as islands; evolution does the rest, and there are scores of different salamanders all around. The Peaks of Otter on the Blue Ridge Parkway produce their own unique species, black and spotted in dark gold; the rangers there keep a live one handy by sticking it in a Baggie and stowing it in the refrigerator, like a piece of cheese.

Newts are the most common of salamanders. Their skin is a lighted green, like water in a sunlit pond, and rows of very bright red dots line their backs. They have gills as larvae; as they grow they turn a luminescent red, lose their gills, and walk out of the water to spend a few years padding around in damp places on the forest floor. Their feet look like fingered baby hands, and they walk in the same leg patterns as all four-footed creatures—dogs, mules, and, for that matter, lesser pandas. When they mature fully, they turn green again and stream to the water in droves. A newt can scent its way home from as far as eight miles away. They are altogether excellent creatures, if somewhat moist, but no one pays the least attention to them, except children.

Once I was camped "alone" at Douthat State Park in the Allegheny Mountains near here, and spent the greater part of one afternoon watching children and newts. There were many times more red-spotted newts at the edge of the lake than there were children; the supply exceeded even that very heavy demand. One child was collecting them in a Thermos mug to take home to Lancaster, Pennsylvania, to feed an ailing cayman. Other children ran to their mothers with squirming fistfuls. One boy was mistreating the newts spectacularly: he squeezed them by their tails and threw them at a shoreline stone, one by one. I tried to reason with him, but nothing worked. Finally he asked me, "Is this one a male?" and in a fit of inspiration I said, "No, it's a baby." He cried, "Oh, isn't he *cute!*" and cradled the newt carefully back into the water.

No one but me disturbed the newts here in the Adams' woods. They hung in the water as if suspended from strings. Their specific gravity put them just a jot below the water's surface, and they could apparently relax just as well with lowered heads as lowered tails; their tiny limbs hung limp in the water. One newt was sunning on a stick in such an extravagant posture I thought she was dead. She was half out of water, her front legs grasping the stick, her nose tilted back to the zenith and then some. The concave arch of her spine stretched her neck past believing; the thin ventral skin was a bright taut yellow. I should not have nudged her—it made her relax the angle of repose—but I had to see if she was dead. Medieval Europeans believed that salamanders were so cold they could put out fires and not be burned themselves; ancient Romans thought that the poison of salamanders was so cold that if anyone ate the fruit of a tree that a salamander had merely touched, that person would die of a terrible coldness. But I survived these mild encounters—my being nibbled and my poking the salamander's neck—and stood up.

The woods were flush with flowers. The redbud trees were in flower, and the sassafras, dully; so also were the tulip trees, catawbas, and the weird pawpaw. On the floor of the little woods, hepatica and dogtooth violet had come and gone; now I saw the pink spring beauty here and there, and Solomon's seal with its pendant flowers, bloodroot, violets, trillium, and May apple in luxuriant stands. The mountains would be brilliant in mountain laurel, rhododendron, and flame azalea, and the Appalachian Trail was probably packed with picnickers. I had seen in the steers' pasture daisies, henbits, and yellow-flowering oxalis; sow thistle and sneezeweed shot up by the barbed-wire fence. Does anything eat flowers? I couldn't recall ever having seen anything actually eat a flower—are they nature's priviledged pets?

But I was much more interested in the leafing of trees. By the path I discovered a wonderful tulip-tree sapling three feet tall. From its tip grew two thin slips of green tissue shaped like two tears; they enclosed, like cupped palms sheltering a flame, a tiny tulip leaf that was curled upon itself and bowed neatly at the middle. The leaf was so thin and etiolated it was translucent, but at the same time it was lambent, minutely, with a kind of pale and sufficient light. It was not wet, nor even damp, but it was clearly moist inside; the wrinkle where it folded in half looked less like a crease than a dimple, like the liquid dip a skater's leg makes on the surface film of still water. A barely concealed, powerful juice swelled its cells, and the leaf was uncurling and rising between the green slips of tissue. I looked around for more leaves like it—that part of the Adams' woods seems to be almost solely tulip trees—but all the other leaves had just lately unfurled, and were waving on pale stalks like new small hands.

The tulip-tree leaf reminded me of a newborn mammal I'd seen the other day, one of the neighborhood children's gerbils. It was less than an inch long, with a piggish snout, clenched eyes, and swollen white knobs where its ears would grow. Its skin was hairless except for an infinitesimal set of whiskers; the skin seemed as thin as the membrane on an onion, tightly packed as a sausage casing, and bulging roundly with wet, bloody meat. It seemed near to bursting with possibilities, like the taut gum over a coming tooth. This three-foot sapling was going somewhere, too; it meant business.

There's a real power here. It is amazing that trees can turn gravel and bitter salts into these soft-lipped lobes, as if I were to bite down on a granite slab and start to swell, bud, and flower. Trees seem to do their feats so effortlessly. Every year a given tree creates absolutely from scratch ninety-nine percent of its living parts. Water lifting up tree trunks can climb one hundred and fifty feet an hour; in full summer a tree can, and does, heave a ton of water every day. A big elm in a single season might make as many as *six million* leaves, wholly intricate, without budging an inch; I couldn't make one. A tree stands there, accumulating deadwood, mute and rigid as an obelisk, but secretly it seethes; it splits, sucks, and stretches; it heaves up tons and hurls them out in a green, fringed fling. No person taps this free power; the dynamo in the tulip tree pumps out ever more tulip tree, and it runs on rain and air.

John Cowper Powys said, "We have no reason for denying to the world of plants a certain slow, dim, vague, large, leisurely semiconsciousness." He may not be right, but I like his adjectives. The patch of bluets in the grass may not be long on brains, but it might be, at least in a very small way, awake. The trees especially seem to bespeak a generosity of spirit. I suspect that the real moral thinkers end up, wherever they may start, in botany. We know nothing for certain, but we seem to see that the world turns upon growing, grows toward growing, and growing green and clean.

I looked away from the tulip leaf at the tip of the sapling, and I looked back. I was trying to determine if I could actually see the bent leaf tip rise and shove against the enclosing flaps. I couldn't tell whether I was seeing or merely imagining progress, but I knew the leaf would be fully erect within the hour. I couldn't wait.

I left the woods, spreading silence before me in a wave, as though I'd stepped not through the forest, but on it. I left the wood silent, but I myself was stirred and quickened. I'll go to the Northwest Territories, I thought, Finland.

"Why leap ye, ye high hills?" The earth was an egg, freshened and splitting; a new pulse struck, and I resounded. Pliny, who, you remember, came up with the Portuguese wind-foals, must have kept his daughters in on windy days, for he also believed that plants conceive in the spring of the western wind Flavonius. In February the plants go into rut; the wind impregnates them, and their buds swell and burst in their time, bringing forth flowers and leaves and fruit. I could smell the loamy force in the wind. I'll go to Alaska, Greenland. I saw hundreds of holes in the ground everywhere I looked; all kinds of creatures were popping out of the dim earth, some for the first time, to be lighted and warmed directly by the sun. It is a fact that the men and women all over the northern hemisphere who dream up new plans for a perpetual motion machine conceive their best ideas in the spring. If I swallowed a seed and some soil, could I grow grapes in my mouth? Once I dug a hole to plant a pine, and found an old gold coin on a stone. Little America, the Yukon. . . . "Why leap ye, ye high hills?"

On my way home, every bird I saw had something in its mouth. A male English sparrow, his mouth stuffed, was hopping in and out of an old nest in a bare tree, and sloshing around in its bottom. A robin on red alert in the grass, trailing half a worm from its bill, bobbed three steps and straightened up, performing unawares the universal robin trick. A mockingbird flew by with a red berry in its beak; the berry flashed in the sun and glowed like a coal from some forge or cauldron of the gods.

Finally I saw some very small children playing with a striped orange kitten, and overheard their mysterious conversation, which has since been ringing in my brain like a gong. The kitten ran into a garden, and the girl called after it, "Sweet Dreams! Sweet Dreams! Where are you?" And the boy said to her crossly, "Don't call Sweet Dreams *'you'!"*

II

Now it is May. The walrus are migrating; Diomede Island Eskimos follow them in boats through the Bering Strait. The Netsilik Eskimos hunt seal. According to Asen Balikci, a seal basks in the sun all day and slips into the water at midnight, to return at dawn to emerge from the same hole. In spring the sun, too, slips below the horizon for only a brief period, and the sky still glows. All the Netsilik hunter has to do in spring is go out at midnight, watch a seal disappear into a given hole, and wait there quietly in the brief twilight, on a spread piece of bearskin. The seal will be up soon, with the sun. The glaciers are calving; brash ice and grease ice clog the bays. From land you can see the widening of open leads on the distant pack ice by watching the "water sky"—the dark patches and streaks on the glaring cloud cover that are breaks in the light reflected from the pack.

You might think the Eskimos would welcome the spring and the coming of summer; they did, but they looked forward more to the coming of winter. I'm talking as usual about the various Eskimo cultures as they were before modernization. Some Eskimos used to greet the sun on its first appearance at the horizon in stunned silence, and with raised arms. But in summer, they well knew, they would have to eat lean fish and birds. Winter's snow would melt to water and soak the thin thawed ground down to the permafrost; the water couldn't drain away, and it would turn the earth into a sop of puddles. Then the mosquitos would come, the mosquitos that could easily drive migrating caribou to a mad frenzy so that they trampled their newborn calves, the famous arctic mosquitos of which it is said, "If there were any more of them, they'd have to be smaller."

In winter the Eskimos could travel with dog sleds and visit; with the coming of warm weather, their pathways, like mine in Virginia, closed. In interior Alaska and northern Canada, breakup is the big event. Old-timers and cheechakos alike lay wagers on the exact day and hour it will occur. For the ice on rivers there does not just simply melt; it rips out in a general holocaust. Upstream, thin ice breaks from its banks and races downriver. Where it rams solid ice it punches it free and shoots it downstream, buckling and shearing: ice adds to ice, exploding a Juggernaut into motion. A grate and roar blast the air, the ice machine razes bridges and fences and trees, and the whole year's ice rushes out like a train in an hour. Breakup: I'd give anything to see it. Now for the people in the bush the waterways are open to navigation but closed to snowmobile and snowshoe, and it's harder for them, too, to get around.

Here in the May valley, fullness is at a peak. All the plants are fully leafed, but intensive insect damage hasn't begun. The leaves are fresh, whole, and perfect. Light in the sky is clear, unfiltered by haze, and the sun hasn't yet withered the grass.

Now the plants are closing in on me. The neighborhood children are growing up; they aren't keeping all the paths open. I feel like buying them all motorbikes. The woods are a clog of green, and I have to follow the manner of the North, or of the past, and take to the waterways to get around. But maybe I think things are more difficult than they are, because once, after I had waded and slogged in tennis shoes a quarter of a mile upstream in Tinker Creek, a boy hailed me from the tangled bank. He had followed me just to pass the time of day, and he was barefoot.

When I'm up to my knees in honeysuckle, I beat a retreat, and visit the duck pond. The duck pond is a small eutrophic pond on cleared land near Carvin's Creek. It is choked with algae and seething with frogs; when I see it, I always remember Jean White's horse.

Several years ago, Jean White's old mare, Nancy, died. It died on private property where it was pastured, and Jean couldn't get permission to bury the horse there. It was just as well, because we were in the middle of a July drought, and the clay ground was fired hard as rock. Anyway, the problem remained: What do you do with a dead horse? Another friend once tried to burn a dead horse, an experiment he never repeated. Jean White made phone calls and enlisted friends who made more phone calls. All experts offered the same suggestion: try the fox farm. The fox farm is south of here; it raises various animals to make into coats. It turned out that the fox farm readily accepts dead horses from far and wide to use as "fresh" meat for the foxes. But it also turned out, oddly enough, that the fox farm was up to its hem in dead horses already, and had room for no more.

It was, as I say, July, and the problem of the dead mare's

final resting place was gathering urgency. Finally someone suggested that Jean try the landfill down where the new interstate highway was being built. Certain key phone calls were made, and, to everybody's amazement, government officials accepted the dead horse. They even welcomed the dead horse, needed the dead horse, for its bulk, which, incidentally, was becoming greater each passing hour. A local dairy farmer donated his time; a crane hauled the dead horse into the farmer's truck, and he drove south. With precious little ceremony he dumped the mare into the landfill on which the new highway would rest—and that was the end of Jean White's horse. If you ever drive through Virginia on the new interstate highway between Christiansburg and Salem, and you feel a slight dip in the paving under your wheels, then loose thy shoe from off thy foot, for the place whereon thou drivest is Jean White's horse.

All this comes to mind at the duck pond, because the duck pond is rapidly turning into a landfill of its own, a landfill paved in frogs. There are a million frogs here, bullfrogs hopping all over each other on tangled mats of algae. And the pond is filling up. Small ponds don't live very long, especially in the South. Decaying matter piles up on the bottom, depleting oxygen, and the shore plants march to the middle. In another couple of centuries, if no one interferes, the duck pond will be a hickory forest.

On an evening in late May, a moist wind from Carvin's Cove shoots down the gap between Tinker and Brushy mountains, tears along Carvin's Creek valley, and buffets my face as I stand by the duck pond. The surface of the duck pond doesn't budge. The algal layer is a rigid plating; if the wind blew hard enough, I imagine it might audibly creak. On warm days in February the primitive plants start creeping over the pond, filamentous green and blue-green algae in sopping strands. From a sunlit shallow edge they green and spread, thickening throughout the water like bright gelatin. When they smother the whole pond they block sunlight, strangle respiration, and snarl creatures in hopeless tangles. Dragonfly nymphs, for instance, are easily able to shed a leg or two to escape a tight spot, but even dragonfly nymphs get stuck in the algae strands and starve.

Several times I've seen a frog trapped under the algae. I would be staring at the pond when the green muck by my feet would suddenly leap into the air and then subside. It looked as though it had been jabbed from underneath by a broom handle. Then it would leap again, somewhere else, a jumping green flare, absolutely silently—this is a very disconcerting way to spend an evening. The frog would always find an open place at last, and break successfully onto the top of the heap, trailing long green slime from its back, and emitting a hollow sound like a pipe thrown into a cavern. Tonight I walked around the pond scaring frogs; a couple of them jumped off, going, in effect, eek, and most grunted, and the pond was still. But one big frog, bright green like a poster-paint frog, didn't jump, so I waved my arm and stamped to scare it, and it jumped suddenly, and I jumped, and then everything in the pond jumped, and I laughed and laughed.

There is a muscular energy in sunlight corresponding to the spiritual energy of wind. On a sunny day, sun's energy on a square acre of land or pond can equal 4500 horsepower. These "horses" heave in every direction, like slaves building pyramids, and fashion, from the bottom up, a new and sturdy world.

The pond is popping with life. Midges are swarming over the center, and the edges are clotted with the jellied egg masses of snails. One spring I saw a snapping turtle lumber from the pond to lay her eggs. Now a green heron picks around in the pondweed and bladderwort; two muskrats at the shallow end are stockpiling cattails. Diatoms, which are algae that look under a microscope like crystals, multiply so fast you can practically watch a submersed green leaf transform into a brown fuzz. In the plankton, single-cell algae, screw fungi, bacteria, and water mold abound. Insect larvae and nymphs carry on their eating business everywhere in the pond. Stillwater caddises, alderfly larvae, and damselfly and dragonfly nymphs stalk on the bottom debris; mayfly nymphs hide in the weeds, mosquito larvae wriggle near the surface, and red-tailed maggots stick their breathing tubes up from between decayed leaves along the shore. Also at the pond's muddy edges it is easy to see the tiny red tubifex worms and bloodworms; the convulsive jerking of hundreds and hundreds together catches my eye.

Once, when the pond was younger and the algae had not yet taken over, I saw an amazing creature. At first all I saw was a slender motion. Then I saw that it was a wormlike creature swimming in the water with a strong, whiplike thrust, and it was two feet long. It was also slender as a thread. It looked like an inked line someone was nervously drawing over and over. Later I learned that it was a horsehair worm. The larvae of horsehair worms live as parasites in land insects; the aquatic adults can get to be a yard long. I don't know how it gets from the insect to the pond, or from the pond to the insect, for that matter, or why on earth it needs such an extreme shape. If the one I saw had been so much as an inch longer or a shave thinner, I doubt if I would ever have come back.

The plankton bloom is what interests me. The plankton animals are all those microscopic drifting animals that so staggeringly outnumber us. In the spring they are said to "bloom," like so many poppies. There may be five times as many of these teeming creatures in spring as in summer. Among them are the protozoans—amoebae and other rhizopods, and millions of various flagellates and ciliates; gelatinous moss animalcules or byrozoans; rotifers—which wheel around either free or in colonies; and all the diverse crustacean minutiae—copepods, ostracods, and cladocerans like the abundant daphnias. All these drifting animals multiply in sundry bizarre fashions, eat tiny plants or each other, die, and drop to the pond's bottom. Many of them have quite refined means of locomotion—they whirl, paddle, swim, slog, whip, and sinuate—but since they are so small, they are no match against even the least current in the water. Even such a sober limnologist as Robert E. Coker characterizes the movement of plankton as "milling around."

A cup of duck-pond water looks like a seething broth. If I carry the cup home and let the sludge settle, the animalcules sort themselves out, and I can concentrate them further by dividing them into two clear glass bowls. One bowl I paint all black except for a single circle where the light shines through; I leave the other bowl clear except for a single black circle against the light. Given a few hours, the light-loving creatures make their feeble way to the clear circle, and the shade-loving creatures to the black. Then, if I want to, I can harvest them with a pipette and examine them under a microscope.

There they loom and disappear as I fiddle with the focus. I run the eyepiece around until I am seeing the drop magnified three hundred times, and I squint at the little rotifer called monostyla. It zooms around excitedly, crashing into strands of spirogyra alga or zipping around the frayed edge of a clump of debris. The creature is a flattened oval; at its "head" is a circular fringe of whirling cilia, and at its "tail" a single long spike, so that it is shaped roughly like a horseshoe crab. But it is so incredibly small, as multicelled animals go, that it is translucent, even transparent, and I have a hard time telling if it is above or beneath a similarly transparent alga. Two monostyla drive into view from opposite directions; they meet, bump, reverse, part. I keep thinking that if I listen closely I will hear the high whine of tiny engines. As their drop heats from the light on the mirror, the rotifers skitter more and more frantically; as it dries, they pale and begin to stagger, and at last can muster only a halting twitch. Then I either wash the whole batch down the sink's drain, or in a rush of sentiment walk out to the road by starlight and dump them in a puddle. Tinker Creek where I live is too fast and rough for most of them.

I don't really look forward to these microscopic forays: I have been almost knocked off my kitchen chair on several occasions when, as I was following with strained eyes the tiny career of a monostyla rotifer, an enormous red roundworm whipped into the scene, blocking everything, and writhing in huge, flapping convulsions that seemed to sweep my face and fill the kitchen. I do it as a moral exercise; the microscope at my forehead is a kind of phylactery, a constant reminder of the facts of creation that I would just as soon forget. You can buy your child a microscope and say grandly, "Look, child, at the Jungle in a Little Drop." The boy looks, plays around with pond water and bread mold and onion sprouts for a month or two, and then starts shooting baskets or racing cars, leaving the microscope on the basement table staring fixedly at its own mirror forever—and you say he's growing up. But in the puddle or pond, in the city reservoir, ditch, or Atlantic Ocean, the rotifers still spin and munch, the daphnia still filter and are filtered, and the copepods still swarm hanging with clusters of eggs. These are real creatures with real organs leading real lives, one by one. I can't pretend they're not there. If I have life, sense, energy, will, so does a rotifer. The monostyla goes to the dark spot on the bowl: To which circle am I heading? I can move around right smartly in a calm; but in a real wind, in a change of weather, in a riptide, am I really moving, or am I "milling around"?

I was created from a clot and set in proud, free motion: so were they. So was this rotifer created, this monostyla with its body like a light bulb in which pale organs hang in loops; so was this paramecium created, with a thousand propulsive hairs jerking in unison, whipping it from here to there across a drop and back. *Ad majorem Dei gloriam?*

Somewhere, and I can't find where, I read about an Eskimo hunter who asked the local missionary priest, "If I did not know about God and sin, would I go to hell?" "No," said the priest, "not if you did not know." "Then why," asked the Eskimo earnestly, "did you tell me?" If I did not know about the rotifers and paramecia, and all the bloom of plankton clogging the dying pond, fine; but since I've seen it I must somehow deal with it, take it into account. "Never lose a holy curiosity," Einstein said; and so I lift my microscope down from the shelf, spread a drop of duck pond on a glass slide, and try to look spring in the eye.

CHAPTER 8

Intricacy

I

A ROSY, COMPLEX LIGHT fills my kitchen at the end of these lengthening June days. From an explosion on a nearby star eight minutes ago, the light zips through space, particle-wave, strikes the planet, angles on the continent, and filters through a mesh of land dust: clay bits, sod bits, tiny wind-borne insects, bacteria, shreds of wing and leg, gravel dust, grits of carbon, and dried cells of grass, bark, and leaves. Reddened, the light inclines into this valley over the green western mountains; it sifts between pine needles on northern slopes, and through all the mountain black-jack oak and haw, whose leaves are unclenching, one by one, and making an intricate, toothed and lobed haze. The light crosses the valley, threads through the screen on my open kitchen window, and gilds the painted wall. A plank of brightness bends from the wall and extends over the goldfish bowl on the table where I sit. The goldfish's side catches the light and bats it my way; I've an eyeful of fish-scale and star.

This Ellery cost me twenty-five cents. He is a deep red-orange, darker than most goldfish. He steers short distances mainly with his slender red lateral fins; they seem to provide impetus for going backward, up, or down. It took me a few days to discover his ventral fins; they are completely transparent and all but invisible—dream fins. He also has a short anal fin, and a tail that is deeply notched and perfectly transparent at the two tapered tips. He can extend his mouth, so that it looks like a length of pipe; he can shift the angle of his eyes in his head so he can look before and behind himself, instead of simply out to his side. His belly, what there is of it, is white ventrally, and a patch of this white extends up his sides—the variegated Ellery. When he opens his gill slits he shows a thin crescent of silver where the flap overlapped—as though all his brightness were sunburn.

For this creature, as I said, I paid twenty-five cents. I had never bought an animal before. It was very simple; I went to a store in Roanoke called "Wet Pets"; I handed the man a quarter, and he handed me a knotted plastic bag bouncing with water in which a green plant floated and the goldfish swam. This fish, two bits worth, has a coiled gut, a spine radiating fine bones, and a brain. Just before I sprinkle his food flakes into his bowl, I rap three times on the bowl's edge; now he is conditioned, and swims to the surface when I rap. And, he has a heart.

Once, years ago, I saw red blood cells whip, one by one, through the capillaries in a goldfish's transparent tail. The goldfish was etherized. Its head lay in a wad of wet cotton wool; its tail lay on a tray under a dissecting microscope, one of those wonderful light-gathering microscopes with two eye-pieces like a stereoscope in which the world's fragments—even the skin on my finger—look brilliant with myriads of colored lights, and as deep as any alpine landscape. The red blood cells in the goldfish's tail streamed and coursed through narrow channels invisible save for glistening threads of thickness in the general translucency. They never wavered or

slowed or ceased flowing, like the creek itself; they streamed
redly around, up, and on, one by one, more, and more, without end. (The energy of that pulse reminds me of something
about the human body: if you sit absolutely perfectly balanced
on the end of your spine, with your legs either crossed tailor-
fashion or drawn up together, and your arms forward on your
legs, then even if you hold your breath, your body will rock
with the energy of your heartbeat, forward and back, effortlessly, for as long as you want to remain balanced.) Those red
blood cells are coursing in Ellery's tail now, too, in just that
way, and through his mouth and eyes as well, and through
mine. I've never forgotten the sight of those cells; I think of
it when I see the fish in his bowl; I think of it lying in bed at
night, imagining that if I concentrate enough I might be able
to feel in my fingers' capillaries the small knockings and flow
of those circular dots, like a string of beads drawn through my
hand.

Something else is happening in the goldfish bowl. There on
the kitchen table, nourished by the simple plank of complex
light, the plankton is blooming. The water yellows and clouds;
a transparent slime coats the leaves of the water plant, elodea;
a blue-green film of single-celled algae clings to the glass. And
I have to clean the doggone bowl. I'll spare you the details:
it's the plant I'm interested in. While Ellery swims in the
stoppered sink, I rinse the algae down the drain of another
sink, wash the gravel, and rub the elodea's many ferny leaves
under running water until they feel clean.

The elodea is not considered much of a plant. Aquarists use
it because it's available and it gives off oxygen completely
submersed; laboratories use it because its leaves are only two
cells thick. It's plentiful, easy to grow, and cheap—like the
goldfish. And, like the goldfish, its cells have unwittingly performed for me on a microscope's stage.

I was in a laboratory, using a very expensive microscope. I
peered through the deep twin eyepieces and saw again that
color-charged, glistening world. A thin, oblong leaf of elodea,

a quarter of an inch long, lay on a glass slide soppin
floodlighted brilliantly from below. In the circl
formed by the two eyepieces trained at the transluc
saw a clean mosaic of almost colorless cells. The cells were
large—eight or nine of them, magnified four hundred and fifty
times, packed the circle—so that I could easily see what I had
come to see: the streaming of chloroplasts.

Chloroplasts bear chlorophyll; they give the green world its
color, and they carry out the business of photosynthesis.
Around the inside perimeter of each gigantic cell trailed a
continuous loop of these bright green dots. They spun like
paramecia; they pulsed, pressed, and thronged. A change of
focus suddenly revealed the eddying currents of the river of
transparent cytoplasm, a sort of "ether" to the chloroplasts, or
"space-time," in which they have their tiny being. Back to the
green dots: they shone, they swarmed in ever-shifting files
around and around the edge of the cell; they wandered, they
charged, they milled, raced, and ran at the edge of apparent
nothingness, the empty-looking inner cell; they flowed and
trooped greenly, up against the vegetative wall.

All the green in the planted world consists of these whole,
rounded chloroplasts wending their ways in water. If you
analyze a molecule of chlorophyll itself, what you get is one
hundred thirty-six atoms of hydrogen, carbon, oxygen, and
nitrogen arranged in an exact and complex relationship
around a central ring. At the ring's center is a single atom of
magnesium. Now: if you remove the atom of magnesium and
in its exact place put an atom of iron, you get a molecule of
hemoglobin. The iron atom combines with all the other atoms
to make red blood, the streaming red dots in the goldfish's tail.

It is, then, a small world there in the goldfish bowl, and a
very large one. Say the nucleus of any atom in the bowl were
the size of a cherry pit: its nearest electron would revolve
around it one hundred seventy-five yards away. A whirling air
in his swim bladder balances the goldfish's weight in the water;

his scales overlap, his feathery gills pump and filter; his eyes work, his heart beats, his liver absorbs, his muscles contract in a wave of extending ripples. The daphnias he eats have eyes and jointed legs. The algae the daphnias eat have green cells stacked like checkers or winding in narrow ribbons like spiral staircases up long columns of emptiness. And so on diminishingly down. We have not yet found the dot so small it is uncreated, as it were, like a metal blank, or merely roughed in—and we never shall. We go down landscape after mobile, sculpture after collage, down to molecular structures like a mob dance in Breughel, down to atoms airy and balanced as a canvas by Klee, down to atomic particles, the heart of the matter, as spirited and wild as any El Greco saints. And it all works. "Nature," said Thoreau in his journal, "is mythical and mystical always, and spends her whole genius on the least work." The creator, I would add, churns out the intricate texture of least works that is the world with a spendthrift genius and an extravagance of care. This is the point.

I am sitting here looking at a goldfish bowl and busting my brain. *Ich kann nicht anders.* I am sitting here, you are sitting there. Say even that you are sitting across this kitchen table from me right now. Our eyes meet; a consciousness snaps back and forth. What we know, at least for starters, is: here we—so incontrovertibly—are. This is our life, these are our lighted seasons, and then we die. (You die, you die; first you go wet, and then you go dry.) In the meantime, in between time, we can see. The scales are fallen from our eyes, the cataracts are cut away, and we can work at making sense of the color-patches we see in an effort to discover *where* we so incontrovertibly are. It's common sense: when you move in, you try to learn the neighborhood.

I am as passionately interested in where I am as is a lone sailor sans sextant in a ketch on the open ocean. What else is he supposed to be thinking about? Fortunately, like the sailor, I have at the moment a situation which allows me to devote considerable hunks of time to seeing what I can see, and trying to piece it together. I've learned the names of some color-patches, but not the meanings. I've read books. I've gathered statistics feverishly: the average temperature of our planet is 57° Fahrenheit. Of the 29% of all land that is above water, over a third is given to grazing. The average size of all living animals, including man, is almost that of a housefly. The earth is mostly granite, which in turn is mostly oxygen. The most numerous of animals big enough to see are the copepods, the mites, and the springtails; of plants, the algae, the sedge. In these Appalachians we have found a coal bed with 120 seams, meaning 120 forests that just happened to fall into water, heaped like corpses in drawers. And so on. These statistics, and all the various facts about subatomic particles, quanta, neutrinos, and so forth, constitute in effect the infrared and ultraviolet light at either end of the spectrum. They are too big and too small to see, to understand; they are more or less invisible to me though present, and peripheral to me in a real sense because I do not understand even what I can easily see. I would like to see it all, to understand it, but I must start somewhere, so I try to deal with the giant water bug in Tinker Creek and the flight of three hundred redwings from an Osage orange, with the goldfish bowl and the snakeskin, and let those who dare worry about the birthrate and population explosion among solar systems.

So I think about the valley. And it occurs to me more and more that everything I have seen is wholly gratuitous. The giant water bug's predations, the frog's croak, the tree with the lights in it are not in any real sense necessary per se to the world or to its creator. Nor am I. The creation in the first place, being itself, is the only necessity, for which I would die, and I shall. The point about that being, as I know it here and see it, is that, as I think about it, it accumulates in my mind as an extravagance of minutiae. The sheer fringe and network of detail assumes primary importance. That there are so many details seems to be the most important and visible fact about

the creation. If you can't see the forest for the trees, then look
at the trees; when you've looked at enough trees, you've seen
a forest, you've got it. If the world is gratuitous, then the
fringe of a goldfish's fin is a million times more so. The first
question—the one crucial one—of the creation of the universe
and the existence of something as a sign and an affront to
nothing, is a blank one. I can't think about it. So it is to the
fringe of that question that I affix my attention, the fringe of
the fish's fin, the intricacy of the world's spotted and speckled
detail.

The old Kabbalistic phrase is "the Mystery of the Splinter-
ing of the Vessels." The words refer to the shrinking or im-
prisonment of essences within the various husk-covered forms
of emanation or time. The Vessels splintered and solar systems
spun; ciliated rotifers whirled in still water, and newts with
gills laid tracks in the silt-bottomed creek. Not only did the
Vessels splinter: they splintered exceeding fine. Intricacy,
then, is the subject, the intricacy of the created world.

You are God. You want to make a forest, something to hold
the soil, lock up solar energy, and give off oxygen. Wouldn't
it be simpler just to rough in a slab of chemicals, a green acre
of goo?

You are a man, a retired railroad worker who makes replicas as a hobby. You decide to make a replica of one tree, the
longleaf pine your great-grandfather planted—just a replica—
it doesn't have to work. How are you going to do it? How
long do you think you might live, how good is your glue? For
one thing, you are going to have to dig a hole and stick your
replica trunk in the ground halfway to China if you want the
thing to stand up. Because you will have to work fairly big;
if your replica is too small, you'll be unable to handle the
slender, three-sided needles, affix them in clusters of three in
fascicles, and attach those laden fascicles to flexible twigs. The
twigs themselves must be covered by "many silvery-white,

fringed, long-spreading scales." Are your pine cones' scales "thin, flat, rounded at the apex, the exposed portions (closed cone) reddish brown, often wrinkled, armed on the back with a small, reflexed prickle, which curves toward the base of the scale"? When you loose the lashed copper wire trussing the replica limbs to the trunk, the whole tree collapses like an umbrella.

You are a starling. I've seen you fly through a longleaf pine without missing a beat.

You are a sculptor. You climb a great ladder; you pour grease all over a growing longleaf pine. Next, you build a hollow cylinder like a cofferdam around the entire pine, and grease its inside walls. You climb your ladder and spend the next week pouring wet plaster into the cofferdam, over and inside the pine. You wait; the plaster hardens. Now open the walls of the dam, split the plaster, saw down the tree, remove it, discard, and your intricate sculpture is ready: this is the shape of part of the air.

You are a chloroplast moving in water heaved one hundred feet above ground. Hydrogen, carbon, oxygen, nitrogen in a ring around magnesium. . . . You are evolution; you have only begun to make trees. You are God—are you tired? finished?

Intricacy means that there is a fluted fringe to the something that exists over against nothing, a fringe that rises and spreads, burgeoning in detail. Mentally reverse positive and negative space, as in the plaster cast of the pine, and imagine emptiness as a sort of person, a boundless person consisting of an elastic, unformed clay. (For the moment forget that the air in our atmosphere is "something," and count it as "nothing," the sculptor's negative space.) The clay man completely surrounds the holes in him, which are galaxies and solar systems. The holes in him part, expand, shrink, veer, circle, spin. He gives like water, he spreads and fills unseeing. Here is a ragged hole, our earth, a hole that makes torn and frayed edges in his side, mountains and pines. And here is the shape of one swift, raveling edge, a feather-hole on a flying goose's hollow wing extended over the planet. Five hundred barbs of emptiness prick into clay from either side of a central, flexible shaft. On each barb are two fringes of five hundred barbules apiece, making a million barbules on each feather, fluted and hooked in a matrix of clasped hollowness. Through the fabric of this form the clay man shuttles unerringly, and through the other feather-holes, and the goose, the pine forest, the planet, and so on.

In other words, even on the perfectly ordinary and clearly visible level, creation carries on with an intricacy unfathomable and apparently uncalled for. The lone ping into being of the first hydrogen atom *ex nihilo* was so unthinkably, violently radical, that surely it ought to have been enough, more than enough. But look what happens. You open the door and all heaven and hell break loose.

Evolution, of course, is the vehicle of intricacy. The stability of simple forms is the sturdy base from which more complex stable forms might arise, forming in turn more complex forms, and so on. The stratified nature of this stability, like a house built on rock on rock on rock, performs, in Jacob Branowski's terms, as the "ratchet" that prevents the whole shebang from "slipping back." Bring a feather into the house, and a piano; put a sculpture on the roof, sure, and fly banners from the lintels—the house will hold.

There are, for instance, two hundred twenty-eight separate and distinct muscles in the head of an ordinary caterpillar. Again, of an ostracod, a common fresh-water crustacean of the sort I crunch on by the thousands every time I set foot in Tinker Creek, I read, "There is one eye situated at the fore-end of the animal. The food canal lies just below the hinge, and around the mouth are the feathery feeding appendages which collect the food. . . . Behind them is a foot which is clawed and this is partly used for removing unwanted particles from the feeding appendages." Or again, there are, as I have said, six million leaves on a big elm. All right . . . but they are toothed, and the teeth themselves are toothed. How many notches and barbs is that to a world? In and out go the intricate leaf edges, and "don't nobody know why." All the theories botanists have devised to explain the functions of various leaf-shapes tumble under an avalanche of inconsistencies. They simply don't know, can't imagine.

I have often noticed that these things, which obsess me, neither bother nor impress other people even slightly. I am horribly apt to approach some innocent at a gathering and, like the ancient mariner, fix him with a wild, glitt'ring eye and say, "Do you know that in the head of the caterpillar of the ordinary goat moth there are two hundred twenty-eight separate muscles?" The poor wretch flees. I am not making chatter; I mean to change his life. I seem to possess an organ that others lack, a sort of trivia machine.

When I was young I thought that all human beings had an organ inside each lower eyelid which caught things that got in the eye. I don't know where I imagined I'd learned this piece of anatomy. Things got in my eye, and then they went away, so I supposed that they had fallen into my eye-pouch. This eye-pouch was a slender, thin-walled purse, equipped with frail digestive powers that enabled it eventually to absorb eyelashes, strands of fabric, bits of grit, and anything else that might stray into the eye. Well, the existence of this eye-pouch, it turned out, was all in my mind, and, it turns out, it is apparently there still, a brain-pouch, catching and absorbing small bits that fall deeply into my open eye.

All I can remember from a required zoology course years ago, for instance, is a lasting impression that there is an item in the universe called a Henle's loop. Its terrestrial abode is in the human kidney. I just refreshed my memory on the subject. The Henle's loop is an attenuated oxbow or U-turn made by an incredibly tiny tube in the nephron of the kidney.

The nephron in turn is a filtering structure which produces urine and reabsorbs nutrients. This business is so important that one fifth of all the heart's pumped blood goes to the kidneys.

There is no way to describe a nephron; you might hazard into a fairly good approximation of its structure if you threw about fifteen yards of string on the floor. If half the string fell into a very narrow loop, that would be the Henle's loop. Two other bits of string that rumpled up and tangled would be the "proximal convoluted tubule" and the "distal convoluted tubule," shaped just so. But the heart of the matter would be a very snarled clump of string, "an almost spherical tuft of parallel capillaries," which is the glomerulus, or Malpighian body. This is the filter to end all filters, supplied with afferent and efferent arterioles and protected by a double-walled capsule. Compared to the glomerulus, the Henle's loop is rather unimportant. By going from here to there in such a round-about way, the Henle's loop packs a great deal of filtering tubule into a very narrow space. But the delicate oxbow of tissue, looping down so far, and then up, is really a peripheral extravagance, which is why I remembered it, and a beautiful one, like a meander in a creek.

Now the point of all this is that there are a million nephrons in each human kidney. I've got two million glomeruli, two million Henle's loops, and I made them all myself, without the least effort. They're undoubtedly my finest work. What an elaboration, what an extravagance! The proximal segment of the tubule, for instance, "is composed of irregular cuboidal cells with characteristic brushlike striations (brush border) at the internal, or luminal, border." Here are my own fringed necessities, a veritable forest of pines.

Van Gogh, you remember, called the world a study that didn't come off. Whether it "came off" is a difficult question. The chloroplasts do stream in the leaf as if propelled by a mighty, invisible breath; but on the other hand, a certain sorrow arises, welling up in Shadow Creek, and from those lonely banks it appears that all our intricate fringes, however beautiful, are really the striations of a universal and undeserved flaying. But, Van Gogh: a *study* it is not. This is the truth of the pervading intricacy of the world's detail: the creation is not a study, a roughed-in sketch; it is supremely, meticulously created, created abundantly, extravagantly, and in fine.

Along with intricacy, there is another aspect of the creation that has impressed me in the course of my wanderings. Look again at the horsehair worm, a yard long and thin as a thread, whipping through the duck pond, or tangled with others of its kind in a slithering Gordian knot. Look at an overwintering ball of buzzing bees, or a turtle under ice breathing through its pumping cloaca. Look at the fruit of the Osage orange tree, big as a grapefruit, green, convoluted as any human brain. Or look at a rotifer's translucent gut: something orange and powerful is surging up and down like a piston, and something small and round is spinning in place like a flywheel. Look, in short, at practically anything—the coot's feet, the mantis's face, a banana, the human ear—and see that not only did the creator create everything, but that he is apt to create *anything*. He'll stop at nothing.

There is no one standing over evolution with a blue pencil to say, "Now that one, there, is absolutely ridiculous, and I won't have it." If the creature makes it, it gets a "stet." Is our taste so much better than the creator's? Utility to the creature is evolution's only aesthetic consideration. Form follows function in the created world, so far as I know, and the creature that functions, however bizarre, survives to perpetuate its form. Of the intricacy of form, I know some answers and not others: I know why the barbules on a feather hook together, and why the Henle's loop loops, but not why the elm tree's leaves zigzag, or why butterfly scales and pollen are shaped just so. But of the *variety* of form itself, of the multiplicity of forms, I know nothing. Except that, apparently, anything goes. This holds for forms of behavior as well as design—the mantis munching her mate, the frog wintering in mud, the spider wrapping a hummingbird, the pine processionary straddling a thread. Welcome aboard. A generous spirit signs on this motley crew.

Take, for instance, the African Hercules beetle, which is so big, according to Edwin Way Teale, "it drones over the countryside at evening with a sound like an approaching airplane." Or, better, take to heart Teale's description of South American honey ants. These ants have abdomens that can stretch to enormous proportions. "Certain members of the colony act as storage vessels for the honeydew gathered by the workers. They never leave the nest. With abdomens so swollen they cannot walk, they cling to the roof of their underground chamber, regurgitating food to the workers when it is needed." I read these things, and those ants are as present to me as if they hung from my kitchen ceiling, or down the vaults of my skull, pulsing live jars, engorged vats, teats, with an eyed animal at the head thinking—what?

Blake said, "He who does not prefer Form to Colour is a Coward!" I often wish the creator had been more of a coward, giving us many fewer forms and many more colors. Here is an interesting form, one closer to home. This is the larva, or nymph, of an ordinary dragonfly. The wingless nymphs are an inch long and fat as earthworms. They stalk everywhere on the floors of valley ponds and creeks, sucking water into their gilled rectums. But it is their faces I'm interested in. According to Howard Ensign Evans, a dragonfly larva's "lower lip is enormously lengthened, and has a double hinge joint so that it can be pulled back beneath the body when not in use; the outer part is expanded and provided with stout hooks, and in resting position forms a 'mask' that covers much of the face of the larva. The lip is capable of being thrust forward suddenly, and the terminal hooks are capable of grasping prey well in front of the larva and pulling it back to the sharp, jagged mandibles. Dragonfly larvae prey on many kinds of small insects occurring in the water, and the larger ones are well able to handle small fish."

The world is full of creatures that for some reason seem stranger to us than others, and libraries are full of books describing them—hagfish, platypuses, lizardlike pangolins four feet long with bright green, lapped scales like umbrella-tree leaves on a bush hut roof, butterflies emerging from anthills, spiderlings wafting through the air clutching tiny silken balloons, horseshoe crabs . . . the creator creates. Does he stoop, does he speak, does he save, succor, prevail? Maybe. But he creates; he creates everything and anything.

Of all known forms of life, only about ten percent are still living today. All other forms—fantastic plants, ordinary plants, living animals with unimaginably various wings, tails, teeth, brains—are utterly and forever gone. That is a great many forms that have been created. Multiplying ten times the number of living forms today yields a profusion that is quite beyond what I consider thinkable. Why so many forms? Why not just that one hydrogen atom? The creator goes off on one wild, specific tangent after another, or millions simultaneously, with an exuberance that would seem to be unwarranted, and with an abandoned energy sprung from an unfathomable font. What is going on here? The point of the dragonfly's terrible lip, the giant water bug, birdsong, or the beautiful dazzle and flash of sunlighted minnows, is not that it all fits together like clockwork—for it doesn't particularly, not even inside the goldfish bowl—but that it all flows so freely wild, like the creek, that it all surges in such a free, fringed tangle. Freedom is the world's water and weather, the world's nourishment freely given, its soil and sap: and the creator loves pizzazz.

II

What I aim to do is not so much learn the names of the shreds of creation that flourish in this valley, but to keep myself open to their meanings, which is to try to impress myself at all times with the fullest possible force of their very reality. I want to have things as multiply and intricately as possible present and visible in my mind. Then I might be able to sit on the hill by the burnt books where the starlings fly over, and see not only the starlings, the grass field, the quarried rock, the viney woods, Hollins Pond, and the mountains beyond, but also, and simultaneously, feathers' barbs, springtails in the soil, crystal in rock, chloroplasts streaming, rotifers pulsing, and the shape of the air in the pines. And, if I try to keep my eye on quantum physics, if I try to keep up with astronomy and cosmology, and really believe it all, I might ultimately be able to make out the landscape of the universe. Why not?

Landscape consists in the multiple, overlapping intricacies and forms that exist in a given space at a moment in time. Landscape is the texture of intricacy, and texture is my present subject. Intricacies of detail and varieties of form build up into textures. A bird's feather is an intricacy; the bird is a form; the bird in space in relation to air, forest, continent, and so on, is a thread in a texture. The moon has its texture, too, its pitted and carved landscapes in even its flattest seas. The planets are more than smooth spheres; the galaxy itself is a fleck of texture, binding and bound. But here on earth texture interests us supremely. Wherever there is life, there is twist and mess: the frizz of an arctic lichen, the tangle of brush along a bank, the dogleg of a dog's leg, the way a line has got to curve, split, or knob. The planet is characterized by its very jaggedness, its random heaps of mountains, its frayed fringes of shore.

Think of a globe, a revolving globe on a stand. Think of a contour globe, whose mountain ranges cast shadows, whose continents rise in bas-relief above the oceans. But then: think of how it *really* is. These heights aren't just suggested; they're there. Pliny, who knew the world was round, figured that when it was all surveyed the earth would be seen to resemble in shape, not a sphere, but a pineapple, pricked by irregularities. When I think of walking across a continent I think of all the neighborhood hills, the tiny grades up which children drag their sleds. It is all so sculptured, three-dimensional, casting a shadow. What if you had an enormous globe in relief that was so huge it showed roads and houses—a geological survey globe, a quarter of a mile to an inch—of the whole world, and the ocean floor! Looking at it, you would know what had to be left out: the free-standing sculptural arrangement of furniture in rooms, the jumble of broken rocks in a creek bed, tools in a box, labyrinthine ocean liners, the shape of snapdragons, walrus. Where is the one thing you care about on earth, the molding of one face? The relief globe couldn't begin to show trees, between whose overlapping boughs birds raise broods, or the furrows in bark, where whole creatures, creatures easily visible, live out their lives and call it world enough.

What do I make of all this texture? What does it mean about the kind of world in which I have been set down? The texture of the world, its filigree and scrollwork, means that there is the possibility for beauty here, a beauty inexhaustible in its complexity, which opens to my knock, which answers in me a call I do not remember calling, and which trains me to the wild and extravagant nature of the spirit I seek.

In the eighteenth century, when educated European tourists visited the Alps, they deliberately blindfolded their eyes to shield themselves from the evidence of the earth's horrid irregularity. It is hard to say if this was not merely affectation, for today, newborn infants, who have not yet been taught our ideas of beauty, repeatedly show in tests that they prefer complex to simple designs. At any rate, after the Romantic Revolution, and after Darwin, I might add, our conscious notions of beauty changed. Were the earth as smooth as a ball bearing, it might be beautiful seen from another planet, as the rings of

Saturn are. But here we live and move; we wander up and down the banks of the creek, we ride a railway through the Alps, and the landscape shifts and changes. Were the earth smooth, our brains would be smooth as well; we would wake, blink, walk two steps to get the whole picture, and lapse into a dreamless sleep. Because we are living people, and because we are on the receiving end of beauty, another element necessarily enters the question. The texture of space is a condition of time. Time is the warp and matter the weft of the woven texture of beauty in space, and death is the hurtling shuttle. Did those eighteenth-century people think they were immortal? Or were their carriages stalled to rigidity, so that they knew they would never move again, and, panicked, they reached for their blindfolds?

What I want to do, then, is add time to the texture, paint the landscape on an unrolling scroll, and set the giant relief globe spinning on its stand.

Last year I had a very unusual experience. I was awake, with my eyes closed, when I had a dream. It was a small dream about time.

I was dead, I guess, in deep black space high up among many white stars. My own consciousness had been disclosed to me, and I was happy. Then I saw far below me a long, curved band of color. As I came closer, I saw that it stretched endlessly in either direction, and I understood that I was seeing all the time of the planet where I had lived. It looked like a woman's tweed scarf; the longer I studied any one spot, the more dots of color I saw. There was no end to the deepness and variety of the dots. At length I started to look for my time, but, although more and more specks of color and deeper and more intricate textures appeared in the fabric, I couldn't find my time, or any time at all that I recognized as being near my time. I couldn't make out so much as a pyramid. Yet as I looked at the band of time, all the individual people, I understood with special clarity, were living at that very moment with great emotion, in intricate detail, in their individual times and places, and they were dying and being replaced by ever more people, one by one, like stitches in which whole worlds of feeling and energy were wrapped, in a never-ending cloth. I remembered suddenly the color and texture of our life as we knew it—these things had been utterly forgotten—and I thought as I searched for it on the limitless band, "That was a good time then, a good time to be living." And I began to remember our time.

I recalled green fields with carrots growing, one by one, in slender rows. Men and women in bright vests and scarves came and pulled the carrots out of the soil and carried them in baskets to shaded kitchens, where they scrubbed them with yellow brushes under running water. I saw white-faced cattle lowing and wading in creeks, with dust on the whorled and curly white hair between their ears. I saw May apples in forests, erupting through leaf-strewn paths. Cells on the root hairs of sycamores split and divided, and apples grew spotted and striped in the fall. Mountains kept their cool caves, and squirrels raced home to their nests through sunlight and shade.

I remembered the ocean, and I seemed to be in the ocean myself, swimming over orange crabs that looked like coral, or off the deep Atlantic banks where whitefish school. Or again I saw the tops of poplars, and the whole sky brushed with clouds in pallid streaks, under which wild ducks flew with outstretched necks, and called, one by one, and flew on.

All these things I saw. Scenes grew in depth and sunlit detail before my eyes, and were replaced by ever more scenes, as I remembered the life of my time with increasing feeling.

At last I saw the earth as a globe in space, and I recalled the ocean's shape and the form of continents, saying to myself with surprise as I looked at the planet, "Yes, that's how it was then; that part there we called . . . 'France.' " I was filled with the deep affection of nostalgia—and then I opened my eyes.

* * *

We all ought to be able to conjure up sights like these at will, so that we can keep in mind the scope of texture's motion in time. It is a pity we can't watch it on a screen. John Dee, the Elizabethan geographer and mathematician, dreamed up a great idea, which is just what we need. You shoot a mirror up into space so that it is traveling faster than the speed of light (there's the rub). Then you can look in the mirror and watch all the earth's previous history unfolding as on a movie screen. Those people who shoot endless time-lapse films of unfurling roses and tulips have the wrong idea. They should train their cameras instead on the melting of pack ice, the green filling of ponds, the tidal swing of the Seven Bore. They should film the glaciers of Greenland, some of which creak along at such a fast clip that even the dogs bark at them. They should film the invasion of the southernmost Canadian tundra by the northernmost spruce-fir-forest, which is happening right now at the rate of a mile every ten years. When the last ice sheet receded from the North American continent, the earth rebounded ten feet. Wouldn't that have been a sight to see?

People say that a good seat in the backyard affords as accurate and inspiring a vantage point on the planet earth as any observation tower on Alpha Centauri. They are wrong. We see through a glass darkly. We find ourselves in the middle of a movie, or, God help us, a take for a movie, and we don't know what's on the rest of the film.

Say you could look through John Dee's mirror whizzing through space; say you could heave our relief globe into motion like a giant top and breathe life on its surface; say you could view a time-lapse film of our planet: What would you see? Transparent images moving through light, "an infinite storm of beauty."

The beginning is swaddled in mists, blasted by random blinding flashes. Lava pours and cools; seas boil and flood. Clouds materialize and shift; now you can see the earth's face through only random patches of clarity. The land shudders and splits, like pack ice rent by a widening lead. Mountains burst up, jutting, and dull and soften before your eyes, clothed in forests like felt. The ice rolls up, grinding green land under water forever; the ice rolls back. Forests erupt and disappear like fairy rings. The ice rolls up—mountains are mowed into lakes, land rises wet from the sea like a surfacing whale—the ice rolls back.

A blue-green streaks the highest ridges, a yellow-green spreads from the south like a wave up a strand. A red dye seems to leak from the north down the ridges and into the valleys, seeping south; a white follows the red, then yellow-green washes north, then red spreads again, then white, over and over, making patterns of color too swift and intricate to follow. Slow the film. You see dust storms, locusts, floods, in dizzying flash-frames.

Zero in on a well-watered shore and see smoke from fires drifting. Stone cities rise, spread, and crumble, like patches of alpine blossoms that flourish for a day an inch above the permafrost, that iced earth no root can suck, and wither in an hour. New cities appear, and rivers sift silt onto their rooftops; more cities emerge and spread in lobes like lichen on rock. The great human figures of history, those intricate, spirited tissues that roamed the earth's surface, are a wavering blur whose split second in the light was too brief an exposure to yield any image but the hunched, shadowless figures of ghosts. The great herds of caribou pour into the valleys like slag, and trickle back, and pour, a brown fluid.

Slow it down more, come closer still. A dot appears, a flesh-flake. It swells like a balloon; it moves, circles, slows, and vanishes. This is your life.

Our life is a faint tracing on the surface of mystery. The surface of mystery is not smooth, any more than the planet is smooth; not even a single hydrogen atom is smooth, let alone a pine. Nor does it fit together; not even the chlorophyll and hemoglobin molecules are a perfect match, for, even after the atom of iron replaces the magnesium, long streamers of disparate atoms trail disjointedly from the rims of the molecules' loops. Freedom cuts both ways. Mystery itself is as fringed and intricate as the shape of the air in time. Forays into mystery cut bays and fine fiords, but the forested mainland itself is implacable both in its bulk and in its most filigreed fringe of detail. "Every religion that does not affirm that God is hidden," said Pascal flatly, "is not true."

What is man, that thou art mindful of him? This is where the great modern religions are so unthinkably radical: the love of God! For we can see that we are as many as the leaves of trees. But it could be that our faithlessness is a cowering cowardice born of our very smallness, a massive failure of imagination. Certainly nature seems to exult in abounding radicality, extremism, anarchy. If we were to judge nature by its common sense or likelihood, we wouldn't believe the world existed. In nature, improbabilities are the one stock in trade. The whole creation is one lunatic fringe. If creation had been left up to me, I'm sure I wouldn't have had the imagination or courage to do more than shape a single, reasonably sized atom, smooth as a snowball, and let it go at that. No claims of any and all revelations could be so far-fetched as a single giraffe.

The question from agnosticism is, Who turned on the lights? The question from faith is, Whatever for? Thoreau climbs Mount Katahdin and gives vent to an almost outraged sense of the reality of the things of this world: "I fear bodies, I tremble to meet them. What is this Titan that has possession of me? Talk of mysteries!—Think of our life in nature,—daily to be shown matter, to come in contact with it,—rocks, trees, wind on our cheeks! the *solid* earth! the *actual* world! the *common* sense! *Contact! Contact!* Who are we? *where* are we?" The Lord God of gods, the Lord God of gods, he knoweth. . . .

Sir James Jeans, British astronomer and physicist, suggested that the universe was beginning to look more like a great thought than a great machine. Humanists seized on the expression, but it was hardly news. We knew, looking around, that a thought branches and leafs, a tree comes to a conclusion. But the question of who is thinking the thought is more fruitful than the question of who made the machine, for a machinist can of course wipe his hands and leave, and his simple machine still hums; but if the thinker's attention strays for a minute, his simplest thought ceases altogether. And, as I have stressed, the place where we so incontrovertibly find ourselves, whether thought or machine, is at least not in any way simple.

Instead, the landscape of the world is "ring-streaked, speckled, and spotted," like Jacob's cattle culled from Laban's herd. Laban had been hard, making Jacob serve seven years in his fields for Rachel, and then giving him instead Rachel's sister, Leah, withholding Rachel until he had served another seven years. When Laban finally sent Jacob on his way, he agreed that Jacob could have all those cattle, sheep, and goats from the herd that were ringstreaked, speckled, and spotted. Jacob pulled some tricks of his own, and soon the strongest and hardiest of Laban's fecund flocks were born ringstreaked, speckled, and spotted. Jacob set out for Canaan with his wives and twelve sons, the fathers of the twelve tribes of Israel, and with these cattle that are Israel's heritage, into Egypt and out of Egypt, just as the intricate speckled and spotted world is ours.

Intricacy is that which is given from the beginning, the birthright, and in intricacy is the hardiness of complexity that ensures against the failure of all life. This is our heritage, the piebald landscape of time. We walk around; we see a shred of the infinite possible combinations of an infinite variety of forms.

Anything can happen; any pattern of speckles may appear in a world ceaselessly bawling with newness. I see red blood stream in shimmering dots inside a goldfish's tail; I see the stout, extensible lip of a dragonfly nymph that can pierce and clasp a goldfish; and I see the clotted snarls of bright algae that snare and starve the nymph. I see engorged, motionless ants regurgitate pap to a colony of pawing workers, and I see sharks limned in light twist in a raised and emerald wave.

The wonder is—given the errant nature of freedom and the burgeoning of texture in time—the wonder is that all the forms are not monsters, that there is beauty at all, grace gratuitous, pennies found, like mockingbird's free fall. Beauty itself is the fruit of the creator's exuberance that grew such a tangle, and the grotesques and horrors bloom from that same free growth, that intricate scramble and twine up and down the conditions of time.

This, then, is the extravagant landscape of the world, given, given with pizzazz, given in good measure, pressed down, shaken together, and running over.

CHAPTER 9

Flood

IT'S SUMMER. We had some deep spring sunshine about a month ago, in a drought; the nights were cold. It's been gray sporadically, but not oppressively, and rainy for a week, and I would think: When is the real hot stuff coming, the mind-melting weeding weather? It was rainy again this morning, the same spring rain, and then this afternoon a different rain came: a pounding, three-minute shower. And when it was over, the cloud dissolved to haze. I can't see Tinker Mountain. It's summer now: the heat is on. It's summer now all summer long.

The season changed two hours ago. Will my life change as well? This is a time for resolutions, revolutions. The animals are going wild. I must have seen ten rabbits in as many minutes. Baltimore orioles are here; brown thrashers seem to be nesting down by Tinker Creek across the road. The coot is still around, big as a Thanksgiving turkey, and as careless; it doesn't even glance at a barking dog.

The creek's up. When the rain stopped today I walked across the road to the downed log by the steer crossing. The steers were across the creek, a black clot on a distant hill. High water had touched my log, the log I sit on, and dumped a smooth slope of muck in its lee. The water itself was an opaque pale green, like pulverized jade, still high and very fast, lightless, like no earthly water. A dog I've never seen before, thin as death, was flushing rabbits.

A knot of yellow, fleshy somethings had grown up by the log. They didn't seem to have either proper stems or proper flowers, but instead only blind, featureless growth, like etiolated potato sprouts in a root cellar. I tried to dig one up from the crumbly soil, but they all apparently grew from a single, well-rooted corm, so I let them go.

Still, the day had an air of menace. A broken whiskey bottle by the log, the brown tip of a snake's tail disappearing between two rocks on the hill at my back, the rabbit the dog nearly caught, the rabies I knew was in the county, the bees who kept unaccountably fumbling at my forehead with their furred feet . . .

I headed over to the new woods by the creek, the motorbike woods. They were strangely empty. The air was so steamy I could barely see. The ravine separating the woods from the field had filled during high water, and a dead tan mud clogged it now. The horny orange roots of one tree on the ravine's jagged bank had been stripped of soil; now the roots hung, an empty net in the air, clutching an incongruous light bulb stranded by receding waters. For the entire time that I walked in the woods, four jays flew around me very slowly, acting generally odd, and screaming on two held notes. There wasn't a breath of wind.

Coming out of the woods, I heard loud shots; they reverberated ominously in the damp air. But when I walked up the road, I saw what it was, and the dread quality of the whole afternoon vanished at once. It was a couple of garbage trucks, huge trash compacters humped like armadillos, and they were making their engines backfire to impress my neighbors' pretty daughters, high school girls who had just been let off the school bus. The long-haired girls strayed into giggling clumps at the corner of the road; the garbage trucks sped away gloriously, as if they had been the Tarleton twins on thoroughbreds cantering away from the gates of Tara. In the distance a white vapor was rising from the waters of Carvin's Cove and catching in trailing tufts in the mountains' sides. I stood on my own porch, exhilarated, unwilling to go indoors.

It was just this time last year that we had the flood. It was Hurricane Agnes, really, but by the time it got here, the weather bureau had demoted it to a tropical storm. I see by a clipping I saved that the date was June twenty-first, the solstice, midsummer's night, the longest daylight of the year; but I didn't notice it at the time. Everything was so exciting, and so very dark.

All it did was rain. It rained, and the creek started to rise. The creek, naturally, rises every time it rains; this didn't seem any different. But it kept raining, and, that morning of the twenty-first, the creek kept rising.

That morning I'm standing at my kitchen window. Tinker Creek is out of its four-foot banks, way out, and it's still coming. The high creek doesn't look like our creek. Our creek splashes transparently over a jumble of rocks; the high creek obliterates everything in flat opacity. It looks like somebody else's creek that has usurped or eaten our creek and is roving frantically to escape, big and ugly, like a blacksnake caught in a kitchen drawer. The color is foul, a rusty cream. Water that has picked up clay soils looks worse than other muddy waters, because the particles of clay are so fine; they spread out and cloud the water so that you can't see light through even an inch of it in a drinking glass.

Everything looks different. Where my eye is used to depth, I see the flat water, near, too near. I see trees I never noticed before, the black verticals of their rain-soaked trunks standing out of the pale water like pilings for a rotted dock. The stillness of grassy banks and stony ledges is gone; I see rushing, a wild sweep and hurry in one direction, as swift and compelling as a waterfall. The Atkins kids are out in their tiny rain gear, staring at the monster creek. It's risen up to their gates; the neighbors are gathering; I go out.

I hear a roar, a high windy sound more like air than like water, like the run-together whaps of a helicopter's propeller after the engine is off, a high million rushings. The air smells damp and acrid, like fuel oil, or insecticide. It's raining.

I'm in no danger; my house is high. I hurry down the road to the bridge. Neighbors who have barely seen each other all winter are there, shaking their heads. Few have ever seen it before: the water is *over* the bridge. Even when I see the bridge now, which I do every day, I still can't believe it: the water was *over* the bridge, a foot or two over the bridge, which at normal times is eleven feet above the surface of the creek.

Now the water is receding slightly; someone has produced empty metal drums, which we roll to the bridge and set up in a square to keep cars from trying to cross. It takes a bit of nerve even to stand on the bridge; the flood has ripped away a wedge of concrete that buttressed the bridge on the bank. Now one corner of the bridge hangs apparently unsupported while water hurls in an arch just inches below.

It's hard to take it all in, it's all so new. I look at the creek at my feet. It smashes under the bridge like a fist, but there is no end to its force; it hurtles down as far as I can see till it lurches round the bend, filling the valley, flattening, mashing, pushed, wider and faster, till it fills my brain.

It's like a dragon. Maybe it's because the bridge we are on is chancy, but I notice that no one can help imagining himself washed overboard, and gauging his chances for survival. You couldn't live. Mark Spitz couldn't live. The water arches where the bridge's supports at the banks prevent its enormous volume from going wide, forcing it to go high; that arch drives down like a diving whale, and would butt you on the bottom. "You'd never know what hit you," one of the men says. But if you survived that part and managed to surface . . . ? How fast can you live? You'd need a windshield. You couldn't keep your head up; the water under the surface is fastest. You'd spin around like a sock in a clothes dryer. You couldn't grab onto a tree trunk without leaving that arm behind. No, you couldn't live. And if they ever found you, your gut would be solid red clay.

It's all I can do to stand. I feel dizzy, drawn, mauled. Below me the floodwater roils to a violent froth that looks like dirty lace, a lace that continuously explodes before my eyes. If I look away, the earth moves backwards, rises and swells, from the fixing of my eyes at one spot against the motion of the flood. All the familiar land looks as though it were not solid and real at all, but painted on a scroll like a backdrop, and that unrolled scroll has been shaken, so the earth sways and the air roars.

Everything imaginable is zipping by, almost too fast to see. If I stand on the bridge and look downstream, I get dizzy; but if I look upstream, I feel as though I am looking up the business end of an avalanche. There are dolls, split wood and kindling, dead fledgling songbirds, bottles, whole bushes and trees, rakes and garden gloves. Wooden, rough-hewn railroad ties charge by faster than any express. Lattice fencing bobs along, and a wooden picket gate. There are so many white plastic gallon milk jugs that when the flood ultimately recedes, they are left on the grassy banks looking from a distance like a flock of white geese.

I expect to see anything at all. In this one way, the creek is more like itself when it floods than at any other time: mediating, bringing things down. I wouldn't be at all surprised to see John Paul Jones coming round the bend, standing on the deck of the *Bon Homme Richard,* or Amelia Earhart waving gaily from the cockpit of her floating Lockheed. Why not a cello, a basket of breadfruit, a casket of antique coins? Here comes the Franklin expedition on snowshoes, and the three magi, plus camels, afloat on a canopied barge!

The whole world is in flood, the land as well as the water. Water streams down the trunks of trees, drips from hat-brims, courses across roads. The whole earth seems to slide like sand down a chute; water pouring over the least slope leaves the grass flattened, silver side up, pointing downstream. Everywhere windfall and flotsam twigs and leafy boughs, wood from woodpiles, bottles, and saturated straw spatter the ground or streak it in curving windrows. Tomatoes in flat gardens are literally floating in mud; they look as though they have been dropped whole into a boiling, brown-gravy stew. The level of the water table is at the top of the toe of my shoes. Pale muddy water lies on the flat so that it all but drowns the grass; it looks like a hideous parody of a light snow on the field, with only the dark tips of the grass blades visible.

When I look across the street, I can't believe my eyes. Right behind the road's shoulder are waves, waves whipped in rhythmically peaking scallops, racing downstream. The hill where I watched the praying mantis lay her eggs is a waterfall that splashes into a brown ocean. I can't even remember where the creek usually runs—it is everywhere now. My log is gone for sure, I think—but in fact, I discover later, it holds, rammed between growing trees. Only the cable suspending the steers' fence is visible, and not the fence itself; the steers' pasture is entirely in flood, a brown river. The river leaps its banks and smashes into the woods where the motorbikes go, devastating all but the sturdiest trees. The water is so deep and wide it seems as though you could navigate the *Queen Mary* in it, clear to Tinker Mountain.

What do animals do in these floods? I see a drowned muskrat go by like he's flying, but they all couldn't die; the water rises after every hard rain, and the creek is still full of muskrats. This flood is higher than their raised sleeping platforms in the banks; they must just race for high ground and hold on. Where do the fish go, and what do they do? Presumably their gills can filter oxygen out of this muck, but I don't know how. They must hide from the current behind any barriers they can find, and fast for a few days. They must: otherwise we'd have no fish; they'd all be in the Atlantic Ocean. What about herons and kingfishers, say? They can't see to eat. It usually seems to me that when I see any animal, its business is urgent enough that it couldn't easily be suspended for forty-eight hours. Crayfish, frogs, snails, rotifers? Most things must simply die. They couldn't live. Then I suppose that when the water goes down and clears, the survivors have a field day with no competition. But you'd think the bottom would be knocked out of the food chain—the whole pyramid would have no base plankton, and it would crumble, or crash with a thud. Maybe enough spores and larvae and eggs are constantly being borne down from slower upstream waters to repopulate . . . I don't know.

Some little children have discovered a snapping turtle as big as a tray. It's hard to believe that this creek could support a predator that size: its shell is a foot and a half across, and its head extends a good seven inches beyond the shell. When the children—in the company of a shrunken terrier—approach it on the bank, the snapper rears up on its thick front legs and hisses very impressively. I had read earlier that since turtles' shells are rigid, they don't have bellows lungs; they have to gulp for air. And, also since their shells are rigid, there's only room for so much inside, so when they are frightened and planning a retreat, they have to expel air from their lungs to make room for head and feet—hence the malevolent hiss.

The next time I look, I see that the children have somehow maneuvered the snapper into a washtub. They're waving a broom handle at it in hopes that it will snap the wood like a matchstick, but the creature will not deign to oblige. The kids are crushed; all their lives they've heard that this is the one thing you do with a snapping turtle—you shove a broom handle near it, and it "snaps it like a matchstick." It's nature's way; it's sure-fire. But the turtle is having none of it. It avoids the broom handle with an air of patiently repressed rage. They let it go, and it beelines down the bank, dives unhesitatingly into the swirling floodwater, and that's the last we see of it.

A cheer comes up from the crowd on the bridge. The truck is here with a pump for the Bowerys' basement, hooray! We roll away the metal drums, the truck makes it over the bridge, to my amazement—the crowd cheers again. State police cruise by; everything's fine here; downstream people are in trouble. The bridge over by the Bings' on Tinker Creek looks like it's about to go. There's a tree trunk wedged against its railing, and a section of concrete is out. The Bings are away, and a young couple is living there, "taking care of the house." What can they do? The husband drove to work that morning as usual; a few hours later, his wife was evacuated from the front door in a *motorboat.*

I walk to the Bings'. Most of the people who are on our bridge eventually end up over there; it's just down the road. We straggle along in the rain, gathering a crowd. The men who work away from home are here, too; their wives have telephoned them at work this morning to say that the creek is rising fast, and they'd better get home while the gettin's good.

There's a big crowd already there; everybody knows that the Bings' is low. The creek is coming in the recreation-room windows; it's halfway up the garage door. Later that day people will haul out everything salvageable and try to dry it: books, rugs, furniture—the lower level was filled from floor to ceiling. Now on this bridge a road crew is trying to chop away the wedged tree trunk with a long-handled ax. The handle isn't so long that they don't have to stand on the bridge, in Tinker Creek. I walk along a low brick wall that was built to retain the creek away from the house at high water. The wall holds just fine, but now that the creek's receding, it's retaining water around the house. On the wall I can walk right out into the flood and stand in the middle of it. Now on the return trip I meet a young man who's going in the opposite direction. The wall is one brick wide; we can't pass. So we clasp hands and lean out backwards over the turbulent water; our feet interlace like teeth on a zipper, we pull together, stand, and continue on our ways. The kids have spotted a rattlesnake draping itself out of harm's way in a bush; now they all want to walk over the brick wall to the bush, to get bitten by the snake.

The little Atkins kids are here, and they are hopping up and down. I wonder if I hopped up and down, would the bridge go? I could stand at the railing as at the railing of a steamboat, shouting deliriously, "Mark three! Quarter-less-three! Half twain! Quarter twain! . . ." as the current bore the broken bridge out of sight around the bend before she sank. . . .

Everyone else is standing around. Some of the women are carrying curious plastic umbrellas that look like diving bells— umbrellas they don't put up, but on; they don't get under, but in. They can see out dimly, like goldfish in bowls. Their voices from within sound distant, but with an underlying cheerfulness that plainly acknowledges, "Isn't this ridiculous?" Some of the men are wearing their fishing hats. Others duck their heads under folded newspapers held not very high in an effort to compromise between keeping their heads dry and letting rain run up their sleeves. Following some form of courtesy, I guess, they lower these newspapers when they speak with you, and squint politely into the rain.

Women are bringing coffee in mugs to the road crew. They've barely made a dent in the tree trunk, and they're giving up. It's a job for power tools; the water's going down anyway, and the danger is past. Some kid starts doing tricks on a skateboard; I head home.

On the same day that I was standing on bridges here over Tinker Creek, a friend, Lee Zacharias, was standing on a bridge in Richmond over the James River. It was a calm day there, with not a cloud in the skies. The James River was up a mere nine feet, which didn't look too unusual. But floating in the river was everything under the bright sun. As Lee watched, chicken coops raced by, chunks of houses, porches, stairs, whole uprooted trees—and finally a bloated dead horse. Lee knew, all of Richmond knew: it was coming.

There the James ultimately rose thirty-two feet. The whole

town was under water, and all the electrical power was out. When Governor Holton signed the emergency relief bill—which listed our county among the federal disaster areas—he had to do it by candlelight.

That night a curious thing happened in the blacked-out Governor's mansion. Governor Holton walked down an upstairs hall and saw, to his disbelief, a lightbulb glowing in a ceiling fixture. It was one of three bulbs, all dead—the whole city was dead—but that one bulb was giving off a faint electrical light. He stared at the thing, scratched his head, and summoned an electrician. The electrician stared at the thing, scratched his head, and announced, "Impossible." The governor went back to bed, and the electrician went home. No explanation has ever been found.

Later Agnes would move on up into Maryland, Pennsylvania, and New York, killing people and doing hundreds of millions of dollars worth of damage. Here in Virginia alone it killed twelve people and ruined 166 million dollars worth of property. But it hit Pennsylvania twice, coming and going. I talked to one of the helicopter pilots who had helped airlift ancient corpses from a flooded cemetery in Wilkes-Barre, Pennsylvania. The flood left the bodies stranded on housetops, in trees; the pilots, sickened, had to be relieved every few hours. The one I talked to, in a little sandwich shop at the Peaks of Otter on the Blue Ridge Parkway, preferred Vietnam. We were lucky here.

This winter I heard a final flood story, about an extra dividend that the flood left the Bings, a surprise as unexpected as a baby in a basket on a stoop.

The Bings came home and their house was ruined, but somehow they managed to salvage almost everything, and live as before. One afternoon in the fall a friend went to visit them; as he was coming in, he met a man coming out, a professor with a large volume under his arm. The Bings led my friend inside and into the kitchen, where they proudly opened the oven door and showed him a giant mushroom—which they were baking to serve to guests the following day. The professor with the book had just been verifying its edibility. I imagined the mushroom, wrinkled, black, and big as a dinner plate, erupting overnight mysteriously in the Bings' living room—from the back of an upholstered couch, say, or from a still-damp rug under an armchair.

Alas, the story as I had fixed it in my mind proved to be only partly true. The Bings often cook wild mushrooms, and they know what they're doing. This particular mushroom had grown outside, under a sycamore, on high ground that the flood hadn't touched. So the flood had nothing to do with it. But it's still a good story, and I like to think that the flood left them a gift, a consolation prize, so that for years to come they will be finding edible mushrooms here and there about the house, dinner on the bookshelf, hors d'oeuvres in the piano. It would have been nice.

CHAPTER 10

Fecundity

I

I WAKENED MYSELF last night with my own shouting. It must have been that terrible yellow plant I saw pushing through the flood-damp soil near the log by Tinker Creek, the plant as fleshy and featureless as a slug, that erupted through the floor of my brain as I slept, and burgeoned into the dream of fecundity that woke me up.

I was watching two huge luna moths mate. Luna moths are those fragile ghost moths, fairy moths, whose five-inch wings are swallow-tailed, a pastel green bordered in silken lavender. From the hairy head of the male sprouted two enormous, furry antennae that trailed down past his ethereal wings. He was on top of the female, hunching repeatedly with a horrible animal vigor.

It was the perfect picture of utter spirituality and utter degradation. I was fascinated and could not turn away my eyes. By watching them I in effect permitted their mating to take place and so committed myself to accepting the consequences—all because I wanted to see what would happen. I wanted in on a secret.

And then the eggs hatched and the bed was full of fish. I was standing across the room in the doorway, staring at the bed. The eggs hatched before my eyes, on my bed, and a thousand chunky fish swarmed there in a viscid slime. The fish were firm and fat, black and white, with triangular bodies and bulging eyes. I watched in horror as they squirmed three feet deep, swimming and oozing about in the glistening, transparent slime. Fish in the bed!—and I awoke. My ears still rang with the foreign cry that had been my own voice.

For nightmare you eat wild carrot, which is Queen Anne's lace, or you chew the black seeds of the male peony. But it was too late for prevention, and there is no cure. What root or seed will erase that scene from my mind? Fool, I thought: child, you child, you ignorant, innocent fool. What did you expect to see—angels? For it was understood in the dream that the bed full of fish was my own fault, that if I had turned away from the mating moths the hatching of their eggs wouldn't have happened, or at least would have happened in secret, elsewhere. I brought it upon myself, this slither, this swarm.

I don't know what it is about fecundity that so appalls. I suppose it is the teeming evidence that birth and growth, which we value, are ubiquitous and blind, that life itself is so astonishingly cheap, that nature is as careless as it is bountiful, and that with extravagance goes a crushing waste that will one day include our own cheap lives, Henle's loops and all. Every glistening egg is a memento mori.

After a natural disaster such as a flood, nature "stages a comeback." People use the optimistic expression without any real idea of the pressures and waste the comeback involves. Now, in late June, things are popping outside. Creatures extrude or vent eggs; larvae fatten, split their shells, and eat them; spores dissolve or explode; root hairs multiply, corn puffs on the stalk, grass yields seed, shoots erupt from the earth turgid and sheathed; wet muskrats, rabbits, and squirrels slide into the sunlight, mewling and blind; and everywhere watery cells divide and swell, swell and divide. I can like it and call it birth and regeneration, or I can play the devil's advocate and call it rank fecundity—and say that it's hell that's a-poppin'.

This is what I plan to do. Partly as a result of my terrible dream, I have been thinking that the landscape of the intricate world that I have painted is inaccurate and lopsided. It is too optimistic. For the notion of the infinite variety of detail and the multiplicity of forms is a pleasing one; in complexity are the fringes of beauty, and in variety are generosity and exuberance. But all this leaves something vital out of the picture. It is not one pine I see, but a thousand. I myself am not one, but legion. And we are all going to die.

In this repetition of individuals is a mindless stutter, an imbecilic fixedness that must be taken into account. The driving force behind all this fecundity is a terrible pressure I also must consider, the pressure of birth and growth, the pressure that splits the bark of trees and shoots out seeds, that squeezes out the egg and bursts the pupa, that hungers and lusts and drives the creature relentlessly toward its own death. Fecundity, then, is what I have been thinking about, fecundity and the pressure of growth. Fecundity is an ugly word for an ugly subject. It is ugly, at least, in the eggy animal world. I don't think it is for plants.

I never met a man who was shaken by a field of identical blades of grass. An acre of poppies and a forest of spruce boggle no one's mind. Even ten square miles of wheat gladdens the hearts of most people, although it is really as unnatural and freakish as the Frankenstein monster; if man were to die, I read, wheat wouldn't survive him more than three years. No, in the plant world, and especially among the flowering plants, fecundity is not an assault on human values. Plants are not our competitors; they are our prey and our nesting materials. We are no more distressed at their proliferation than an owl is at a population explosion among field mice.

After the flood last year I found a big tulip-tree limb that had been wind-thrown into Tinker Creek. The current dragged it up on some rocks on the bank, where receding waters stranded it. A month after the flood I discovered that it was growing new leaves. Both ends of the branch were completely exposed and dried. I was amazed. It was like the old fable about the corpse's growing a beard; it was as if the woodpile in my garage were suddenly to burst greenly into leaf. The way plants persevere in the bitterest of circumstances is utterly heartening. I can barely keep from unconsciously ascribing a will to these plants, a do-or-die courage, and I have to remind myself that coded cells and mute water pressure have no idea how grandly they are flying in the teeth of it all.

In the lower Bronx, for example, enthusiasts found an ailanthus tree that was fifteen feet long growing from the corner of a garage roof. It was rooted in and living on "dust and roofing cinders." Even more spectacular is a desert plant, *Ibervillea sonorae*—a member of the gourd family—that Joseph Wood Krutch describes. If you see this plant in the desert, you see only a dried chunk of loose wood. It has neither roots nor stems; it's like an old gray knothole. But it is alive. Each year before the rainy season comes, it sends out a few roots and shoots. If the rain arrives, it grows flowers and fruits; these soon wither away, and it reverts to a state as quiet as driftwood.

Well, the New York Botanical Garden put a dried *Ibervillea sonorae* on display in a glass case. "For seven years," says Joseph Wood Krutch, "without soil or water, simply lying in the case, it put forth a few anticipatory shoots and then, when no rainy season arrived, dried up again, hoping for better luck next year." That's what I call flying in the teeth of it all.

(It's hard to understand why no one at the New York Botanical Garden had the grace to splash a glass of water on the thing. Then they could say on their display case label, "This is a live plant." But by the eighth year what they had was a dead plant, which is precisely what it had looked like all along. The sight of it, reinforced by the label "Dead *Ibervillea sonorae,*" would have been most melancholy to visitors to the botanical garden. I suppose they just threw it away.)

The growth pressure of plants can do an impressive variety of tricks. Bamboo can grow three feet in twenty-four hours, an accomplishment that is capitalized upon, *legendarily,* in that exquisite Asian torture in which a victim is strapped to a mesh bunk a mere foot above a bed of healthy bamboo plants whose wood-like tips have been sharpened. For the first eight hours he is fine, if jittery; then he starts turning into a collander, by degrees.

Down at the root end of things, blind growth reaches astonishing proportions. So far as I know, only one real experiment has ever been performed to determine the extent and rate of root growth, and when you read the figures, you see why. I have run into various accounts of this experiment, and the only thing they don't tell you is how many lab assistants were blinded for life.

The experimenters studied a single grass plant, winter rye. They let it grow in a greenhouse for four months; then they gingerly spirited away the soil—under microscopes, I imagine—and counted and measured all the roots and root hairs. In four months the plant had set forth 378 miles of roots— that's about three miles a day—in 14 million distinct roots. This is mighty impressive, but when they get down to the root hairs, I boggle completely. In those same four months the rye plant created 14 *billion* root hairs, and those little strands placed end-to-end just about wouldn't quit. In a single *cubic inch* of soil, the length of the root hairs totaled 6000 miles.

Other plants use the same water power to heave the rock earth around as though they were merely shrugging off a silken cape. Rutherford Platt tells about a larch tree whose root had cleft a one-and-one-half ton boulder and hoisted it a foot into the air. Everyone knows how a sycamore root will buckle a sidewalk, a mushroom will shatter a cement basement floor. But when the first real measurements of this awesome pressure were taken, nobody could believe the figures.

Rutherford Platt tells the story in *The Great American Forest*, one of the most interesting books ever written: "In 1875, a Massachusetts farmer, curious about the growing power of expanding apples, melons and squashes, harnessed a squash to a weightlifting device which had a dial like a grocer's scale to indicate the pressure exerted by the expanding fruit. As the days passed, he kept piling on counterbalancing weight; he could hardly believe his eyes when he saw his vegetables quietly exerting a lifting force of 5 thousand pounds per square inch. When nobody believed him, he set up exhibits of harnessed squashes and invited the public to come and see. The *Annual Report of the Massachusetts Board of Agriculture*, 1875, reported: 'Many thousands of men, women, and children of all classes of society visited it. *Mr. Penlow* watched it day and night, making hourly observations; *Professor Parker* was moved to write a poem about it; *Professor Seelye* declared that he positively stood in awe of it.'"

All this is very jolly. Unless perhaps I were strapped down above a stand of growing, sharpened bamboo, I am unlikely to feel the faintest queasiness either about the growth pressure of plants, or their fecundity. Even when the plants get in the way of human "culture," I don't mind. When I read how many thousands of dollars a city like New York has to spend to keep underground water pipes free of ailanthus, ginko, and sycamore roots, I cannot help but give a little cheer. After all, water pipes are almost always an excellent source of water. In a town where resourcefulness and beating the system are highly prized, these primitive trees can fight city hall and win.

But in the animal world things are different, and human feelings are different. While we're in New York, consider the cockroaches under the bed and the rats in the early morning clustered on the porch stoop. Apartment houses are hives of swarming roaches. Or again: in one sense you could think of

Manhattan's land as high-rent, high-rise real estate; in another sense you could see it as an enormous breeding ground for rats, acres and acres of rats. I suppose that the rats and the cockroaches don't do so much actual damage as the roots do; nevertheless, the prospect does not please. Fecundity is anathema only in the animal. "Acres and acres of rats" has a suitably chilling ring to it that is decidedly lacking if I say, instead, "acres and acres of tulips."

The landscape of earth is dotted and smeared with masses of apparently identical individual animals, from the great Pleistocene herds that blanketed grasslands to the gluey gobs of bacteria that clog the lobes of lungs. The oceanic breeding grounds of pelagic birds are as teeming and cluttered as any human Calcutta. Lemmings blacken the earth and locusts the air. Grunion run thick in the ocean, corals pile on pile, and protozoans explode in a red tide stain. Ants take to the skies in swarms, mayflies hatch by the millions, and molting cicadas coat the trunks of trees. Have you seen the rivers run red and lumpy with salmon?

Consider the ordinary barnacle, the rock barnacle. Inside every one of those millions of hard white cones on the rocks— the kind that bruises your heel as you bruise its head—is of course a creature as alive as you or I. Its business in life is this: when a wave washes over it, it sticks out twelve feathery feeding appendages and filters the plankton for food. As it grows, it sheds its skin like a lobster, enlarges its shell, and reproduces itself without end. The larvae "hatch into the sea in milky clouds." The barnacles encrusting a single half mile of shore can leak into the water a million million larvae. How many is that to a human mouthful? In sea water they grow, molt, change shape wildly, and eventually, after several months, settle on the rocks, turn into adults, and build shells. Inside the shells they have to shed their skins. Rachel Carson was always finding the old skins; she reported: "Almost every container of sea water that I bring up from the shore is flecked with white, semitransparent objects. . . . Seen under the microscope, every detail of structure is perfectly represented. . . . In the little cellophane-like replicas I can count the joints of the appendages; even the bristles, growing at the bases of the joints, seem to have been slipped intact out of their casings." All in all, rock barnacles may live four years.

My point about rock barnacles is those million million larvae "in milky clouds" and those shed flecks of skin. Sea water seems suddenly to be but a broth of barnacle bits. Can I fancy that a million million human infants are more real?

What if God has the same affectionate disregard for us that we have for barnacles? I don't know if each barnacle larva is of itself unique and special, or if we the people are essentially as interchangeable as bricks. My brain is full of numbers; they swell and would split my skull like a shell. I examine the trapezoids of skin covering the back of my hands like blown dust motes moistened to clay. I have hatched, too, with millions of my kind, into a milky way that spreads from an unknown shore.

I have seen the mantis's abdomen dribbling out eggs in wet bubbles like tapioca pudding glued to a thorn. I have seen a film of a termite queen as big as my face, dead white and featureless, glistening with slime, throbbing and pulsing out rivers of globular eggs. Termite workers, who looked like tiny longshoremen unloading the *Queen Mary,* licked each egg as fast as it was extruded to prevent mold. The whole world is an incubator for incalculable numbers of eggs, each one coded minutely and ready to burst.

The egg of a parasite chalcid wasp, a common small wasp, multiplies unassisted, making ever more identical eggs. The female lays a single fertilized egg in the flaccid tissues of its live prey, and that one egg divides and divides. As many as two thousand new parasitic wasps will hatch to feed on the host's body with identical hunger. Similarly—only more so—Edwin Way Teale reports that a lone aphid, without a partner, breeding "unmolested" for one year, would produce so many living aphids that, although they are only a tenth of an inch long, together they would extend into space twenty-five hundred *light-years*. Even the average goldfish lays five thousand eggs, which she will eat as fast as she lays, if permitted. The sales manager of Ozark Fisheries in Missouri, which raises commercial goldfish for the likes of me, said, "We produce, measure, and sell our product by the ton." The intricacy of Ellery and aphids multiplied mindlessly into tons and light-years is more than extravagance; it is holocaust, parody, glut.

The pressure of growth among animals is a kind of terrible hunger. These billions must eat in order to fuel their surge to sexual maturity so that they may pump out more billions of eggs. And what are the fish on the bed going to eat, or the hatched mantises in the Mason jar going to eat, but each other? There is a terrible innocence in the benumbed world of the lower animals, reducing life there to a universal chomp. Edwin Way Teale, in *The Strange Lives of Familiar Insects*—a book I couldn't live without—describes several occasions of meals mouthed under the pressure of a hunger that knew no bounds.

You remember the dragonfly nymph, for instance, which stalks the bottom of the creek and the pond in search of live prey to snare with its hooked, unfolding lip. Dragonfly nymphs are insatiable and mighty. They clasp and devour whole minnows and fat tadpoles. Well, a dragonfly nymph, says Teale, "has even been seen climbing up out of the water on a plant to attack a helpless dragonfly emerging, soft and rumpled, from its nymphal skin." Is this where I draw the line?

It is between mothers and their offspring that these feedings have truly macabre overtones. Look at lacewings. Lacewings are those fragile green insects with large, rounded transparent wings. The larvae eat enormous numbers of aphids, the adults mate in a fluttering rush of instinct, lay eggs, and die by the millions in the first cold snap of fall. Sometimes, when a female lays her fertile eggs on a green leaf atop a slender stalked thread, she is hungry. She pauses in her laying, turns around, and eats her eggs one by one, then lays some more, and eats them, too.

Anything can happen, and anything does; what's it all about? Valerie Eliot, T. S. Eliot's widow, wrote in a letter to the London *Times:* "My husband, T. S. Eliot, loved to recount how late one evening he stopped a taxi. As he got in the driver said: 'You're T. S. Eliot.' When asked how he knew, he replied: 'Ah, I've got an eye for a celebrity. Only the other evening I picked up Bertrand Russell, and I said to him, "Well, Lord Russell, what's it all about," and, do you know, he couldn't tell me.' " Well, Lord God, asks the delicate, dying lacewing whose mandibles are wet with the juice secreted by her own ovipositor, what's it all about? ("And do you know . . .")

Planarians, which live in the duck pond, behave similarly. They are those dark laboratory flatworms that can regenerate themselves from almost any severed part. Arthur Koestler writes, "during the mating season the worms become cannibals, devouring everything alive that comes their way, including their own previously discarded tails which were in the process of growing a new head." Even such sophisticated mammals as the great predator cats occasionally eat their cubs. A mother cat will be observed licking the area around the umbilical cord of the helpless newborn. She licks, she licks, she licks until something snaps in her brain, and she begins eating, starting there, at the vulnerable belly.

Although mothers devouring their own offspring is patently the more senseless, somehow the reverse behavior is the more appalling. In the death of the parent in the jaws of its offspring I recognize a universal drama that chance occurrence has merely telescoped, so that I can see all the players at once. Gall gnats, for instance, are common small flies. Sometimes, according to Teale, a gall gnat larva, which does not resemble the adult in the least, and which has certainly not mated, nevertheless produces within its body eggs, live eggs, which then hatch within its soft tissues. Sometimes the eggs hatch alive even within the quiescent body of the pupa. The same incredible thing occasionally occurs within the fly genus *Miastor,* again to both larvae and pupae. "These eggs hatch within their bodies and the ravenous larvae which emerge immediately begin devouring their parents." In this case, I know what it's all about, and I wish I didn't. The parents die, the next generation lives, *ad majorem gloriam,* and so it goes. If the new generation hastens the death of the old, it scarcely matters; the old has served its one purpose, and the direct processing of proteins is tidily all in the family. But think of the invisible swelling of ripe eggs inside the pupa as wrapped and rigid as a mummified Egyptian queen! The eggs burst, shatter her belly, and emerge alive, awake, and hungry from a mummy case which they crawl over like worms and feed on till its gone. And then they turn to the world.

"To prevent a like fate," Teale continues, "some of the ichneumon flies, those wasplike parasites which deposit their eggs in the body tissues of caterpillars, have to scatter their eggs while in flight at times when they are unable to find their prey and the eggs are ready to hatch within their bodies."

You are an ichneumon. You mated and your eggs are fertile. If you can't find a caterpillar on which to lay your eggs, your young will starve. When the eggs hatch, the young will eat any body in which they find themselves, so if you don't kill them by emitting them broadcast over the landscape, they'll eat you alive. But if you let them drop over the fields you will probably be dead yourself, of old age, before they even hatch to starve, and the whole show will be over and done, and a wretched one it was. You feel them coming, and coming, and you struggle to rise. . . .

Not that the ichneumon is making any conscious choice. If she were, her dilemma would be truly the stuff of tragedy; Aeschylus need have looked no further than the ichneumon. That is, it would be the stuff of real tragedy if only Aeschylus and I could convince you that the ichneumon is really and truly as alive as we are, and that what happens to it matters. Will you take it on faith?

Here is one last story. It shows that the pressures of growth gang aft a-gley. The clothes moth, whose caterpillar eats wool, sometimes goes into a molting frenzy which Teale blandly describes as "curious": "A curious paradox in molting is the action of a clothes-moth larva with insufficient food. It sometimes goes into a 'molting frenzy,' changing its skin repeatedly and getting smaller and smaller with each change." Smaller and smaller . . . can you imagine the frenzy? Where shall we send our sweaters? The diminution process could, in imagination, extend to infinity, as the creature frantically shrinks and shrinks and shrinks to the size of a molecule, then an electron, but never can shrink to absolute nothing and end its terrible hunger. I feel like Ezra: "And when I heard this thing, I rent my garment and my mantle, and plucked off the hair of my head and of my beard, and sat down astonished."

II

I am not kidding anyone if I pretend that these awesome pressures to eat and breed are wholly mystifying. The million million barnacle larvae in a half mile of shore water, the rivers of termite eggs, and the light-years of aphids ensure the living presence, in a scarcely concerned world, of ever more rock barnacles, termites, and aphids.

It's chancy out there. Dog whelks eat rock barnacles, worms invade their shells, shore ice razes them from the rocks and grinds them to a powder. Can you lay aphid eggs faster than chickadees can eat them? Can you find a caterpillar, can you beat the killing frost?

As far as lower animals go, if you lead a simple life you probably face a boring death. Some animals, however, lead such complicated lives that not only do the chances for any one animal's death at any minute multiply greatly, but so also do the *varieties* of the deaths it might die. The ordained paths of some animals are so rocky they are preposterous. The horsehair worm in the duck pond, for instance, wriggling so serenely near the surface, is the survivor of an impossible series of squeaky escapes. I did a bit of research into the life cycles of these worms, which are shaped exactly like hairs from a horse's tail, and learned that although scientists are not exactly sure what happens to any one species of them, they think it might go something like this:

You start with long strands of eggs wrapped around vegetation in the duck pond. The eggs hatch, the larvae emerge, and each seeks an aquatic host, say a dragonfly nymph. The larva bores into the nymph's body, where it feeds and grows and somehow escapes. Then if it doesn't get eaten it swims over to the shore where it encysts on submersed plants. This is all fairly improbable, but not impossibly so.

Now the coincidences begin. First, presumably, the water level of the duck pond has to drop. This exposes the vegetation so that the land host organism can get at it without drowning. Horsehair worms have various land hosts, such as crickets, beetles, and grasshoppers. Let's say ours can only make it if a grasshopper comes along. Fine. But the grasshopper had best hurry, for there is only so much fat stored in the encysted worm, and it might starve. Well, here comes just the right species of grasshopper, and it is obligingly feeding on shore vegetation. Now I have not observed any extensive grazing of grasshoppers on any grassy shores, but obviously it must occur. Bingo, then, the grasshopper just happens to eat the encysted worm.

The cyst bursts. The worm emerges in all its hideous length, up to thirty-six inches, inside the body of the grasshopper, on which it feeds. I presume that the worm must eat enough of its host to stay alive, but not so much that the grasshopper will keel over dead far from water. Entomologists have found tiger beetles dead and dying on the water whose insides were almost perfectly empty except for the white coiled bodies of horsehair worms. At any rate, now the worm is almost an adult, ready to reproduce. But first it's got to get out of this grasshopper.

Biologists don't know what happens next. If at the critical stage the grasshopper is hopping in a sunny meadow away from a duck pond or ditch, which is entirely likely, then the story is over. But say it happens to be feeding near the duck pond. The worm perhaps bores its way out of the grasshopper's body, or perhaps is excreted. At any rate, there it is on the grass, drying out. Now the biologists have to go so far as to invoke a "heavy rain," falling from heaven at this fortuitous moment, in order to get the horsehair worm back into the water where it can mate and lay more seemingly doomed eggs. You'd be thin, too.

Other creatures have it just about as easy. A blood fluke starts out as an egg in human feces. If it happens to fall into fresh water it will live only if it happens to encounter a certain species of snail. It changes in the snail, swims out, and now needs to find a human being in the water in order to bore through his skin. It travels around in the man's blood, settles down in the blood vessels of his intestine, and turns into a sexually mature blood fluke, either male or female. Now it has to find another fluke, of the opposite sex, who also just happens to have traveled the same circuitous route and landed in the same unfortunate man's intestinal blood vessels. Other flukes lead similarly improbable lives, some passing through as many as four hosts.

But it is for gooseneck barnacles that I reserve the largest measure of awe. Recently I saw photographs taken by members of the *Ra* expedition. One showed a glob of tar as big as a softball, jetsam from a larger craft, which Heyerdahl and his crew spotted in the middle of the Atlantic Ocean. The tar had been in the sea for a long time; it was overgrown with gooseneck barnacles. The gooseneck barnacles were entirely incidental, but for me they were the most interesting thing about the whole expedition. How many gooseneck barnacle larvae must be dying out there in the middle of vast oceans for every one that finds a glob of tar to fasten to? You've seen gooseneck barnacles washed up on the beach; they grow on old ship's timber, driftwood, strips of rubber—anything that's been afloat in the sea long enough. They do not resemble rock barnacles in the least, although the two are closely related. They have pinkish shells extending in a flattened oval from a flexible bit of "gooseneck" tissue that secures them to the substratum.

I have always had a fancy for these creatures, but I'd always assumed that they lived near shores, where chance floating holdfasts are more likely to occur. What are they doing—what are the larvae doing—out there in the middle of the ocean? They drift and perish, or, by some freak accident in a world where anything can happen, they latch and flourish. If I dangled my hand from the deck of the *Ra* into the sea, could a gooseneck barnacle fasten there? If I gathered a cup of ocean water, would I be holding a score of dying and dead barnacle larvae? Should I throw them a chip? What kind of a world is this, anyway? Why not make fewer barnacle larvae and give them a decent chance? Are we dealing in life, or in death?

I have to look at the landscape of the blue-green world again. Just think: in all the clean beautiful reaches of the solar system, our planet alone is a blot; our planet alone has death. I have to acknowledge that the sea is a cup of death and the land is a stained altar stone. We the living are survivors huddled on flotsam, living on jetsam. We are escapees. We wake in terror, eat in hunger, sleep with a mouthful of blood.

Death: W. C. Fields called death "the Fellow in the Bright Nightgown." He shuffles around the house in all the corners I've forgotten, all the halls I dare not call to mind or visit for fear I'll glimpse the hem of his shabby, dazzling gown disappearing around a turn. This is the monster evolution loves. How could it be?

The faster death goes, the faster evolution goes. If an aphid lays a million eggs, several might survive. Now, my right hand, in all its human cunning, could not make one aphid in a thousand years. But these aphid eggs—which run less than a dime a dozen, which run absolutely free—can make aphids as effortlessly as the sea makes waves. Wonderful things, wasted. It's a wretched system. Arthur Stanley Eddington, the British physicist and astronomer who died in 1944, suggested that all of "Nature" could conceivably run on the same deranged scheme. "If indeed she has no greater aim than to provide a home for her greatest experiment, Man, it would be just like her methods to scatter a million stars whereof one might haply achieve her purpose." I doubt very much that this is the aim, but it seems clear on all fronts that this is the method.

Say you are the manager of the Southern Railroad. You figure that you need three engines for a stretch of track between Lynchburg and Danville. It's a mighty steep grade. So at fantastic effort and expense you have your shops make nine thousand engines. Each engine must be fashioned just so, every rivet and bolt secure, every wire twisted and wrapped, every needle on every indicator sensitive and accurate.

You send all nine thousand of them out on the runs. Although there are engineers at the throttles, no one is manning the switches. The engines crash, collide, derail, jump, jam, burn. . . . At the end of the massacre you have three engines, which is what the run could support in the first place. There are few enough of them that they can stay out of each others' paths.

You go to your board of directors and show them what you've done. And what are they going to say? You know what they're going to say. They're going to say: it's a hell of a way to run a railroad.

Is it a better way to run a universe?

Evolution loves death more than it loves you or me. This is easy to write, easy to read, and hard to believe. The words are simple, the concept clear—but you don't believe it, do you? Nor do I. How could I, when we're both so lovable? Are my values then so diametrically opposed to those that nature preserves? This is the key point.

Must I then part ways with the only world I know? I had thought to live by the side of the creek in order to shape my life to its free flow. But I seem to have reached a point where I must draw the line. It looks as though the creek is not buoying me up but dragging me down. Look: Cock Robin may die the most gruesome of slow deaths, and nature is no less pleased; the sun comes up, the creek rolls on, the survivors still sing. I cannot feel that way about your death, nor you about mine, nor either of us about the robin's—or even the barnacles'. We value the individual supremely, and nature values him not a whit. It looks for the moment as though I might have to reject this creek life unless I want to be utterly brutalized. Is human culture with its values my only real home after all? Can it possibly be that I should move my anchor-hold to the side of a library? This direction of thought brings me abruptly to a fork in the road where I stand paralyzed, unwilling to go on, for both ways lead to madness.

Either this world, my mother, is a monster, or I myself am a freak.

Consider the former: the world is a monster. Any three-year-old can see how unsatisfactory and clumsy is this whole business of reproducing and dying by the billions. We have not yet encountered any god who is as merciful as a man who flicks a beetle over on its feet. There is not a people in the world who behaves as badly as praying mantises. But wait, you say, there is no right and wrong in nature; right and wrong is a human concept. Precisely: we are moral creatures, then, in an amoral world. The universe that suckled us is a monster that does not care if we live or die—does not care if it itself grinds to a halt. It is fixed and blind, a robot programmed to kill. We are free and seeing; we can only try to outwit it at every turn to save our skins.

This view requires that a monstrous world running on

chance and death, careening blindly from nowhere to nowhere, somehow produced wonderful us. I came from the world, I crawled out of a sea of amino acids, and now I must whirl around and shake my fist at that sea and cry Shame! If I value anything at all, then I must blindfold my eyes when I near the Swiss Alps. We must as a culture disassemble our telescopes and settle down to backslapping. We little blobs of soft tissue crawling around on this one planet's skin are right, and the whole universe is wrong.

Or consider the alternative.

Julian of Norwich, the great English anchorite and theologian, cited, in the manner of the prophets, these words from God: "See, I am God: see, I am in all things: see, I never lift my hands off my works, nor ever shall, without end. . . . How should anything be amiss?" But now not even the simplest and best of us sees things the way Julian did. It seems to us that plenty is amiss. So much is amiss that I must consider the second fork in the road, that creation itself is blamelessly, benevolently askew by its very free nature, and that it is only human feeling that is freakishly amiss. The frog that the giant water bug sucked had, presumably, a rush of pure feeling for about a second, before its brain turned to broth. I, however, have been sapped by various strong feelings about the incident almost daily for several years.

Do the barnacle larvae care? Does the lacewing who eats her eggs care? If they do not care, then why am I making all this fuss? If I am a freak, then why don't I hush?

Our excessive emotions are so patently painful and harmful to us as a species that I can hardly believe that they evolved. Other creatures manage to have effective matings and even stable societies without great emotions, and they have a bonus in that they need not ever mourn. (But some higher animals have emotions that we think are similar to ours: dogs, elephants, otters, and the sea mammals mourn their dead. Why do that to an otter? What creator could be so cruel, not to kill otters, but to let them care?) It would seem that emotions are the curse, not death—emotions that appear to have devolved upon a few freaks as a special curse from Malevolence.

All right then. It is our emotions that are amiss. We are freaks, the world is fine, and let us all go have lobotomies to restore us to a natural state. We can leave the library then, go back to the creek lobotomized, and live on its banks as untroubled as any muskrat or reed. You first.

Of the two ridiculous alternatives, I rather favor the second. Although it is true that we are moral creatures in an amoral world, the world's amorality does not make it a monster. Rather, I am the freak. Perhaps I don't need a lobotomy, but I could use some calming down, and the creek is just the place for it. I must go down to the creek again. It is where I belong, although as I become closer to it, my fellows appear more and more freakish, and my home in the library more and more limited. Imperceptibly at first, and now consciously, I shy away from the arts, from the human emotional stew. I read what the men with telescopes and microscopes have to say about the landscape. I read about the polar ice, and I drive myself deeper and deeper into exile from my own kind. But, since I cannot avoid the library altogether—the human culture that taught me to speak in its tongue—I bring human values to the creek, and so save myself from being brutalized.

What I have been after all along is not an explanation but a picture. This is the way the world is, altar and cup, lit by the fire from a star that has only begun to die. My rage and shock at the pain and death of individuals of my kind is the old, old mystery, as old as man, but forever fresh, and completely unanswerable. My reservations about the fecundity and waste of life among other creatures is, however, mere squeamishness. After all, I'm the one having the nightmares. It is true that many of the creatures live and die abominably, but I am not called upon to pass judgment. Nor am I called upon to live in that same way, and those creatures who are mercifully unconscious.

I don't want to cut this too short. Let me pull the camera back and look at that fork in the road from a distance, in the larger context of the speckled and twining world. It could be that the fork will disappear, or that I will see it to be but one of many interstices in a network, so that it is impossible to say which line is the main part and which is the fork.

The picture of fecundity and its excesses and of the pressures of growth and its accidents is of course no different from the picture I painted before of the world as an intricate texture of a bizarre variety of forms. Only now the shadows are deeper. Extravagance takes on a sinister, wastrel air, and exuberance blithers. When I added the dimension of time to the landscape of the world, I saw how freedom grew the beauties and horrors from the same live branch. This landscape is the same as that one, with a few more details added, and a different emphasis. I see squashes expanding with pressure and a hunk of wood rapt on the desert floor. The rye plant and the Bronx ailanthus are literally killing themselves to make seeds, and the animals to lay eggs. Instead of one goldfish swimming in its intricate bowl, I see tons and tons of goldfish laying and eating billions and billions of eggs. The point of all the eggs is of course to make goldfish one by one—nature loves the *idea* of the individual, if not the individual himself—and the point of a goldfish is pizzazz. This is familiar ground. I merely failed to mention that it is death that is spinning the globe.

It is harder to take, but surely it's been thought about. I cannot really get very exercised over the hideous appearance and habits of some deep-sea jellies and fishes, and I exercise easy. But about the topic of my own death I am decidedly touchy. Nevertheless, the two phenomena are two branches of the same creek, the creek that waters the world. Its source is freedom, and its network of branches is infinite. The graceful mockingbird that falls drinks there and sips in the same drop a beauty that waters its eyes and a death that fledges and flies. The petals of tulips are flaps of the same doomed water that swells and hatches in the ichneumon's gut.

That something is everywhere and always amiss is part of the very stuff of creation. It is as though each clay form had baked into it, fired into it, a blue streak of nonbeing, a shaded emptiness like a bubble that not only shapes its very structure but that also causes it to list and ultimately explode. We could have planned things more mercifully, perhaps, but our plan would never get off the drawing board until we agreed to the very compromising terms that are the only ones that being offers.

The world has signed a pact with the devil; it had to. It is a covenant to which every thing, even every hydrogen atom, is bound. The terms are clear: if you want to live, you have to die; you cannot have mountains and creeks without space, and space is a beauty married to a blind man. The blind man is Freedom, or Time, and he does not go anywhere without his great dog Death. The world came into being with the signing of the contract. A scientist calls it the Second Law of Thermodynamics. A poet says, "The force that through the green fuse drives the flower/Drives my green age." This is what we know. The rest is gravy.

CHAPTER 11

Stalking

I

SUMMER: I GO DOWN to the creek again, and lead a creek life. I watch and stalk.

The Eskimos' life changes in summer, too. The caribou flee from the inland tundra's mosquitos to the windy shores of the Arctic Ocean, and coastal Eskimos hunt them there. In the old days before they had long-range rifles, the men had to approach the wary animals very closely for a kill. Sometimes, waiting for a favorable change of weather so they could rush in unseen and unscented, the Eskimos would have to follow the fleet herds on foot for days, sleepless.

Also in summer they dredge for herring with nets from shoreline camps. In the open water off the Mackenzie River delta, they hunt the white whale (the beluga) and bearded seal. They paddle their slender kayaks inland to fresh water and hunt muskrats, too, which they used to snare or beat with sticks.

To travel from camp to camp in summer, coastal Eskimos ply the open seas in big umiaks paddled by women. They eat fish, goose or duck eggs, fresh meat, and anything else they can get, including fresh "salad" of greens still raw in a killed caribou's stomach and dressed with the delicate acids of digestion.

On St. Lawrence Island, women and children are in charge of netting little birds. They have devised a cruel and ingenious method: after they net a few birds with great effort and after much stalking, they thread them alive and squawking through their beaks' nostrils, and fly them like living kites at the end of long lines. The birds fly frantically, trying to escape, but they cannot, and their flapping efforts attract others of their kind, curious—and the Eskimos easily net the others.

They used to make a kind of undershirt out of bird skins, which they wore under fur parkas in cold weather, and left on inside the igloos after they'd taken the parkas off. It was an elaborate undertaking, this making of a bird-skin shirt, requiring thousands of tiny stitches. For thread they had the stringy sinew found along a caribou's backbone. The sinew had to be dried, frayed, and twisted into a clumsy thread. Its only advantages were that it swelled in water, making seams more or less waterproof, and it generally contained a minute smear of fat, so if they were starving they could suck their sewing thread and add maybe five minutes to their lives. For needles they had shards of bone, which got thinner and shorter every time they pushed through tough skins, so that an old needle might be little more than a barely enclosed slit. When the Eskimos first met the advanced culture of the south, men and women alike admired it first and foremost for its sturdy sewing needles. For it is understood that without good clothing, you perish. A crewman from a whaler with a paper of needles in his pocket could save many lives, and was welcome everywhere as the rich and powerful always are.

I doubt that they make bird-skin shirts anymore, steel needles or no. They do not do many of the old things at all any more, except in my mind, where they hunt and stitch well, with an animal skill, in silhouette always against white oceans of ice.

Down here, the heat is on. Even a bird-skin shirt would be too much. In the cool of the evening I take to the bridges over the creek. I am prying into secrets again, and taking my chances. I might see anything happen; I might see nothing but light on the water. I walk home exhilarated or becalmed, but always changed, alive. "It scatters and gathers," Heraclitus said, "it comes and goes." And I want to be in the way of its passage, and cooled by its invisible breath.

In summer, I stalk. Summer leaves obscure, heat dazzles, and creatures hide from the red-eyed sun, and me. I have to seek things out. The creatures I seek have several senses and free will; it becomes apparent that they do not wish to be seen. I can stalk them in either of two ways. The first is not what you think of as true stalking, but it is the *Via negativa,* and as fruitful as actual pursuit. When I stalk this way I take my stand on a bridge and wait, emptied. I put myself in the way of the creature's passage, like spring Eskimos at a seal's breathing hole. Something might come; something might go. I am Newton under the apple tree, Buddha under the bo. Stalking the other way, I forge my own passage seeking the creature. I wander the banks; what I find, I follow, doggedly, like Eskimos haunting the caribou herds. I am Wilson squinting after the traces of electrons in a cloud chamber; I am Jacob at Peniel wrestling with the angel.

Fish are hard to see either way. Although I spend most of the summer stalking muskrats, I think it is fish even more than muskrats that by their very mystery and hiddenness crystalize the quality of my summer life at the creek. A thick spawning of fish, a bedful of fish, is too much, horror; but I walk out of my way in hopes of glimpsing three bluegills bewitched in a pool's depth or rising to floating petals or bubbles.

The very act of trying to see fish makes them almost impossible to see. My eyes are awkward instruments whose casing is clumsily outsized. If I face the sun along a bank I cannot see into the water; instead of fish I see water striders, the reflected undersides of leaves, birds' bellies, clouds and blue sky. So I cross to the opposite bank and put the sun at my back. Then I can see into the water perfectly within the blue shadow made by my body; but as soon as that shadow looms across them, the fish vanish in a flurry of flashing tails.

Occasionally by waiting still on a bridge or by sneaking smoothly into the shade of a bankside tree, I see fish slowly materialize in the shallows, one by one, swimming around and around in a silent circle, each one washed in a blue like the sky's and all as tapered as tears. Or I see them suspended in a line in deep pools, parallel to the life-giving current, literally "streamlined." Because fish have swim bladders filled with gas that balances their weight in the water, they are actually hanging from their own bodies, as it were, as gondolas hang from balloons. They wait suspended and seemingly motionless in clear water; they look dead, under a spell, or captured in amber. They look like the expressionless parts hung in a mobile, which has apparently suggested itself to mobile designers. Fish! They manage to be so water-colored. Theirs is not the color of the bottom but the color of the light itself, the light dissolved like a powder in the water. They disappear and reappear as if by spontaneous generation: sleight of fish.

I am coming around to fish as spirit. The Greek acronym for some of the names of Christ yields *ichthys,* Christ as fish, and fish as Christ. The more I glimpse the fish in Tinker Creek, the more satisfying the coincidence becomes, the richer the symbol, not only for Christ but for the spirit as well. The people must live. Imagine for a Mediterranean people how much easier it is to haul up free, fed fish in nets than to pasture hungry herds on those bony hills and feed them through a winter. To say that holiness is a fish is a statement of the abundance of grace; it is the equivalent of affirming in a purely materialistic culture that money does indeed grow on trees.

"Not as the world gives do I give to you"; these fish are spirit food. And revelation is a study in stalking: "Cast the net on the right side of the ship, and ye shall find."

Still—of course—there is a risk. More men in all of time have died at fishing than at any other human activity except perhaps the making of war. You go out so far . . . and you are blown, or stove, or swamped, and never seen again. Where are the fish? Out in the underwater gaps, out where the winds are, wary, adept, invisible. You can lure them, net them, troll for them, club them, clutch them, chase them up an inlet, stun them with plant juice, catch them in a wooden wheel that runs all night—and you still might starve. They are there, they are certainly there, free, food, and wholly fleeting. You can see them if you want to; catch them if you can.

It scatters and gathers; it comes and goes. I might see a monstrous carp heave out of the water and disappear in a smack of foam, I might see a trout emerge in a riffle under my dangling hand, or I might see only a flash of back parts fleeing. It is the same all summer long, all year long, no matter what I seek. Lately I have given myself over almost entirely to stalking muskrats—eye food. I found out the hard way that waiting is better than pursuing; now I usually sit on a narrow pedestrian bridge at a spot where the creek is shallow and wide. I sit alone and alert, but stilled in a special way, waiting and watching for a change in the water, for the tremulous ripples rising in intensity that signal the appearance of a living muskrat from the underwater entrance to its den. Muskrats are cautious. Many, many evenings I wait without seeing one. But sometimes it turns out that the focus of my waiting is mis-directed, as if Buddha had been expecting the fall of an apple. For when the muskrats don't show, something else does.

I positively ruined the dinner of a green heron on the creek last week. It was fairly young and fairly determined not to fly away, but not to be too foolhardy, either. So it had to keep an eye on me. I watched it for half an hour, during which time it stalked about in the creek moodily, expanding and contracting its incredible, brown-streaked neck. It made only three lightning-quick stabs at strands of slime for food, and all three times occurred when my head was turned slightly away.

The heron was in calm shallows; the deepest water it walked in went two inches up its orange legs. It would go and get something from the cattails on the side, and, when it had eaten it—tossing up its beak and contracting its throat in great gulps—it would plod back to a dry sandbar in the center of the creek which seemed to serve as its observation tower. It wagged its stubby tail up and down; its tail was so short it did not extend beyond its folded wings.

Mostly it just watched me warily, as if I might shoot it, or steal its minnows for my own supper, if it did not stare me down. But my only weapon was stillness, and my only wish its continued presence before my eyes. I knew it would fly away if I made the least false move. In half an hour it got used to me—as though I were a bicycle somebody had abandoned on the bridge, or a branch left by high water. It even suffered me to turn my head slowly, and to stretch my aching legs very slowly. But finally, at the end, some least motion or thought set it off, and it rose, glancing at me with a cry, and winged slowly away upstream, around a bend, and out of sight.

I find it hard to see anything about a bird that it does not want seen. It demands my full attention. Several times waiting for muskrats, however, I have watched insects doing various special things who were, like the mantis laying her eggs, happily oblivious to my presence. Twice I was not certain what I had seen.

Once it was a dragonfly flying low over the creek in an unusual rhythm. I looked closely; it was dipping the tip of its abdomen in the water very quickly, over and over. It was flying in a series of tight circles, just touching the water at the very bottom arc of each circle. The only thing I could imagine it was doing was laying eggs, and this later proved to be the case. I actually saw this, I thought—I actually saw a dragonfly laying her eggs not five feet away.

It is this peculiar stitching motion of the dragonfly's abdomen that earned it the name "darning needle"—parents used to threaten their children by saying that, if the children told lies, dragonflies would hover over their faces as they slept and sew their lips together. Interestingly, I read that only the great speed at which the egg-laying female dragonfly flies over the water prevents her from being "caught by the surface tension and pulled down." And at that same great speed the dragonfly I saw that day whirred away, downstream: a drone, a dot, and then gone.

Another time I saw a water strider behaving oddly. When there is nothing whatsoever to see, I watch the water striders skate over the top of the water, and I watch the six dots of shade—made by their feet dimpling the water's surface—slide dreamily over the bottom silt. Their motion raises tiny ripples or wavelets ahead of them over the water's surface, and I had noticed that when they feel or see these ripples coming towards them, they tend to turn away from the ripples' source. In other words, they avoid each other. I figure this behavior has the effect of distributing them evenly over an area, giving them each a better chance at whatever it is they eat.

But one day I was staring idly at the water when something out of the ordinary triggered my attention. A strider was skating across the creek purposefully instead of randomly. Instead of heading away from ripples made by another insect, it was racing towards them. At the center of the ripples I saw that some sort of small fly had fallen into the water and was struggling to right itself. The strider acted extremely "interested"; it jerked after the fly's frantic efforts, following it across the creek and back again, inching closer and closer like Eskimos stalking caribou. The fly could not escape the surface tension. Its efforts were diminishing to an occasional buzz; it floated against the bank, and the strider pursued it there—but

I could not see what happened, because overhanging grasses concealed the spot.

Again, only later did I learn what I had seen. I read that striders are attracted to any light. According to William H. Amos, "Often the attracting light turns out to be the reflections off the ripples set up by an insect trapped on the surface, and it is on such creatures that the striders feed." They suck them dry. Talk about living on jetsam! At any rate, it will be easy enough to watch for this again this summer. I especially want to see if the slow ripples set up by striders themselves reflect less light than the ripples set up by trapped insects—but it might be years before I happen to see another insect fall on the water among striders. I was lucky to have seen it once. Next time I will know what is happening, and if they want to play the last bloody act offstage, I will just part the curtain of grasses and hope I sleep through the night.

II

Learning to stalk muskrats took me several years.

I've always known there were muskrats in the creek. Sometimes when I drove late at night my headlights' beam on the water would catch the broad lines of ripples made by a swimming muskrat, a bow wave, converging across the water at the raised dark vee of its head. I would stop the car and get out: nothing. They eat corn and tomatoes from my neighbors' gardens, too, by night, so that my neighbors were always telling me that the creek was full of them. Around here, people call them "mushrats"; Thoreau called them "Musquashes." They are not of course rats at all (let alone squashes). They are more like diminutive beavers, and, like beavers, they exude a scented oil from musk glands under the base of the tail—hence the name. I had read in several respectable sources that muskrats are so wary they are almost impossible to observe. One expert who made a full-time study of large populations, mainly by examining "sign" and performing autopsies on corpses, said he often went for weeks at a time without seeing a single living muskrat.

One hot evening three years ago, I was standing more or less *in* a bush. I was stock-still, looking deep into Tinker Creek from a spot on the bank opposite the house, watching a group of blue-gills stare and hang motionless near the bottom of a deep, sunlit pool. I was focused for depth. I had long since lost myself, lost the creek, the day, lost everything but still amber depth. All at once I couldn't see. And then I could: a young muskrat had appeared on top of the water, floating on its back. Its forelegs were folded langorously across its chest; the sun shone on its upturned belly. Its youthfulness and rodent grin, coupled with its ridiculous method of locomotion, which consisted of a lazy wag of the tail assisted by an occasional dabble of a webbed hind foot, made it an enchanting picture of decadence, dissipation, and summer sloth. I forgot all about the fish.

But in my surprise at having the light come on so suddenly, and at having my consciousness returned to me all at once and bearing an inverted muskrat, I must have moved and betrayed myself. The kit—for I know now it was just a young kit—righted itself so that only its head was visible above water, and swam downstream, away from me. I extricated myself from the bush and foolishly pursued it. It dove sleekly, reemerged, and glided for the opposite bank. I ran along the bankside brush, trying to keep it in sight. It kept casting an alarmed look over its shoulder at me. Once again it dove, under a floating mat of brush lodged in the bank, and disappeared. I never saw it again. (Nor have I ever, despite all the muskrats I have seen, again seen a muskrat floating on its back.) But I did not know muskrats then; I waited panting, and watched the shadowed bank. Now I know that I cannot outwait a muskrat who knows I am there. The most I can do is get "there" quietly, while it is still in its hole, so that it never knows, and wait there until it emerges. But then all I knew was that I wanted to see more muskrats.

I began to look for them day and night. Sometimes I would see ripples suddenly start beating from the creek's side, but as I crouched to watch, the ripples would die. Now I know what this means, and have learned to stand perfectly still to make out the muskrat's small, pointed face hidden under overhanging bank vegetation, watching me. That summer I haunted the bridges, I walked up creeks and down, but no muskrats ever appeared. You must just have to be there, I thought. You must have to spend the rest of your life standing in bushes. It was a once-in-a-lifetime thing, and you've had your once.

Then one night I saw another, and my life changed. After that I knew where they were in numbers, and I knew when to look. It was late dusk; I was driving home from a visit with friends. Just on the off chance I parked quietly by the creek, walked out on the narrow bridge over the shallows, and looked upstream. Someday, I had been telling myself for weeks, someday a muskrat is going to swim right through that channel in the cattails, and I am going to see it. That is precisely what happened. I looked up into the channel for a muskrat, and there it came, swimming right toward me. Knock; seek; ask. It seemed to swim with a side-to-side, sculling motion of its vertically flattened tail. It looked bigger than the upside-down muskrat, and its face more reddish. In its mouth it clasped a twig of tulip tree. One thing amazed me: it swam right down the middle of the creek. I thought it would hide in the brush along the edge; instead, it plied the waters as obviously as an aquaplane. I could just look and look.

But I was standing on the bridge, not sitting, and it saw me. It changed its course, veered towards the bank, and disappeared behind an indentation in the rushy shoreline. I felt a rush of such pure energy I thought I would not need to breathe for days.

*   *   *

That innocence of mine is mostly gone now, although I felt almost the same pure rush last night. I have seen many muskrats since I learned to look for them in that part of the creek. But still I seek them out in the cool of the evening, and still I hold my breath when rising ripples surge from under the creek's bank. The great hurrah about wild animals is that they exist at all, and the greater hurrah is the actual moment of seeing them. Because they have a nice dignity, and prefer to have nothing to do with me, not even as the simple objects of my vision. They show me by their very wariness what a prize it is simply to open my eyes and behold.

Muskrats are the bread and butter of the carnivorous food chain. They are like rabbits and mice: if you are big enough to eat mammals, you eat them. Hawks and owls prey on them, and foxes; so do otters. Minks are their special enemies; minks live near large muskrat populations, slinking in and out of their dens and generally hanging around like mantises outside a beehive. Muskrats are also subject to a contagious blood disease that wipes out whole colonies. Sometimes, however, their whole populations explode, just like lemmings', which are their near kin; and they either die by the hundreds or fan out across the land migrating to new creeks and ponds.

Men kill them, too. One Eskimo who hunted muskrats for a few weeks each year strictly as a sideline says that in fourteen years he killed 30,739 muskrats. The pelts sell, and the price is rising. Muskrats are the most important fur animal on the North American continent. I don't know what they bring on the Mackenzie River delta these days, but around here, fur dealers, who paid $2.90 in 1971, now pay $5.00 a pelt. They make the pelts into coats, calling the fur anything but muskrat: "Hudson seal" is typical. In the old days, after they had sold the skins, trappers would sell the meat, too, calling it "marsh rabbit." Many people still stew muskrat.

Keeping ahead of all this slaughter, a female might have as many as five litters a year, and each litter contains six or seven or more muskrats. The nest is high and dry under the bank;

only the entrance is under water, usually by several feet, to foil enemies. Here the nests are marked by simple holes in a creek's clay bank; in other parts of the country muskrats build floating, conical winter lodges which are not only watertight, but edible to muskrats.

The very young have a risky life. For one thing, even snakes and raccoons eat them. For another, their mother is easily confused, and may abandon one or two of a big litter here or there, forgetting as it were to count noses. The newborn hanging on their mother's teats may drop off if the mother has to make a sudden dive into the water, and sometimes these drown. The just-weaned young have a rough time, too, because new litters are coming along so hard and fast that they have to be weaned before they really know how to survive. And if the just-weaned young are near starving, they might eat the newborn—if they can get to them. Adult muskrats, including their own mothers, often kill them if they approach too closely. But if they live through all these hazards, they can begin a life of swimming at twilight and munching cattail roots, clover, and an occasional crayfish. Paul Errington, a usually solemn authority, writes, "The muskrat nearing the end of its first month may be thought of as an independent enterprise in a very modest way."

The wonderful thing about muskrats in my book is that they cannot see very well, and are rather dim, to boot. They are extremely wary if they know I am there, and will outwait me every time. But with a modicum of skill and a minimum loss of human dignity, such as it is, I can be right "there," and the breathing fact of my presence will never penetrate their narrow skulls.

What happened last night was not only the ultimate in muskrat dimness, it was also the ultimate in human intrusion, the limit beyond which I am certain I cannot go. I would never have imagined I could go that far, actually to sit beside a feeding muskrat as beside a dinner partner at a crowded table.

What happened was this. Just in the past week I have been frequenting a different place, one of the creek's nameless feeder streams. It is mostly a shallow trickle joining several pools up to three feet deep. Over one of these pools is a tiny pedestrian bridge known locally, if at all, as the troll bridge. I was sitting on the troll bridge about an hour before sunset, looking upstream about eight feet to my right where I know the muskrats have a den. I had just lighted a cigarette when a pulse of ripples appeared at the mouth of the den, and a muskrat emerged. He swam straight toward me and headed under the bridge.

Now the moment a muskrat's eyes disappear from view under a bridge, I go into action. I have about five seconds to switch myself around so that I will be able to see him very well when he emerges on the other side of the bridge. I can easily hang my head over the other side of the bridge, so that when he appears from under me, I will be able to count his eyelashes if I want. The trouble with this maneuver is that, once his beady eyes appear again on the other side, I am stuck. If I move again, the show is over for the evening. I have to remain in whatever insane position I happen to be caught, for as long as I am in his sight, so that I stiffen all my muscles, bruise my ankles on the concrete, and burn my fingers on the cigarette. And if the muskrat goes out on a bank to feed, there I am with my face hanging a foot over the water, unable to see anything but crayfish. So I have learned to take it easy on these five-second flings.

When the muskrat went under the bridge, I moved so I could face downstream comfortably. He reappeared, and I had a good look at him. He was eight inches long in the body, and another six in the tail. Muskrat tails are black and scaled, flattened not horizontally, like beavers' tails, but vertically, like a belt stood on edge. In the winter, muskrats' tails sometimes freeze solid, and the animals chew off the frozen parts up to about an inch of the body. They must swim entirely with their hind feet, and have a terrible time steering. This one used his tail as a rudder and only occasionally as a propeller; mostly he swam with a pedaling motion of his hind feet, held very straight and moving down and around, "toeing down" like a bicycle racer. The soles of his hind feet were strangely pale; his toenails were pointed in long cones. He kept his forelegs still, tucked up to his chest.

The muskrat clambered out on the bank across the stream from me, and began feeding. He chomped down on a ten-inch weed, pushing it into his mouth steadily with both forepaws as a carpenter feeds a saw. I could hear his chewing; it sounded like somebody eating celery sticks. Then he slid back into the water with the weed still in his mouth, crossed under the bridge, and, instead of returning to his den, rose erect on a submerged rock and calmly polished off the rest of the weed. He was about four feet away from me. Immediately he swam under the bridge again, hauled himself out on the bank, and unerringly found the same spot on the grass, where he devoured the weed's stump.

All this time I was not only doing an elaborate about-face every time his eyes disappeared under the bridge, but I was also smoking a cigarette. He never noticed that the configuration of the bridge metamorphosed utterly every time he went under it. Many animals are the same way: they can't see a thing unless it's moving. Similarly, every time he turned his head away, I was free to smoke the cigarette, although of course I never knew when he would suddenly turn again and leave me caught in some wretched position. The galling thing was, he was downwind of me and my cigarette: was I really going through all this for a creature without any sense whatsoever?

After the weed stump was gone, the muskrat began ranging over the grass with a nervous motion, chewing off mouthfuls of grass and clover near the base. Soon he had gathered a huge, bushy mouthful; he pushed into the water, crossed under the bridge, swam towards his den, and dove.

When he launched himself again shortly, having apparently cached the grass, he repeated the same routine in a business-like fashion, and returned with another shock of grass.

Out he came again. I lost him for a minute when he went under the bridge; he did not come out where I expected him. Suddenly to my utter disbelief he appeared on the bank next to me. The troll bridge itself is on a level with the low bank; there I was, and there he was, at my side. I could have touched him with the palm of my hand without straightening my elbow. He was ready to hand.

Foraging beside me he walked very humped up, maybe to save heat loss through evaporation. Generally, whenever he was out of water he assumed the shape of a shmoo; his shoulders were as slender as a kitten's. He used his forepaws to part clumps of grass extremely tidily; I could see the flex in his narrow wrists. He gathered mouthfuls of grass and clover less by actually gnawing than by biting hard near the ground, locking his neck muscles, and pushing up jerkily with his forelegs.

His jaw was underslung, his black eyes close set and glistening, his small ears pointed and furred. I will have to try and see if he can cock them. I could see the water-slicked long hairs of his coat, which gathered in rich brown strands that emphasized the smooth contours of his body, and which parted to reveal the paler, softer hair like rabbit fur underneath. Despite his closeness, I never saw his teeth or belly.

After several minutes of rummaging about in the grass at my side, he eased into the water under the bridge and paddled to his den with the jawful of grass held high, and that was the last I saw of him.

In the forty minutes I watched him, he never saw me, smelled me, or heard me at all. When he was in full view of course I never moved except to breathe. My eyes would move, too, following his, but he never noticed. I even swallowed a couple of times: nothing. The swallowing thing interested me because I had read that, when you are trying to hand-tame wild birds, if you inadvertently swallow, you ruin everything. The bird, according to this theory, thinks you are swallowing in anticipation, and off it goes. The muskrat never twitched. Only once, when he was feeding from the opposite bank about eight feet away from me, did he suddenly rise upright, all alert—and then he immediately resumed foraging. But he never knew I was there.

I never knew I was there, either. For that forty minutes last night I was as purely sensitive and mute as a photographic plate; I received impressions, but I did not print out captions. My own self-awareness had disappeared; it seems now almost as though, had I been wired with electrodes, my EEG would have been flat. I have done this sort of thing so often that I have lost self-consciousness about moving slowly and halting suddenly; it is second nature to me now. And I have often noticed that even a few minutes of this self-forgetfulness is tremendously invigorating. I wonder if we do not waste most of our energy just by spending every waking minute saying hello to ourselves. Martin Buber quotes an old Hasid master who said, "When you walk across the fields with your mind pure and holy, then from all the stones, and all growing things, and all animals, the sparks of their soul come out and cling to you, and then they are purified and become a holy fire in you." This is one way of describing the energy that comes, using the specialized Kabbalistic vocabulary of Hasidism.

I have tried to show muskrats to other people, but it rarely works. No matter how quiet we are, the muskrats stay hidden. Maybe they sense the tense hum of consciousness, the buzz from two human beings who in the silence cannot help but be aware of each other, and so of themselves. Then too, the other people invariably suffer from a self-consciousness that prevents their stalking well. It used to bother me, too: I just could not bear to lose so much dignity that I would completely alter my whole way of being for a muskrat. So I would move or look around or scratch my nose, and no muskrats would show, leaving me alone with my dignity for days on end, until I decided that it was worth my while to learn—from the muskrats themselves—how to stalk.

* * *

The old, classic rule for stalking is, "Stop often 'n' set frequent." The rule cannot be improved upon, but muskrats will permit a little more. If a muskrat's eyes are out of sight, I can practically do a buck-and-wing on his tail, and he'll never notice. A few days ago I approached a muskrat feeding on a bank by the troll bridge simply by taking as many gliding steps towards him as possible while his head was turned. I spread my weight as evenly as I could, so that he wouldn't feel my coming through the ground, and so that no matter when I became visible to him, I could pause motionless until he turned away again without having to balance too awkwardly on one leg.

When I got within ten feet of him, I was sure he would flee, but he continued to browse nearsightedly among the mown clovers and grass. Since I had seen just about everything I was ever going to see, I continued approaching just to see when he would break. To my utter bafflement, he never broke. I broke first. When one of my feet was six inches from his back, I refused to press on. He could see me perfectly well, of course, but I was stock-still except when he lowered his head. There was nothing left to do but kick him. Finally he returned to the water, dove, and vanished. I do not know to this day if he would have permitted me to keep on walking right up his back.

It is not always so easy. Other times I have learned that the only way to approach a feeding muskrat for a good look is to commit myself to a procedure so ridiculous that only a total unselfconsciousness will permit me to live with myself. I have to ditch my hat, line up behind a low boulder, and lay on my belly to inch snake-fashion across twenty feet of bare field until I am behind the boulder itself and able to hazard a slow peek around it. If my head moves from around the boulder when the muskrat's head happens to be turned, then all is well. I can be fixed into position and still by the time he looks around. But if he sees me move my head, then he dives into the water, and the whole belly-crawl routine was in vain. There is no way to tell ahead of time; I just have to chance it and see.

I have read that in the unlikely event that you are caught in a stare-down with a grizzly bear, the best thing to do is talk to him softly and pleasantly. Your voice is supposed to have a soothing effect. I have not yet had occasion to test this out on grizzly bears, but I can attest that it does not work on muskrats. It scares them witless. I have tried time and again. Once I watched a muskrat feeding on a bank ten feet away from me; after I had looked my fill I had nothing to lose, so I offered a convivial greeting. Boom. The terrified muskrat flipped a hundred and eighty degrees in the air, nose-dived into the grass at his feet, and disappeared. The earth swallowed him; his tail shot straight up in the air and then vanished into the ground without a sound. Muskrats make several emergency escape holes along a bank for just this very purpose, and they don't like to feed too far away from them. The entire event was most impressive, and illustrates the relative power in nature of the word and the sneak.

Stalking is a pure form of skill, like pitching or playing chess. Rarely is luck involved. I do it right or I do it wrong; the muskrat will tell me, and that right early. Even more than baseball, stalking is a game played in the actual present. At every second, the muskrat comes, or stays, or goes, depending on my skill.

Can I stay still? How still? It is astonishing how many people cannot, or will not, hold still. I could not, or would not, hold still for thirty minutes inside, but at the creek I slow down, center down, empty. I am not excited; my breathing is slow and regular. In my brain I am not saying, Muskrat! Muskrat! There! I am saying nothing. If I must hold a position, I do not "freeze." If I freeze, locking my muscles, I will tire and break. Instead of going rigid, I go calm. I center down wherever I am; I find a balance and repose. I retreat—not inside myself, but outside myself, so that I am a tissue of senses. Whatever

I see is plenty, abundance. I am the skin of water the wind plays over; I am petal, feather, stone.

III

Living this way by the creek, where the light appears and vanishes on the water, where muskrats surface and dive, and redwings scatter, I have come to know a special side of nature. I look to the mountains, and the mountains still slumber, blue and mute and rapt. I say, it gathers; the world abides. But I look to the creek, and I say: it scatters, it comes and goes. When I leave the house the sparrows flee and hush; on the banks of the creek jays scream in alarm, squirrels race for cover, tadpoles dive, frogs leap, snakes freeze, warblers vanish. Why do they hide? I will not hurt them. They simply do not want to be seen. "Nature," said Heraclitus, "is wont to hide herself." A fleeing mockingbird unfurls for a second a dazzling array of white fans . . . and disappears in the leaves. Shane! . . . Shane! Nature flashes the old mighty glance—the come-hither look—drops the handkerchief, turns tail, and is gone. The nature I know is old touch-and-go.

I wonder whether what I see and seem to understand about nature is merely one of the accidents of freedom, repeated by chance before my eyes, or whether it has any counterpart in the worlds beyond Tinker Creek. I find in quantum mechanics a world symbolically similar to my world at the creek.

Many of us are still living in the universe of Newtonian physics, and fondly imagine that real, hard scientists have no use for these misty ramblings, dealing as scientists do with the measurable and known. We think that at least the physical causes of physical events are perfectly knowable, and that, as the results of various experiments keep coming in, we gradually roll back the cloud of unknowing. We remove the veils one by one, painstakingly, adding knowledge to knowledge

and whisking away veil after veil, until at last we reveal the
nub of things, the sparkling equation from whom all blessings
flow. Even wildman Emerson accepted the truly pathetic fal-
lacy of the old science when he wrote grudgingly towards the
end of his life, "When the microscope is improved, we shall
have the cells analysed, and all will be electricity, or somewhat
else." All we need to do is perfect our instruments and our
methods, and we can collect enough data like birds on a string
to predict physical events from physical causes.

But in 1927 Werner Heisenberg pulled out the rug, and
our whole understanding of the universe toppled and collapsed. For some reason it has not yet trickled down to the
man on the street that some physicists now are a bunch of
wild-eyed, raving mystics. For they have perfected their instruments and methods just enough to whisk away the crucial veil,
and what stands revealed is the Cheshire cat's grin.

The Principle of Indeterminacy, which saw the light in the
summer of 1927, says in effect that you cannot know both a
particle's velocity and position. You can guess statistically
what any batch of electrons might do, but you cannot predict
the career of any one particle. They seem to be as free as
dragonflies. You can perfect your instruments and your methods till the cows come home, and you will never ever be able
to measure this one basic thing. It cannot be done. The electron is a muskrat; it cannot be perfectly stalked. And nature
is a fan dancer born with a fan; you can wrestle her down,
throw her on the stage and grapple with her for the fan with
all your might, but it will never quit her grip. She comes that
way; the fan is attached.

It is not that we lack sufficient information to know both a
particle's velocity and its position; that would have been a
perfectly ordinary situation well within the understanding of
classical physics. Rather, we know now for sure that there is
no knowing. You can determine the position, and your figure
for the velocity blurs into vagueness; or, you can determine
the velocity, but whoops, there goes the position. The use of

instruments and the very fact of an observer seem to bollix the observations; as a consequence, physicists are saying that they cannot study nature per se, but only their own investigation of nature. And I can only see bluegills within my own blue shadow, from which they immediately flee.

The Principle of Indeterminacy turned science inside-out. Suddenly determinism goes, causality goes, and we are left with a universe composed of what Eddington calls, "mind-stuff." Listen to these physicists: Sir James Jeans, Eddington's successor, invokes "fate," saying that the future "may rest on the knees of whatever gods there be." Eddington says that "the physical world is entirely abstract and without 'actuality' apart from its linkage to consciousness." Heisenberg himself says, "method and object can no longer be separated. *The scientific world-view has ceased to be a scientific view in the true sense of the word.*" Jeans says that science can no longer remain opposed to the notion of free will. Heisenberg says, "there is a higher power, not influenced by our wishes, which finally decides and judges." Eddington says that our dropping causality as a result of the Principle of Indeterminacy "leaves us with no clear distinction between the Natural and the Supernatural." And so forth.

These physicists are once again mystics, as Kepler was, standing on a rarefied mountain pass, gazing transfixed into an abyss of freedom. And they got there by experimental method and a few wild leaps such as Einstein made. What a pretty pass!

All this means is that the physical world as we understand it now is more like the touch-and-go creek world I see than it is like the abiding world of which the mountains seem to speak. The physicists' particles whiz and shift like rotifers in and out of my microscope's field, and that this valley's ring of granite mountains is an airy haze of those same particles I must believe. The whole universe is a swarm of those wild, wary energies, the sun that glistens from the wet hairs on a musk-rat's back and the stars which the mountains obscure on the horizon but which catch from on high in Tinker Creek. It is all touch and go. The heron flaps away; the dragonfly departs at thirty miles an hour; the water strider vanishes under a screen of grass; the muskrat dives, and the ripples roll from the bank, and flatten, and cease altogether.

Moses said to God, "I beseech thee, shew me thy glory." And God said, "Thou canst not see my face: for there shall no man see me, and live." But he added, "There is a place by me, and thou shalt stand upon a rock: and it shall come to pass, while my glory passeth by, that I will put thee in a clift of the rock, and will cover thee with my hand while I pass by: And I will take away mine hand, and thou shalt see my back parts: but my face shall not be seen." So Moses went up on Mount Sinai, waited still in a clift of the rock, and saw the back parts of God. Forty years later he went up on Mount Pisgah, and saw the promised land across the Jordan, which he was to die without ever being permitted to enter.

Just a glimpse, Moses: a clift in the rock here, a mountaintop there, and the rest is denial and longing. You have to stalk everything. Everything scatters and gathers; everything comes and goes like fish under a bridge. You have to stalk the spirit, too. You can wait forgetful anywhere, for anywhere is the way of his fleet passage, and hope to catch him by the tail and shout something in his ear before he wrests away. Or you can pursue him wherever you dare, risking the shrunken sinew in the hollow of the thigh; you can bang at the door all night till the innkeeper relents, if he ever relents; and you can wail till you're hoarse or worse the cry for incarnation always in John Knoepfle's poem: "and christ is red rover . . . and the children are calling/come over come over." I sit on a bridge as on Pisgah or Sinai, and I am both waiting becalmed in a clift of the rock and banging with all my will, calling like a child beating on a door: come on out! . . . I know you're there.

And then occasionally the mountains part. The tree with the lights in it appears, the mockingbird falls, and time unfurls across space like an oriflamme. Now we rejoice. The news, after all, is not that muskrats are wary, but that they can be seen. The hem of the robe was a Nobel Prize to Heisenberg; he did not go home in disgust. I wait on the bridges and stalk along banks for those moments I cannot predict, when a wave begins to surge under the water, and ripples strengthen and pulse high across the creek and back again in a texture that throbs. It is like the surfacing of an impulse, like the materialization of fish, this rising, this coming to a head, like the ripening of nutmeats still in their husks, ready to split open like buckeyes in a field, shining with newness. "Surely the Lord is in this place; and I knew it not." The fleeing shreds I see, the back parts, are a gift, an abundance. When Moses came down from the clift in Mount Sinai, the people were afraid of him: the very skin on his face shone.

Do the Eskimos' faces shine, too? I lie in bed alert: I am with the Eskimos on the tundra who are running after the click-footed caribou, running sleepless and dazed for days, running spread out in scraggling lines across the glacier-ground hummocks and reindeer moss, in sight of the ocean, under the long-shadowed pale sun, running silent all night long.

CHAPTER 12

Nightwatch

I STOOD IN THE LUCAS MEADOW in the middle of a barrage of grasshoppers. There must have been something about the rising heat, the falling night, the ripeness of grasses—something that mustered this army in the meadow where they have never been in such legions before. I must have seen a thousand grasshoppers, alarums and excursions clicking over the clover, knee-high to me.

I had stepped into the meadow to feel the heat and catch a glimpse of the sky, but these grasshoppers demanded my attention, and became an event in themselves. Every step I took detonated the grass. A blast of bodies like shrapnel exploded around me; the air burst and whirred. There were grasshoppers of all sizes, grasshoppers yellow, green and black, short-horned, long-horned, slant-faced, band-winged, spur-throated, cone-headed, pygmy, spotted, striped and barred. They sprang in salvos, dropped in the air, and clung unevenly to stems and blades with their legs spread for balance, as redwings ride cattail reeds. They clattered around my ears; they ricocheted off my calves with an instant clutch and release of tiny legs.

I was in shelter, but open to the sky. The meadow was clean, the world new, and I washed by my walk over the waters of the dam. A new, wild feeling descended upon me and caught me up. What if these grasshoppers were locusts, I thought; what if I were the first man in the world, and stood in a swarm?

I had been reading about locusts. Hordes of migrating locusts have always appeared in arid countries, and then disappeared as suddenly as they had come. You could actually watch them lay eggs all over a plain, and the next year there would be no locusts on the plain. Entomologists would label their specimens, study their structure, and never find a single one that was alive—until years later they would be overrun again. No one knew in what caves or clouds the locusts hid between plagues.

In 1921 a Russian naturalist named Uvarov solved the mystery. Locusts are grasshoppers: they are the same animal. Swarms of locusts are ordinary grasshoppers gone berserk.

If you take ordinary grasshoppers of any of several species from any of a number of the world's dry regions—including the Rocky Mountains—and rear them in glass jars under crowded conditions, they go into the migratory phase. That is, they turn into locusts. They literally and physically change from Jekyll to Hyde before your eyes. They will even change, all alone in their jars, if you stimulate them by a rapid succession of artificial touches. Imperceptibly at first, their wings and wing-covers elongate. Their drab color heightens, then saturates more and more, until it locks at the hysterical locust yellows and pinks. Stripes and dots appear on the wing-covers; these deepen to a glittering black. They lay more egg-pods than grasshoppers. They are restless, excitable, voracious. You now have jars full of plague.

Under ordinary conditions, inside the laboratory and out in the deserts, the eggs laid by these locusts produce ordinary solitary grasshoppers. Only under special conditions—such as droughts that herd them together in crowds near available food—do the grasshoppers change. They shun food and shelter and seek only the jostle and clack of their kind. Their ranks swell; the valleys teem. One fine day they take to the air.

In full flight their millions can blacken the sky for nine hours, and when they land, it's every man to your tents, O Israel. "A fire devoureth before them; and behind them a flame burneth: the land is as the garden of Eden before them, and behind them a desolate wilderness; yea, and nothing shall escape them." One writer says that if you feed one a blade of grass, "the eighteen components of its jaws go immediately into action, lubricated by a brown saliva which looks like motor oil." Multiply this action by millions, and you hear a new sound: "The noise their myriad jaws make when engaged in their work of destruction can be realized by any one who has fought a prairie fire or heard the flames passing along before a brisk wind, the low crackling and rasping." Every contour of the land, every twig, is inches deep in bodies, so the valleys seethe and the hills tremble. Locusts: it is an old story.

A man lay down to sleep in a horde of locusts, Will Barker says. Instantly the suffocating swarm fell on him and knit him in a clicking coat of mail. The metallic mouth parts meshed and pinched. His friends rushed in and woke him at once. But when he stood up, he was bleeding from the throat and wrists.

The world has locusts, and the world has grasshoppers. I was up to my knees in the world.

Not one of these insects in this meadow could change into a locust under any circumstance. I am King of the Meadow, I thought, and raised my arms. Instantly grasshoppers burst all around me, describing in the air a blur of angular trajectories which ended in front of my path in a wag of grasses. As *if* I were king, dilly-dilly.

A large gray-green grasshopper hit with a clack on my shirt, and stood on my shoulder, panting. "Boo," I said, and it clattered off. It landed on a grass head several yards away. The grass bucked and sprang from the impact like a bronc, and the grasshopper rode it down. When the movement ceased, I couldn't see the grasshopper.

I walked on, one step at a time, both instigating and receiving this spray of small-arms fire. I had to laugh. I'd been had. I wanted to see the creatures, and they were gone. The only way I could see them in their cunning was to frighten them in their innocence. No charm or cleverness of mine could conjure or draw them; I could only flush them, triggering the grossest of their instincts, with the physical bluntness of my passage. To them I was just so much trouble, a horde of commotion, like any rolling stone. Wait! Where did you go? Does not any one of you, with your eighteen mouthparts, wish to have a word with me here in the Lucas meadow? Again I raised my arms: there you are. And then gone. The grasses slammed. I was exhilarated, flush. I was the serf of the meadow, exalted; I was the bride who waits with her lamp filled. A new wind was stirring; I had received the grasshoppers the way I received this wind. All around the meadow's rim the highest trees heaved soundlessly.

I walked back toward the cottage, maneuvering the whole squadron from one end of the meadow to the other. I'd been had all along by grasshoppers, muskrats, mountains—and like any sucker, I come back for more. They always get you in the end, and when you know it from the beginning, you have to laugh. You come for the assault, you come for the flight—but really you know you come for the laugh.

This is the fullness of late summer now; the green of what is growing and grown conceals. I can watch a muskrat feed on a bank for ten minutes, harvesting shocks of grass that bristle and droop from his jaws, and when he is gone I cannot see any difference in the grass. If I spread the patch with my hands and peer closely, I am hard put to locate any damage from even the most intense grazing. Nothing even looks trampled. Does everything else but me pass so lightly? When the praying mantis egg cases hatched in June, over a period of several days, I watched the tiny translucent mantises leap about leggily on the egg case, scraggle down the hedge's twigs, and disappear in the grass. In some places I could see them descend in a line like a moving bridge from stem to ground. The instant they crossed the horizon and entered the grass, they vanished as if they had jumped off the edge of the world.

Now it is early September, and the paths are clogged. I look to water to see sky. It is the time of year when a honeybee beats feebly at the inside back window of every parked car. A frog flies up for every foot of bank, bubbles tangle in a snare of blue-green algae, and Japanese beetles hunch doubled on the willow leaves. The sun thickens the air to jelly; it bleaches, flattens, dissolves. The skies are a milky haze—nowhere, do-nothing summer skies. Every kid I see has a circular grid on his forehead, a regular cross-hatching of straight lines, from spending his days leaning into screen doors.

I had come to the Lucas place to spend a night there, to let come what may. The Lucas place is paradise enow. It has everything: old woods, young woods, cliffs, meadows, slow water, fast water, caves. All it needs is a glacier extending a creaking foot behind the cottage. This magic garden is just on the other side of the oxbow in Tinker Creek; it is secluded because it is hard to approach. I could have followed the rock cliff path through the old woods, but in summer that path is wrapped past finding in saplings, bushes, kudzu, and poison oak. I could have tacked down the shorn grass terraces next to the cliff, but to get there I would have had to pass a vicious dog, who is waiting for the day I forget to carry a stick. So I planned on going the third way, over the dam.

I made a sandwich, filled a canteen, and slipped a palm-sized flashlight into my pocket. Then all I had to do was grab a thin foam pad and my sleeping bag, walk down the road, over the eroded clay hill where the mantis laid her eggs, along the creek downstream to the motorbike woods, and through the woods' bike trail to the dam.

I like crossing the dam. If I fell, I might not get up again. The dam is three or four feet high; a thick green algae, combed by the drag and sudden plunge of the creek's current, clings to its submersed, concrete brim. Below is a jumble of fast water and rocks. But I face this threat every time I cross the dam, and it is always exhilarating. The tightest part is at the very beginning. That day as always I faced the current, planted my feet firmly, stepped sideways instead of striding, and I soon emerged dripping in a new world.

Now, returning from my foray into the grasshopper meadow, I was back where I started, on the bank that separates the cottage from the top of the dam, where my sleeping bag, foam pad, and sandwich lay. The sun was setting invisibly behind the cliffs' rim. I unwrapped the sandwich and looked back over the way I had come, as if I could have seen the grasshoppers spread themselves again over the wide meadow and hide enfolded in its thickets and plush.

This is what I had come for, just this, and nothing more. A fling of leafy motion on the cliffs, the assault of real things, living and still, with shapes and powers under the sky—this is my city, my culture, and all the world I need. I looked around.

What I call the Lucas place is only a part of the vast Lucas property. It is one of the earliest clearings around here, a garden in the wilderness; every time I cross the dam and dry my feet on the bank, I feel like I've just been born. Now to my right the creek's dammed waters were silent and deep, overhung by and reflecting bankside tulip and pawpaw and ash. The creek angled away out of sight upstream; this was the oxbow, and the dam spanned its sharpest arc. Downstream the creek slid over the dam and slapped along sandstone ledges and bankside boulders, exhaling a cooling breath of mist before disappearing around the bend under the steep wooded cliff.

I stood ringed and rimmed in heights, locked and limned, in a valley within a valley. Next to the cliff fell a grassy series

of high terraces, suitable for planting the hanging gardens of
Babylon. Beyond the terraces, forest erupted again wherever
it could eke a roothold on the sheer vertical rock. In one place,
three caves cut into the stone vaults, their entrances hidden by
honeysuckle. One of the caves was so small only a child could
enter it crawling; one was big enough to explore long after
you have taken the initiatory turns that shut out the light; the
third was huge and shallow, filled with cut wood and chicken
wire, and into its nether wall extended another tiny cave in
which a groundhog reared her litter this spring.

Ahead of me in the distance I could see where the forested
cliffs mined with caves gave way to overgrown terraces that
once must have been cleared. Now they were tangled in saplings swathed in honeysuckle and wild rose brambles. I always
remember trying to fight my way up that steepness one winter
when I first understood that even January is not muscle
enough to subdue the deciduous South. There were clear
trails through the undergrowth—I saw once I was in the thick
of it—but they were rabbit paths, unfit for anyone over seven
inches tall. I had emerged scratched, pricked, and panting in
the Lucas peach orchard, which is considerably more conve-
niently approached by the steep gravel drive that parallels the
creek.

In the flat at the center of all this rimrock was the sunlit
grasshopper meadow, and facing the meadow, tucked up between the grass terrace and the creek's dam, was the heart of
the city, the Lucas cottage.

I stepped to the porch. My footfall resounded; the cliffs rang
back the sound, and the clover and grasses absorbed it. The
Lucas cottage was in fact mostly porch, airy and winged. Gray-
painted two-by-fours wobbled around three sides of the cottage, split, smashed, and warped long past plumb. Beams at
the porch's four corners supported a low, peaked roof that
vaulted over both the porch and the cottage impartially, lending so much importance to the already huge porch that it made
the cottage proper seem an afterthought, as Adam seems

sometimes an afterthought in Eden. For years an old inlaid chess table with a broken carved pedestal leaned against the cottage on one wing of the porch; the contrasting brown patches of weathered inlay curled up in curves like leaves.

The cottage was scarcely longer than the porch was deep. It was a one-room cottage; you could manage (I've thought this through again and again—building more spartan mansions, o my soul) a cot, a plank window-desk, a chair (two for company, as the man says), and some narrow shelves. The cottage is mostly windows—there are five—and the windows are entirely broken, so that my life inside the cottage is mostly Tinker Creek and mud dauber wasps.

It's a great life—luxurious, really. The cottage is wired for electricity; a bare-bulb socket hangs from the unfinished wood ceiling. There is a stovepipe connection in the roof. Beyond the porch on the side away from the creek is a big brick fireplace suitable for grilling whole steers. The steers themselves are fattening just five minutes away, up the hill and down into the pasture. The trees that shade the cottage are walnuts and pecans. In the spring the edge of the upstream creek just outside the cottage porch comes up in yellow daffodils, all the way up to the peach orchard.

That day it was dark inside the cottage, as usual; the five windows framed five films of the light and living world. I crunched to the creekside window, walking on the layer of glass shards on the floor, and stood to watch the creek lurch over the dam and round the shaded bend under the cliff, while bumblebees the size of ponies fumbled in the fragrant flowers that flecked the bank. A young cottontail rabbit bounded into view and froze. It crouched under my window with its ears flattened to its skull and its body motionless, the picture of adaptive invisibility. With one ridiculous exception. It was so very young, and its shoulder itched so maddeningly, that it whapped away at the spot noisily with a violent burst of a hind leg—and then resumed its frozen alert. Over the dam's drop of waters, two dog-faced sulphur butterflies were fighting.

They touched and parted, ascending in a vertical climb, as
though they were racing up an invisible spiraling vine.

All at once something wonderful happened, although at first
it seemed perfectly ordinary. A female goldfinch suddenly
hove into view. She lighted weightlessly on the head of a
bankside purple thistle and began emptying the seedcase,
sowing the air with down.

The lighted frame of my window filled. The down rose and
spread in all directions, wafting over the dam's waterfall and
wavering between the tulip trunks and into the meadow. It
vaulted towards the orchard in a puff; it hovered over the
ripening pawpaw fruit and staggered up the steep-faced terrace. It jerked, floated, rolled, veered, swayed. The thistledown faltered toward the cottage and gusted clear to the
motorbike woods; it rose and entered the shaggy arms of
pecans. At last it strayed like snow, blind and sweet, into the
pool of the creek upstream, and into the race of the creek over
rocks down. It shuddered onto the tips of growing grasses,
where it poised, light, still wracked by errant quivers. I was
holding my breath. Is this where we live, I thought, in this
place at this moment, with the air so light and wild?

The same fixity that collapses stars and drives the mantis to
devour her mate eased these creatures together before my
eyes: the thick adept bill of the goldfinch, and the feathery,
coded down. How could anything be amiss? If I myself were
lighter and frayed, I could ride these small winds, too, taking
my chances, for the pleasure of being so purely played.

The thistle is part of Adam's curse. "Cursed is the ground
for thy sake; in sorrow shalt thou eat of it all the days of thy
life; Thorns also and thistles shall it bring forth to thee." A
terrible curse: But does the goldfinch eat thorny sorrow with
the thistle, or do I? If this furling air is fallen, then the fall was
happy indeed. If this creekside garden is sorrow, then I seek
martyrdom. This crown of thorns sits light on my skull, like
wings. The Venetian Baroque painter Tiepolo painted Christ
as a red-lipped infant clutching a goldfinch; the goldfinch

seems to be looking around in search of thorns. Creation itself was the fall, a burst into the thorny beauty of the real.

The goldfinch here on the fringed thistletop was burying her head with each light thrust deeper into the seedcase. Her fragile legs braced to her task on the vertical, thorny stem; the last of the thistledown sprayed and poured. Is there anything I could eat so lightly, or could I die so fair? With a ruffle of feathered wings the goldfinch fluttered away, out of range of the broken window's frame and toward the deep blue shade of the cliffs where late fireflies already were rising alight under trees. I was weightless; my bones were taut skins blown with buoyant gas; it seemed that if I inhaled too deeply, my shoulders and head would waft off. Alleluia.

Later I lay half out of my sleeping bag on a narrow shelf of flat ground between the cottage porch and the bank to the dam. I lay where a flash flood would reach me, but we have had a flood; the time is late. The night was clear; when the fretwork of overhead foliage rustled and parted, I could see the pagan stars.

Sounds fell all about me; I vibrated like still water ruffed by wind. Cicadas—which Donald E. Carr calls "the guns of August"—were out in full force. Their stridulations mounted over the meadow and echoed from the rim of cliffs, filling the air with a plaintive, mysterious urgency. I had heard them begin at twilight, and was struck with the way they actually do "start up," like an out-of-practice orchestra, creaking and grinding and all out of synch. It had sounded like someone playing a cello with a wide-toothed comb. The frogs added their unlocatable notes, which always seem to me to be so arbitrary and anarchistic, and crickets piped in, calling their own tune which they have been calling since the time of Pliny, who noted bluntly of the cricket, it "never ceaseth all night long to creak very shrill."

Earlier a bobwhite had cried from the orchardside cliff, now here, now there, and his round notes swelled sorrowfully over the meadow. A bobwhite who is still calling in summer is lorn; he has never found a mate. When I first read this piece of information, every bobwhite call I heard sounded tinged with desperation, suicidally miserable. But now I am somehow cheered on my way by that solitary signal. The bobwhite's very helplessness, his obstinate Johnny-two-notedness, takes on an aura of dogged pluck. God knows what he is thinking in those pendant silences between calls. God knows what I am. But: bob*white*. (Somebody showed me once how to answer a bobwhite in the warbling, descending notes of the female. It works like a charm. But what can I do with a charmed circle of male bobwhites but weep? Still, I am brutalized enough that I give the answering call occasionally, just to get a rise out of the cliffs, and a bitter laugh.) Yes, it's tough, it's tough, that goes without saying. But isn't waiting itself and longing a wonder, being played on by wind, sun, and shade?

In his famous *Camping and Woodcraft,* Horace Kephart sounds a single ominous note. He writes in parentheses: "Some cannot sleep well in a white tent under a full moon." Every time I think of it, I laugh. I like the way that handy woodsy tip threatens us with the thrashings of the spirit.

I was in no tent under leaves, sleepless and glad. There was no moon at all; along the world's coasts the sea tides would be springing strong. The air itself also has lunar tides: I lay still. Could I feel in the air an invisible sweep and surge, and an answering knock in my lungs? Or could I feel the starlight? Every minute on a square mile of this land—on the steers and the orchard, on the quarry, the meadow, and creek—one ten thousandth of an ounce of starlight spatters to earth. What percentage of an ounce did that make on my eyes and cheeks and arms, tapping and nudging as particles, pulsing and stroking as waves? Straining after these tiny sensations, I nearly rolled off the world when I heard, and at the same time felt through my hips' and legs' bones on the ground, the bang and shudder of distant freight trains coupling.

Night risings and fallings filled my mind, free excursions carried out invisibly while the air swung up and back and the starlight rained. By day I had watched water striders dimple and jerk over the deep bankside water slowed by the dam. But I knew that sometimes a breath or call stirs the colony, and new forms emerge with wings. They cluster at night on the surface of their home waters and then take to the air in a rush. Migrating, they sail over meadows, under trees, cruising, veering towards a steady gleam in a flurry of glistening wings: "phantom ships in the air."

Now also in the valley night a skunk emerged from his underground burrow to hunt pale beetle grubs in the dark. A great horned owl folded his wings and dropped from the sky, and the two met on the bloodied surface of earth. Spreading over a distance, the air from that spot thinned to a frail sweetness, a tinctured wind that bespoke real creatures and real encounters at the edge . . . events, events. Over my head black hunting beetles crawled up into the high limbs of trees, killing more caterpillars and pupae than they would eat.

I had read once about a mysterious event of the night that is never far from my mind. Edwin Way Teale described an occurrence so absurd that it vaults out of the world of strange facts and into that startling realm where power and beauty hold sovereign sway.

The sentence in Teale is simple: "On cool autumn nights, eels hurrying to the sea sometimes crawl for a mile or more across dewy meadows to reach streams that will carry them to salt water." These are adult eels, silver eels, and this descent that slid down my mind is the fall from a long spring ascent the eels made years ago. As one-inch elvers they wriggled and heaved their way from the salt sea up the coastal rivers of America and Europe, upstream always into "the quiet upper reaches of rivers and brooks, in lakes and ponds—sometimes as high as 8,000 feet above sea level." There they had lived without breeding "for at least eight years." In the late summer of the year they reached maturity, they stopped eating, and their dark color vanished. They turned silver; now they are heading to the sea. Down streams to rivers, down rivers to the sea, south in the North Atlantic where they meet and pass billions of northbound elvers, they are returning to the Sargasso Sea, where, in floating sargassum weed in the deepest waters of the Atlantic, they will mate, release their eggs, and die. This, the whole story of eels at which I have only just hinted, is extravagant in the extreme, and food for another kind of thought, a thought about the meaning of such wild, incomprehensible gestures. But it was feeling with which I was concerned under the walnut tree by the side of the Lucas cottage and dam. My mind was on that meadow.

Imagine a chilly night and a meadow; balls of dew droop from the curved blades of grass. All right: the grass at the edge of the meadow begins to tremble and sway. Here come the eels. The largest are five feet long. All are silver. They stream into the meadow, sift between grasses and clover, veer from your path. There are too many to count. All you see is a silver slither, like twisted ropes of water falling roughly, a one-way milling and mingling over the meadow and slide to the creek. Silver eels in the night: a barely-made-out seething as far as you can squint, a squirming, jostling torrent of silver eels in the grass. If I saw that sight, would I live? If I stumbled across it, would I ever set foot from my door again? Or would I be seized to join that compelling rush, would I cease eating, and pale, and abandon all to start walking?

Had this place always been so, and had I not known it? There were blowings and flights, tossings and heaves up the air and down to grass. Why didn't God let the animals in Eden name the man; why didn't I wrestle the grasshopper on my shoulder and pin him down till he called my name? I was thistledown, and now I seemed to be grass, the receiver of grasshoppers and eels and mantises, grass the windblown and final receiver.

For the grasshoppers and thistledown and eels went up and came down. If you watch carefully the hands of a juggler, you see they are almost motionless, held at precise angles, so that the balls seem to be of their own volition describing a perfect circle in the air. The ascending arc is the hard part, but our eyes are on the smooth and curving fall. Each falling ball seems to trail beauty as its afterimage, receding faintly down the air, almost disappearing, when lo, another real ball falls, shedding its transparent beauty, and another. . . .

And it all happens so dizzyingly fast. The goldfinch I had seen was asleep in a thicket; when she settled to sleep, the weight of her breast locked her toes around her perch. Wasps were asleep with their legs hanging loose, their jaws jammed into the soft stems of plants. Everybody grab a handle: we're spinning headlong down.

I am puffed clay, blown up and set down. That I fall like Adam is not surprising: I plunge, waft, arc, pour, and dive. The surprise is how good the wind feels on my face as I fall. And the other surprise is that I ever rise at all. I rise when I receive, like grass.

I didn't know, I never have known, what spirit it is that descends into my lungs and flaps near my heart like an eagle rising. I named it full-of-wonder, highest good, voices. I shut my eyes and saw a tree stump hurled by wind, an enormous tree stump sailing sideways across my vision, with a wide circular brim of roots and soil like a tossed top hat.

And what if those grasshoppers had been locusts descending, I thought, and what if I stood awake in a swarm? I cannot ask for more than to be so wholly acted upon, flown at, and lighted on in throngs, probed, knocked, even bitten. A little blood from the wrists and throat is the price I would willingly pay for that pressure of clacking weights on my shoulders, for the scent of deserts, groundfire in my ears—for being so in the clustering thick of things, rapt and enwrapped in the rising and falling real world.

CHAPTER 13

The Horns of the Altar

I

THERE WAS A SNAKE at the quarry with me tonight. It lay shaded by cliffs on a flat sandstone ledge above the quarry's dark waters. I was thirty feet away, sitting on the forest path overlook, when my eye caught the dark scrawl on the rocks, the lazy sinuosity that can only mean snake. I approached for a better look, edging my way down the steep rock cutting, and saw that the snake was only twelve or thirteen inches long. Its body was thick for its length. I came closer still, and saw the unmistakable undulating bands of brown, the hourglasses: copperhead.

I never step a foot out of the house, even in winter, without a snakebite kit in my pocket. Mine is a small kit in rubber casing about the size of a shotgun shell; I slapped my pants instinctively to fix in my mind its location. Then I stomped hard on the ground a few times and sat down beside the snake.

The young copperhead was motionless on its rock. Although it lay in a loose sprawl, all I saw at first was a camouflage pattern of particolored splotches confused by the rushing speckles of light in the weeds between us, and by the deep twilight dark of the quarry pond beyond the rock. Then suddenly the form of its head emerged from the confusion: burnished brown, triangular, blunt as a stone ax. Its head and the first four inches of its body rested on airy nothing an inch above the rock. I admired the snake. Its scales shone with newness, bright and buffed. Its body was perfect, whole and unblemished. I found it hard to believe it had not just been created on the spot, or hatched fresh from its mother, so unscathed and clean was its body, so unmarked by any passage.

Did it see me? I was only four feet away, seated on the weedy cliff behind the sandstone ledge; the snake was between me and the quarry pond. I waved an arm in its direction: nothing moved. Its low-forehead glare and lipless reptile smirk revealed nothing. How could I tell where it was looking, what it was seeing? I squinted at its head, staring at those eyes like the glass eyes of a stuffed warbler, at those scales like shields canted and lapped just so, to frame an improbable, unfathomable face.

Yes, it knew I was there. There was something about its eyes, some alien alertness . . . what on earth must it be like to have scales on your face? All right then, copperhead. I know you're here, you know I'm here. This is a big night. I dug my elbows into rough rock and dry soil and settled back on the hillside to begin the long business of waiting out a snake.

The only other poisonous snake around here is the timber rattler, *Crotalus horridus horridus.* These grow up to six feet long in the mountains, and as big as your thigh. I've never seen one in the wild; I don't know how many have seen me. I see copperheads, though, sunning in the dust, disappearing into rock cliff chinks, crossing dirt roads at twilight. Copperheads have no rattle, of course, and, at least in my experience, they do not give way. You walk around a copperhead—if you see it. Copperheads are not big enough or venomous enough to kill adult humans readily, but they do account for far and away the greatest number of poisonous snakebites in North America: there are so many of them, and people, in the Eastern woodlands. It always interests me when I read about new studies being done on pit vipers; the team of herpetologists always seems to pick my neck of the woods for its fieldwork. I infer that we have got poisonous snakes as East Africa has zebras or the tropics have orchids—they are our specialty, our stock-in-trade. So I try to keep my eyes open. But I don't worry: you have to live pretty far out to be more than a day from a hospital. And worrying about getting it in the face from a timber rattler is like worrying about being struck by a meteorite: life's too short. Anyway, perhaps the actual bite is painless.

One day I was talking about snakes to Mrs. Mildred Sink, who operates a switchboard. A large pane separated us, and we were talking through a circular hole in the glass. She was seated in a dark room little bigger than a booth. As we talked, red lights on her desk would flash. She would glance at them, then back at me, and, finishing her point with careful calmness, she would fix on me a long, significant look to hold my attention while her hand expertly sought the button and pushed it. In this way she handled incoming calls and told me her snake story.

When she was a girl, she lived in the country just north of here. She had a brother four years old. One bright summer day her brother and her mother were sitting quietly in the big room of the log cabin. Her mother had her sewing in her lap and was bent over it in concentration. The little boy was playing with wooden blocks on the floor. "Ma," he said, "I saw a snake." "Where?" "Down by the spring." The woman stitched the hem of a cotton dress, gathering the material with her needle and drawing it smooth with her hand. The little boy piled his blocks carefully, this way and that. After a while he said, "Ma, it's too dark in here, I can't see." She looked up and the boy's leg was swollen up as big around as his body.

Mrs. Sink nodded at me emphatically and then heeded the flashing light on the panel before her. She turned away; this caller was taking time. I waved and caught her eye; she waved, and I left.

The copperhead in front of me was motionless; its head still hung in the air above the sandstone rock. I thought of poking at it with a weed, but rejected the notion. Still, I wished it would do something. Marston Bates tells about an English ecologist, Charles Elton, who said, with his Britishness fully unfurled, "All cold-blooded animals . . . spend an unexpectedly large proportion of their time doing nothing at all, or at any rate nothing in particular." That is precisely what this one was doing.

I noticed its tail. It tapered to nothingness. I started back at the head and slid my eye down its body slowly: taper, taper, taper, scales, tiny scales, air. Suddenly the copperhead's tail seemed to be the most remarkable thing I had ever seen. I wished I tapered like that somewhere. What if I were a shaped balloon blown up through the tip of a finger?

Here was this blood-filled, alert creature, this nerved rope of matter, really here instead of not here, splayed soft and solid on a rock by the slimmest of chances. It was a thickening of the air spread from a tip, a rush into being, eyeball and blood, through a pin-hole rent. Every other time I had ever seen this rock it had been a flat sandstone rock over the quarry pond; now it hosted and bore this chunk of fullness that parted the air around it like a driven wedge. I looked at it from the other direction. From tail to head it spread like the lines of a crescendo, widening from stillness to a turgid blast; then at the bulging jaws it began contracting again, diminuendo, till at the tip of its snout the lines met back at the infinite point that corners every angle, and that space once more ceased being a snake.

* * *

While this wonder engaged me, something happened that was so unusual and unexpected that I can scarcely believe I saw it. It was ridiculous.

Night had been rising like a ground vapor from the blackened quarry pool. I heard a mosquito sing in my ear; I waved it away. I was looking at the copperhead. The mosquito landed on my ankle; again, I idly brushed it off. To my utter disbelief, it lighted on the copperhead. It squatted on the copperhead's back near its "neck," and bent its head to its task. I was riveted. I couldn't see the mosquito in great detail, but I could make out its lowered head that seemed to bore like a well drill through surface rock to fluid. Quickly I looked around to see if I could find anyone—any hunter going to practice shooting beer cans, any boy on a motorbike—to whom I could show this remarkable sight while it lasted.

To the best of my knowledge, it lasted two or three full minutes; it seemed like an hour. I could imagine the snake, like the frog sucked dry by the giant water bug, collapsing to an empty bag of skin. But the snake never moved, never indicated any awareness. At last the mosquito straightened itself, fumbled with its forelegs about its head like a fly, and sluggishly took to the air, where I lost it at once. I looked at the snake; I looked beyond the snake to the ragged chomp in the hillside where years before men had quarried stone; I rose, brushed myself off, and walked home.

Is this what it's like, I thought then, and think now: a little blood here, a chomp there, and still we live, trampling the grass? Must everything whole be nibbled? Here was a new light on the intricate texture of things in the world, the actual plot of the present moment in time after the fall: the way we the living are nibbled and nibbling—not held aloft on a cloud in the air but bumbling pitted and scarred and broken through a frayed and beautiful land.

II

When I reached home, I turned first to the bookshelf, to see if I could possibly have seen what I thought I had. All I could find was this sentence in Will Barker's book, *Familiar Insects of North America:* "The bite of the female [Mosquito, *Culex pipiens*] is effected with a little drill than can puncture many types of body covering—even the leathery skin of a frog or the overlapping scales on a snake." All right then; maybe I *had* seen it. Anything can happen in any direction; the world is more chomped than I'd dreamed.

It is mid-September now; I can see in the fading light the jagged holes in the leaves of the mock-orange hedge outside my study window. The more closely I look, the more I doubt that there is a single whole, unblemished leaf left on the bush. I go out again and examine the leaves one by one, first of the mock orange outside my study, then of the cherry tree in the yard. In the blue light I see scratched and peeled stems, leaves that are half-eaten, rusted, blighted, blistered, mined, snipped, smutted, pitted, puffed, sawed, bored, and rucked. Where have I been all summer while the world has been eaten?

I remember something else I saw this week. I passed on the road by the creek a small boy bearing aloft an enormous foot-long snapping turtle. The boy was carrying the turtle—which was stretching and snapping wildly in the air—at arm's length, and his arms must have been tired, for he asked me plaintively, "Do you have a box?" when I was on foot myself and quite clearly did not have a box. I admired the turtle, but the boy was worried. "He's got bleachers," he said. "Bleachers?" "You know, they suck your blood." Oh. I had noticed the black leech drooping like a tar tear down the turtle's thick shell. The boy showed me another one, almost two inches long, fixed to the granular skin under the turtle's foreleg. "Will they kill him?" the boy asked. "Will he live?" Many, if not most, of the wild turtles I see harbor leeches. I assured him

that the turtle would live. For most creatures, being parasi-
tized is a way of life—if you call that living.

I think of the fox that Park Service Ranger Gene Parker told
me about. The fox sprawled naked and pink-skinned in a
mountain field, unable to rise, dying of mange. I think of the
swimming bluegill I saw at the Lawsons', upstream in Tinker
Creek on the other side of Tinker Mountain. One of its eyes
was blinded by an overgrowth of white water mold, a white
that spread halfway down its back in filmy lumps like soaked
cotton batting. It had been injured, perhaps when a fisherman
had hooked it and tossed it back, perhaps when a flood dashed
it on rocks, and the fungus had spread from the injured site.
I think of Joseph Wood Krutch's description of a scientist he
met in the field, who was gleefully bearing a bloody jar
squirming with yard after yard of some unthinkable parasite
he had just found in the belly of a rabbit. Suddenly the lives
of the parasites—some sort of hellish hagiography—come to
mind. I remember the blood worms and flukes, whose parasitic life cycles require the living bodies of as many as four
hosts. How many of the grasshoppers that hurtled around me
in the Lucas meadow bore inside their guts the immense coiled
larvae of horsehair worms?

I received once as a gift a small, illustrated layman's guide
to insect pests. These are insects that for one reason or another
are in the way of human culture—or economics. By no means
all are parasites. Nevertheless, the book reads like the devil's
summa theologica. The various insects themselves include cot-
tony-cushion scales, bean beetles, borers, weevils, bulb flies,
thrips, cutworms, stink bugs, screw-worms, sawflies, poultry
lice, cheese skippers, cheese mites, cluster flies, puss caterpillars, itch mites, and long-tailed mealy bugs. Of cockroaches
the book says, "When very abundant, they may also eat human
hair, skin, and nails." (The key word, *skin,* is buried.) The
full-color pictures show warbled beef and fly-blown gashes,
blighted trees and blasted corn, engorged ticks and seething

ham, pus-eyed hogs and the wormy nostrils of sheep.

In another book I learn that ten percent of all the world's species are parasitic insects. It is hard to believe. What if you were an inventor, and you made ten percent of your inventions in such a way that they could only work by harassing, disfiguring, or totally destroying the other ninety percent? These things are not well enough known.

There is, for instance, a species of louse for almost every species of everything else. In addition to sucking blood, lice may also eat hair, feathers, the dry scales of moths, and other lice. Birdbanders report that wild birds are universally infested with lice, to each its own. Songbirds often squat in the dust near ant hills and spray themselves with a shower of living ants; it is thought that the formic acid in the ants discourages the presence of lice. "Each species of auk has its own species of louse, found on all individuals examined." The European cuckoo is the sole host to three species of lice, and the glossy ibis to five, each specializing in eating a different part of the host's body. Lice live in the hollow quills of birds' feathers, in wart hog bristles, in Antarctic seals' flippers and pelican pouches.

Fleas are almost as widely distributed as lice, but much more catholic in their choice of hosts. Immature fleas, interestingly, feed almost entirely on the feces of their parents and other adults, while mature fleas live on sucked blood.

Parasitic two-winged insects, such as flies and mosquitos, abound. It is these that cause hippos to live in the mud and frenzied caribou to trample their young. Twenty thousand head of domestic livestock died in Europe from a host of black flies that swarmed from the banks of the Danube in 1923. Some parasitic flies live in the stomachs of horses, zebras, and elephants; others live in the nostrils and eyes of frogs. Some feed on earthworms, snails, and slugs; others attack and successfully pierce mosquitos already engorged on stolen blood. Still others live on such delicate fare as the brains of ants, the blood of nestling songbirds, or the fluid in the wings of lace-wings and butterflies.

The lives of insects and their parasites are horribly en-twined. The usual story is that the larva of the parasite eats the other insect alive in any of several stages and degrees of con-sciousness. It is above all parasitic *Hymenoptera*—which for the sake of simplicity I shall call wasps—that specialize in this behavior. Some species of wasps are so "practiced" as parasites that the female will etch a figure-eight design on the egg of another insect in which she has just laid her egg, and other wasps will avoid ovipositing on those marked, already parasi-tized eggs. There are over one hundred thousand species of parasitic wasps, so that, although many life histories are known, many others are still mysterious. British entomologist R. R. Askew says, "The field is wide open, the prospect invit-ing." The field may be wide open, but—although most of my favorite entomologists seem to revel in these creatures—the prospect is, to me at least, scarcely inviting.

Consider this story of Edwin Way Teale's. He brought a monarch butterfly caterpillar inside to photograph just as it was about to pupate. The pale green caterpillar had hung itself upside-down from a leaf, as monarch caterpillars have done from time immemorial, in the form of a letter J.

"All that night it remained as it was. The next morning, at eight o'clock, I noticed that the curve in the 'J' had become shallower. Then, suddenly, as though a cord within had been severed, the larva straightened out and hung limp. Its skin was baggy and lumpy. It began to heave as the lumps within pushed and moved. At 9:30 A.M., the first of the six white, fat-bodied grubs appeared through the skin of the caterpillar. Each was about three eighths of an inch in length." This was the work of a parasitic wasp.

There is a parasitic wasp that travels on any adult female praying mantis, feeding on her body wherever she goes. When the mantis lays her eggs, the wasp lays hers, inside the frothy mass of bubbles before it hardens, so that the early-hatching wasp larvae emerge inside the case to eat the developing mantis eggs. Others eat cockroach eggs, ticks, mites, and houseflies. Many seek out and lay eggs on the caterpillars of butterflies and moths; sometimes they store paralyzed, living caterpillars, on which eggs have been laid, in underground burrows where they stay "fresh" for as long as nine months. Askew, who is apparently very alert, says, "The mass of yellowish cocoons of the braconid *Apanteles glomeratus* beneath the shrivelled remains of a large white butterfly caterpillar are a familiar sight."

There are so many parasitic wasps that some parasitic wasps have parasitic wasps. One startled entomologist, examining the gall made by a vegetarian oak gall wasp, found parasitism of the fifth order. This means that he found the remains of an oak gall wasp which had a parasitic wasp which had another which had another which had another which had another, if I count it aright.

Other insect orders also include fascinating parasites. Among true bugs are bed-bugs, insects that parasitize dozens of species of bats, and those that parasitize bed-bugs. Parasitic beetles as larvae prey on other insects, and as adults on bees and kangaroos. There is a blind beetle that lives on beavers. The cone-nose bug, or kissing bug, bites the lips of sleeping people, sucking blood and injecting an excruciating toxin.

There is an insect order that consists entirely of parasitic insects called, singly and collectively, stylops, which is interesting because of the grotesquerie of its form and its effects. Stylops parasitize diverse other insects such as leaf hoppers, ants, bees, and wasps. The female spends her entire life inside the body of her host, with only the tip of her bean-shaped body protruding. She is a formless lump, having no wings, legs, eyes, or antennae; her vestigial mouth and anus are tiny, degenerate, and nonfunctional. She absorbs food—her host— through the skin of her abdomen, which is "inflated, white, and soft."

The sex life of a stylops is equally degenerate. The female has a wide, primitive orifice called a "brood canal" near her vestigial mouthparts, out in the open air. The male inserts his sperm into the brood canal, from whence it flows into her disorganized body and fertilizes the eggs that are floating freely there. The hatched larvae find their way to the brood canal and emerge into the "outside world."

The unfortunate insects on which the stylops feed, although they live normal life spans, frequently undergo inexplicable changes. Their colors brighten. The gonads of males and females are "destroyed," and they not only lose their secondary sexual characteristics, they actually acquire those of the opposite sex. This happens especially to bees, in which the differences between the sexes are pronounced. "A stylopsised insect," says Askew, "may sometimes be described as an intersex."

Finally, completing this whirlwind survey of parasitic insects, there are, I was surprised to learn, certain parasitic moths. One moth caterpillar occurs regularly in the *horns* of African ungulates. One adult, winged moth lives on the skin secretions between the hairs of the fur of the three-fingered sloth. Another adult moth sucks mammal blood in southeast Asia. Last of all, there are the many eye-moths, which feed as winged adults about the open eyes of domestic cattle, sucking blood, pus, and tears.

Let me repeat that these parasitic insects comprise ten percent of all known animal species. How can this be understood? Certainly we give our infants the wrong idea about their fellow creatures in the world. Teddy bears should come with tiny stuffed bear-lice; ten percent of all baby bibs and rattles sold should be adorned with colorful blowflies, maggots, and screw-worms. What kind of devil's tithe do we pay? What percentage of the world's species that are *not* insects are parasitic? Could it be, counting bacteria and viruses, that we live in a world in which half the creatures are running from—or limping from—the other half?

The creator is no puritan. A creature need not work for a living; creatures may simply steal and suck and be blessed for all that with a share—an enormous share—of the sunlight and air. There is something that profoundly fails to be exuberant about these crawling, translucent lice and white, fat-bodied grubs, but there is an almost manic exuberance about a creator who turns them out, creature after creature after creature, and sets them buzzing and lurking and flying and swimming about. These parasites are our companions at life, wending their dim, unfathomable ways into the tender tissues of their living hosts, searching as we are simply for food, for energy to grow and breed, to fly or creep on the planet, adding more shapes to the texture of intricacy and more life to the universal dance. Parasitism: this itch, this gasp in the lung, this coiled worm in the gut, hatching egg in the sinew, warble-hole in the hide—is a sort of rent, paid by all creatures who live in the real world with us now. It is not an extortionary rent: Wouldn't you pay it, don't you, a little blood from the throat and wrists for the taste of the air? Ask the turtle. True, for some creatures it is a slow death; for others, like the stylopsised bee, it is a strange, transfigured life. For most of us Western humans directly it is a pinprick or scabrous itch here and there from a world we learned early could pinch, and no surprise. Or it is the black burgeoning of disease, the dank baptismal lagoon into which we are dipped by blind chance many times over against our wishes, until one way or another we die. Chomp. It is the thorn in the flesh of the world, another sign, if any be needed, that the world is actual and fringed, pierced here and there, and through and through, with the toothed conditions of time and the mysterious, coiled spring of death.

Outright predators, of course, I understand. I am among them. There is no denying that the feats of predators can be just as gruesome as those of the unlovely parasites: the swathing and sipping of trapped hummingbirds by barn spiders, the occasional killing and eating of monkeys by chimpanzees. If I were to eat as the delicate ladybug eats, I would go through in just nine days the entire population of Boys Town. Nevertheless, the most rapacious lurk and charge of any predator is not nearly so sinister as the silent hatching of barely visible, implanted eggs. With predators, at least you have a chance.

One night this summer I had gone looking for muskrats, and was waiting on the long pedestrian bridge over the widest part of the creek. No muskrat came, but a small event occurred in a spider's web strung from the lower rung of the bridge's handrail. As I watched, a tiny pale-green insect flew directly into the spider's web. It jerked violently, bringing the spider charging. But the fragile insect, which was no larger than a fifth of the spider's abdomen, extricated itself from the gluey strands in a flurry, dropped in a deadfall to the hard bridge surface a foot below, stood, shook itself, and flew away. I felt as I felt on the way back from lobar pneumonia, stuffed with penicillin and taking a few steps outside: *vive la chance.*

Recently I have been keeping an informal list of the ones that got away, of living creatures I have seen in various states of disarray. It started with spiders. I used to see a number of daddy-longlegs, or harvestmen, in the summer, and I got in the idle habit of counting their legs. It didn't take me long to notice that hardly ever did an adult of any size cross my path which was still hitting on all eight cylinders. Most had seven legs, some had six. Even in the house I noticed that the larger spiders tended to be missing a leg or two.

Then last September I was walking across a gravel path in full sunlight, when I nearly stepped on a grasshopper. I poked its leg with a twig to see it hop, but no hop came. So I crouched down low on my hands and knees, and sure enough, her swollen ovipositor was sunk into the gravel. She was pulsing faintly—with a movement not nearly so strained as the egg-laying mantis's was—and her right antenna was broken off near the base. She'd been around. I thought of her in the Lucas meadow, too, where so many grasshoppers leaped about me. One of those was very conspicuously lacking one of its big, springlike hind legs—a grasslunger. It seemed to move fairly well from here to there, but then of course I didn't know where it had been aiming.

Nature seems to catch you by the tail. I think of all the butterflies I have seen whose torn hind wings bore the jagged marks of birds' bills. There were four or five tiger swallowtails missing one of their tails, and a fritillary missing two thirds of a hind wing. The birds, too, who make up the bulk of my list, always seem to have been snatched at from behind, except for the killdeer I saw just yesterday, who was missing all of its toes; its slender shank ended in a smooth, gray knob. Once I saw a swallowtailed sparrow, who on second look proved to be a sparrow from whose tail the central wedge of feathers had been torn. I've seen a completely tailless sparrow, a tailless robin, and a tailless grackle. Then my private list ends with one bob-tailed and one tailless squirrel, and a muskrat kit whose tail bore a sizeable nick near the spine.

The testimony of experts bears out the same point: it's rough out there. Gerald Durrell, defending the caging of animals in well-kept zoos, says that the animals he collects from the wild are all either ridden with parasites, recovering from various wounds, or both. Howard Ensign Evans finds the butterflies in his neck of the woods as tattered as I do. A southwest Virginia naturalist noted in his journal for April, 1896, "Mourning-cloaks are plentiful but broken, having lived through the winter." Trappers have a hard time finding unblemished skins. Cetologists photograph the scarred hides of living whales, striated with gashes as long as my body, and hilly with vast colonies of crustaceans called whale lice.

Finally, Paul Siple, the Antarctic explorer and scientist, writes of the Antarctic crab-eater seal, which lives in the pack ice off the continent: "One seldom finds a sleek silvery adult crab-eater that does not bear ugly scars—or two-foot long parallel slashes—on each side of its body, received when it managed somehow to wriggle out of the jaws of a killer whale that had seized it."

I think of those crab-eater seals, and the jaws of the killer whales lined with teeth that are, according to Siple, "as large as bananas." How did they get away? How did not one or two, but most of them get away? Of course any predator that decimates its prey will go hungry, as will any parasite that kills its host species. Predator and prey offenses and defenses (and fecundity is a defense) usually operate in such a way that both populations are fairly balanced, stable in the middle as it were, and frayed and nibbled at the edges, like a bitten apple that still bears its seeds. Healthy caribou can outrun a pack of wolves; the wolves cull the diseased, old, and injured, who stray behind the herd. All this goes without saying. But it is truly startling to realize how on the very slender bridge of chance some of the most "efficient" predators operate. Wolves literally starve to death in valleys teeming with game. How many crab-eater seals can one killer whale *miss* in a lifetime?

Still, it is to the picture of the "sleek silvery" crab-eater seals that I return, seals drawn up by scientists from the Antarctic ice pack, seals bearing again and again the long gash marks of unthinkable teeth. Any way you look at it, from the point of view of the whale or the seal or the crab, from the point of view of the mosquito or copperhead or frog or dragonfly or minnow or rotifer, it is chomp or fast.

III

It is chomp or fast. Earlier this evening I brought in a handful of the gnawed mock-orange hedge and cherry tree leaves; they are uncurling now, limp and bluish, on the top of this desk. They didn't escape, but their time was almost up

anyway. Already outside a corky ring of tissue is thickening
around the base of each leaf stem, strangling each leaf one by
one. The summer is old. A gritty, colorless dust cakes the
melons and squashes, and worms fatten within on the bright,
sweet flesh. The world is festering with suppurating sores.
Where is the good, whole fruit? The world "Hath really neither joy, nor love, nor light,/Nor certitude, nor peace, nor
help for pain." I've been there, seen it, done it, I suddenly
think, and the world is old, a hungry old man, fatigued and
broken past mending. Have I walked too much, aged beyond
my years? I see the copperhead shining new on a rock altar
over a fetid pool where a forest should grow. I see the knob-
footed killdeer, the tattered butterflies and birds, the snapping
turtle festooned with black leeches. There are the flies that
make a wound, the flies that find a wound, and a hungry world
that won't wait till I'm decently dead.

"In nature," wrote Huston Smith, "the emphasis is in what
is rather than what ought to be." I learn this lesson in a new
way every day. It must be, I think tonight, that in a certain
sense only the newborn in this world are whole, that as adults
we are expected to be, and necessarily, somewhat nibbled. It's
par for the course. Physical wholeness is not something we
have barring accident; it is itself accidental, an accident of
infancy, like a baby's fontanel or the egg-tooth on a hatchling.
Are the five-foot silver eels that migrate as adults across meadows by night actually scarred with the bill marks of herons,
flayed by the sharp teeth of bass? I think of the beautiful sharks
I saw from a shore, hefted and held aloft in a light-shot wave.
Were those sharks sliced with scars, were there mites in their
hides and worms in their hearts? Did the mockingbird that
plunged from the rooftop, folding its wings, bear in its buoyant quills a host of sucking lice? Is our birthright and heritage
to be, like Jacob's cattle on which the life of a nation was
founded, "ring-streaked, speckled, and spotted" not with the
spangling marks of a grace like beauty rained down from
eternity, but with the blotched assaults and quarryings of time?

"We are all of us clocks," says Eddington, "whose faces tell the passing years." The young man proudly names his scars for his lover; the old man alone before a mirror erases his scars with his eyes and sees himself whole.

Through the window over my desk comes a drone, drone, drone, the weary winding of cicadas' horns. If I were blasted by a meteorite, I think, I could call it blind chance and die cursing. But we live creatures are eating each other, who have done us no harm. We're all in this Mason jar together, snapping at anything that moves. If the pneumococcus bacteria had flourished more vitally, if it had colonized my other lung successfully, living and being fruitful after its created kind, then I would have died my death, and my last ludicrous work would have been an Easter egg, an Easter egg painted with beaver and deer, an Easter egg that was actually in fact, even as I painted it and the creatures burgeoned in my lung, fertilized. It is ridiculous. What happened to manna? Why doesn't everything eat manna, into what rare air did the manna dissolve that we harry the free live things, each other?

An Eskimo shaman said, "Life's greatest danger lies in the fact that men's food consists entirely of souls." Did he say it to the harmless man who gave him tuberculosis, or to the one who gave him tar paper and sugar for wolfskin and seal? I wonder how many bites I have taken, parasite and predator, from family and friends; I wonder how long I will be permitted the luxury of this relative solitude. Out here on the rocks the people don't mean to grapple, to crush and starve and betray, but with all the good will in the world, we do, there's no other way. We want it; we take it out of each other's hides; we chew the bitter skins the rest of our lives.

But the sight of the leeched turtle and the frayed flighted things means something else. I think of the green insect shaking the web from its wings, and of the whale-scarred crab-eater seals. They demand a certain respect. The only way I can reasonably talk about all this is to address you directly and frankly as a fellow survivor. Here we so incontrovertibly are. *Sub specie aeternitatis* this may all look different, from inside the blackened gut beyond the narrow craw, but now, although we hear the buzz in our ears and the crashing of jaws at our heels, we can look around as those who are nibbled but unbroken, from the shimmering vantage of the living. Here may not be the cleanest, newest place, but that clean timeless place that vaults on either side of this one is noplace at all. "Your fathers did eat manna in the wilderness, and are dead." There are no more chilling, invigorating words than these of Christ's, "Your fathers did eat manna in the wilderness, and are dead."

Alaskan Eskimos believe in many souls. An individual soul has a series of afterlives, returning again and again to earth, but only rarely as a human. "Since its appearances as a human being are rare, it is thought a great privilege to be here as we are, with human companions who also, in this reincarnation, are privileged and therefore greatly to be respected." To be here as we are. I love the little facts, the ten percents, the fact of the real and legged borers, the cuticle-covered, secretive grubs, the blister beetles, blood flukes and mites. But there are plenty of ways to pile the facts, and it is easy to overlook some things. "The fact is," said Van Gogh, "the fact is that we are painters in real life, and the important thing is to breathe as hard as ever we can breathe."

So I breathe. I breathe at the open window above my desk, and a moist fragrance assails me from the gnawed leaves of the growing mock orange. This air is as intricate as the light that filters through forested mountain ridges and into my kitchen window; this sweet air is the breath of leafy lungs more rotted than mine; it has sifted through the serrations of many teeth. I have to love these tatters. And I must confess that the thought of this old yard breathing alone in the dark turns my mind to something else.

I cannot in all honesty call the world old when I've seen it new. On the other hand, neither will honesty permit me suddenly to invoke certain experiences of newness and beauty as binding, sweeping away all knowledge. But I am thinking now of the tree with the lights in it, the cedar in the yard by the creek I saw transfigured.

That the world is old and frayed is no surprise; that the world could ever become new and whole beyond uncertainty was, and is, such a surprise that I find myself referring all subsequent kinds of knowledge to it. And it suddenly occurs to me to wonder: Were the twigs of the cedar I saw really bloated with galls? They probably were; they almost surely were. I have seen those "cedar apples" swell from that cedar's green before and since: reddish-gray, rank, malignant. All right then. But knowledge does not vanquish mystery, or obscure its distant lights. I still now and will tomorrow steer by what happened that day, when some undeniably new spirit roared down the air, bowled me over, and turned on the lights. I stood on grass like air, air like lightning coursed in my blood, floated my bones, swam in my teeth. I've been there, seen it, been done by it. I know what happened to the cedar tree, I saw the cells in the cedar tree pulse charged like wings beating praise. Now, it would be too facile to pull everything out of the hat and say that mystery vanquishes knowledge. Although my vision of the world of the spirit would not be altered a jot if the cedar had been purulent with galls, those galls actually do matter to my understanding of this world. Can I say then that corruption is one of beauty's deep-blue speckles, that the frayed and nibbled fringe of the world is a tallith, a prayer shawl, the intricate garment of beauty? It is very tempting, but I honestly cannot. But I can, however, affirm that corruption is not beauty's very heart. And I can I think call the vision of the cedar and the knowledge of these wormy quarryings twin fiords cutting into the granite cliffs of mystery, and say that the new is always present simultaneously with the old, however hidden. The tree with the lights in it does not go out; that light still shines on an old world, now feebly, now bright.

I am a frayed and nibbled survivor in a fallen world, and I

am getting along. I am aging and eaten and have done my share of eating too. I am not washed and beautiful, in control of a shining world in which everything fits, but instead am wandering awed about on a splintered wreck I've come to care for, whose gnawed trees breathe a delicate air, whose bloodied and scarred creatures are my dearest companions, and whose beauty beats and shines not *in* its imperfections but overwhelmingly in spite of them, under the wind-rent clouds, upstream and down. Simone Weil says simply, "Let us love the country of here below. It is real; it offers resistance to love."

I am a sacrifice bound with cords to the horns of the world's rock altar, waiting for worms. I take a deep breath, I open my eyes. Looking, I see there are worms in the horns of the altar like live maggots in amber, there are shells of worms in the rock and moths flapping at my eyes. A wind from noplace rises. A sense of the real exults me; the cords loose; I walk on my way.

CHAPTER 14

Northing

I

IN SEPTEMBER the birds were quiet. They were molting in the valley, the mockingbird in the spruce, the sparrow in the mock orange, the doves in the cedar by the creek. Everywhere I walked the ground was littered with shed feathers, long, colorful primaries and shaftless white down. I garnered this weightless crop in pockets all month long, and inserted the feathers one by one into the frame of a wall mirror. They're still there; I look in the mirror as though I'm wearing a ceremonial headdress, inside-out.

In October the great restlessness came, the *Zugunruhe,* the restlessness of birds before migration. After a long, unseasonable hot spell, one morning dawned suddenly cold. The birds were excited, stammering new songs all day long. Titmice, which had hidden in the leafy shade of mountains all summer, perched on the gutter; chickadees staged a conventicle in the locusts, and a sparrow, acting very strange, hovered like a hummingbird inches above a roadside goldenrod.

I watched at the window; I watched at the creek. A new wind lifted the hair on my arms. The cold light was coming and going between oversized, careening clouds; patches of blue, like a ragged flock of protean birds, shifted and stretched, flapping and racing from one end of the sky to the other. Despite the wind, the air was moist; I smelled the rich vapor of loam around my face and wondered again why all that death—all those rotten leaves that one layer down are black sops roped in white webs of mold, all those millions of dead summer insects—didn't smell worse. When the wind quickened, a stranger, more subtle scent leaked from beyond the mountains, a disquieting fragrance of wet bark, salt marsh, and mud flat.

The creek's water was still warm from the hot spell. It bore floating tulip leaves as big as plates, and sinking tulip leaves, downstream, and out of sight. I watched the leaves fall on water, first on running water, and then on still. It was as different as visiting Cornwall, and visiting Corfu. But those winds and flickering lights and the mad cries of jays stirred me. I was wishing: colder, colder than this, colder than anything, and let the year hurry down!

The day before, in a dry calm, all the summer's ants took wing and swarmed, shining at the front door, at the back door, all up and down the road. I tried in vain to induce them to light on my upraised arm. Now at the slow part of the creek I suddenly saw migrating goldfinches in flocks hurling themselves from willow to willow over the reeds. They ascended in a sudden puff and settled, spreading slowly, like a blanket shaken over a bed, till some impulse tossed them up again, twenty and thirty together in sprays, and they tilted their wings, veered, folded, and spattered down.

I followed the goldfinches downstream until the bank beside me rose to a cliff and blocked the light on the willows and water. Above the cliff rose the Adams' woods, and in the cliff nested—according not only to local observation but also to the testimony of the county agricultural agent—hundreds of the area's copperheads. This October restlessness was worse than any April's or May's. In the spring the wish to wander is partly composed of an unnamable irritation, born of long inactivity; in the fall the impulse is more pure, more inexplicable, and more urgent. I could use some danger, I suddenly thought, so I abruptly abandoned the creek to its banks and climbed the cliff. I wanted some height, and I wanted to see the woods.

The woods were as restless as birds.

I stood under tulips and ashes, maples, sourwood, sassafras, locusts, catalpas, and oaks. I let my eyes spread and unfix, screening out all that was not vertical motion, and I saw only leaves in the air—or rather, since my mind was also unfixed, vertical trails of yellow color-patches falling from nowhere to nowhere. Mysterious streamers of color unrolled silently all about me, distant and near. Some color chips made the descent violently; they wrenched from side to side in a series of diminishing swings, as if willfully fighting the fall with all the tricks of keel and glide they could muster. Others spun straight down in tight, suicidal circles.

Tulips had cast their leaves on my path, flat and bright as doubloons. I passed under a sugar maple that stunned me by its elegant unself-consciousness: it was as if a man on fire were to continue calmly sipping tea.

In the deepest part of the woods was a stand of ferns. I had just been reading in Donald Culross Peattie that the so-called "seed" of ferns was formerly thought to bestow the gift of invisibility on its bearer, and that Genghis Khan wore such a seed in his ring, "and by it understood the speech of birds." If I were invisible, might I also be small, so that I could be borne by winds, spreading my body like a sail, like a vaulted leaf, to anyplace at all? Mushrooms erupted through the forest mold, the fly amanita in various stages of thrust and spread, some big brown mushrooms rounded and smooth as loaves, and some eerie purple ones I'd never noticed before, the color of Portuguese men-of-war, murex, a deep-sea, pressurized color, as if the earth heavy with trees and rocks had pressed and leached all other hues away.

A squirrel suddenly appeared, and, eying me over his shoulder, began eating a mushroom. Squirrels and box turtles are immune to the poison in mushrooms, so it is not safe to eat a mushroom on the grounds that squirrels eat it. This squirrel plucked the nibbled mushroom cap from its base and, holding it Ubangi-like in his mouth, raced up the trunk of an oak. Then I moved, and he went into his tail-furling threat. I can't imagine what predator this routine would frighten, or even slow. Or did he take me for another male squirrel? It was clear that, like a cat, he seemed always to present a large front. But he might have fooled me better by holding still and not letting me see what insubstantial stuff his tail was. He flattened his body against the tree trunk and stretched himself into the shape of a giant rectangle. By some trick his legs barely protuded at the corners, like a flying squirrel's. Then he made a wave run down his tail held low against the trunk, the same flicking wave, over and over, and he never took his eyes from mine. Next, frightened more—or emboldened?—he ran up to a limb, still mouthing his mushroom cap, and, crouching close to the trunk, presented a solid target, coiled. He bent his tail high and whipped it furiously, with repeated snaps, as if a piece of gluey tape were stuck to the tip.

When I left the squirrel to cache his mushroom in peace, I almost stepped on another squirrel, who was biting the base of his tail, his flank, and scratching his shoulder with a hind paw. A chipmunk was streaking around with the usual calamitous air. When he saw me he stood to investigate, tucking his front legs tightly against his breast, so that only his paws were visible, and he looked like a supplicant modestly holding his hat.

The woods were a rustle of affairs. Woolly bears, those orange-and-black-banded furry caterpillars of the Isabella moth, were on the move. They crossed my path in every direction; they would climb over my foot, my finger, urgently seeking shelter. If a skunk finds one, he rolls it over and over on the ground, very delicately, brushing off the long hairs before he eats it. There seemed to be a parade of walking sticks that day, too; I must have seen five or six of them, or the same one five or six times, which kept hitching a ride on my pants leg. One entomologist says that walking sticks, along with monarch butterflies, are able to feign death—although I don't know how you could determine if a walking stick was feigning death or twigginess. At any rate, the female walking stick is absolutely casual about her egg-laying, dribbling out her eggs "from wherever she happens to be, and they drop willy-nilly"—which I suppose might mean that my pants and I were suddenly in the walking-stick business.

I heard a clamor in the underbrush beside me, a rustle of an animal's approach. It sounded as though the animal was about the size of a bobcat, a small bear, or a large snake. The commotion stopped and started, coming ever nearer. The agent of all this ruckus proved to be, of course, a towhee.

The more I see of these bright birds—with black backs, white tail bars, and rufous patches on either side of their white breasts—the more I like them. They are not even faintly shy. They are everywhere, in treetops and on the ground. Their song reminds me of a child's neighborhood rallying cry—ee-ockee—with a heartfelt warble at the end. But it is their call that is especially endearing. The towhee has the brass and grace to call, simply and clearly, "tweet." I know of no other bird that stoops to literal tweeting.

The towhee never saw me. It crossed the path and kicked its way back into the woods, cutting a wide swath in the leaf litter like a bulldozer, and splashing the air with clods.

The bark of trees was cool to my palm. I saw a hairy wood-pecker beating his skull on a pine, and a katydid dying on a stone.

I could go. I could simply angle off the path, take one step after another, and be on my way. I could walk to Point Bar-

row, Mount McKinley, Hudson's Bay. My summer jacket is
put away; my winter jacket is warm.

In autumn the winding passage of ravens from the north
heralds the great fall migration of caribou. The shaggy-necked
birds spread their wing tips to the skin of convection currents
rising, and hie them south. The great deer meet herd on herd
in arctic and subarctic valleys, milling and massing and gathering force like a waterfall, till they pour across the barren
grounds wide as a tidal wave. Their coats are new and fine.
Their thin spring coats—which had been scraped off in great
hunks by the southern forests and were riddled with blackfly
and gadfly stings, warble and botfly maggots—are gone, and
a lustrous new pelage has appeared, a luxurious brown fur
backed by a plush layer of hollow hairs that insulate and waterproof. Four inches of creamy fat cover even their backs. A
loose cartilage in their fetlocks makes their huge strides click,
mile upon mile over the tundra south to the shelter of trees,
and you can hear them before they've come and after they've
gone, rumbling like rivers, ticking like clocks.

The Eskimos' major caribou hunt is in the fall, when the
deer are fat and their hides thick. If some whim or weather
shifts the northern caribou into another valley, some hidden,
unexpected valley, then even to this day some inland Eskimo
tribes may altogether starve.

Up on the Arctic Ocean coasts, Eskimos dry the late summer's fish on drying racks, to use throughout the winter as
feed for dogs. The newly forming sea ice is elastic and flexible.
It undulates without cracking as the roiling sea swells and
subsides, and it bends and sags under the Eskimos' weight as
they walk, spreading leviathan ripples out toward the horizon,
so that they seem to be walking and bouncing on the fragile
sheath of the world's balloon. During these autumn days Eskimo adults and children alike play at cat's cradle, a game they
have always known. The intricate string patterns looped from
their fingers were thought to "tangle the sun" and so "delay

its disappearance." Later when the sun sets for the winter, children will sled down any snowy slope, using as sleds frozen seal embryos pulled with thongs through the nose.

These northings drew me, present northings, past northings, the thought of northings. In the literature of arctic exploration, the talk is of northing. An explorer might scrawl in his tattered journal, "Latitude 82° 15′ N. We accomplished 20 miles of northing today, in spite of the shifting pack." Shall I go northing? My legs are long.

A skin-colored sandstone ledge beside me was stained with pokeberry juice, like an altar bloodied. The edges of the scarlet were dissolved, faded to lymph like small blood from a wound. As I looked, a maple leaf suddenly screeched across the rock, arched crabwise on its points, and a yellow-spotted dog appeared from noplace, bearing in its jaws the leg of a deer. The hooves of the deer leg were pointed like a dancer's toes. I have felt dead deer legs before; some local butchers keep them as weapons. They are greaseless and dry; I can feel the little bones. The dog was coming towards me on the path. I spoke to him and stepped aside; he loped past, looking neither to the right or the left.

In a final, higher part of the woods, some of the trees were black and gray, leafless, but wrapped in fresh green vines. The path was a fairway of new gold leaves strewn at the edges with bright vines and dotted with dark green seedlings pushing up through the leaf cover. One seedling spruce grew from a horse's hoofmark deep in dried mud.

There was a little hollow in the woods, broad, like a flat soup-bowl, with grass on the ground. This was the forest pasture of the white mare Itch. Water had collected in a small pool five feet across, in which gold leaves floated, and the water reflected the half-forgotten, cloud-whipped sky. To the right was a stand of slender silver-barked tulip saplings with tall limbless trunks leaning together, leafless. In the general litter and scramble of these woods, the small grazed hollow looked very old, like the site of druidical rites, or like a theatrical set, with the pool at center stage, and the stand of silver saplings the audience in thrall. There at the pool lovers would meet in various guises, and there Bottom in his ass's head would bleat at the reflection of the moon.

I started home. And one more event occurred that day, one more confrontation with restless life bearing past me.

I approached a long, slanting mown field near the house. A flock of forty robins had commandeered the area, and I watched them from a fringe of trees. I see robins in flocks only in the fall. They were spaced evenly on the grass, ten yards apart. They looked like a marching band with each member in place, but facing in every direction. Distributed among them were the fledglings from summer's last brood, young robins still mottled on the breast, embarking on their first trip to unknown southern fields. At any given moment as I watched, half of the robins were on the move, sloping forward in a streamlined series of hops.

I stepped into the field, and they all halted. They stopped short, drew up, and looked at me, every one. I stopped too, suddenly as self-conscious as if I were before a firing squad. What are you going to do? I looked over the field, at all those cocked heads and black eyes. I'm staying here. You all go on. I'm staying here.

A kind of northing is what I wish to accomplish, a single-minded trek toward that place where any shutter left open to the zenith at night will record the wheeling of all the sky's stars as a pattern of perfect, concentric circles. I seek a reduction, a shedding, a sloughing off.

At the seashore you often see a shell, or fragment of a shell, that sharp sands and surf have thinned to a wisp. There is no way you can tell what kind of shell it had been, what creature it had housed; it could have been a whelk or a scallop, a cowrie, limpet, or conch. The animal is long since dissolved, and its blood spread and thinned in the general sea. All you hold in your hand is a cool shred of shell, an inch long, pared so thin it passes a faint pink light, and almost as flexible as a straight razor. It is an essence, a smooth condensation of the air, a curve. I long for the North where unimpeded winds would hone me to such a pure slip of bone. But I'll not go northing this year. I'll stalk that floating pole and frigid air by waiting here. I wait on bridges; I wait, struck, on forest paths and meadow's fringes, hilltops and banksides, day in and day out, and I receive a southing as a gift. The North washes down the mountains like a waterfall, like a tidal wave, and pours across the valley; it comes to me. It sweetens the persimmons and numbs the last of the crickets and hornets; it fans the flames of the forest maples, bows the meadow's seeded grasses, and pokes its chilling fingers under the leaf litter, thrusting the springtails and earthworms, the sowbugs and beetle grubs deeper into the earth. The sun heaves to the south by day, and at night wild Orion emerges looming like the Specter of the Brocken over Dead Man Mountain. Something is already here, and more is coming.

II

A few days later the monarchs hit. I saw one, and then another, and then others all day long, before I consciously understood that I was witnessing a migration, and it wasn't until another two weeks had passed that I realized the enormity of what I had seen.

Each of these butterflies, the fruit of two or three broods of this summer, had hatched successfully from one of those emerald cases that Teale's caterpillar had been about to form when the parasitic larvae snapped it limp, eating their way out of its side. They had hatched, many of them, just before a thunderstorm, when winds lifted the silver leaves of trees and birds sought the shelter of shrubbery, uttering cries. They were butterflies, going south to the Gulf states or farther, and some of them had come from Hudson's Bay.

Monarchs were everywhere. They skittered and bobbed, rested in the air, lolled on the dust—but with none of their usual insouciance. They had but one unwearying thought: South. I watched from my study window: three, four . . . eighteen, nineteen, one every few seconds, and some in tandem. They came fanning straight towards my window from the northwest, and from the northeast, materializing from behind the tips of high hemlocks, where Polaris hangs by night. They appeared as Indian horsemen appear in movies: first dotted, then massed, silent, at the rim of a hill.

Each monarch butterfly had a brittle black body and deep orange wings limned and looped in black bands. A monarch at rest looks like a fleck of tiger, stilled and wide-eyed. A monarch in flight looks like an autumn leaf with a will, vitalized and cast upon the air from which it seems to suck some thin sugar of energy, some leaf-like or sap. As each one climbed up the air outside my window, I could see the more delicate, ventral surfaces of its wings, and I had a sense of bunched legs and straining thorax, but I could never focus well into the flapping and jerking before it vaulted up past the window and out of sight over my head.

I walked out and saw a monarch do a wonderful thing: it climbed a hill without twitching a muscle. I was standing at the bridge over Tinker Creek, at the southern foot of a very steep hill. The monarch beat its way beside me over the bridge at eye level, and then, flailing its wings exhaustedly, ascended straight up in the air. It rose vertically to the enormous height of a bankside sycamore's crown. Then, fixing its wings at a precise angle, it glided *up* the steep road, losing altitude extremely slowly, climbing by checking its fall, until it came to rest at a puddle in front of the house at the top of the hill.

I followed. It panted, skirmished briefly westward, and then, returning to the puddle, began its assault on the house. It struggled almost straight up the air next to the two-story brick wall, and then scaled the roof. Wasting no effort, it followed the roof's own slope, from a distance of two inches. Puff, and it was out of sight. I wondered how many more hills and houses it would have to climb before it could rest. From the force of its will it would seem it could flutter through walls.

Monarchs are "tough and powerful, as butterflies go." They fly over Lake Superior without resting; in fact, observers there have discovered a curious thing. Instead of flying directly south, the monarchs crossing high over the water take an inexplicable turn towards the east. Then when they reach an invisible point, they all veer south again. Each successive swarm repeats this mysterious dogleg movement, year after year. Entomologists actually think that the butterflies might be "remembering" the position of a long-gone, looming glacier. In another book I read that geologists think that Lake Superior marks the site of the highest mountain that ever existed on this continent. I don't know. I'd like to see it. Or I'd like to be it, to feel when to turn. At night on land migrating monarchs slumber on certain trees, hung in festoons with wings folded together, thick on the trees and shaggy as bearskin.

Monarchs have always been assumed to taste terribly bitter, because of the acrid milkweed on which the caterpillars feed. You always run into monarchs and viceroys when you read about mimicry: viceroys look enough like monarchs that keen-eyed birds who have tasted monarchs once will avoid the viceroys as well. New studies indicate that milkweed-fed monarchs are not so much evil-tasting as literally nauseating, since milkweed contains "heart poisons similar to digitalis" that make the bird ill. Personally, I like an experiment performed by an entomologist with real spirit. He had heard all his life, as I have, that monarchs taste unforgettably bitter, so he tried some. "To conduct what was in fact a field experiment the doctor first went South, and he ate a number of monarchs in the field. . . . The monarch butterfly, Dr. Urquhart learned, has no more flavor than dried toast." Dried toast? It was hard for me, throughout the monarch migration, in the middle of all that beauty and real splendor, to fight down the thought that what I was really seeing in the air was a vast and fluttering tea tray for shut-ins.

It is easy to coax a dying or exhausted butterfly onto your finger. I saw a monarch walking across a gas station lot; it was walking south. I placed my index finger in its path, and it clambered aboard and let me lift it to my face. Its wings were faded but unmarked by hazard; a veneer of velvet caught the light and hinted at the frailest depth of lapped scales. It was a male; his legs clutching my finger were short and atrophied; they clasped my finger with a spread fragility, a fineness as of some low note of emotion or pure strain of spirit, scarcely perceived. And I knew that those feet were actually tasting me, sipping with sensitive organs the vapor of my finger's skin: butterflies taste with their feet. All the time he held me, he opened and closed his glorious wings, senselessly, as if sighing.

The closing of his wings fanned an almost imperceptible redolence at my face, and I leaned closer. I could barely scent a sweetness, I could almost name it . . . fireflies, sparklers— honeysuckle. He smelled like honeysuckle; I couldn't believe it. I knew that many male butterflies exuded distinctive odors from special scent glands, but I thought that only laboratory instruments could detect those odors compounded of many, many butterflies. I had read a list of the improbable scents of butterflies: sandalwood, chocolate, heliotrope, sweet pea. Now this live creature here on my finger had an odor that even I could sense—this flap actually smelled, this chip that took its temperature from the air like any envelope or hammer, this programmed wisp of spread horn. And he smelled of honeysuckle. Why not caribou hoof or Labrador tea, tundra lichen or dwarf willow, the brine of Hudson's Bay or the vapor of rivers milky with fine-ground glacial silt? This honeysuckle was an odor already only half-remembered, a breath of the summer past, the Lucas cliffs and overgrown fence by

Tinker Creek, a drugged sweetness that had almost cloyed on those moisture-laden nights, now refined to a wary trickle in the air, a distillation pure and rare, scarcely known and mostly lost, and heading south.

I walked him across the gas station lot and lowered him into a field. He took to the air, pulsing and gliding; he lighted on sassafras, and I lost him.

For weeks I found paired monarch wings, bodiless, on the grass or on the road. I collected one such wing and freed it of its scales; first I rubbed it between my fingers, and then I stroked it gently with the tip of an infant's silver spoon. What I had at the end of this delicate labor is lying here on this study desk: a kind of resilient scaffolding, like the webbing over a hot-air balloon, black veins stretching the merest something across the nothingness it plies. The integument itself is perfectly transparent; through it I can read the smallest print. It is as thin as the skin peeled from sunburn, and as tough as a parchment of flensed buffalo hide. The butterflies that were eaten here in the valley, leaving us their wings, were, however, few: most lived to follow the valley south.

The migration lasted in full force for five days. For those five days I was inundated, drained. The air was alive and unwinding. Time itself was a scroll unraveled, curved and still quivering on a table or altar stone. The monarchs clattered in the air, burnished like throngs of pennies, here's one, and here's one, and more, and more. They flapped and floundered; they thrust, splitting the air like the keels of canoes, quickened and fleet. It looked as though the leaves of the autumn forest had taken flight, and were pouring down the valley like a waterfall, like a tidal wave, all the leaves of hardwoods from here to Hudson's Bay. It was as if the season's color were draining away like lifeblood, as if the year were molting and shedding. The year was rolling down, and a vital curve had been reached, the tilt that gives way to headlong rush. And when the monarchs had passed and were gone, the skies were vacant, the air poised. The dark night into which

the year was plunging was not a sleep but an awakening, a new
and necessary austerity, the sparer climate for which I longed.
The shed trees were brittle and still, the creek light and cold,
and my spirit holding its breath.

III

Before the aurora borealis appears, the sensitive needles of
compasses all over the world are restless for hours, agitating
on their pins in airplanes and ships, trembling in desk drawers,
in attics, in boxes on shelves.

I had a curious dream last night that stirred me. I visited the
house of my childhood, and the basement there was covered
with a fine sifting of snow. I lifted a snow-covered rug and
found underneath it a bound sheaf of ink drawings I had made
when I was six. Next to the basement, but unattached to it,
extended a prayer tunnel.

The prayer tunnel was a tunnel fully enclosed by solid snow.
It was cylindrical, and its diameter was the height of a man.
Only an Eskimo, and then only very rarely, could survive in
the prayer tunnel. There was, however, no exit or entrance;
but I nevertheless understood that if I—if almost anyone—
volunteered to enter it, death would follow after a long and
bitter struggle. Inside the tunnel it was killingly cold, and a
hollow wind like broadswords never ceased to blow. But there
was little breatheable air, and that soon gone. It was utterly
without light, and from all eternity it snowed the same fine,
unmelting, wind-hurled snow.

I have been reading the apophthegmata, the sayings of
fourth- and fifth-century Egyptian desert hermits. Abba Moses
said to a disciple, "Go and sit in your cell, and your cell will
teach you everything."

A few weeks before the monarch migration I visited Carvin's Cove, a reservoir in a gap between Tinker and Brushy
mountains, and there beside the forest path I saw, it occurs to

me now, Abba Moses, in the form of an acorn. The acorn was screwing itself into the soil. From a raw split in its husk burst a long white root that plunged like an arrow into the earth. The acorn itself was loose, but the root was fixed: I thought if I could lift the acorn and stand, I would heave the world. Beside the root erupted a greening shoot, and from the shoot spread two furred, serrated leaves, tiny leaves of chestnut oak, the size of two intricate grains of rice. That acorn was pressured, blown, driven down with force and up with furl, making at once a power dive to grit and *grand jeté en l'air.*

Since then the killing frost has struck. If I got lost now on the mountains or in the valley, and acted foolishly, I would be dead of hypothermia and my brain wiped smooth as a plate long before the water in my flesh elongated to crystal slivers that would pierce and shatter the walls of my cells. The harvest is in, the granaries full. The broadleaf trees of the world's forests have cast their various fruits: "Oak, a nut; Sycamore, achenes; California Laurel, a drupe; Maple, a samara; Locust, a legume; Pomegranate, a berry; Buckeye, a capsule; Apple, a pome." Now the twin leaves of the seedling chestnut oak on the Carvin's Cove path have dried, dropped, and blown; the acorn itself is shrunk and sere. But the sheath of the stem holds water and the white root still delicately sucks, porous and permeable, mute. The death of the self of which the great writers speak is no violent act. It is merely the joining of the great rock heart of the earth in its roll. It is merely the slow cessation of the will's sprints and the intellect's chatter: it is waiting like a hollow bell with stilled tongue. *Fuge, tace, quiesce.* The waiting itself is the thing.

Last year I saw three migrating Canada geese flying low over the frozen duck pond where I stood. I heard a heart-stopping blast of speed before I saw them; I felt the flayed air slap at my face. They thundered across the pond, and back, and back again: I swear I have never seen such speed, such single-mindedness, such flailing of wings. They froze the duck pond as they flew; they rang the air; they disappeared. I think of this now, and my brain vibrates to the blurred bastinado of feathered bone. "Our God shall come," it says in a psalm for Advent, "and shall not keep silence; there shall go before him a consuming fire, and a mighty tempest shall be stirred up round about him." It is the shock I remember. Not only does something come if you wait, but it pours over you like a waterfall, like a tidal wave. You wait in all naturalness without expectation or hope, emptied, translucent, and that which comes rocks and topples you; it will shear, loose, launch, winnow, grind.

I have glutted on richness and welcome hyssop. This distant silver November sky, these sere branches of trees, shed and bearing their pure and secret colors—this is the real world, not the world gilded and pearled. I stand under wiped skies directly, naked, without intercessors. Frost winds have lofted my body's bones with all their restless sprints to an airborne raven's glide. I am buoyed by a calm and effortless longing, an angled pitch of the will, like the set of the wings of the monarch which climbed a hill by falling still.

There is the wave breast of thanksgiving—a catching God's eye with the easy motions of praise—and a time for it. In ancient Israel's rites for a voluntary offering of thanksgiving, the priest comes before the altar in clean linen, empty-handed. Into his hands is placed the breast of the slain unblemished ram of consecration: and he waves it as a wave offering before the Lord. The wind's knife has done its work. Thanks be to God.

CHAPTER 15

The Waters of Separation

They will question thee concerning what they should expend.
Say: "The abundance."   —THE KORAN

"FAIR WEATHER cometh out of the north: with God is terrible majesty."

Today is the winter solstice. The planet tilts just so to its star, lists and holds circling in a fixed tension between veering and longing, and spins helpless, exalted, in and out of that fleet blazing touch. Last night Orion vaulted and spread all over the sky, pagan and lunatic, his shoulder and knee on fire, his sword three suns at the ready—for what?

And today was fair, hot, even; I woke and my fingers were hot and dry to their own touch, like the skin of a stranger. I stood at the window, the bay window on which one summer a waxen-looking grasshopper had breathed puff puff, and thought, I won't see this year again, not again so innocent; and longing wrapped round my throat like a scarf. "For the Heavenly Father desires that we should see," said Ruysbroeck, "and that is why He is ever saying to our inmost spirit one deep unfathomable word and nothing else." But what is that word? Is this mystery or coyness? A cast-iron bell hung from the arch of my rib cage; when I stirred it rang, or it tolled, a

long syllable pulsing ripples up my lungs and down the gritty
sap inside my bones, and I couldn't make it out; I felt the
voiced vowel like a sigh or a note but I couldn't catch the
consonant that shaped it into sense. I wrenched myself from
the window. I stepped outside.

Here by the mock-orange hedge was a bee, a honeybee,
sprung from its hive by the heat. Instantly I had a wonderful
idea. I had recently read that ancient Romans thought that
bees were killed by echoes. It seemed a far-fetched and pleasing notion, that a spoken word or falling rock given back by
cliffs—that airy nothing which nevertheless bore and spread
the uncomprehended impact of something—should stun these
sturdy creatures right out of the air. I could put it to the test.
It was as good an excuse for a walk as any; it might still the
bell, even, or temper it true.

I knew where I could find an echo; I'd have to take my
chances on finding another December bee. I tied a sweater
around my waist and headed for the quarry. The experiment
didn't pan out, exactly, but the trip led on to other excursions
and vigils up and down the landscape of this brief year's end
day.

It was hot; I never needed the sweater. A great tall cloud
moved elegantly across an invisible walkway in the upper air,
sliding on its flat foot like an enormous proud snail. I smelled
silt on the wind, turkey, laundry, leaves . . . my God what a
world. There is no accounting for one second of it. On the
quarry path through the woods I saw again the discarded
aquarium; now, almost a year later, still only one side of the
aquarium's glass was shattered. I could plant a terrarium here,
I thought; I could transfer the two square feet of forest floor
under the glass to *above* the glass, framing it, hiding a penny,
and saying to passers-by look! look! here is two square feet of
the world.

I waited for an hour at the quarry, roving, my eyes filtering
the air for flecks, until at last I discovered a bee. It was wander-

ing listlessly among dried weeds on the stony bank where I
had sat months ago and watched a mosquito pierce and suck
a copperhead on a rock; beyond the bank, fingers of ice
touched the green quarry pond in the shade of the sheared
bare cliffs beyond. The setup was perfect. Hello! I tried tenta-
tively: Hello! faltered the cliffs under the forest; and did the
root tips quiver in the rock? But that is no way to kill a
creature, saying hello. Goodbye! I shouted; Goodbye! came
back, and the bee drifted unconcerned among the weeds.

It could be, I reasoned, that ancient Roman naturalists knew
this fact that has escaped us because it works only in Latin. My
Latin is sketchy. *Habeas corpus!* I cried; *Deus absconditus! Veni!*
And the rock cliff batted it back: *Veni!* and the bee droned on.

That was that. It was almost noon; the tall cloud was gone.
To West Virginia, where it snubbed on a high ridge, snared
by trees, and sifted in shards over the side? I watched the bee
as long as I could, catching it with my eyes and losing it, until
it rose suddenly in the air like a lost balloon and vanished into
the forest. I stood alone. I still seemed to hear the unaccus-
tomed sound of my own voice honed to a quaver by rock,
thrown back down my throat and cast dying around me, lorn:
could that have been heard at Hollins Pond, or behind me,
across the creek, up the hill the starlings fly over? Was anybody there to hear? I felt again the bell resounding faint under
my ribs. I'm coming, when I can. I quit the quarry, my spurt
of exuberance drained, my spirit edgy and taut.

The quarry path parallels Tinker Creek far upstream from
my house, and when the woods broke into clearing and pasture, I followed the creek banks down. When I drew near the
tear-shaped island, which I had never before approached from
this side of the creek, a fence barred my way, a feeble wire
horse fence that wobbled across the creek and served me as
a sagging bridge to the island. I stood, panting, breathing the
frail scent of fresh water and feeling the sun heat my hair.

The December grass on the island was blanched and sere,

pale against the dusty boles of sycamores, noisy underfoot. Behind me, the way I had come, rose the pasture belonging to twilight, a horse of a perpetually different color whose name was originally Midnight, and who one spring startled the neighborhood by becoming brown. Far before me Tinker Mountain glinted and pitched in the sunlight. The Lucas orchard spanned the middle distance, its wan peach limbs swept and poised just so, row upon row, like a stageful of thin innocent dancers who will never be asked to perform; below the orchard rolled the steers' pasture yielding to flood plain fields and finally the sycamore log bridge to the island where in horror I had watched a green frog sucked to a skin and sunk. A fugitive, empty sky vaulted overhead, apparently receding from me the harder I searched its dome for a measure of distance.

Downstream at the island's tip where the giant water bug clasped and ate the living frog, I sat and sucked at my own dry knuckles. It was the way that frog's eyes crumpled. His mouth was a gash of terror; the shining skin of his breast and shoulder shivered once and sagged, reduced to an empty purse; but oh those two snuffed eyes! They crinkled, the comprehension poured out of them as if sense and life had been a mere incidental addition to the idea of eyes, a filling like any jam in a jar that is soon and easily emptied; they flattened, lightless, opaque, and sank. Did the giant water bug have the frog by the back parts, or by the hollow of the thigh? Would I eat a frog's leg if offered? Yes.

In addition to the wave breast of thanksgiving, in which the wave breast is waved before the Lord, there is another voluntary offering performed at the same time. In addition to the wave breast of thanksgiving, there is the heave shoulder. The wave breast is waved before the altar of the Lord; the heave shoulder is heaved. What I want to know is this: Does the priest heave it *at* the Lord? Does he *throw* the shoulder of the ram of consecration—a ram that, before the priest slayed and chunked it, had been perfect and whole, not "Blind, or broken, or maimed, or having a wen, or scurvy, or scabbed . . . bruised, or crushed, or broken, or cut"—does he hurl it across the tabernacle, between the bloodied horns of the altar, at God? Now look what you made me do. And then he eats it. This heave is a violent, desperate way of catching God's eye. It is not inappropriate. We are people; we are permitted to have dealings with the creator and we must speak up for the creation. God *look* at what you've done to this creature, look at the sorrow, the cruelty, the long damned waste! Can it possibly, ludicrously be for *this* that on this unconscious planet with my innocent kind I play softball all spring, to develop my throwing arm? How high, how far, could I heave a little shred of frog shoulder at the Lord? How high, how far, how long until I die?

I fingered the winterkilled grass, looping it round the tip of my finger like hair, ruffling its tips with my palms. Another year has twined away, unrolled and dropped across nowhere like a flung banner painted in gibberish. "The last act is bloody, however brave be all the rest of the play; at the end they throw a little earth upon your head, and it's all over forever." Somewhere, everywhere, there is a gap, like the shuddering chasm of Shadow Creek which gapes open at my feet, like a sudden split in the window or hull of a high-altitude jet, into which things slip, or are blown, out of sight, vanished in a rush, blasted, gone, and can no more be found. For the living there is rending loss at each opening of the eye, each *augenblick,* as a muskrat dives, a heron takes alarm, a leaf floats spinning away. There is death in the pot for the living's food, fly-blown meat, muddy salt, and plucked herbs bitter as squill. If you can get it. How many people have prayed for their daily bread and famished? They die their daily death as utterly as did the frog, *people,* played with, dabbled upon, when God knows they loved their life. In a winter famine, desperate Algonquian Indians "ate broth made of smoke, snow, and buckskin, and the rash of pellagra appeared like tattooed flowers on their emaciated bodies—the roses of starvation, in a French physician's description; and those who starved died covered with roses." Is this beauty, these gratuitous roses, or a mere display of force?

Or is beauty itself an intricately fashioned lure, the cruelest hoax of all? There is a certain fragment of an ancient and involved Eskimo tale I read in Farley Mowat that for years has risen, unbidden, in my mind. The fragment is a short scenario, observing all the classical unities, simple and cruel, and performed by the light of a soapstone seal-oil lamp.

A young man in a strange land falls in love with a young woman and takes her to wife in her mother's tent. By day the women chew skins and boil meat while the young man hunts. But the old crone is jealous; she wants the boy. Calling her daughter to her one day, she offers to braid her hair; the girl sits pleased, proud, and soon is strangled by her own hair. One thing Eskimos know is skinning. The mother takes her curved hand knife shaped like a dancing skirt, skins her daughter's beautiful face, and presses that empty flap smooth on her own skull. When the boy returns that night he lies with her, in the tent on top of the world. But he is wet from hunting; the skin mask shrinks and slides, uncovering the shriveled face of the old mother, and the boy flees in horror, forever.

Could it be that if I climbed the dome of heaven and scrabbled and clutched at the beautiful cloth till I loaded my fists with a wrinkle to pull, that the mask would rip away to reveal a toothless old ugly, eyes glazed with delight?

A wind rose, quickening; it seemed at the same instant to invade my nostrils and vibrate my gut. I stirred and lifted my head. No, I've gone through this a million times, beauty is not a hoax—how many days have I learned not to stare at the back of my hand when I could look out at the creek? Come on, I say to the creek, surprise me; and it does, with each new drop. Beauty is real. I would never deny it; the appalling thing is that I forget it. Waste and extravagance go together up and down the banks, all along the intricate fringe of spirit's free incursions into time. On either side of me the creek snared and kept the sky's distant lights, shaped them into shifting substance and bore them speckled down.

This Tinker Creek! It was low today, and clear. On the still side of the island the water held pellucid as a pane, a gloss on runes of sandstone, shale, and snail-inscribed clay silt; on the faster side it hosted a blinding profusion of curved and pitched surfaces, flecks of shadow and tatters of sky. These are the waters of beauty and mystery, issuing from a gap in the granite world; they fill the lodes in my cells with a light like petaled water, and they churn in my lungs mighty and frigid, like a big ship's screw. And these are also the waters of separation: they purify, acrid and laving, and they cut me off. I am spattered with a sop of ashes, burnt bone knobs, and blood; I range wild-eyed, flying over fields and plundering the woods, no longer quite fit for company.

Bear with me one last time. In the old Hebrew ordinance for the waters of separation, the priest must find a red heifer, a red heifer unblemished, which has never known the yoke, and lead her outside the people's camp, and sacrifice her, burn her wholly, without looking away: "burn the heifer in his sight; her skin, and her flesh, and her blood, with her dung, shall he burn." Into the stinking flame the priest casts the wood of a cedar tree for longevity, hyssop for purgation, and a scarlet thread for a vein of living blood. It is from these innocent ashes that the waters of separation are made, anew each time, by steeping them in a vessel with fresh running water. This special water purifies. A man—any man—dips a sprig of hyssop into the vessel and sprinkles—merely sprinkles!—the water upon the unclean, "upon him that touched a bone, or one slain, or one dead." So. But I never signed up for this role. The bone touched me.

I stood, alone, and the world swayed. I am a fugitive and a vagabond, a sojourner seeking signs. Isak Dinesen in Kenya, her heart utterly broken by loss, stepped out of the house at sunrise, seeking a sign. She saw a rooster lunge and rip a chameleon's tongue from its root in the throat and gobble it down. And then Isak Dinesen had to pick up a stone and smash the chameleon. But I had seen that sign, more times than I had ever sought it; today I saw an inspiriting thing, a pretty thing, really, and small.

I was standing lost, sunk, my hands in my pockets, gazing toward Tinker Mountain and feeling the earth reel down. All at once I saw what looked like a Martian spaceship whirling towards me in the air. It flashed borrowed light like a propeller. Its forward motion greatly outran its fall. As I watched, transfixed, it rose, just before it would have touched a thistle, and hovered pirouetting in one spot, then twirled on and finally came to rest. I found it in the grass; it was a maple key, a single winged seed from a pair. Hullo. I threw it into the wind and it flew off again, bristling with animate purpose, not like a thing dropped or windblown, pushed by the witless winds of convection currents hauling round the world's rondure where they must, but like a creature muscled and vigorous, or a creature spread thin to that other wind, the wind of the spirit which bloweth where it listeth, lighting, and raising up, and easing down. O maple key, I thought, I must confess I thought, o welcome, cheers.

And the bell under my ribs rang a true note, a flourish as of blended horns, clarion, sweet, and making a long dim sense I will try at length to explain. Flung is too harsh a word for the rush of the world. Blown is more like it, but blown by a generous, unending breath. That breath never ceases to kindle, exuberant, abandoned; frayed splinters spatter in every direction and burgeon into flame. And now when I sway to a fitful wind, alone and listing, I will think, maple key. When I see a photograph of earth from space, the planet so startlingly painterly and hung, I will think, maple key. When I shake your hand or meet your eyes I will think, two maple keys. If I am a maple key falling, at least I can twirl.

* * *

Thomas Merton wrote, "There is always a temptation to diddle around in the contemplative life, making itsy-bitsy statues." There is always an enormous temptation in all of life to diddle around making itsy-bitsy friends and meals and journeys for itsy-bitsy years on end. It is so self-conscious, so apparently moral, simply to step aside from the gaps where the creeks and winds pour down, saying, I never merited this grace, quite rightly, and then to sulk along the rest of your days on the edge of rage. I won't have it. The world is wilder than that in all directions, more dangerous and bitter, more extravagant and bright. We are making hay when we should be making whoopee; we are raising tomatoes when we should be raising Cain, or Lazarus.

Ezekiel excoriates false prophets as those who have "not gone up into the gaps." The gaps are the thing. The gaps are the spirit's one home, the altitudes and latitudes so dazzlingly spare and clean that the spirit can discover itself for the first time like a once-blind man unbound. The gaps are the clifts in the rock where you cower to see the back parts of God; they are the fissures between mountains and cells the wind lances through, the icy narrowing fiords splitting the cliffs of mystery. Go up into the gaps. If you can find them; they shift and vanish too. Stalk the gaps. Squeak into a gap in the soil, turn, and unlock—more than a maple—a universe. This is how you spend this afternoon, and tomorrow morning, and tomorrow afternoon. *Spend* the afternoon. You can't take it with you.

I live in tranquility and trembling. Sometimes I dream. I am interested in Alice mainly when she eats the cooky that makes her smaller. I would pare myself or be pared that I too might pass through the merest crack, a gap I know is there in the sky. I am looking just now for the cooky. Sometimes I open, pried like a fruit. Or I am porous as old bone, or translucent, a tinted condensation of the air like a watercolor wash, and I gaze around me in bewilderment, fancying I cast no shadow. Some-

times I ride a bucking faith while one hand grips and the other
flails the air, and like any daredevil I gouge with my heels for
blood, for a wilder ride, for more.

There is not a guarantee in the world. Oh your *needs* are
guaranteed, your needs are absolutely guaranteed by the most
stringent of warranties, in the plainest, truest words: knock;
seek; ask. But you must read the fine print. "Not as the world
giveth, give I unto you." That's the catch. If you can catch it
it will catch you up, aloft, up to any gap at all, and you'll come
back, for you will come back, transformed in a way you may
not have bargained for—dribbling and crazed. The waters of
separation, however lightly sprinkled, leave indelible stains.
Did you think, before you were caught, that you needed, say,
life? Do you think you will keep your life, or anything else you
love? But no. Your needs are all met. But not as the world
giveth. You see the needs of your own spirit met whenever
you have asked, and you have learned that the outrageous
guarantee holds. You see the creatures die, and you know you
will die. And one day it occurs to you that you must not need
life. Obviously. And then you're gone. You have finally understood that you're dealing with a maniac.

I think that the dying pray at the last not "please," but
"thank you," as a guest thanks his host at the door. Falling
from airplanes the people are crying thank you, thank you, all
down the air; and the cold carriages draw up for them on the
rocks. Divinity is not playful. The universe was not made in
jest but in solemn incomprehensible earnest. By a power that
is unfathomably secret, and holy, and fleet. There is nothing
to be done about it, but ignore it, or see. And then you walk
fearlessly, eating what you must, growing wherever you can,
like the monk on the road who knows precisely how vulnerable he is, who takes no comfort among death-forgetting men,
and who carries his vision of vastness and might around in his
tunic like a live coal which neither burns nor warms him, but
with which he will not part.

*   *   *

I used to have a cat, an old fighting tom, who sprang
through the open window by my bed and pummeled my chest,
barely sheathing his claws. I've been bloodied and mauled,
wrung, dazzled, drawn. I taste salt on my lips in the early
morning; I surprise my eyes in the mirror and they are ashes,
or fiery sprouts, and I gape appalled, or full of breath. The
planet whirls alone and dreaming. Power broods, spins, and
lurches down. The planet and the power meet with a shock.
They fuse and tumble, lightning, ground fire; they part, mute,
submitting, and touch again with hiss and cry. The tree with
the lights in it buzzes into flame and the cast-rock mountains
ring.

Emerson saw it. "I dreamed that I floated at will in the great
Ether, and I saw this world floating also not far off, but dimin-
ished to the size of an apple. Then an angel took it in his hand
and brought it to me and said, 'This must thou eat.' And I ate
the world." All of it. All of it intricate, speckled, gnawed,
fringed, and free. Israel's priests offered the wave breast and
the heave shoulder together, freely, in full knowledge, for
thanksgiving. They waved, they heaved, and neither gesture
was whole without the other, and both meant a wide-eyed and
keen-eyed thanks. Go your way, eat the fat, and drink the
sweet, said the bell. A sixteenth-century alchemist wrote of the
philosopher's stone, "One finds it in the open country, in the
village and in the town. It is in everything which God created.
Maids throw it on the street. Children play with it." The giant
water bug ate the world. And like Billy Bray I go my way, and
my left foot says "Glory," and my right foot says "Amen": in
and out of Shadow Creek, upstream and down, exultant, in a
daze, dancing, to the twin silver trumpets of praise.

AN AMERICAN
CHILDHOOD

for my parents
PAM LAMBERT DOAK
and
FRANK DOAK

A grant from the John
Simon Guggenheim Memorial Foundation
aided this work.

I have loved, O Lord, the beauty
of thy house and the place
where dwelleth thy glory.

Psalm 26

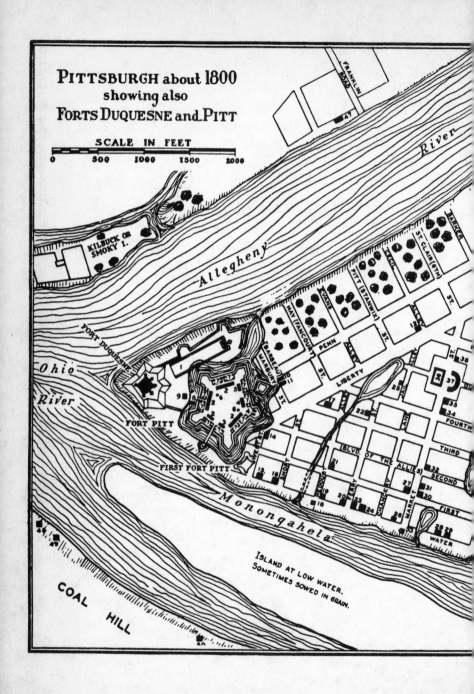

PITTSBURGH about 1800
showing also
FORTS DUQUESNE and PITT

SCALE IN FEET

0   500   1000   1500   2000

FRANKLIN ROAD

River

Allegheny

Kilbuck or
Smoky I.

Ohio
River

FORT DUQUESNE

FORT PITT

FIRST FORT PITT

Monongahela

ISLAND AT LOW WATER.
SOMETIMES SOWED IN GRAIN.

COAL HILL

St. CLAIR (9TH)

PITT (STANWIX)

WAY (FANCOURT)

PENN

LIBERTY

(BLVD. OF THE ALLIES)

FOURTH

THIRD

SECOND

FIRST

WATER

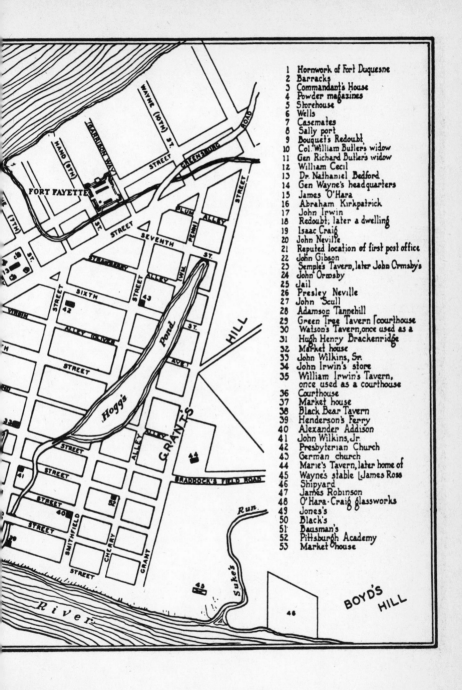

1 Hornwork of Fort Duquesne
2 Barracks
3 Commandant's House
4 Powder magazines
5 Storehouse
6 Wells
7 Casemates
8 Sally port
9 Bouquet's Redoubt
10 Col. William Butler's widow
11 Gen Richard Butler's widow
12 William Cecil
13 Dr. Nathaniel Bedford
14 Gen Wayne's headquarters
15 James O'Hara
16 Abraham Kirkpatrick
17 John Irwin
18 Redoubt; later a dwelling
19 Isaac Craig
20 John Neville
21 Reputed location of first post office
22 John Gibson
23 Semple's Tavern, later John Ormsby's
24 John Ormsby
25 Jail
26 Presley Neville
27 John Scull
28 Adamson Tannehill
29 Green Tree Tavern [courthouse
30 Watson's Tavern, once used as a
31 Hugh Henry Brackenridge
32 Market house
33 John Wilkins, Sr.
34 John Irwin's store
35 William Irwin's Tavern,
   once used as a courthouse
36 Courthouse
37 Market house
38 Black Bear Tavern
39 Henderson's Ferry
40 Alexander Addison
41 John Wilkins, Jr.
42 Presbyterian Church
43 German church
44 Marie's Tavern, later home of
45 Wayne's stable [James Ross
46 Shipyard
47 James Robinson
48 O'Hara-Craig glassworks
49 Jones's
50 Black's
51 Bausman's
52 Pittsburgh Academy
53 Market house

Prologue

WHEN EVERYTHING ELSE HAS GONE from my brain—the President's name, the state capitals, the neighborhoods where I lived, and then my own name and what it was on earth I sought, and then at length the faces of my friends, and finally the faces of my family—when all this has dissolved, what will be left, I believe, is topology: the dreaming memory of land as it lay this way and that.

I will see the city poured rolling down the mountain valleys like slag, and see the city lights sprinkled and curved around the hills' curves, rows of bonfires winding. At sunset a red light like housefires shines from the narrow hillside windows; the houses' bricks burn like glowing coals.

The three wide rivers divide and cool the mountains. Calm old bridges span the banks and link the hills. The Allegheny River flows in brawling from the north, from near the shore of Lake Erie, and from Lake Chautauqua in New York and eastward. The Monongahela River flows in shallow and slow from the south, from West Virginia. The Allegheny and the Monongahela meet and form the westward-wending Ohio.

Where the two rivers join lies an acute point of flat land from which rises the city. The tall buildings rise lighted to their tips. Their lights illumine other buildings' clean sides, and illumine the narrow city canyons below, where people move, and shine reflected red and white at night from the black waters.

When the shining city, too, fades, I will see only those forested mountains and hills, and the way the rivers lie flat and moving among them, and the way the low land lies wooded among them, and the blunt mountains rise in darkness from the rivers' banks, steep from the rugged south and rolling from the north, and from farther, from the inclined eastward plateau where the high ridges begin to run so long north and south unbroken that to get around them you practically have to navigate Cape Horn.

In those first days, people said, a squirrel could run the long length of Pennsylvania without ever touching the ground. In those first days, the woods were white oak and chestnut, hickory, maple, sycamore, walnut, wild ash, wild plum, and white pine. The pine grew on the ridgetops where the mountains' lumpy spines stuck up and their skin was thinnest.

The wilderness was uncanny, unknown. Benjamin Franklin had already invented his stove in Philadelphia by 1753, and Thomas Jefferson was a schoolboy in Virginia; French soldiers had been living in forts along Lake Erie for two generations. But west of the Alleghenies in western Pennsylvania, there was not even a settlement, not even a cabin. No Indians lived there, or even near there.

Wild grapevines tangled the treetops and shut out the sun. Few songbirds lived in the deep woods. Bright Carolina parakeets—red, green, and yellow—nested in the dark forest. There were ravens then, too. Woodpeckers rattled the big trees' trunks, ruffed grouse whirred their tail feathers in the fall, and every long once in a while a nervous gang of empty-headed turkeys came hustling and kicking through the leaves—but no one heard any of this, no one at all.

In 1753, young George Washington surveyed for the English this point of land where rivers met. To see the forest-blurred lay of the land, he rode his horse to a ridgetop and climbed a tree. He judged it would make a good spot for a fort. And an English fort it became, and a depot for Indian traders to the Ohio country, and later a French fort and way station to New Orleans.

But it would be another ten years before any settlers lived there on that land where the rivers met, lived to draw in the flowery scent of June rhododendrons with every breath. It would be another ten years before, for the first time on earth, tall men and women lay exhausted in their cabins, sleeping in the sweetness, worn out from planting corn.

IN 1955, WHEN I WAS TEN, my father's reading went to his head.

My father's reading during that time, and for many years before and after, consisted for the most part of *Life on the Mississippi*. He was a young executive in the old family firm, American Standard; sometimes he traveled alone on business. Traveling, he checked into a hotel, found a bookstore, and chose for the night's reading, after what I fancy to have been long deliberation, yet another copy of *Life on the Mississippi*. He brought all these books home. There were dozens of copies of *Life on the Mississippi* on the living-room shelves. From time to time, I read one.

Down the Mississippi hazarded the cub riverboat pilot, down the Mississippi from St. Louis to New Orleans. His chief, the pilot Mr. Bixby, taught him how to lay the boat in her marks and dart between points; he learned to pick a way fastidiously inside a certain snag and outside a shifting shoal in the black dark; he learned to clamber down a memorized channel in his head. On tricky crossings the leadsmen sang out the soundings, so familiar I seemed to have heard them the length of my life: "Mark four! . . . Quarter-less-four! . . . Half three! . . . Mark three! . . . Quarter-less . . ." It was an old story.

When all this reading went to my father's head, he took action. From Pittsburgh he went down the river. Although no one else that our family knew kept a boat on the Allegheny River, our father did, and now he was going all the way with it. He quit the firm his great-grandfather had founded a hundred years earlier down the river at his family's seat in Louisville, Kentucky; he sold his own holdings in the firm. He was taking off for New Orleans.

New Orleans was the source of the music he loved: Dixieland jazz, O Dixieland. In New Orleans men would blow it in the air and beat it underfoot, the music that hustled and snapped, the music whose zip matched his when he was a man-about-town at home in Pittsburgh, working for the family firm; the music he tapped his foot to when he was a man-about-town in New York for a few years after college working for the family firm by day and by night hanging out at Jimmy Ryan's on Fifty-second Street with Zutty Singleton, the black drummer who befriended him, and the rest of the house band. A certain kind of Dixieland suited him best. They played it at Jimmy Ryan's, and Pee Wee Russell and Eddie Condon played it too—New Orleans Dixieland chilled a bit by its journey up the river, and smoothed by its sojourns in Chicago and New York.

Back in New Orleans where he was headed they would play the old stuff, the hot, rough stuff—bastardized for tourists maybe, but still the big and muddy source of it all. Back in New Orleans where he was headed the music would smell like the river itself, maybe, like a thicker, older version of the Allegheny River at Pittsburgh, where he heard the music beat in the roar of his boat's inboard motor; like a thicker, older version of the wide Ohio River at Louisville, Kentucky, where at his family's summer house he'd spent his boyhood summers mucking about in boats.

Getting ready for the trip one Saturday, he roamed around our big brick house snapping his fingers. He had put a record on: Sharkey Bonano, "Li'l Liza Jane." I was reading Robert Louis Stevenson on the sunporch: *Kidnapped.* I looked up from my book and saw him outside; he had wandered out to the lawn and was standing in the wind between the buckeye trees and looking up at what must have been a small patch of wild sky. Old Low-Pockets. He was six feet four, all lanky and leggy; he had thick brown hair and shaggy brows, and a mild and dreamy expression in his blue eyes.

When our mother met Frank Doak, he was twenty-seven: witty, boyish, bookish, unsnobbish, a good dancer. He had grown up an only child in Pittsburgh, attended Shady Side Academy, and Washington and Jefferson College in Pennsylvania, where he studied history. He was a lapsed Presbyterian and a believing Republican. "Books make the man," read the blue bookplate in all his books. "Frank Doak." The bookplate's woodcut showed a square-rigged ship under way in a steep following sea. Father had hung around jazz in New York, and halfheartedly played the drums; he had smoked marijuana, written poems, begun a novel, painted in oils, imagined a career as a riverboat pilot, and acted for more than ten seasons in amateur and small-time professional theater. At American Standard, Amstan Division, he was the personnel manager.

But not for long, and never again; Mother told us he was quitting to go down the river. I was sorry he'd be leaving the Manufacturers' Building downtown. From his office on the fourteenth floor, he often saw suicides, which he reported at dinner. The suicides grieved him, but they thrilled us kids. My sister Amy was seven.

People jumped from the Sixth Street bridge into the Allegheny River. Because the bridge was low, they shinnied all the way up the steel suspension cables to the bridge towers before they jumped. Father saw them from his desk in silhouette, far away. A man vigorously climbed a slanting cable. He slowed near the top, where the cables hung almost vertically; he paused on the stone tower, seeming to sway against the sky, high over the bridge and the river below. Priests, firemen, and others—presumably family members or passersby—gathered on the bridge. In about half the cases, Father said, these people talked the suicide down. The ones who jumped kicked off from the tower so they'd miss the bridge, and fell tumbling a long way down.

Pittsburgh was a cheerful town, and had far fewer suicides than most other cities its size. Yet people jumped so often that Father and his colleagues on the fourteenth floor had a betting pool going. They guessed the date and time of day the next jumper would appear. If a man got talked down before he jumped, he still counted for the betting pool, thank God; no manager of American Standard ever wanted to hope, even in the smallest part of himself, that the fellow would go ahead and jump. Father said he and the other men used to gather at the biggest window and holler, "No! Don't do it, buddy, don't!" Now he was leaving American Standard to go down the river, and he was a couple of bucks in the hole.

While I was reading *Kidnapped* on this Saturday morning, I heard him come inside and roam from the kitchen to the pantry to the bar, to the dining room, the living room, and the sunporch, snapping his fingers. He was snapping the fingers of both hands, and shaking his head, to the record—"Li'l Liza Jane"—the sound that was beating, big and jivey, all over the house. He walked lightly, long-legged, like a soft-shoe hoofer barely in touch with the floor. When he played the drums, he played lightly, coming down soft with the steel brushes that sounded like a Slinky falling, not making the beat but just sizzling along with it. He wandered into the sunporch, unseeing; he was snapping his fingers lightly, too, as if he were feeling between them a fine layer of Mississippi silt. The big buckeyes outside the glass sunporch walls were waving.

A week later, he bade a cheerful farewell to us—to Mother, who had encouraged him, to us oblivious daughters, ten and seven, and to the new baby girl, six months old. He loaded his twenty-four-foot cabin cruiser with canned food, pushed off from the dock of the wretched boat club that Mother hated, and pointed his bow downstream, down the Allegheny River. From there it was only a few miles to the Ohio River at Pittsburgh's point, where the Monongahela came in. He wore on westward down the Ohio; he watched West Virginia float past his port bow and Ohio past his starboard. It was 138 river miles to New Martinsville, West Virginia, where he lingered for some races. Back on the move, he tied up nights at club docks he'd seen on the charts; he poured himself water for drinks from dockside hoses. By day he rode through locks, twenty of them in all. He conversed with the lockmasters, those lone men who paced silhouetted in overalls on the concrete lock-chamber walls and threw the big switches that flooded or drained the locks: "Hello, up there!" "So long, down there!"

He continued down the river along the Kentucky border with Ohio, bumping down the locks. He passed through Cincinnati. He moved along down the Kentucky border with Indiana. After 640 miles of river travel, he reached Louisville, Kentucky. There he visited relatives at their summer house on the river.

It was a long way to New Orleans, at this rate another couple of months. He was finding the river lonesome. It got dark too early. It was September; people had abandoned their pleasure boats for the season; their children were back in school. There were no old salts on the docks talking river talk. People weren't so friendly as they were in Pittsburgh. There was no music except the dreary yacht-club jukeboxes playing "How Much Is That Doggie in the Window?" Jazz had come up the river once and for all; it wasn't still coming, he couldn't hear it across the water at night rambling and blowing and banging along high and tuneful, sneaking upstream to Chicago to get educated. He wasn't free so much as loose. He was living alone on beans in a boat and having witless conversations with lockmasters. He mailed out sad postcards.

From phone booths all down the Ohio River he talked to Mother. She told him that she was lonesome, too, and that three children—maid and nanny or no—were a handful. She said, further, that people were starting to talk. She knew Father couldn't bear people's talking. For all his dreaminess, he prized respectability above all; it was our young mother, whose circumstances bespoke such dignity, who loved to shock the world. After only six weeks, then—on the Ohio River at Louisville—he sold the boat and flew home.

I was just waking up then, just barely. Other things were changing. The highly entertaining new baby, Molly, had taken up residence in a former guest room. The great outer world hove into view and began to fill with things that had apparently been there all along: mineralogy, detective work, lepidopterology, ponds and streams, flying, society. My younger sister Amy and I were to start at private school that year: the Ellis School, on Fifth Avenue. I would start dancing school.

Children ten years old wake up and find themselves here, discover themselves to have been here all along; is this sad? They wake like sleepwalkers, in full stride; they wake like people brought back from cardiac arrest or from drowning: *in medias res,* surrounded by familiar people and objects, equipped with a hundred skills. They know the neighborhood, they can read and write English, they are old hands at the commonplace mysteries, and yet they feel themselves to have just stepped off the boat, just converged with their bodies, just flown down from a trance, to lodge in an eerily familiar life already well under way.

I woke in bits, like all children, piecemeal over the years.
I discovered myself and the world, and forgot them, and
discovered them again. I woke at intervals until, by that September when Father went down the river, the intervals of
waking tipped the scales, and I was more often awake than not.
I noticed this process of waking, and predicted with terrifying
logic that one of these years not far away I would be awake
continuously and never slip back, and never be free of myself
again.

Consciousness converges with the child as a landing tern
touches the outspread feet of its shadow on the sand: precisely,
toe hits toe. The tern folds its wings to sit; its shadow dips and
spreads over the sand to meet and cup its breast.

Like any child, I slid into myself perfectly fitted, as a diver
meets her reflection in a pool. Her fingertips enter the fingertips on the water, her wrists slide up her arms. The diver wraps
herself in her reflection wholly, sealing it at the toes, and wears
it as she climbs rising from the pool, and ever after.

I never woke, at first, without recalling, chilled, all those
other waking times, those similar stark views from similarly
lighted precipices: dizzying precipices from which the distant,
glittering world revealed itself as a brooding and separated
scene—and so let slip a queer implication, that I myself was
both observer and observable, and so a possible object of my
own humming awareness. Whenever I stepped into the porcelain bathtub, the bath's hot water sent a shock traveling up my
bones. The skin on my arms pricked up, and the hair rose on
the back of my skull. I saw my own firm foot press the tub, and
the pale shadows waver over it, as if I were looking down from
the sky and remembering this scene forever. The skin on my
face tightened, as it had always done whenever I stepped into
the tub, and remembering it all drew a swinging line, loops
connecting the dots, all the way back. You again.

Part One

THE STORY STARTS BACK IN 1950, when I was five. Oh, the great humming silence of the empty neighborhoods in those days, the neighborhoods abandoned everywhere across continental America—the city residential areas, the new "suburbs," the towns and villages on the peopled highways, the cities, towns, and villages on the rivers, the shores, in the Rocky and Appalachian mountains, the piedmont, the dells, the bayous, the hills, the Great Basin, the Great Valley, the Great Plains—oh, the silence!

For every morning the neighborhoods emptied, and all vital activity, it seemed, set forth for parts unknown.

The men left in a rush: they flung on coats, they slid kisses at everybody's cheeks, they slammed house doors, they slammed car doors; they ground their cars' starters till the motors caught with a jump.

And the Catholic schoolchildren left in a rush; I saw them from our dining-room windows. They burst into the street buttoning their jackets; they threw dry catalpa pods at the stop sign and at each other. They hugged their brown-and-tan workbooks to them, clumped and parted, and proceeded to-ward St. Bede's church school almost by accident.

The men in their oval, empty cars drove slowly among the schoolchildren. The boys banged the cars' fenders with their hands, with their jackets' elbows, or their books. The men in cars inched among the children; they edged around corners and vanished from sight. The waving knots of children zig-zagged and hollered up the street and vanished from sight. And inside all the forgotten houses in all the abandoned neighborhoods, the day of silence and waiting had begun.

The war was over. People wanted to settle down, appar-ently, and calmly blow their way out of years of rationing. They wanted to bake sugary cakes, burn gas, go to church together, get rich, and make babies.

I had been born at the end of April 1945, on the day Hitler died; Roosevelt had died eighteen days before. My father had been 4-F in the war, because of a collapsing lung—despite his repeated and chagrined efforts to enlist. Now—five years after V-J Day—he still went out one night a week as a volunteer to the Civil Air Patrol; he searched the Pittsburgh skies for new enemy bombers. By day he worked downtown for American Standard.

Every woman stayed alone in her house in those days, like a coin in a safe. Amy and I lived alone with our mother most of the day. Amy was three years younger than I. Mother and Amy and I went our separate ways in peace.

The men had driven away and the schoolchildren had paraded out of sight. Now a self-conscious and stricken silence overtook the neighborhood, overtook our white corner house and myself inside. "Am I living?" In the kitchen I watched the unselfconscious trees through the screen door, until the trees' autumn branches like fins waved away the silence. I forgot myself, and sank into dim and watery oblivion.

A car passed. Its rush and whine jolted me from my blankness. The sound faded again and I faded again down into my hushed brain until the icebox motor kicked on and prodded me awake. "You are living," the icebox motor said. "It is morning, morning, here in the kitchen, and you are in it," the icebox motor said, or the dripping faucet said, or any of the hundred other noisy things that only children can't stop hearing. Cars started, leaves rubbed, trucks' brakes whistled, sparrows peeped. Whenever it rained, the rain spattered, dripped and ran, for the entire length of the shower, for the entire length of days-long rains, until we children were almost insane from hearing it rain because we couldn't stop hearing it rain. "Rinso white!" cried the man on the radio. "Rinso blue." The silence, like all silences, was made poignant and distinct by its sounds.

What a marvel it was that the day so often introduced itself with a firm footfall nearby. What a marvel it was that so many times a day the world, like a church bell, reminded me to recall and contemplate the durable fact that I was here, and had awakened once more to find myself set down in a going world.

In the living room the mail slot clicked open and envelopes clattered down. In the back room, where our maid, Margaret Butler, was ironing, the steam iron thumped the muffled ironing board and hissed. The walls squeaked, the pipes knocked, the screen door trembled, the furnace banged, and the radiators clanged. This was the fall the loud trucks went by. I sat mindless and eternal on the kitchen floor, stony of head and solemn, playing with my fingers. Time streamed in full flood beside me on the kitchen floor; time roared raging beside me down its swollen banks; and when I woke I was so startled I fell in.

Who could ever tire of this heart-stopping transition, of this breakthrough shift between seeing and knowing you see, between being and knowing you be? It drives you to a life of concentration, it does, a life in which effort draws you down so very deep that when you surface you twist up exhilarated with a yelp and a gasp.

Who could ever tire of this radiant transition, this surfacing to awareness and this deliberate plunging to oblivion—the theater curtain rising and falling? Who could tire of it when the sum of those moments at the edge—the conscious life we so dread losing—is all we have, the gift at the moment of opening it?

Six xylophone notes chimed evenly from the radio in the back room where Margaret was ironing, and then seven xylophone notes chimed. With carefully controlled emotion, a radio woman sang:

> What will the weather be?
> Tell us, Mister Weather Man.

Mother picked up Amy, who was afraid of the trucks. She called the painters on the phone; it was time to paint the outside trim again. She ordered groceries on the phone. Larry, from Lloyd's Market, delivered. He joked with us in the kitchen while Mother unpacked the groceries' cardboard box.

I wandered outside. It was afternoon. No cars passed on the empty streets; no people passed on the empty sidewalks. The brick houses, the frame and stucco houses, white and red behind their high hedges, were still. A small woman appeared at the far, high end of the street, in silhouette against the sky; she pushed a black baby carriage tall and chromed as a hearse. The leaves in the Lombardy poplars were turning brown.

"Lie on your back," my mother said. She was kind, imaginative. She had joined me in one of the side yards. "Look at the clouds and figure out what they look like. A hat? I see a camel."

Must I? Could this be anybody's idea of something worth doing?

I was hoping the war would break out again, here. I was hoping the streets would fill and I could shoot my cap gun at people instead of at mere sparrows. My project was to ride my swing all around, over the top. I bounced a ball against the house; I fired gravel bits from an illegal slingshot Mother gave me. Sometimes I looked at the back of my hand and tried to memorize it. Sometimes I dreamed of a coal furnace, a blue lake, a redheaded woodpecker who turned into a screeching hag. Sometimes I sang uselessly in the yard, "Blithar, blithar, blithar, blithar."

It rained and it cleared and I sent Popsicle sticks and twigs down the gritty rivulet below the curb. Soon the separated neighborhood trees lost their leaves, one by one. On Saturday afternoons I watched the men rake leaves into low heaps at the curb. They tried to ignite the heaps with matches. At length my father went into the house and returned with a yellow can of lighter fluid. The daylight ended early, before all the men had burned all their leaves.

It snowed and it cleared and I kicked and pounded the snow. I roamed the darkening snowy neighborhood, oblivious. I bit and crumbled on my tongue the sweet, metallic worms of ice that had formed in rows on my mittens. I took a mitten off to fetch some wool strands from my mouth. Deeper the blue shadows grew on the sidewalk snow, and longer; the blue shadows joined and spread upward from the streets like rising water. I walked wordless and unseeing, dumb and sunk in my skull, until—what was that?

The streetlights had come on—yellow, bing—and the new light woke me like noise. I surfaced once again and saw: it was winter now, winter again. The air had grown blue dark; the skies were shrinking; the streetlights had come on; and I was here outside in the dimming day's snow, alive.

THE INTERIOR LIFE is often stupid. Its egoism blinds it and deafens it; its imagination spins out ignorant tales, fascinated. It fancies that the western wind blows on the Self, and leaves fall at the feet of the Self for a reason, and people are watching. A mind risks real ignorance for the sometimes paltry prize of an imagination enriched. The trick of reason is to get the imagination to seize the actual world—if only from time to time.

When I was five, growing up in Pittsburgh in 1950, I would not go to bed willingly because something came into my room. This was a private matter between me and it. If I spoke of it, it would kill me.

Who could breathe as this thing searched for me over the very corners of the room? Who could ever breathe freely again? I lay in the dark.

My sister Amy, two years old, was asleep in the other bed. What did she know? She was innocent of evil. Even at two she composed herself attractively for sleep. She folded the top

sheet tidily under her prettily outstretched arm; she laid her
perfect head lightly on an unwrinkled pillow, where her thick
curls spread evenly in rays like petals. All night long she slept
smoothly in a series of pleasant and serene, if artificial-looking,
positions, a faint smile on her closed lips, as if she were posing
for an ad for sheets. There was no messiness in her, no rough-
ness for things to cling to, only a charming and charmed
innocence that seemed then to protect her, an innocence I
needed but couldn't muster. Since Amy was asleep, further-
more, and since when I needed someone most I was afraid to
stir enough to wake her, she was useless.

I lay alone and was almost asleep when the damned thing
entered the room by flattening itself against the open door and
sliding in. It was a transparent, luminous oblong. I could see
the door whiten at its touch; I could see the blue wall turn pale
where it raced over it, and see the maple headboard of Amy's
bed glow. It was a swift spirit; it was an awareness. It made
noise. It had two joined parts, a head and a tail, like a Chinese
dragon. It found the door, wall, and headboard; and it swiped
them, charging them with its luminous glance. After its fleet,
searching passage, things looked the same, but weren't.

I dared not blink or breathe; I tried to hush my whooping
blood. If it found another awareness, it would destroy it.

Every night before it got to me it gave up. It hit my wall's
corner and couldn't get past. It shrank completely into itself
and vanished like a cobra down a hole. I heard the rising roar
it made when it died or left. I still couldn't breathe. I knew—it
was the worst fact I knew, a very hard fact—that it could return
again alive that same night.

Sometimes it came back, sometimes it didn't. Most often,
restless, it came back. The light stripe slipped in the door, ran
searching over Amy's wall, stopped, stretched lunatic at the
first corner, raced wailing toward my wall, and vanished into
the second corner with a cry. So I wouldn't go to bed.

* * *

It was a passing car whose windshield reflected the corner streetlight outside. I figured it out one night.

Figuring it out was as memorable as the oblong itself. Figuring it out was a long and forced ascent to the very rim of being, to the membrane of skin that both separates and connects the inner life and the outer world. I climbed deliberately from the depths like a diver who releases the monster in his arms and hauls himself hand over hand up an anchor chain till he meets the ocean's sparkling membrane and bursts through it; he sights the sunlit, becalmed hull of his boat, which had bulked so ominously from below.

I recognized the noise it made when it left. That is, the noise it made called to mind, at last, my daytime sensations when a car passed—the sight and noise together. A car came roaring down hushed Edgerton Avenue in front of our house, stopped at the corner stop sign, and passed on shrieking as its engine shifted up the gears. What, precisely, came into the bedroom? A reflection from the car's oblong windshield. Why did it travel in two parts? The window sash split the light and cast a shadow.

Night after night I labored up the same long chain of reasoning, as night after night the thing burst into the room where I lay awake and Amy slept prettily and my loud heart thrashed and I froze.

There was a world outside my window and contiguous to it. If I was so all-fired bright, as my parents, who had patently no basis for comparison, seemed to think, why did I have to keep learning this same thing over and over? For I had learned it a summer ago, when men with jackhammers broke up Edgerton Avenue. I had watched them from the yard; the street came up in jagged slabs like floes. When I lay to nap, I listened. One restless afternoon I connected the new noise in my bedroom with the jackhammer men I had been seeing outside. I understood abruptly that these worlds met, the outside and the inside. I traveled the route in my mind: You walked downstairs from here, and outside from downstairs. "Outside," then, was conceivably just beyond my windows. It was the same world I reached by going out the front or the back door. I forced my imagination yet again over this route.

The world did not have me in mind; it had no mind. It was a coincidental collection of things and people, of items, and I myself was one such item—a child walking up the sidewalk, whom anyone could see or ignore. The things in the world did not necessarily cause my overwhelming feelings; the feelings were inside me, beneath my skin, behind my ribs, within my skull. They were even, to some extent, under my control.

I could be connected to the outer world by reason, if I chose, or I could yield to what amounted to a narrative fiction, to a tale of terror whispered to me by the blood in my ears, a show in light projected on the room's blue walls. As time passed, I learned to amuse myself in bed in the darkened room by entering the fiction deliberately and replacing it by reason deliberately.

When the low roar drew nigh and the oblong slid in the door, I threw my own switches for pleasure. It's coming after me; it's a car outside. It's after me. It's a car. It raced over the wall, lighting it blue wherever it ran; it bumped over Amy's maple headboard in a rush, paused, slithered elongate over the corner, shrank, flew my way, and vanished into itself with a wail. It was a car.

OUR PARENTS AND GRANDPARENTS, and all their friends, seemed insensible to their own prominent defect, their limp, coarse skin.

We children had, for instance, proper hands; our fluid, pliant fingers joined their skin. Adults had misshapen, knuckly hands loose in their skin like bones in bags; it was a wonder they could open jars. They were loose in their skins all over, except at the wrists and ankles, like rabbits.

We were whole, we were pleasing to ourselves. Our crystalline eyes shone from firm, smooth sockets; we spoke in pure, piping voices through dark, tidy lips. Adults were coming apart, but they neither noticed nor minded. My revulsion was rude, so I hid it. Besides, we could never rise to the absolute figural splendor they alone could on occasion achieve. Our beauty was a mere absence of decrepitude; their beauty, when they had it, was not passive but earned; it was grandeur; it was a party to power, and to artifice, even, and to knowledge. Our beauty was, in the long run, merely elfin. We could not, finally, discount the fact that in some sense they owned us, and they owned the world.

Mother let me play with one of her hands. She laid it flat on a living-room end table beside her chair. I picked up a transverse pinch of skin over the knuckle of her index finger and let it drop. The pinch didn't snap back; it lay dead across her knuckle in a yellowish ridge. I poked it; it slid over intact. I left it there as an experiment and shifted to another finger. Mother was reading *Time* magazine.

Carefully, lifting it by the tip, I raised her middle finger an inch and released it. It snapped back to the tabletop. Her insides, at least, were alive. I tried all the fingers. They all worked. Some I could lift higher than others.

"That's getting boring."

"Sorry, Mama."

I refashioned the ridge on her index-finger knuckle; I made the ridge as long as I could, using both my hands. Moving quickly, I made parallel ridges on her other fingers—a real mountain chain, the Alleghenies; Indians crept along just below the ridgetops, eyeing the frozen lakes below them through the trees.

. Skin was earth; it was soil. I could see, even on my own skin, the joined trapezoids of dust specks God had wetted and stuck with his spit the morning he made Adam from dirt. Now, all these generations later, we people could still see on our skin the inherited prints of the dust specks of Eden.

I loved this thought, and repeated it for myself often. I don't know where I got it; my parents cited Adam and Eve only in jokes. Someday I would count the trapezoids, with the aid of a mirror, and learn precisely how many dust specks Adam comprised—one single handful God wetted, shaped, blew into, and set firmly into motion and left to wander about in the fabulous garden bewildered.

The skin on my mother's face was smooth, fair, and tender; it took impressions readily. She napped on her side on the couch. Her face skin pooled on the low side; it piled up in the low corners of her deep-set eyes and drew down her lips and cheeks. How flexible was it? I pushed at a puddle of it by her nose.

She stirred and opened her eyes. I jumped back.

She reminded me not to touch her face while she was sleeping. Anybody's face.

When she sat up, her cheek and brow bone bore a deep red gash, the mark of a cushion's welting. It was textured inside precisely with the upholstery's weave and brocade.

Another day, after a similar nap, I spoke up about this gash. I told her she had a mark on her face where she'd been sleeping.

"Do I?" she said; she ran her fingers through her hair. Her hair was short, blond, and wavy. She wore it swept back from her high, curved forehead. The skin on her forehead was both tight and soft. It would only barely shift when I tried to move it. She went to the kitchen. She was not interested in the hideous mark on her face. "It'll go away," I said. "What?" she called.

I noticed the hair on my father's arms and legs; each hair sprang from a dark dot on his skin. I lifted a hair and studied the puckered tepee of skin it pulled with it. Those hairs were in there tight. The greater the strain I put on the hair, the more puckered the tepee became, and shrunken within, concave. I could point it every which way.

"Ouch! Enough of that."

"Sorry, Daddy."

At the beach I felt my parent's shinbones. The bones were flat and curved, like the slats in a Venetian blind. The long edges were sharp as swords. But they had unexplained and, I thought, possibly diseased irregularities: nicks, bumps, small hard balls, shallow ridges, and soft spots. I was lying between my parents on an enormous towel through which I could feel the hot sand.

Loose under their shinbones, as in a hammock, hung the

relaxed flesh of their calves. You could push and swing this like a baby in a sling. Their heels were dry and hard, sharp at the curved edge. The bottoms of their toes had flattened, holding the imprint of life's smooth floors even when they were lying down. I would not let this happen to me. Under certain conditions, the long bones of their feet showed under their skin. The bones rose up long and miserably thin in skeletal rays on the slopes of their feet. This terrible sight they ignored also.

In fact, they were young. Mother was twenty-two when I was born, and Father twenty-nine; both appeared to other adults much younger than they were. They were a handsome couple. I felt it overwhelmingly when they dressed for occasions. I never lost a wondering awe at the transformation of an everyday, tender, nap-creased mother into an exalted and dazzling beauty who chatted with me as she dressed.

Her blue eyes shone and caught the light, and so did the platinum waves in her hair and the pearls at her ears and throat. She was wearing a black dress. The smooth skin on her breastbone rent my heart, it was so familiar and beloved; the black silk bodice and the simple necklace set off its human fineness. Mother was perhaps a bit vain of her long and perfect legs, but not too vain for me; despite her excited pleasure, she did not share my view of her beauty.

"Look at your father," she said. We were all in the dressing room. I found him in one of the long mirrors, where he waggled his outthrust chin over the last push of his tie knot. For me he made his big ears jiggle on his skull. It was a wonder he could ever hear anything; his head was loose inside him.

Father's enormousness was an everyday, stunning fact; he was taller than everyone else. He was neither thin nor stout; his torso was supple, his long legs nimble. Before the dressing-room mirror he produced an anticipatory soft-shoe, and checked to see that his cuffs stayed down.

Now they were off. I hoped they knocked them dead; I

hoped their friends knew how witty they were, and how splendid. Their parties at home did not seem very entertaining, although they laughed loudly and often fetched the one-man percussion band from the basement, or an old trumpet, or a snare drum. We children could have shown them how to have a better time. Kick the Can, for instance, never palled. A private game called Spider Cow, played by the Spencer children, also had possibilities: The spider cow hid and flung a wet washcloth at whoever found it, and erupted from hiding and chased him running all over the house.

But implicitly and emphatically, my parents and their friends were not interested. They never ran. They did not choose to run. It went with being old, apparently, and having their skin half off.

THERE WAS A BIG SNOW that same year, 1950. Traffic vanished; in the first week, nothing could move. The mailman couldn't get to us; the milkman couldn't come. Our long-legged father walked four miles with my sled to the dairy across Fifth Avenue and carried back milk.

We had a puppy, who was shorter than the big snow. Our parents tossed it for fun in the yard and it disappeared, only to pop up somewhere else at random like a loon in a lake. After a few days of this game, the happy puppy went crazy and died. It had distemper. While it was crazy it ran around the house crying, upstairs and down.

One night during the second week of the big snow I saw Jo Ann Sheehy skating on the street. I remembered this sight for its beauty and strangeness.

I was aware of the Sheehy family; they were Irish Catholics from a steep part of the neighborhood. One summer when I was walking around the block, I had to walk past skinny Tommy Sheehy and his fat father, who were hunched on their porch doing nothing. Tommy's eleven-year-old sister, Jo Ann, brought them iced tea.

"Go tell your maid she's a nigger," Tommy Sheehy said to me.

What?

He repeated it, and I did it, later, when I got home. That night, Mother came into our room after Amy was asleep. She explained, and made sure I understood. She was steely. Where had my regular mother gone? Did she hate me? She told me a passel of other words that some people use for other people. I was never to use such words, and never to associate with people who did so long as I lived; I was to apologize to Margaret Butler first thing in the morning; and I was to have no further dealings with the Sheehys.

The night Jo Ann Sheehy skated on the street, it was dark inside our house. We were having dinner in the dining room—my mother, my father, my sister Amy, who was two, and I. There were lighted ivory candles on the table. The only other light inside was the blue fluorescent lamp over the fish tank, on a sideboard. Inside the tank, neon tetras, black mollies, and angelfish circled, illumined, through the lightshot water. When I turned the fluorescent lamp off, I had learned, the fish still circled their tank in the dark. The still water in the tank's center barely stirred.

Now we sat in the dark dining room, hushed. The big snow outside, the big snow on the roof, silenced our words and the scrape of our forks and our chairs. The dog was gone, the world outside was dangerously cold, and the big snow held the houses down and the people in.

Behind me, tall chilled windows gave out onto the narrow front yard and the street. A motion must have caught my mother's eye; she rose and moved to the windows, and Father and I followed. There we saw the young girl, the transfigured Jo Ann Sheehy, skating alone under the streetlight.

She was turning on ice skates inside the streetlight's yellow cone of light—illumined and silent. She tilted and spun. She wore a short skirt, as if Edgerton Avenue's asphalt had been the ice of an Olympic arena. She wore mittens and a red knitted cap below which her black hair lifted when she turned. Under her skates the street's packed snow shone; it illumined her from below, the cold light striking her under her chin.

I stood at the tall window, barely reaching the sill; the glass fogged before my face, so I had to keep moving or hold my breath. What was she doing out there? Was everything beautiful so bold? I expected a car to run over her at any moment: the open street was a fatal place, where I was forbidden to set foot.

Once, the skater left the light. She winged into the blackness beyond the streetlight and sped down the street; only her white skates showed, and the white snow. She emerged again under another streetlight, in the continuing silence, just at our corner stop sign where the trucks' brakes hissed. Inside that second cone of light she circled backward and leaning. Then she reversed herself in an abrupt half-turn—as if she had skated backward into herself, absorbed her own motion's impetus, and rebounded from it; she shot forward into the dark street and appeared again becalmed in the first streetlight's cone. I exhaled; I looked up. Distant over the street, the night sky was moonless and foreign, a frail, bottomless black, and the cold stars speckled it without moving.

This was for many years the center of the maze, this still, frozen evening inside, the family's watching through glass the Irish girl skate outside on the street. Here were beauty and mystery outside the house, and peace and safety within. I watched passive and uncomprehending, as in summer I watched Lombardy poplar leaves turn their green sides out, and then their silver sides out—watched as if the world were a screen on which played interesting scenes for my pleasure. But there was danger in this radiant sight, in the long glimpse of the lone girl skating, for it was night, and killingly cold. The

open street was fatal and forbidden. And the apparently invul-
nerable girl was Jo Ann Sheehy, Tommy Sheehy's sister, part
of the Sheehy family, whose dark ways were a danger and a
crime.

"Tell your maid she's a nigger," he had said, and when I
said to Margaret, "You're a nigger," I had put myself in
danger—I felt at the time, for Mother was so enraged—of
being put out, tossed out in the cold, where I would go crazy
and die like the dog.

That night Jo Ann alone outside in the cold had performed
recklessly. My parents did not disapprove; they loved the
beauty of it, and the queerness of skating on a street. The next
morning I saw from the dining-room windows the street
shrunken again and ordinary, tracked by tires, and the streetlights inconspicuous, and Jo Ann Sheehy walking to school in
a blue plaid skirt.

Jo ANN SHEEHY and the Catholic schoolchildren carried brown-and-tan workbooks, which they filled, I knew, with gibberish they not only had to memorize, they had to believe.

Every morning they filed into the subterranean maw of St. Bede's, the low stone school attached to the high stone church just a block up Edgerton Avenue. From other Protestant children, I gathered St. Bede's was a cave where Catholic children had to go to fill their brown-and-tan workbooks in the dark, possibly kneeling; they wrote down whatever the Pope said. (Whatever the Pope said, I thought, it was no prize; it didn't work; our Protestant lives were much sunnier, without our half trying.) Every afternoon, authorities "let out" the surviving children to return to their lightless steep houses, where they knelt before writhing crucifixes, bandied racial epithets about, and ate stewed fish.

One afternoon the following spring, I was sitting stilled on the side-yard swing; I was watching transparent circles swim in the sky. When I focused on them, the circles parted, as fish

flew from a finger poked in their tank. Apparently it was my
eyes, and not the sky, that produced the transparent circles,
each with a dimple or nucleus, but I always failed to find any
in my eyes in a mirror; I had tried the night before.

Now St. Bede's was, as the expression had it, letting out; Jo
Ann Sheehy would walk by again, and all the other Catholic
children, and perhaps the nuns. I kept an eye out for the nuns.

From my swing seat I saw the girls appear in bunches. There
came Jo Ann Sheehy up the dry sidewalk with two other girls;
her black hair fell over her blue blazer's back. Behind them,
running back and forth across the street, little boys were
throwing gravel bits. The boys held their workbooks tightly.
Probably, if they lost them, they would be put to death.

In the leafy distance up Edgerton I could see a black phalanx. It blocked the sidewalk; it rolled footlessly forward like
a tank. The nuns were coming. They had no bodies, and
imitation faces. I quitted the swing and banged through the
back door and ran in to Mother in the kitchen.

I didn't know the nuns taught the children; the Catholic
children certainly avoided them on the streets, almost as much
as I did. The nuns seemed to be kept in St. Bede's as in a
prison, where their faces had rotted away—or they lived eyeless in the dark by choice, like bats. Parts of them were manufactured. Other parts were made of mushrooms.

In the kitchen, Mother said it was time I got over this. She
took me by the hand and hauled me back outside; we crossed
the street and caught up with the nuns. "Excuse me," Mother
said to the black phalanx. It wheeled around. "Would you just
please say hello to my daughter here? If you could just let her
see your faces."

I saw the white, conical billboards they had as mock-up
heads; I couldn't avoid seeing them, those white boards like
pillories with circles cut out and some bunched human flesh
pressed like raw pie crust into the holes. Like mushrooms and
engines, they didn't have hands. There was only that discon-
nected saucerful of whitened human flesh at their tops. The

rest, concealed by a chassis of soft cloth over hard cloth, was cylinders, drive shafts, clean wiring, and wheels.

"Why, hello," some of the top parts said distinctly. They teetered toward me. I was delivered to my enemies, and had no place to hide; I could only wail for my young life so unpityingly snuffed.

THESE ARE THE FEW, floating scenes from early childhood, from before time and understanding pinned events down to the fixed and coherent world. Soon the remembered scenes would grow in vividness and depth, as like any child I elaborated a picture of the place, and as my feelings met actual people, and as the interesting things of the world engaged my loose mind like a gear, and set it in forward motion.

A young child knows Mother as a smelled skin, a halo of light, a strength in the arms, a voice that trembles with feeling. Later the child wakes and discovers this mother—and adds facts to impressions, and historical understanding to facts.

When she was in her twenties, my mother's taste ran to modernism. In our living room on Edgerton Avenue we had a free-form blond coffee table, Jean Arp style, shaped something like a kidney, and also something like a boomerang. Over a heat register Mother hung a black iron Calder-like mobile. The mobile's disks spun and orbited slowly before a window all winter when the heat was on, and replaced for me the ensorcerizing waving of tree leaves. On the wall above the couch she hung a large print of Gauguin's *Fatata te miti;* those enormous rounded women, with their muscular curving backs, sat before a blue river in a flat and speckled jungle. On an end table she placed the first piece of art she ever bought: a Yoruba wood sculpture, a long-headed abstract woman with pointy breasts and a cold coil of wire around her neck.

Mother must have cut a paradoxical figure in her modernist living room, with her platinum blond hair, her brisk motions, her slender, urbane frame, her ironic wit (one might even say "lip")—and her wee Scotticisms. "Sit you doon," Mother said cordially to guests. If the room was too bright, she asked one of us to douse the glim. When we were babies, she bade each of us in turn, "Put your wee headie down." If no one could locate Amy when she was avoiding her nap, it was because she'd found herself a hidey-hole. Sometimes after school we discovered in our rooms a wee giftie. If Mother wanted a favor, she asked, heartrendingly, "Would you grant me a boon?"

This was all the more remarkable because Mother was no more Scotch, nor Scotch-Irish, than the Pope. She was, if anyone cared to inquire, Pennsylvania Dutch and French. But the Pittsburgh in which we lived—and that Pittsburgh only— was so strongly Scotch-Irish it might have been seventeenth- century Donegal; almost all old Pittsburgh families were Scotch-Irish. Scotticisms fairly flew in the air. And Mother picked up every sort of quaint expression.

She delighted in using queer nouns from the mountains, too. Her family hailed from Somerset, the mountain-county seat near Pittsburgh: Whiskey Rebellion country. They were pretty well educated, but they heard plenty of mountain terms.

"Where's the woolly brush?" "I need a gummy"—that is, a gum band, or rubber band. She keenly enjoyed these archa- isms, and whenever she used one, she stopped enthusiastically in midsentence to list the others: "And do you know what a poke is?" We did indeed.

Her speech was an endlessly interesting, swerving path of old punch lines, heartfelt cris de coeur, puns new and old, dramatic true confessions, challenges, witty one-liners, we Scotticisms, tag lines from Frank Sinatra songs, obsolete mountain nouns, and moral exhortations.

"I'll show him," she'd say. "I'll show him which way the bear went through the buckwheat. It'll be Katy-bar-the-door around here." "He'll be gone," Father would add wistfully, "where the woodbine twineth."

Mother woke Amy and me in the mornings by dashing into our room, wrenching aside the window curtains, cranking open our old leaded windows, shouting mysteriously, "It smells like a French whorehouse in here," and dashing out. When we got downstairs we might find her—that same morning—sitting half asleep, crumpled-of-skin in her soft bathrobe, staring at her foot in its slipper, or even with her eyes closed. If we began to whisper, we soon heard her murmur affectionately if unconvincingly into her bathrobe collar, "I'm awake."

She moved vigorously, laughed easily, spoke rapidly and boldly, and analyzed with restless force. Her moods shifted; her utterances changed key and pitch. She was fond of ending any long explanation with the sudden, puzzling kicker, "And that's why I can't imitate four Hawaiians." She stroked our heads tenderly, called us each a dozen endearing names; she thrilled, apparently, to tales of our adventures, and admired inordinately our drawings and forts. She taught us to curtsy; she taught us to play poker.

Mother's Somerset family were respectable Millers and good-looking, prominent, wild Lamberts. The Lambert women were beautiful; they married rich men. The Lambert men were charmers; they drank hard and came to early ends. They flourished during Prohibition, and set a dashing, doomed tone for the town.

Mother's handsome father was the mayor. He was so well liked that no one in town voted for his opponent. He won a contest by writing the slogan: "When better automobiles are built, Buick will build them." He and a friend journeyed to Detroit to pick up the contest prize. The trip was a famous spree; it lasted a month. He died not long after, at forty-one, when Mother was seven, and left her forever full of longing.

Late at night on Christmas Eve, she carried us each to our high bedroom, and darkened the room, and opened the window, and held us awed in the freezing stillness, saying—and we could hear the edge of tears in her voice—"Do you hear them? Do you hear the bells, the little bells, on Santa's sleigh?" We marveled and drowsed, smelling the piercingly cold night and the sweetness of Mother's warm neck, hearing in her voice so much pent emotion, feeling the familiar strength in the crook of her arms, and looking out over the silent streetlights and the chilled stars over the rooftops of the town. "Very faint, and far away—can you hear them coming?" And we could hear them coming, very faint and far away, the bells on the flying sleigh.

NEXT TO ONE OF OUR SIDE YARDS ran a short, dirty dead-end alley. We couldn't see the alley from the house; our parents had planted a row of Lombardy poplars to keep it out of sight. I found an old dime there.

High above the darkest part of the alley, in a teetering set of rooms, lived a terrible old man and a terrible old woman, brother and sister.

Doc Hall appeared only high against the sky, just outside his door at the top of two rickety flights of zigzag stairs. There he stood, grimy with coal dust, in a black suit wrinkled as underwear, and yelled unintelligibly, furiously, down at us children who played on his woodpile. We looked fearfully overhead and saw him stamp his aerial porch, a raven messing up his pile of sticks and littering the ground below. We couldn't understand his curses, but we scattered.

Doc Hall's grim sister went to early Mass at St. Bede's; she passed our house every morning. She was shapeless and sooty, dressed in black; she leaned squeezing a black cane, and walked downcast. No one knew what Mass might be; my parents shuddered to think. She crawled back and down the alley.

The alley ended at an empty, padlocked garage. In summer a few hairs of grass grew down the alley's center. Down the alley's side, broken glass, old nails, and pellets of foil and candy wrappers spiked the greasy black soil out of which a dirty catalpa and a dirty sycamore grew.

When I found the dime I was crouched in the alley digging dirt with a Popsicle stick under one of the Lombardy poplars. I struck the dime and dug around it; it was buried on edge. I pulled it out, cleaned it between my fingers, and pocketed it. Later I showed it to my father, who had been until then my only imaginable source of income. He read the date—1919— and told me it was an old dime, which might be worth more than ten cents.

He explained that the passage of time had buried the dime; soil tends to pile up around things. In Rome, he went on— looking out the kitchen window as I leaned against a counter looking up at him—in Rome, he had seen old doorways two or three stories underground. Where children had once tumbled directly outside from their doors, now visitors had to climb two flights of stairs to meet the light of the street. I stopped listening for a minute. I imagined that if the Roman children had, by awful chance, sat still in their doorways long enough, sat dreaming and forgetting to move, they, too, would have been buried in dirt, up to their chins, over their heads!—only by then, of course, they would be very old. Which was, in fact—the picture swept over me—precisely what had happened to all those Roman children, whether they sat still or not.

I turned the warm dime in my fingers. Father told me that, in general, the older a coin was, the greater its value. The older coins were farther down. I decided to devote my life to unearthing treasure. Beneath my 1919 dime, buried in the little Pittsburgh alley, might be coins older still, coins deeper down, coins from ancient times, from forgotten peoples and times, gold coins, even—pieces of eight, doubloons.

I continually imagined these old, deeply buried coins, and dreamed of them; the alley was thick with them. After I'd unearthed all the layers of wealth I could reach with a Popsicle stick, I would switch to a spade and delve down to the good stuff: to the shining layers of antique Spanish gold, of Roman gold—maybe brass-bound chests of it, maybe diamonds and rubies, maybe dulled gold from days so long past that people didn't manufacture coins at all, but simply carried bags of raw gold or ore in lumps.

That's all. It was the long years of these same few thoughts that wore tracks in my interior life. These things were mine, I figured, because I knew where to look. Because I was willing. Treasure was something you found in the alley. Treasure was something you dug up out of the dirt in a chaotic, half-forbidden, forsaken place far removed from the ordinary comings and goings of people who earned salaries in the light: under some rickety back stairs, near a falling-down pile of discarded lumber, with people yelling at you to get away from there. That I never found another old coin in that particular alley didn't matter at all.

I WALKED. My mother had given me the freedom of the streets as soon as I could say our telephone number. I walked and memorized the neighborhood. I made a mental map and located myself upon it. At night in bed I rehearsed the small world's scheme and set challenges: Find the store using backyards only. Imagine a route from the school to my friend's house. I mastered chunks of town in one direction only; I ignored the other direction, toward the Catholic church.

On a bicycle I traveled over the known world's edge, and the ground held. I was seven. I had fallen in love with a red-haired fourth-grade boy named Walter Milligan. He was tough, Catholic, from an iffy neighborhood. Two blocks beyond our school was a field—Miss Frick's field, behind Henry Clay Frick's mansion—where boys played football. I parked my bike on the sidelines and watched Walter Milligan play. As he ran up and down the length of the field, following the football, I ran up and down the sidelines, following him. After the game I rode my bike home, delirious. It was the closest we had been, and the farthest I had traveled from home.

(My love lasted two years and occasioned a bit of talk. I knew it angered him. We spoke only once. I caught him between classes in the school's crowded hall and said, "I'm sorry." He looked away, apparently enraged; his pale freckled skin flushed. He jammed his fists in his pockets, looked down, looked at me for a second, looked away, and brought out gently, "That's okay." That was the whole of it: beginning, middle, and end.)

Across the street from Walter Milligan's football field was Frick Park. Frick Park was 380 acres of woods in residential Pittsburgh. Only one trail crossed it; the gravelly walk gave way to dirt and led down a forested ravine to a damp streambed. If you followed the streambed all day you would find yourself in a distant part of town reached ordinarily by a long streetcar ride. Near Frick Park's restful entrance, old men and women from other neighborhoods were lawn bowling on the bowling green. The rest of the park was wild woods.

My father forbade me to go to Frick Park. He said bums lived there under bridges; they had been hanging around unnoticed since the Depression. My father was away all day; my mother said I could go to Frick Park if I never mentioned it.

I roamed Frick Park for many years. Our family moved from house to house, but we never moved so far I couldn't walk to Frick Park. I watched the men and women lawn bowling—so careful the players, so dull the game. After I got a bird book I found, in the deep woods, a downy woodpecker working a tree trunk; the woodpecker looked like a jackhammer man banging Edgerton Avenue to bits. I saw sparrows, robins, cardinals, juncos, chipmunks, squirrels, and—always disappointingly, emerging from their magnificent ruckus in the leaves—pedigreed dachshunds, which a woman across the street bred.

I never met anyone in the woods except the woman who walked her shiny dachshunds there, but I was cautious, and hoped I was braving danger. If a bum came after me I would disarm him with courtesy ("Good afternoon"). I would sneak him good food from home; we would bake potatoes together under his bridge; he would introduce me to his fellow bums; we would all feed the squirrels.

The deepest ravine, over which loomed the Forbes Avenue bridge, was called Fern Hollow. There in winter I searched for panther tracks in snow. In summer and fall I imagined the woods extending infinitely. I was the first human being to see these shadowed trees, this land; I would make my pioneer clearing here, near the water. Mine would be one of those famously steep farms: "How'd you get so beat up?" "Fell out of my cornfield." In spring I pried flat rocks from the damp streambed and captured red and black salamanders. I brought the salamanders home in a bag once and terrified my mother with them by mistake, when she was on the phone.

In the fall I walked to collect buckeyes from lawns. Buckeyes were wealth. A ripe buckeye husk splits. It reveals the shining brown sphere inside only partially, as an eyelid only partially discloses an eye's sphere. The nut so revealed looks like the calm brown eye of a buck, apparently. It was odd to imagine the settlers who named it having seen more male deer's eyes in the forest than nuts on a lawn.

Walking was my project before reading. The text I read was the town; the book I made up was a map. First I had walked across one of our side yards to the blackened alley with its buried dime. Now I walked to piano lessons, four long blocks north of school and three zigzag blocks into an Irish neighborhood near Thomas Boulevard.

I pushed at my map's edges. Alone at night I added newly memorized streets and blocks to old streets and blocks, and imagined connecting them on foot. From my parents' earliest injunctions I felt that my life depended on keeping it all straight—remembering where on earth I lived, that is, in relation to where I had walked. It was dead reckoning. On darkening evenings I came home exultant, secretive, often from some exotic leafy curb a mile beyond what I had known at lunch, where I had peered up at the street sign, hugging the cold pole, and fixed the intersection in my mind. What joy, what relief, eased me as I pushed open the heavy front door!—joy and relief because, from the very trackless waste, I had located home, family, and the dinner table once again.

An infant watches her hands and feels them move. Gradually she fixes her own boundaries at the complex incurved rim of her skin. Later she touches one palm to another and tries for a game to distinguish each hand's sensation of feeling and being felt. What is a house but a bigger skin, and a neighborhood map but the world's skin ever expanding?

SOME BOYS TAUGHT ME to play football. This was fine sport. You thought up a new strategy for every play and whispered it to the others. You went out for a pass, fooling everyone. Best, you got to throw yourself mightily at someone's running legs. Either you brought him down or you hit the ground flat out on your chin, with your arms empty before you. It was all or nothing. If you hesitated in fear, you would miss and get hurt: you would take a hard fall while the kid got away, or you would get kicked in the face while the kid got away. But if you flung yourself wholeheartedly at the back of his knees—if you gathered and joined body and soul and pointed them diving fearlessly—then you likely wouldn't get hurt, and you'd stop the ball. Your fate, and your team's score, depended on your concentration and courage. Nothing girls did could compare with it.

Boys welcomed me at baseball, too, for I had, through enthusiastic practice, what was weirdly known as a boy's arm. In winter, in the snow, there was neither baseball nor football, so the boys and I threw snowballs at passing cars. I got in trouble throwing snowballs, and have seldom been happier since.

On one weekday morning after Christmas, six inches of new snow had just fallen. We were standing up to our boot tops in snow on a front yard on trafficked Reynolds Street, waiting for cars. The cars traveled Reynolds Street slowly and evenly; they were targets all but wrapped in red ribbons, cream puffs. We couldn't miss.

I was seven; the boys were eight, nine, and ten. The oldest two Fahey boys were there—Mikey and Peter—polite blond boys who lived near me on Lloyd Street, and who already had four brothers and sisters. My parents approved Mickey and Peter Fahey. Chickie McBride was there, a tough kid, and Billy Paul and Mackie Kean too, from across Reynolds, where the boys grew up dark and furious, grew up skinny, knowing, and skilled. We had all drifted from our houses that morning looking for action, and had found it here on Reynolds Street.

It was cloudy but cold. The cars' tires laid behind them on the snowy street a complex trail of beige chunks like crenellated castle walls. I had stepped on some earlier; they squeaked. We could have wished for more traffic. When a car came, we all popped it one. In the intervals between cars we reverted to the natural solitude of children.

I started making an iceball—a perfect iceball, from perfectly white snow, perfectly spherical, and squeezed perfectly translucent so no snow remained all the way through. (The Fahey boys and I considered it unfair actually to throw an iceball at somebody, but it had been known to happen.)

I had just embarked on the iceball project when we heard tire chains come clanking from afar. A black Buick was moving toward us down the street. We all spread out, banged together some regular snowballs, took aim, and, when the Buick drew nigh, fired.

A soft snowball hit the driver's windshield right before the driver's face. It made a smashed star with a hump in the middle.

Often, of course, we hit our target, but this time, the only time in all of life, the car pulled over and stopped. Its wide black door opened; a man got out of it, running. He didn't even close the car door.

He ran after us, and we ran away from him, up the snowy Reynolds sidewalk. At the corner, I looked back; incredibly, he was still after us. He was in city clothes: a suit and tie, street shoes. Any normal adult would have quit, having sprung us into flight and made his point. This man was gaining on us. He was a thin man, all action. All of a sudden, we were running for our lives.

Wordless, we split up. We were on our turf; we could lose ourselves in the neighborhood backyards, everyone for himself. I paused and considered. Everyone had vanished except Mikey Fahey, who was just rounding the corner of a yellow brick house. Poor Mikey, I trailed him. The driver of the Buick sensibly picked the two of us to follow. The man apparently had all day.

He chased Mikey and me around the yellow house and up a backyard path we knew by heart: under a low tree, up a bank, through a hedge, down some snowy steps, and across the grocery store's delivery driveway. We smashed through a gap in another hedge, entered a scruffy backyard and ran around its back porch and tight between houses to Edgerton Avenue; we ran across Edgerton to an alley and up our own sliding woodpile to the Halls' front yard; he kept coming. We ran up Lloyd Street and wound through mazy backyards toward the steep hilltop at Willard and Lang.

He chased us silently, block after block. He chased us silently over picket fences, through thorny hedges, between houses, around garbage cans, and across streets. Every time I glanced back, choking for breath, I expected he would have quit. He must have been as breathless as we were. His jacket strained over his body. It was an immense discovery, pounding into my hot head with every sliding, joyous step, that this ordinary adult evidently knew what I thought only children who trained at football knew: that you have to fling yourself at what you're doing, you have to point yourself, forget yourself, aim, dive.

Mikey and I had nowhere to go, in our own neighborhood or out of it, but away from this man who was chasing us. He impelled us forward; we compelled him to follow our route. The air was cold; every breath tore my throat. We kept running, block after block; we kept improvising, backyard after backyard, running a frantic course and choosing it simultaneously, failing always to find small places or hard places to slow him down, and discovering always, exhilarated, dismayed, that only bare speed could save us—for he would never give up, this man—and we were losing speed.

He chased us through the backyard labyrinths of ten blocks before he caught us by our jackets. He caught us and we all stopped.

We three stood staggering, half blinded, coughing, in an obscure hilltop backyard: a man in his twenties, a boy, a girl. He had released our jackets, our pursuer, our captor, our hero: he knew we weren't going anywhere. We all played by the rules. Mikey and I unzipped our jackets. I pulled off my sopping mittens. Our tracks multiplied in the backyard's new snow. We had been breaking new snow all morning. We didn't look at each other. I was cherishing my excitement. The man's lower pants legs were wet; his cuffs were full of snow, and there was a prow of snow beneath them on his shoes and socks. Some trees bordered the little flat backyard, some messy winter trees. There was no one around: a clearing in a grove, and we the only players.

It was a long time before he could speak. I had some difficulty at first recalling why we were there. My lips felt swollen; I couldn't see out of the sides of my eyes; I kept coughing.

"You stupid kids," he began perfunctorily.

We listened perfunctorily indeed, if we listened at all, for the chewing out was redundant, a mere formality, and beside the point. The point was that he had chased us passionately without giving up, and so he had caught us. Now he came down to earth. I wanted the glory to last forever.

But how could the glory have lasted forever? We could have run through every backyard in North America until we got to Panama. But when he trapped us at the lip of the Panama Canal, what precisely could he have done to prolong the drama of the chase and cap its glory? I brooded about this for the next few years. He could only have fried Mikey Fahey and me in boiling oil, say, or dismembered us piecemeal, or staked us to anthills. None of which I really wanted, and none of which any adult was likely to do, even in the spirit of fun. He could only chew us out there in the Panamanian jungle, after months or years of exalting pursuit. He could only begin, "You stupid kids," and continue in his ordinary Pittsburgh accent with his normal righteous anger and the usual common sense.

If in that snowy backyard the driver of the black Buick had cut off our heads, Mikey's and mine, I would have died happy, for nothing has required so much of me since as being chased all over Pittsburgh in the middle of winter—running terrified, exhausted—by this sainted, skinny, furious redheaded man who wished to have a word with us. I don't know how he found his way back to his car.

OUR PARENTS WOULD SOONER HAVE left us out of Christmas than leave us out of a joke. They explained a joke to us while they were still laughing at it; they tore a still kicking joke apart, so we could see how it worked. When we got the first Tom Lehrer album in 1954, Mother went through the album with me, cut by cut, explaining. B.V.D.s are men's underwear. Radiation makes you sterile, and lead protects from radiation, so the joke is . . .

Our father kept in his breast pocket a little black notebook. There he noted jokes he wanted to remember. Remembering jokes was a moral obligation. People who said, "I can never remember jokes," were like people who said, obliviously, "I can never remember names," or "I don't bathe."

"No one tells jokes like your father," Mother said. Telling a good joke well—successfully, perfectly—was the highest art. It was an art because it was up to you: if you did not get the laugh, you had told it wrong. Work on it, and do better next time. It would have been reprehensible to blame the joke, or, worse, the audience.

As we children got older, our parents discussed with us every technical, theoretical, and moral aspect of the art. We tinkered with a joke's narrative structure: "Maybe you should begin with the Indians." We polished the wording. There is a Julia Randall story set in Baltimore which we smoothed together for years. How does the lady word the question? Does she say, "How are you called?" No that is needlessly awkward. She just says, "What's your name?" And he says, "Folks generally call me Bominitious." No, he can just say, "They call me Bominitious."

We analyzed many kinds of pacing. We admired with Father the leisurely meanders of the shaggy-dog story. "A young couple moved to the Swiss Alps," one story of his began, "with their grand piano"; and ended, to a blizzard of thrown napkins, ". . . Oppernockity tunes but once." "Frog goes into a bank," another story began, to my enduring pleasure. The joke was not great, but with what a sweet light splash you could launch it! "Frog goes into a bank," you said, and your canoe had slipped delicately and surely into the water, into Lake Champlain with painted Indians behind every tree, and there was no turning back.

Father was also very fond of stories set in bars that starred zoo animals or insects. These creatures apparently came into bars all over America, either accompanied or alone, and sat down to face incredulous, sarcastic bartenders. (It was a wonder the bartenders were always so surprised to see talking dogs or drinking monkeys or performing ants, so surprised year after year, when clearly this sort of thing was the very essence of bar life.) In the years he had been loose, swinging aloft in the airy interval between college and marriage, Father had frequented bars in New York, listening to jazz. Bars had no place whatever in the small Pittsburgh world he had grown up in, and lived in now. Bars were so far from our experience that I had assumed, in my detective work, that their customers were ipso facto crooks. Father's bar jokes—"and there were the regulars, all sitting around"—gave him the raffish air of a man who was at home anywhere. (How poignant were his "you knows" directed at me: you know how bartenders are; you know how the regulars would all be sitting around. For either I, a nine-year-old girl, knew what he was talking about, then or ever, or nobody did. Only because I read a lot, I often knew.)

Our mother favored a staccato, stand-up style; if our father could perorate, she could condense. Fellow goes to a psychiatrist. "You're crazy." "I want a second opinion!" "You're ugly." "How do you get an elephant out of the theater? You can't; it's in his blood."

What else in life so required, and so rewarded, such care? "Tell the girls the one about the four-by-twos, Frank." "Let's see. Let's see." "Fellow goes into a lumberyard . . ." "Yes, but it's tricky. It's a matter of point of view." And Father would leave the dining room, rubbing his face in concentration, or as if he were smearing on greasepaint, and return when he was ready.

"Ready with the four-by-twos?" Mother said.

Our father hung his hands in his pockets and regarded the far ceiling with fond reminiscence.

"Fellow comes into a lumberyard," he began.

"Says to the guy, 'I need some four-by-twos.' 'You mean two-by-fours?' 'Just a minute. I'll find out.' He walks out to the parking lot, where his buddies are waiting in the car. They roll down the car window. He confers with them awhile and comes back across the parking lot and says to the lumberyard guy, 'Yes. I mean two-by-fours.'

"Lumberyard guy says, 'How long do you want them?' 'Just a minute,' fellow says, 'I'll find out.' He goes out across the parking lot and confers with the people in the car and comes back across the parking lot to the lumberyard and says to the guy, 'A long time. We're building a house.' "

After any performance Father rubbed the top of his face with both hands, as if it had all been a dream. He sat back down at the dining-room table, laughing and shaking his head. "And when you tell a joke," Mother said to Amy and me, "laugh. It's mean not to."

We were brought up on the classics. Our parents told us all the great old American jokes, practically by number. They collaborated on, and for our benefit specialized in, the pains-taking paleontological reconstruction of vanished jokes from extant tag lines. They could vivify old *New Yorker* cartoons, source of many tag lines. The lines themselves—"Back to the old drawing board," and "I say it's spinach and I say the hell with it," and "A simple yes or no will suffice"—were no longer funny; they were instead something better, they were fixtures in the language. The tag lines of old jokes were the most powerful expressions we learned at our parents' knees. A few words suggested a complete story and a wealth of feelings. Learning our culture backward, Amy and Molly and I heard only later about *The Divine Comedy* and the Sistine Chapel ceiling, and still later about the Greek and Roman myths, which held no residue of feeling for us at all—certainly not the vibrant suggestiveness of old American jokes and car-toons.

Our parents reserved a few select jokes, such as "Archibald a Soulbroke," like vintage wines for extraordinary occasions. We heard about or witnessed those rare moments—maybe three or four in a lifetime—when circumstances combined to float our father to the top of the world, from which precarious eminence he would consent to fling himself into "Archibald a Soulbroke."

Telling "Archibald a Soulbroke" was for Father an exhila-rating ordeal, like walking a tightrope over Niagara Falls. It was a long, absurdly funny, excruciatingly tricky tour de force he had to tell fast, and it required beat-perfect concentration. He had to go off alone and rouse himself to an exalted, super-human pitch in order to pace the hot coals of its dazzling verbal surface. Often enough he returned from his prayers to a crowd whose moment had passed. We knew that when we were grown, the heavy, honorable mantle of this heart-pounding joke would fall on us.

There was another very complicated joke, also in a select category, which required a long weekend with tolerant friends.

You had to tell a joke that was not funny. It was a long, pointless story about a construction job that ended with someone's throwing away a brick. There was nothing funny about it at all, and when your friends did not laugh, you had to pretend you'd muffed it. (Your husband in the crowd could shill for you: " 'Tain't funny, Pam. You told it all wrong.")

A few days later, if you could contrive another occasion for joke telling, and if your friends still permitted you to speak, you set forth on another joke, this one an old nineteenth-century chestnut about angry passengers on a train. The lady plucks the lighted, smelly cigar from the man's mouth and flings it from the moving train's window. The man seizes the little black poodle from her lap and hurls the poor dog from the same window. When at last the passengers draw unspeaking into the station, what do they see coming down the platform but the black poodle, and guess what it has in its mouth? "The cigar," say your friends, bored sick and vowing never to spend another weekend with you. "No," you say, triumphant, "the brick." This was Mother's kind of joke. Its very riskiness excited her. It wasn't funny, but it was interesting to set up, and it elicited from her friends a grudging admiration.

How long, I wondered, could you stretch this out? How boldly could you push an audience—not, in Mother's terms, to "slay them," but to please them in some grand way? How could you convince the listeners that you knew what you were doing, that the payoff would come? Or conversely, how long could you lead them to think you were stupid, a dumb blonde, to enhance their surprise at the punch line, and heighten their pleasure in the good story you had controlled all along? Alone, energetic and trying to fall asleep, or walking the residential streets long distances every day, I pondered these things.

Our parents were both sympathetic to what professional comedians call flop sweat. Boldness was all at our house, and of course you would lose some. Anyone could be misled by poor judgment into telling a "woulda hadda been there." Telling a funny story was harder than telling a joke; it was trying out, as a tidy unit, some raveling shred of the day's fabric. You learned to gauge what sorts of thing would "tell." You learned that some people, notably your parents, could rescue some things by careful narration from the category "woulda hadda been there" to the category "it tells."

At the heart of originating a funny story was recognizing it as it floated by. You scooped the potentially solid tale from the flux of history. Once I overheard my parents arguing over a thirty-year-old story's credit line. "It was my mother who said that," Mother said. "Yes, but"—Father was downright smug—"I was the one who noticed she said that."

The sight gag was a noble form, and the running gag was a noble form. In combination they produced the top of the line, the running sight gag, like the sincere and deadpan Nairobi Trio interludes on Ernie Kovacs. How splendid it was when my parents could get a running sight gag going. We heard about these legendary occasions with a thrill of family pride, as other children hear about their progenitors' war exploits.

The sight gag could blur with the practical joke—not a noble form but a friendly one, which helps the years pass. My parents favored practical jokes of the sort you set up and then retire from, much as one writes books, possibly because imagining people's reactions beats witnessing them. They procured a living hen and "hypnotized" it by setting it on the sink before the bathroom mirror in a friend's cottage by the New Jersey shore. They spent weeks constructing a ten-foot sea monster—from truck inner tubes, cement blocks, broom-

sticks, lumber, pillows—and set it afloat in a friend's pond. On
Sanibel Island, Florida, they baffled the shell collectors each
Saint Patrick's Day by boiling a bucketful of fine shells in
green dye and strewing the green shells up and down the
beach before dawn. I woke one Christmas morning to find in
my stocking, hung from the mantel with care, a leg. Mother
had charmed a department store display manager into lending
her one.

When I visited my friends, I was well advised to rise when
their parents entered the room. When my friends visited me,
they were well advised to duck.

Central in the orders of merit, and the very bread and butter
of everyday life, was the crack. Our mother excelled at the
crack. We learned early to feed her lines just to watch her
speed to the draw. If someone else fired a crack simultaneously, we compared their concision and pointedness and
declared a winner.

Feeding our mother lines, we were training as straight men.
The straight man's was an honorable calling, a bit like that of
the rodeo clown: despised by the ignorant masses, perhaps,
but revered among experts who understood the skills required
and the risks run. We children mastered the deliberate misun-
derstanding, the planted pun, the Gracie Allen know-nothing
remark, which can make of any interlocutor an instant hero.

How very gracious is the straight man!—or, in this case, the
straight girl. She spreads before her friend a gift-wrapped,
beribboned gag line he can claim for his own, if only he will
pick it up instead of pausing to contemplate what a nitwit he's
talking to.

OUR FATHER'S PARENTS LIVED IN PITTSBURGH; Amy and I dined with them, rather formally, every Friday night until dancing school swept us away. Our grandfather's name was, like our father's, Frank Doak. He was a banker, a potbellied, bald man with thin legs: a generous-hearted, joking, calm Pittsburgher of undistinguished Scotch-Irish descent, who held his peace. Our grandmother's name was Meta Waltenburger Doak. We children called her Oma, accenting both syllables. She was an imperious and kindhearted grande dame of execrable taste, a tall, potbellied redhead, the proud descendant and heir of well-to-do Germans in Louisville, Kentucky, who boasted that she never worked a day in her life. Our father was their only child.

Every summer these grandparents moved to their summer house on the shore of Lake Erie, near North Madison, Ohio, and every summer Amy and I moved in with them for a month or two. With them also lived Mary Burinda, a thin woman who still carried a buzzing trace of Hungarian at the tip of her tongue, and who cooked and cleaned and warmly befriended

both our grandmother and us; and Henry Watson, a Pittsburgh man who drove the car, tended the grounds, and served
dinner.

Oma was odd about money. One ordinary summer afternoon at Lake Erie, I found a penny in the sand.

"Money!" Oma said. "If you've found money, don't touch
it with your bare hands. You don't know who has touched it."

My bare hands? Oma, Amy, and I had been swimming at
the beach below the house when I found the penny. Now I
was to bring it to Oma for safekeeping, and go wash my hands
in the Lake as well as I could. This washing ought to hold
calamity at bay until we could get to the bathhouse to take
showers.

Oma had told me that when she was in her teens, she had
sewed rows of lace on her chemises, to bring her bust forward.
It was hard to believe. By the time I knew her, her bust was
enormous. Walking beside Amy and me up the path to the
bathhouse, she cut an imposing figure: her legs were long and
fine, her hips slender, her carriage erect. She wore her red hair
short, in waves. Her face was round; her head was round and
slightly flattened vertically, like Raggedy Ann's. Her blue
eyes were small, stubby-lashed; her nose was short and bulbous. The expression on her thin lips was sometimes peevish,
sometimes doting.

In the bathhouse Amy and I peeled down our bathing suits.
Stuck to my belly skin, as if by suction, were flat bits of big
Lake Erie sand—gray and smooth, like hammered dots. I
pried them off with a fingernail. My buttocks were cold, my
arms hot.

We all stood in the women's shower; we stamped our sandy
feet on the shower's cedar-slat floor, and turned on the water.
Oma soaped her soft arms with the red sponge. When it was
my turn to use the red sponge, I got sand in it. I washed myself
down with soap and sand—a delicate operation on sunburned

shoulders, a pleasingly rough one on poison-ivy-covered shins.

Peering cheerfully down at me through the sharp strands of water, Oma said, "Have you washed your hands very well with soap?" She stuck her round head under the nozzle, screwed her eyes tight shut, and wagged her chin.

I mistook bodies for persons, and admired Oma above all for her freckles. Also, she could float. She could float on her back in Lake Erie, she said, and read a book. Sadly, I never saw her perform this feat, for she was not so much of a reader that she felt the need of reading while bathing, but I often saw her float for long periods. Her vast tight abdomen rose in the air; her fingers joined over it. She could easily have held a book. Her small round head in its white rubber cap lay half submerged. From the shore I could see an expression of benignity or complacency on her features, features which had been rather bunched together, centered around her nose, by the tight bathing cap and its strap. She rocked over the little waves, calm as a plank. She wore white tennis shoes into the water, for our part of Lake Erie was bumpy with glacial stones. When she floated, her tennis shoes stuck straight up.

From the bathhouse we climbed two flights of stairs to the house proper, a mid-twenties white frame house with five bedrooms and three bathrooms upstairs, and more on the third floor, where Henry Watson lived.

Now Henry was pushing a mower over the back lawn. Politely he asked us how the water was; he didn't like the water.

Henry rarely wore his full uniform at the Lake; he wore only the heavy black pants, a white shirt, and suspenders. When he drove, he put on his cap. Famously, Henry loved summers at the Lake. He took pride in the cool lawns with their bluish, cylindrical grass. Mornings he cleared the horsetail beside the long path from the bathhouse. He washed the glass porch walls. He stood in the driveway up to his ankles in foam, a ridged black garden hose in his hand, washing the car. Vapor rose low from the hot asphalt driveway; it was warm in the nostrils, sweet, smelling of soft soap. Henry's gold-rimmed glasses flashed.

In Pittsburgh, during the rest of the year, Henry went home every night to the Homewood section. By day he waited at curbs while my grandmother tried on shoes. He served dinner, nightly, in his white uniform jacket. Here at the Lake he had one friend, another chauffeur, named Cicero. He slept on the third floor. On a kitchen counter was his drinking glass.

Inside, Oma and Amy and I found Mary Burinda standing on the back of a flower-print couch. She held against a living-room window a curtain rod from which depended heavy, flower-print curtains. "Here, Mrs. Doak? Or lower?" Our grandfather was watching the Cleveland Indians on television in the same room. Henry would join him when he finished mowing.

"No, higher, I should think. But not now."

Mary climbed from the couch. She was thin, sallow-skinned, full of love, quick to laugh. She always wore her white uniform. By choice, she rarely came to the beach. I asked her how long it would be until dinner. She looked at her black watch. Two hours, she said. You *kids*. How was the water?

Mary was forty-five, to Oma's sixty-five. She had lived with them twenty-four years. Almost all of her family, she told me, had died one day during the 1918 flu epidemic; her parents and most of her brothers and sisters had died one after the other in the house. Both at the Lake and in Pittsburgh she had a room and a private bath; over the bed hung a crucifix, the most bizarre object I had ever seen. Of Mary's Catholicism, Oma used to say, with a tinge of admiration, "She's stubborn."

Mary and Henry ate in the kitchen. We ate on the enclosed porch. From the porch we could see the tall fir trunks on the back lawn, and the lake below and far down the cliff, the lake beating in waves over the stones and up onto the sand, and blurring offshore with the sky.

Oma settled in for a phone call. She combed her wet hair and shaped its waves with a freckled forefinger. She sat to her Florentine leather desk, by the tall living-room windows. I joined my grandfather at the Cleveland Indians game; Amy rolled around bored on the floor. I could hear Oma. She placed the call with the operator and apparently got a busy signal, for she hung up, called the operator, and shouted that she'd like to try again. There was a silence. Then she lost her temper. "But I just *told* you. I'm calling Marie Phillips in Pittsburgh—I just this minute finished telling you. Have you already *lost* the number I gave you?"

Oma had grown up an only child, in some luxury. There was something Victorian about her. Her grasp of the great world was slender. She believed that there was not only a telephone operator assigned to her, but also a burglar. She and my grandfather had Cadillacs, one at a time. She referred to the car as "the machine": "Henry is coming around with the machine."

At the Lake, Oma wore cotton sundresses and low-heeled sandals. She relaxed there; we all did. She barely resembled the formidable woman she was in Pittsburgh the rest of the year. In Pittsburgh, she dressed. She wore jewelry by the breastful, by the armload: diamonds, rubies, emeralds. She wore big rings like engine bearings, and vast, slithering mink coats. She wore purple and green silk, purple and green linen, purple and green wool—dresses, suits, robes—and leather high-heeled pumps, which drew attention to her long, energetic legs and thin ankles. She looked imposing. She looked, we at our house tended to think—for how females looked occupied most of females' attention—terrible. We were all blondes; we disliked purple, we disliked green, and were against the rest of it, too.

*   *   *

American Standard Corporation started as a plumbing brass foundry in Louisville, Kentucky. Oma's grandfather, Theodore Ahrens, came over from Hamburg, Germany, in 1848 and opened that foundry, which kept growing. The family kept holdings in the firm. Our grandmother was not ashamed that she was German. Amy and I were ashamed of being one-fourth German because of her (never guessing that our own mother, whose hatred of things German was an ordinary part of family politics, was in fact half German herself).

I thought Oma was brilliant to have accepted the suit of Frank Doak. He was an uncommonly kind and good-natured man. Oma had met him in 1914, while she was visiting Pittsburgh cousins. He was from an ordinary Scotch-Irish family so devotedly Presbyterian they forbade looking at the Sunday funnies. (William Doak had immigrated from Ulster in 1848 with a cargo of woolens. He wrote home depressed that the socks weren't selling well. The name Doak was a corruption of McDougal.) Oma had been a spoiled, fun-loving, red-haired beauty; our grandfather handled her with the same solid calm that is reputedly so effective on racehorses.

By the time I knew him, our grandfather was a vice-president of Pittsburgh's Fidelity Trust Bank. He looked very like a cartoonist's version of "vested interests." In fact, he almost always wore a vest, and a gold watch on a chain; he was short and heavy; he had a small white mustache; he smoked cigars. At home, his thin legs crossed under his belly, he read the financial section of the paper, tolerant of children who might have been driven, in the long course of waiting for dinner, to beating their fingertips on his scalp.

From almost every room at the Lake house, you could see Lake Erie and its mild shore. From my bed as soon as I woke, I gauged the waves' height: two inches, three. The waves disintegrated on the big beach; from the high cliff where our house stood, their breaking sounded like poured raw rice. By afternoon, the waves were two or three feet high. They seemed to rattle the glass porch windows; they broke on the long beaches like seas. On the horizon we saw ore boats—lakers—bringing iron ore east from the Masabi ore range near Lake Superior. Ships had been carrying iron ore bound for Pittsburgh across Lake Erie since the time of Carnegie and Frick. Sometimes a dusting of ore washed up or blew up on the sand beach. It lay in scalloped windrows, as did the powdery purple garnet grains after storms.

Canada, we knew, lay across the Lake. Many times I planned to run away to Canada; I would lie on the canvas raft and paddle with my hands. Instead I took up bicycle exploring. I rode a bicycle all morning for months, for years. I saw apple orchards, nurseries, and cornfields.

The land I toured mornings on a bike was flat and fertile. The Ohio settlers had a crazy way of clearing this land of forest. Father told me about it one night after dinner (our parents visited the Lake every summer). The pioneers, he said—the Scotch-Irish, German, and English pioneers—came in and sawed halfway through the trunk of every tree they wanted to fell, every tree in—was I to believe this?—several acres. Then when a wind came up they felled some big trees at the forest's upwind edge, and those trees took the whole forest down, just knocked those half-cut trees before them like dominoes. I laughed—what a good idea. Father laughed. When you saw through a tree trunk, he said, the first half is a lot easier than the second half. They never had to saw through the second halves.

I rode past cantaloupe stands and truck farms planted in tomatoes. I rode past sandy woods and frame houses with green shutters and screened porches full of kids. I played baseball with some of the kids. I got a book on birds, took up bird-watching, and saw a Baltimore oriole in an apple orchard. I straddled my bike in amazement, bare feet on the cool morning road, and watched the brilliant thing bounce singing from treetop to treetop in the sun.

I learned to whistle; I whistled "The Wayward Wind." I

sang "The Wayward Wind," too, at the top of my lungs for
an hour one evening, bored on the porch, hurling myself from
chair to chair singing, and wondering when these indulgent
grandparents would stop me. At length my grandfather
looked up from his paper and said, "That's a sad song you're
singing. Do you know that?" And I was amazed he knew that.
Did he yearn to wander, my banker grandfather, like the man
in "The Wayward Wind"?

Afternoons we swam at our own beach. When Grandfather
joined us I stared at the skin on his legs. It consisted of many
scaly layers of fragile translucency, which together appeared
bluish. On it, white starbursts appeared at random, and red
streaks were visible somewhere inside. The stars and stripes
forever. The skin on Oma's legs was similarly translucent; the
freckles seemed to float flat just below the first few layers.

I found a beachful of neighborhood kids to swim with; I
came home only to eat. Evenings Amy and I played cards with
Oma and Mary on the porch, or, when we were younger, we
colored in coloring books with Oma. Oma was a tidy hand
with a crayon. She fought with us over the crayons as an equal.
The big woodland silk moths banged at the glass walls beside
our bare shoulders under the lamp.

We left the Lake by rising at three, eating the last of the
sweet cantaloupe by lamplight, and driving through horse-
and-buggy Mennonite country back to Pittsburgh. We re-
traced one of the routes the old Indian traders had used in the
1750s, back from the Lake Erie country to the Forks of the
Ohio, where they could load up on trinkets and, pretty soon,
buy a drink. In Pittsburgh, Oma would go back to work.
Although she claimed never to have worked, in fact she and
a partner directed the Presbyterian Hospital gift shop as
volunteers full time for twenty years. And in Pittsburgh this
year, Amy and I would start new schools.

Now in the embarrassing Cadillac we pulled up in front of
our house. From the capacious row of jump seats Amy and I
were delivered—suntanned, cheerful, covered with poison

ivy, and in possession of suitcases full of new green and purple dresses—to our mother.

The rivalry between our mother and Oma was intense; it was a long, civilized antagonism. Our mother had won the moral battle—we children were shamed, for instance, by Oma's bursts of bigotry—but Mother fought on for autonomy, seeking to prevent our being annexed to Oma's big tribe of Louisville Germans. When I was a baby, Oma had several times hauled me downriver to Louisville for Christmas as a prize; Mother put a stop to it.

If Oma had a great deal of shockingly loose money, we had, we fancied, good taste. Oma had a green-and-blue blown-glass sculpture of two intertwined swans, full of bubbles; we had a black iron Calder-style mobile. Oma had a servant and a companion. We had help. Our "help" shared our drinking glasses. At our parents' parties, friends ate lasagna and danced; at our grandparents' parties, guests ate sauerbraten and went to the theater.

Matters of taste are not, it turns out, moral issues. We thought we were grander than Oma morally, that she was bigoted and vain, quite as if we ourselves were neither. Actually it was her taste we most deplored. We thought that merely possessing a gaudy figurine was a worse offense than wholeheartedly embracing snobbery. We could not see how clearly she saw us, two small children just about to start prep school, who enjoyed the fruits of her family's prosperity, and who had barely peeped beyond Pittsburgh. She never said a word against our mother. But like our mother, she never gave up the struggle, even, apparently, after she suffered a stroke—for after her stroke she earnestly asked our father from time to time, "Have you ever thought of marrying?"

He pressed her freckled hand. Of course we loved her.

It was not, in retrospect, a fair fight. For at our house, we were all so young.

WE HAD MOVED WHEN I WAS EIGHT. We moved from Edgerton Avenue to Richland Lane, a hushed dead-end street on the far side of Frick Park. We expanded into a brick house on two lots. There was a bright sunporch under buckeye trees; there was a golden sandstone wall with fireplace and bench that Mother designed, which ran the length of the living room.

It was into this comfortable house that the last of us sisters, Molly, was born, two years later. It was from this house that Father would leave to go down the river to New Orleans, and to this house that he would return early, from the river at Louisville. Here Mother told the contractor where she wanted kitchen walls knocked out. Here on the sunporch Amy tended her many potentially well-dressed dolls, all of whom were, unfortunately, always sick in bed. Here I began a life of reading books, and drawing, and playing at the sciences. Here also I began to wake in earnest, and shed superstition, and plan my days.

* * *

Every August when Amy and I returned from the Lake, we saw that workmen had altered the house in our absence—the dining room seemed bigger, the kitchen was lighter—but we couldn't recall how it had been. I thought Mother was a genius for thinking up these improvements, for the house always seemed fine to me, yet it got better and better.

This August, the summer I was ten, we returned from the Lake and found our shared room uncannily tidy and stilled, dark, while summer, the summer in which we had been immersed, played outside the closed windows like a movie. So it always was, those first few minutes in an emptied room. They made you self-conscious; you felt yourself living your life. As soon as you unzipped your suitcase and opened the window, you broke the spell; you plunged again into the rush and weather.

While we were gone, Molly had learned to crawl. She pulled herself up and stood singing in her playpen on the flat part of the front lawn; the buckeye boughs stirred far overhead, and waved over her round arms their speckled lights.

Usually when it was hot the family swam at the distant country-club pool. Now that we were back from the Lake, all that resumed—a nasty comedown after the Lake, to whose neighborhood beach I had gone alone, and where we were all kids among kids who owned the beach and our days. There, at the Lake, if you wanted to leave, you simply kicked the bike's kickstand and sprang into the seat and away, in one skilled gesture like cowboys' mounting horses, rode away on the innocent Ohio roads under old, still trees. At the country club, you often wanted to leave as soon as you had come, but there was no leaving to be had. The country-club pool drew a society as complex and constraining, if not so entertaining, as any European capital's drawing room did. You forgot an old woman's name at some peril to your entire family. What if you actually, physically, ran into her? Knocked her off her pins? It was no place for children.

One country-club morning this August, I saw a red blotch moving in a dense hedge by the club's baby pool. I crept up on the red blotch in my cold bathing suit and discovered that it was a rose-breasted grosbeak. I had never seen one. This living, wild bird, which could fetch up any place it pleased, had inexplicably touched down at our country club. It scratched around in a hedge between the baby pool and the sixth hole. The dumb cluck, why a country club?

Mother said Father was going down the river in his boat pretty soon. It sounded like a swell idea.

One windy Saturday morning, after the Lake and before the new private school started, I hung around the house. It was too early for action in the neighborhood. To wake up, I read on the sunporch.

The sunporch would wake anybody up; Father had now put on the record: Sharkey Bonano, "Li'l Liza Jane." He was bopping around, snapping his fingers; now he had wandered outside and stood under the big buckeye trees. I could see him through the sunporch's glass walls. He peered up at a patch of sky as if it could tell him, old salt that he was, right there on Richland Lane, how the weather would be next week on the Ohio River.

I was starting *Kidnapped*. It began in Scotland; David Balfour's father asked that a letter be delivered "when the house is redd up." Some people in Pittsburgh redd up houses, too. The hardworking parents of my earliest neighborhood friends said it: You kids redd up this room. It meant clean up, or ready up. I never expected to find "redd up" in so grand a thing as a book. Apparently it was Scots. I hadn't heard the phrase since we moved.

I rode back to Edgerton Avenue from time to time after we moved—to look around, and to fix in my mind the route back: past the lawn bowlers in Frick Park, past the football field, and beyond the old elementary schoolyard, where a big older boy had said to me, "Why, you're a regular Ralph Kiner." Touring that old neighborhood, I saw the St. Bede's nuns. I sped past them, careless, on my bike.

"Redd up," David Balfour's father said in *Kidnapped*. I was reading on the sunporch, on the bright couch. "Oh, Li'l Liza!" said the music on the record, "Li'l Liza Jane." Next week Father was going down the river to New Orleans. Maybe they'd let him sit in a set on the drums; maybe Zutty Singleton would be there and holler out to him—"Hey, Frank!"

The wind rattled the windowed sunporch walls beside me. I could see, without getting up, some green leaves blowing down from the buckeye branches overhead. Everything in the room was bright, even the bookshelves, even Amy's melancholy dolls. The blue shadows of fast clouds ran over the far walls and floor. Father snapped his fingers and wandered, tall and loose-limbed, over the house.

I was ten years old now, up into the double numbers, where I would likely remain till I died. I am awake now forever, I thought suddenly; I have converged with myself in the present. My hands were icy from holding *Kidnapped* up; I always read lying down. I felt time in full stream, and I felt consciousness in full stream joining it, like the rivers.

Part Two

WE LIVED IN A CLEAN CITY whose center was new; after the war, a few business leaders and Democratic Mayor David L. Lawrence had begun cleaning it up. Beneath the new city, and tucked up its hilly alleys, lay the old Pittsburgh, and the old foothill land beneath it. It was all old if you dug far enough. Our Pittsburgh was like Rome, or Jericho, a palimpsest, a sliding pile of cities built ever nearer the sky, and rising ever higher over the rivers. If you dug, you found things.

Oma's chauffeur, Henry Watson, dug a hole in our yard on Edgerton Avenue to plant a maple tree when I was born, and again when Amy was born three years later. When he dug the hole for Amy's maple, he found an arrowhead—smaller than a dime and sharp. Our mother continually remodeled each of the houses we lived in: the workmen knocked out walls and found brick walls under the plaster and oak planks under the brick. City workers continually paved the streets: they poured asphalt over the streetcar tracks, streetcar tracks their fathers had wormed between the old riverworn cobblestones, cobblestones laid smack into the notorious nineteenth-century mud.

Long stretches of that mud were the same pioneer roads that General John Forbes's troops had hacked over the mountains from Carlisle, or General Braddock's troops had hacked from the Chesapeake and the Susquehanna, widening with their axes the woodland paths the Indians had worn on deer trails.

Many old stone houses had slate-shingle roofs. I used to find blown shingles cracked open on the sidewalk; some of them bore—inside, where no one had been able to look until now— fine fossil prints of flat leaves. I heard there were dinosaur bones under buildings. The largest coal-bearing rock sequence in the world ran under Pittsburgh and popped out at Coal Hill, just across the Monongahela. (Then it ducked far underground and ran up into Nova Scotia, dove into the water and crossed under the Atlantic, and rolled up again thick with coal in Wales.) There were layers of natural gas beneath Pittsburgh, and pools of petroleum the pioneers called Seneca oil, because only Indians would fool with it.

We children lived and breathed our history—our Pittsburgh history, so crucial to the country's story and so typical of it as well—without knowing or believing any of it. For how can anyone know or believe stories she dreamed in her sleep, information for which and to which she feels herself to be in no way responsible? A child is asleep. Her private life unwinds inside her skin and skull; only as she sheds childhood, first one decade and then another, can she locate the actual, historical stream, see the setting of her dreaming private life—the nation, the city, the neighborhood, the house where the family lives—as an actual project under way, a project living people willed, and made well or failed, and are still making, herself among them. I breathed the air of history all unaware, and walked oblivious through its littered layers.

Outside in the neighborhoods, learning our way around the streets, we played among the enormous stone monuments of the millionaires—both those tireless Pittsburgh founders of the heavy industries from which the nation's wealth derived (they told us at school) and the industrialists' couldn't-lose bankers and backers, all of whom began as canny boys, the stories of whose rises to riches adults still considered inspirational to children.

We were unthinkingly familiar with the moguls' immense rough works as so much weird scenery on long drives. We saw the long, low-slung stripes of steel factories by the rivers; we saw pyramidal heaps of yellow sand at glassworks by the shining railroad tracks; we saw rusty slag heaps on the outlying hilltops, and coal barges tied up at the docks. We recognized, on infrequent trips downtown, the industries' smooth corporate headquarters, each to its own soaring building—Gulf Oil, Alcoa, U.S. Steel, Koppers Company, Pittsburgh Plate Glass, Mellon Bank. Our classmates' fathers worked in these buildings, or at nearby corporate headquarters for Westinghouse Electric, Jones & Laughlin Steel, Rockwell Manufacturing, American Standard, Allegheny Ludlum, Westinghouse Air Brake, and H. J. Heinz.

The nineteenth-century industrialists' institutions—galleries, universities, hospitals, churches, Carnegie libraries, the Carnegie Museum, Frick Park, Mellon Park—were, many of them, my stomping grounds. These absolute artifacts of philanthropy littered the neighborhoods with marble. Millionaires' encrusted mansions, now obsolete and turned into parks or art centers, weighed on every block. They lent their expansive, hushed moods to the Point Breeze neighborhoods where we children lived and where those fabulous men had lived also, or rather had visited at night in order to sleep. Everywhere I looked, it was the Valley of the Kings, their dynasty just ended, and their monuments intact but already out of fashion.

All these immensities wholly dominated the life of the city. So did their several peculiar social legacies: their powerful Calvinist mix of piety and acquisitiveness, which characterized the old and new Scotch-Irish families and the nation they helped found; the walled-up hush of what was, by my day, old money—amazing how fast it ages if you let it alone—and the clang and roar of making that money; the owners' Presbyterian churches, their anti-Catholicism, anti-Semitism, Republicanism, and love of continuous work; their dogmatic practicality, their easy friendliness, their Pittsburgh-centered innocence, and, paradoxically, their egalitarianism.

For all the insularity of the old guard, Pittsburgh was always an open and democratic town. "Best-natured people I ever went among," a Boston visitor noted two centuries earlier. In colonial days, everybody went to balls, regardless of rank. No one had any truck with aristocratic pretensions—hadn't they hated the British lords in Ulster? People who cared to rave about their bloodlines, Mother told us, had stayed in Europe, which deserved them. We were vaguely proud of living in a city so full of distinctive immigrant groups, among which we never thought to number ourselves. We had no occasion to visit the steep hillside neighborhoods—Polish, Hungarian, Rumanian, Italian, Slav—of the turn-of-the-century immigrants who poured the steel and stirred the glass and shoveled the coal.

We children played around the moguls' enormous pale stone houses, restful as tombs, houses set back just so on their shaded grounds. Henry Clay Frick's daughter, unthinkably old, lived alone in her proud, sinking mansion; she had lived alone all her life. No one saw her. Men mowed the wide lawns and seeded them, and pushed rollers over them, over the new grass seed and musket balls and arrowheads, over the big trees' roots, bones, shale, coal.

We knew bits of this story, and we knew none of it. Odd facts stuck in the mind: On the Pennsylvania frontier in the eighteenth century, people pressed hummingbirds as if they were poppies, between pages of heavy books, and mailed them back to Ulster and Scotland as curiosities. Money was so scarce in the western Pennsylvania mountains that, as late as the mid-nineteenth century, people substituted odds and ends like road contracts, feathers, and elderberries.

We knew that before big industry there had been small industry here—H. J. Heinz setting up a roadside stand to sell horseradish roots from his garden. There were the makers of cannonballs for the Civil War. There were the braggart and rowdy flatboat men and keelboat men, and the honored steamboat builders and pilots. There were local men getting rich in iron and glass manufacturing and trade downriver. There was a whole continentful of people passing through, native-born and immigrant men and women who funneled down Pittsburgh, where two rivers converged to make a third river. It was the gateway to the West; they piled onto flatboats and launched out into the Ohio River singing, to head for new country. There had been a Revolutionary War, and before that the French and Indian War. And before that, and first of all, had been those first settlers come walking bright-eyed in, into nowhere from out of nowhere, the people who, as they said, "broke wilderness," the pioneers. This was the history.

I treasured some bits; they provided doll-like figures for imagination's travels and wars. There in private imagination were the vivid figures of history in costume, tricked out as if for amateur outdoor drama: a moving, clumsy, insignificant spectacle like everything else the imagination proposes to itself for pure pleasure only—nothing real, nobody gets hurt, it's only ketchup.

WHILE FATHER WAS MOTORING down the river, my reading was giving me a turn.

At a neighbor boy's house, I ran into Kimon Nicolaides' *The Natural Way to Draw*. This was a manual for students who couldn't get to Nicolaides' own classes at New York's Art Students League. I was amazed that there were books about things one actually did. I had been drawing in earnest, but at random, for two years. Like all children, when I drew I tried to reproduce schema. The idea of drawing from life had astounded me two years previously, but I had gradually let it slip, and my drawing, such as it was, had sunk back into facile sloth. Now this book would ignite my fervor for conscious drawing, and bind my attention to both the vigor and the detail of the actual world.

For the rest of August, and all fall, this urgent, hortatory book ran my life. I tried to follow its schedules: every day, sixty-five gesture drawings, fifteen memory drawings, an hour-long contour drawing, and "The Sustained Study in Crayon, Clothed" or "The Sustained Study in Crayon, Nude."

While Father was gone, I outfitted an attic bedroom as a studio, and moved in. Every summer or weekend morning at eight o'clock I taped that day's drawing schedule to a wall. Since there was no model, nude or clothed, I drew my baseball mitt.

I drew my baseball mitt's gesture—its tense repose, its expectancy, which ran up its hollows like a hand. I drew its contours—its flat fingertips strung on square rawhide thongs. I drew its billion grades of light and dark in detail, so the glove weighed vivid and complex on the page, and the trapezoids small as dust motes in the leather fingers cast shadows, and the pale palm leather was smooth as a belly and thick. "Draw anything," said the book. "Learning to draw is really a matter of learning to see," said the book. "Imagine that your pencil point is touching the model instead of the paper." "All the student need concern himself with is reality."

With my pencil point I crawled over the mitt's topology. I slithered over each dip and rise; I checked my bearings, admired the enormous view, and recorded it like Meriwether Lewis mapping the Rockies.

One thing struck me as odd and interesting. A gesture drawing took forty-five seconds; a Sustained Study took all morning. From any still-life arrangement or model's pose, the artist could produce either a short study or a long one. Evidently, a given object took no particular amount of time to draw; instead the artist took the time, or didn't take it, at pleasure. And, similarly, things themselves possessed no fixed and intrinsic amount of interest; instead things were interesting as long as you had attention to give them. How long does it take to draw a baseball mitt? As much time as you care to give it. Not an infinite amount of time, but more time than you first imagined. For many days, so long as you want to keep drawing that mitt, and studying that mitt, there will always be a new and finer layer of distinctions to draw out and lay in. Your attention discovers—seems thereby to produce—an array of interesting features in any object, like a lamp.

By noon, all this drawing would have gone to my head. I slipped into the mitt, quit the attic, quit the house, and headed up the street, looking for a ball game.

My friend had sought permission from his father for me to borrow *The Natural Way to Draw;* it was his book. Grown men and growing children rarely mingled then. I had lived two doors away from this family for several years, and had never clapped eyes on my good friend's father; still, I now regarded him as a man after my own heart. Had he another book about drawing? He had; he owned a book about pencil drawing. This book began well enough, with the drawing of trees. Then it devoted a chapter to the schematic representation of shrubbery. At last it dwindled into its true subject, the drawing of buildings.

My friend's father was an architect. All his other books were about buildings. He had been a boy who liked to draw, according to my friend, so he became an architect. Children who drew, I learned, became architects; I had thought they became painters. My friend explained that it was not proper to become a painter; it couldn't be done. I resigned myself to architecture school and a long life of drawing buildings. It was a pity, for I disliked buildings, considering them only a stiffer and more ample form of clothing, and no more important.

I began reading books, reading books to delirium. I began by vanishing from the known world into the passive abyss of reading, but soon found myself engaged with surprising vigor because the things in the books, or even the things surrounding the books, roused me from my stupor. From the nearest library I learned every sort of surprising thing—some of it, though not much of it, from the books themselves. The Homewood branch of Pittsburgh's Carnegie Library system was in a Negro section of town—Homewood. This branch was our nearest library; Mother drove me to it every two weeks for many years, until I could drive myself. I only very rarely saw other white people there.

I understood that our maid, Margaret Butler, had friends in Homewood. I never saw her there, but I did see Henry Watson.

I was getting out of Mother's car in front of the library when Henry appeared on the sidewalk; he was walking with some other old men. I had never before seen him at large; it must have been his day off. He had gold-rimmed glasses, a gold front tooth, and a frank, open expression. It would embarrass him, I thought, if I said hello to him in front of his friends. I was wrong. He spied me, picked me up—books and all— swung me as he always did, and introduced Mother and me to his friends. Later, as we were climbing the long stone steps to the library's door, Mother said, "That's what I mean by good manners."

The Homewood Library had graven across its enormous stone facade: FREE TO THE PEOPLE. In the evenings, neighborhood people—the men and women of Homewood— browsed in the library, and brought their children. By day, the two vaulted rooms, the adults' and children's sections, were almost empty. The kind Homewood librarians, after a trial period, had given me a card to the adult section. This was an enormous silent room with marble floors. Nonfiction was on the left.

Beside the farthest wall, and under leaded windows set ten feet from the floor, so that no human being could ever see anything from them—next to the wall, and at the farthest remove from the idle librarians at their curved wooden counter, and from the oak bench where my mother waited in her camel's-hair coat chatting with the librarians or reading— stood the last and darkest and most obscure of the tall nonfiction stacks: NEGRO HISTORY and NATURAL HISTORY. It was in Natural History, in the cool darkness of a bottom shelf, that I found *The Field Book of Ponds and Streams.*

The Field Book of Ponds and Streams was a small, blue-bound book printed in fine type on thin paper, like *The Book of Common Prayer.* Its third chapter explained how to make sweep nets, plankton nets, glass-bottomed buckets, and killing jars. It specified how to mount slides, how to label insects on their pins, and how to set up a freshwater aquarium.

One was to go into "the field" wearing hip boots and perhaps a head net for mosquitoes. One carried in a "rucksack" half a dozen corked test tubes, a smattering of screwtop baby-food jars, a white enamel tray, assorted pipettes and eyedroppers, an artillery of cheesecloth nets, a notebook, a hand lens, perhaps a map, and *The Field Book of Ponds and Streams.* This field—unlike the fields I had seen, such as the field where Walter Milligan played football—was evidently very well watered, for there one could find, and distinguish among, daphniae, planaria, water pennies, stonefly larvae, dragonfly nymphs, salamander larvae, tadpoles, snakes, and turtles, all of which one could carry home.

That anyone had lived the fine life described in Chapter 3 astonished me. Although the title page indicated quite plainly that one Ann Haven Morgan had written *The Field Book of Ponds and Streams,* I nevertheless imagined, perhaps from the authority and freedom of it, that its author was a man. It would be good to write him and assure him that someone had found his book, in the dark near the marble floor at Homewood Library. I would, in the same letter or in a subsequent one, ask him a question outside the scope of his book, which was where I personally might find a pond, or a stream. But I did not know how to address such a letter, of course, or how to learn if he was still alive.

I was afraid, too, that my letter would disappoint him by betraying my ignorance, which was just beginning to attract my own notice. What, for example, was this noisome-sounding substance called cheesecloth, and what do scientists do with it? What, when you really got down to it, was enamel? If candy could, notoriously, "eat through enamel," why would anyone make trays out of it? Where—short of robbing a museum—might a fifth-grade student at the Ellis School on Fifth Avenue obtain such a legendary item as a wooden bucket?

The Field Book of Ponds and Streams was a shocker from beginning to end. The greatest shock came at the end.

When you checked out a book from the Homewood Library, the librarian wrote your number on the book's card and stamped the due date on a sheet glued to the book's last page. When I checked out The Field Book of Ponds and Streams for the second time, I noticed the book's card. It was almost full. There were numbers on both sides. My hearty author and I were not alone in the world, after all. With us, and sharing our enthusiasm for dragonfly larvae and single-celled plants, were, apparently, many Negro adults.

Who were these people? Had they, in Pittsburgh's Homewood section, found ponds? Had they found streams? At home, I read the book again; I studied the drawings; I reread Chapter 3; then I settled in to study the due-date slip. People read this book in every season. Seven or eight people were reading this book every year, even during the war.

Every year, I read again The Field Book of Ponds and Streams. Often, when I was in the library, I simply visited it. I sat on the marble floor and studied the book's card. There we all were. There was my number. There was the number of someone else who had checked it out more than once. Might I contact this person and cheer him up? For I assumed that, like me, he had found pickings pretty slim in Pittsburgh.

The people of Homewood, some of whom lived in visible poverty, on crowded streets among burned-out houses—they dreamed of ponds and streams. They were saving to buy microscopes. In their bedrooms they fashioned plankton nets. But their hopes were even more vain than mine, for I was a child, and anything might happen; they were adults, living in Homewood. There was neither pond nor stream on the streetcar routes. The Homewood residents whom I knew had little

money and little free time. The marble floor was beginning to
chill me. It was not fair.

I had been driven into nonfiction against my wishes. I
wanted to read fiction, but I had learned to be cautious about
it.

"When you open a book," the sentimental library posters
said, "anything can happen." This was so. A book of fiction
was a bomb. It was a land mine you wanted to go off. You
wanted it to blow your whole day. Unfortunately, hundreds
of thousands of books were duds. They had been rusting out
of everyone's way for so long that they no longer worked.
There was no way to distinguish the duds from the live mines
except to throw yourself at them headlong, one by one.

The suggestions of adults were uncertain and incoherent.
They gave you Nancy Drew with one hand and *Little Women*
with the other. They mixed good and bad books together
because they could not distinguish between them. Any book
which contained children, or short adults, or animals, was felt
to be a children's book. So also was any book about the sea—as
though danger or even fresh air were a child's prerogative—
or any book by Charles Dickens or Mark Twain. Virtually all
British books, actually, were children's books; no one understood children like the British. Suited to female children were
love stories set in any century but this one. Consequently one
had read, exasperated often to fury, *Pickwick Papers, Désirée,
Wuthering Heights, Lad, a Dog, Gulliver's Travels, Gone With the
Wind, Robinson Crusoe,* Nordhoff and Hall's *Bounty* trilogy,
*Moby-Dick, The Five Little Peppers, Innocents Abroad, Lord Jim, Old
Yeller.*

The fiction stacks at the Homewood Library, their volumes
alphabetized by author, baffled me. How could I learn to
choose a novel? That I could not easily reach the top two
shelves helped limit choices a little. Still, on the lower shelves
I saw too many books: Mary Johnson, *Sweet Rocket;* Samuel
Johnson, *Rasselas;* James Jones, *From Here to Eternity.* I checked

out the last because I had heard of it; it was good. I decided to check out books I had heard of. I had heard of *The Mill on the Floss.* I read it, and it was good. On its binding was printed a figure, a man dancing or running; I had noticed this figure before. Like so many children before and after me, I learned to seek out this logo, the Modern Library colophon.

The going was always rocky. I couldn't count on Modern Library the way I could count on, say, *Mad* magazine, which never failed to slay me. *Native Son* was good, *Walden* was pretty good, *The Interpretation of Dreams* was okay, and *The Education of Henry Adams* was awful. *Ulysses,* a very famous book, was also awful. *Confessions* by Augustine, whose title promised so much, was a bust. *Confessions* by Jean-Jacques Rousseau was much better, though it fell apart halfway through.

In fact, it was a plain truth that most books fell apart halfway through. They fell apart as their protagonists quit, without any apparent reluctance, like idiots diving voluntarily into buckets, the most interesting part of their lives, and entered upon decades of unrelieved tedium. I was forewarned, and would not so bobble my adult life; when things got dull, I would go to sea.

Jude the Obscure was the type case. It started out so well. Halfway through, its author forgot how to write. After Jude got married, his life was over, but the book went on for hundreds of pages while he stewed in his own juices. The same thing happened in *The Little Shepherd of Kingdom Come,* which Mother brought me from a fair. It was simply a hazard of reading. Only a heartsick loyalty to the protagonists of the early chapters, to the eager children they had been, kept me reading chronological narratives to their bitter ends. Perhaps later, when I had become an architect, I would enjoy the latter halves of books more.

This was the most private and obscure part of life, this Homewood Library: a vaulted marble edifice in a mostly de-

cent Negro neighborhood, the silent stacks of which I plun-
dered in deep concentration for many years. There seemed
then, happily, to be an infinitude of books.

I no more expected anyone else on earth to have read a
book I had read than I expected someone else to have twirled
the same blade of grass. I would never meet those Homewood
people who were borrowing *The Field Book of Ponds and
Streams;* the people who read my favorite books were invisible
or in hiding, underground. Father occasionally raised his big
eyebrows at the title of some volume I was hurrying off with,
quite as if he knew what it contained—but I thought he must
know of it by hearsay, for none of it seemed to make much
difference to him. Books swept me away, one after the other,
this way and that; I made endless vows according to their
lights, for I believed them.

THE INTERIOR LIFE EXPANDS AND FILLS; it approaches the edge of skin; it thickens with its own vivid story; it even begins to hear rumors, from beyond the horizon skin's rim, of nations and wars. You wake one day and discover your grandmother; you wake another day and notice, like any curious naturalist, the boys.

There were already boys then: not tough boys—much as I missed their inventiveness and easy democracy—but the polite boys of Richland Lane. The polite boys of Richland Lane aspired to the Presbyterian ministry. Their fathers were surgeons, lawyers, architects, and businessmen, who sat on the boards of churches and hospitals. Early on warm weekday evenings, we children played rough in the calm yards and cultivated woods, grabbing and bruising each other often enough in the course of our magnificently organized games. On Saturday afternoons, these same neighborhood boys appeared wet-combed and white-shirted at the front door, to take me gently to the movies on the bus. And there were the dancing-school boys, who materialized at the front door on Valentine's Day, holding heart-shaped boxes of chocolates.

I was ten when I met the dancing-school boys; it was that same autumn, 1955. Father was motoring down the river. The new sandstone wall was up in the living room.

Outside the city, the mountainside maples were turning; the oaks were green. Everywhere in the spreading Mississippi watershed, from the Allegheny and the Ohio here in Pittsburgh to the Missouri and the Cheyenne and the Bighorn draining the Rocky Mountains, yellow and red leaves, silver-maple and black-oak leaves, or pale cottonwood leaves and aspen, slipped down to the tight surface of the moving water. A few leaves fell on the decks of Father's boat when he tied up at an Ohio island for lunch; he raked them off with his fingers, probably, and thought it damned strange to be raking leaves at all.

Molly, the new baby, had grown less mysterious; she smiled and crawled over the grass or the rug. The family had begun spending summers around a country-club pool. Amy and I had started at a girls' day school, the Ellis School; I belted on the green jumper I would wear, in one size or another, for the next eight years, until I left Pittsburgh altogether. I was taking piano lessons, art classes. And I started dancing school.

The dancing-school boys, it turned out, were our boys, the boys, who ascended through the boys' private school as we ascended through the girls'. I was suprised to see them that first Friday afternoon in dancing school. I was surprised, that is, to see that I already knew them, that I already knew almost everyone in the room; I was surprised that dancing school, as an institution, was eerily more significant than all my other lessons and classes, and that it was not peripheral at all, but central.

For here we all were. I'd seen the boys in, of all places, church—one of the requisite Presbyterian churches of Pittsburgh. I'd seen them at the country club, too. I knew the girls from church, the country club, and school. Here we all were at dancing school; here we all were, dressed to the teeth and sitting on rows of peculiar painted and gilded chairs. Here we all were, boys and girls, plunged by our conspiring elders into the bewildering social truth that we were meant to make each other's acquaintance. Dancing school.

There in that obscure part of town, there in that muffled enormous old stone building, among those bizarre and mismatched adults who seemed grimly to dance their lives away in that dry and claustrophobic ballroom—there, it proved, was the unlikely arena where we were foreordained to assemble, Friday after Friday, for many years until the distant and seemingly unrelated country clubs took over the great work of providing music for us later and later into the night until the time came when we should all have married each other up, at last.

"Isn't he cute?" Bebe would whisper to me as we sat in the girls' row on the edge of the ballroom floor. I had never before seen a painted chair; my mother favored wood for its own sake. The lugubrious instructors were demonstrating one of several fox-trots.

Which?

"Ronny," she whispered one week, and "Danny," the next. I would find that one in the boys' row. He'd fastened his fists to his seat and was rocking back and forth from his hips all unconsciously, open-mouthed.

Sure.

"Isn't he cute?" Mimsie would ask at school, and I would think of this Ricky or Dick, recall some stray bit of bubbling laughter in which he had been caught helpless, pawing at his bangs with his bent wrist, his saliva whitening his braces' rubber bands and occasionally forming a glassy pane at the corner of his mouth; I would remember the way his head bobbed, and imagine those two parallel rods at the back of his neck, which made a thin valley where a short tip of hair lay tapered and curled; the way he scratched his ear by wincing, raising a shoulder, and rubbing the side of his head on his jacket's sleeve seam. Cute?

You bet he was cute. They all were.

Onstage the lonely pianist played "Mountain Greenery." Sometimes he played "Night and Day." It was Friday afternoon; we could have been sled riding. On Fridays, our unrelated private schools, boys' and girls', released us early. On Fridays, dancing school met, an hour later each year, until at last we met in the dark, disrupting our families' dinners, and at last certain boys began to hold our hands, carefully looking away, after a given dance, to secure us for the next one.

We all wore white cotton gloves. Only with the greatest of effort could I sometimes feel, or fancy I felt, the warmth of a boy's hand—through his glove and my glove—on my right palm. My gloved left hand lay lightly, always lightly, on his jacket shoulder. His gloved right hand lay, forgotten by both of us, across the clumsy back of my dress, across its lumpy velvet bow or its long cold zipper concealed by brocade.

Between dances when we held hands, we commonly interleaved our fingers, as if for the sheer challenge of it, for our thick cotton gloves permitted almost no movement, and we quickly cut off the circulation in each other's fingers. If for some reason we had released each other's hands quickly, without thinking, our gloves would have come off and dropped to the ballroom floor together still entwined, while our numbed bare fingers slowly regained sensation and warmth.

We were all on some list. We were to be on that list for life, it turned out, unless we left. I had no inkling of this crucial fact, although the others, I believe, did. I was mystified to see that whoever devised the list misunderstood things so. The best-liked girl in our class, my friend Ellin Hahn, was conspicuously excluded. Because she was precisely fifty percent Jewish, she had to go to Jewish dancing school. The boys courted her anyway, one after the other, and only made do with the rest of us at dancing school. From other grades at our school, all sorts of plain, unintelligent, lifeless girls were included. These were quiet or silly girls, who seemed at school to recognize their rather low places, but who were unreasonably exuberant at dancing school, and who were gradually revealed to have known all along that in the larger arena they occupied very high places indeed. And these same lumpish, plain, very rich girls wound up marrying, to my unending stupefaction, the very liveliest and handsomest of the boys.

The boys. There were, essentially, a dozen or so of them and a dozen or so of us, so it was theoretically possible, as it were, to run through all of them by the time you finished school. We saw our dancing-school boys everywhere we went. Yet they were by no means less extraordinary for being familiar. They were familiar only visually: their eyebrows we could study in quick glimpses as we danced, eyebrows that met like spliced ropes over their noses; the winsome whorls of their hair we could stare at openly in church, hair that radiated spirally from the backs of their quite individual skulls; the smooth skin on their pliant torsos at the country-club pool, all so fascinating, each so different; and their weird little graceful bathing suits: the boys. Richard, Rich, Richie, Ricky, Ronny, Donny, Dan.

They called each other witty names, like Jag-Off. They could dribble. They walked clumsily but assuredly through the world, kicking things for the hell of it. By way of conversation, they slugged each other on their interesting shoulders.

They moved in violent jerks from which we hung back, impressed and appalled, as if from horses slamming the slats of their stalls. This and, as we would have put it, their messy eyelashes. In our heartless, condescending, ignorant way we loved their eyelashes, the fascinating and dreadful way the black hairs curled and tangled. That's the kind of vitality they had, the boys, that's the kind of novelty and attraction: their very eyelashes came out amok, and unthinkably original. That we loved, that and their cloddishness, their broad, vaudevillian reactions. They were always doing slow takes. Their breathtaking lack of subtlety in every particular, we thought— and then sometimes a gleam of consciousness in their eyes, as surprising as if you'd caught a complicit wink from a brick.

Ah, the boys. How little I understood them! How little I even glimpsed who they were. How little any of us did, if I may extrapolate. How completely I condescended to them when we were ten and they were in many ways my betters. And when we were fifteen, how little I understood them still, or again. I still thought they were all alike, for all practical purposes, no longer comical beasts now but walking gods who conferred divine power with their least glances. In fact, they were neither beasts nor gods, as I should have guessed. If they were alike it was in this, that all along the boys had been in the process of becoming responsible members of an actual and moral world we small-minded and fast-talking girls had never heard of.

They had been learning self-control. We had failed to develop any selves worth controlling. We were enforcers of a code we never questioned; we were vigilantes of the trivial. They had been accumulating information about the world outside our private schools and clubs. We had failed to notice that there was such a thing. The life of Pittsburgh, say, or the United States, or assorted foreign continents, concerned us no more than Jupiter did, or its moons.

The boys must have shared our view that we were, as girls, in the long run, negligible—not any sort of factor in anybody's day, or life, no sort of creatures to be reckoned with, or even reckoned in, at all. For they could perhaps see that we possessed neither self-control nor information, so the world could not be ours.

There was something ahead of the boys, we all felt, but we didn't know what it was. To a lesser extent and vicariously, it was ahead of us, too. From the quality of attention our elders gave to various aspects of our lives, we could have inferred that we were being prepared for a life of ballroom dancing. But we knew that wasn't it. Only children practiced ballroom dancing, for which they were patently unsuited. It was something, however, that ballroom dancing obliquely prepared us for, just as, we were told, the study of Latin would obliquely prepare us for something else, also unspecified.

Whatever we needed in order to meet the future, it was located at the unthinkable juncture of Latin class and dancing school. With the declension of Latin nouns and the conjugation of Latin verbs, it had to do with our minds' functioning; presumably this held true for the five steps of the fox-trot as well. Learning these things would permanently alter the structure of our brains, whether we wanted it to or not.

So the boys, with the actual world before them, had when they were small a bewildered air, and an endearing and bravura show of manliness. On the golden-oak ballroom floor, every darkening Friday afternoon while we girls rustled in our pastel dresses and felt at our hair ineffectually with our cotton gloves, the boys in their gloves, standing right in plain view between dances, exploded firecrackers. I would be waltzing with some arm-pumping tyke of a boy when he whispered excitedly in my ear, "Guess what I have in my pocket?" I knew. It was a cherry bomb. He slammed the thing onto the oak floor when no one was looking but a knot of his friends. The instructors flinched at the bang and stiffened; the knot of boys scattered as if shot; we could taste the sharp gunpowder in the air, and see a dab of gray ash on the floor. And when he laughed, his face reddened and gave off a vaporous heat. He seemed tickled inside his jiggling bones; he flapped his arms and slapped himself and tears fell on his tie.

They must have known, those little boys, that they would inherit corporate Pittsburgh, as indeed they have. They must have known that it was theirs by rights as boys, a real world, about which they had best start becoming informed. And they must have known, too, as Pittsburgh Presbyterian boys, that they could only just barely steal a few hours now, a few years now, to kid around, to dribble basketballs and explode fire-crackers, before they were due to make a down payment on a suitable house.

Soon they would enter investment banking and take their places in the management of Fortune 500 corporations. Soon in their scant spare time they would be serving on the boards of schools, hospitals, country clubs, and churches. No wonder they laughed so hard. These were boys who wore ties from the moment their mothers could locate their necks.

I assumed that like me the boys dreamed of running away to sea, of curing cancer, of playing for the Pirates, of painting in Paris, of tramping through the Himalayas, for we were all children together. And they may well have dreamed these things, and more, then and later. I don't know.

Those boys who confided in me later, however, when we were all older, dreamed nothing of the kind. One wanted to be top man at Gulf Oil. One wanted to accumulate a million dollars before he turned thirty. And one wanted to be major-ity leader in the U.S. Senate.

But these, the boys who confided in me, were the ones I would love when we were in our teens, and they were, accord-ing to my predilection, not the dancing-school boys at all, but other, oddball boys. I would give my heart to one oddball boy after another—to older boys, to prep-school boys no one knew, to him who refused to go to college, to him who was a hood, and all of them wonderfully skinny. I loved two such boys deeply, one after the other and for years on end, and forsook everything else in life, and rightly so, to begin learn-ing with them that unplumbed intimacy that is life's chief joy. I loved them deeply, one after the other, for years on end, I say, and hoped to change their worldly ambitions and save them from the noose. But they stood firm.

And it could be, I think, that only those oddball boys, none of whom has inherited Pittsburgh at all, longed to star in the world of money and urban power; and it could be that the central boys, our boys, who are now running Pittsburgh responsibly, longed to escape. I don't know. I never knew them well enough to tell.

AMY WAS A LOOKER; I privately thought she must be the most beautiful child on earth. She inherited our father's thick, wavy hair. Her eyes were big, and so were her lashes; her nose was delicate and fluted, her skin translucent. Her mouth curved quaintly; her lips fitted appealingly, as a cutter's bow dents and curls the water under way. Plus she was quiet. And little, and tidy, and calm, and more or less obedient. She had an endearing way—it attracted even me—of standing with her legs tight together, and peering up and around with wild, stifled hilarity and parodied curiosity, as if to see if—by chance—anybody has noticed small her and found her amusing.

At the top of Richland Lane lived Amy's friend Tibby, a prematurely sophisticated blond tot, best remembered for having drawled conversationally to Mother, when she, Tibby, was only six and still missing her front teeth, "I love your hair, Mrs. Doak." When Tibby and Amy were eight, Amy brought home yet another straight-A report card. Shortly afterward, Mother overheard Tibby say exasperated to Amy, "How can you be so smart in school and so dumb after school?" In fact, as the years passed, after school became Amy's bailiwick, and she was plenty smart at it.

When Amy wasn't playing with Tibby, she played with her dolls. They were a hostile crew. Lying rigidly in their sickbeds, they shot at each other a series of haughty expletives. She had picked these up from Katy Keene comic books; Katy Keene was a society girl with a great many clothes. Amy pronounced every consonant of these expletives: Humph, pshaw.

"I'll show you, you vixen!" cried a flat-out and staring piece of buxom plastic from its Naturalizer shoe box.

"Humph!"

"Pshaw!"

"Humph!"

"Pshaw!"

We all suffered a bit for want of more of these words.

I had made several attempts to snuff baby Amy in her cradle. Mother had repeatedly discovered me pouring glasses of water carefully into her face. So when Molly had appeared, Mother had led me to believe the new baby was a kind of present for me. Actually, the baby displaced Amy. I liked everything about her—the strong purity of her cheeriness, bewilderment, outrage; her big dumb baldness, pointy fingers, little teeth, the works.

Molly possessed a dingy blanket, which she trailed behind her like a travois on her crawls. During this period, she held the belief that when she herself could not see, she was invisible. Consequently, in order to hide, she draped her head in this blanket. When it was time for her nap, we found her a pyramidal woolly mound on the pantry floor, a veritable monadnock, her fat foot protruding from the blanket's edge. She barely breathed from suspense. It broke her heart to be discovered and bundled away, day after day; she tried hard to hide ever more motionless.

When the spirit of Lister seized Mother, she flung the ap-

palling blanket into the washing machine. Molly wept incon-
solably, so Mother carried her to the basement to let her watch
the thing go around in the dryer. Molly plumped down intently, straight-backed, before the dryer as if it were a television screen; her big head rolled around and around on her tiny
neck. Mother, Amy, and I watched from the top of the stairs,
trying not to let her hear us. Finally, Mother cut the blanket
in two so she could wash one easily, and that particular joke
was over.

After Father got back from his river trip, he needed something to do. He had an income, but the days themselves, if
not the coffers, needed filling. So he joined as its business
manager an offbeat outfit that made radio spots in its recording
studio, and also rented the studio to all comers. The company
was small enough so that he got to do some acting, which he
loved. He practiced around the house, saying in rotund tones,
for my amusement, "Hello, Horatio." The line came from a
story I liked, about one of his friends' acting lessons at the
American Academy in New York. The budding actors stood
in the opened window over Fifty-sixth Street and intoned,
over and over again, "Hello, Horatio." The idea was to say
"Hello, Horatio" not loudly but deeply, in a voice so resonant
that passersby far below would look up. That was the test. The
window was high above the street. Did anyone look up? Then
the actor had boomed his speech well. Once I was playing
mumblety-peg with my friend Pin Ford on the side lawn under
the buckeye trees when I heard it from my parents' upstairs
window: "Hello, Horatio!" I looked right up.

Pittsburgh was a great town for radio—KDKA was the
world's first commercial radio station—and a great town for
KDKA's funny-voiced radio characters, like Omicron, a little
fellow from outer space. Father's senior partner in the recording studio was the voice of some of these characters. Father ran
the business end of the enterprise, and sales, and in those years
he had a good time. The people there called him Paco. He did

some straight advertising spots, and got called from his desk to help out with crowd noises—what radio people call Walla Walla talk. A mere two people, he said, could sound like a great crowd—a lively cocktail party or a muted full house at the theater—if they continuously muttered, "Pork chops and Lyonnaise potatoes."

This was not the way any other man we knew lived. Our father had been reared, for instance, cheek by jowl with Oma's best friend's son, Edgar Speer. They played together summers at Lake Erie; they spent holidays together. Our family still spent some holidays with the Speers and their boys, but now Edgar Speer—Uncle Ed—was pretty busy; he was executive vice-president of U.S. Steel, and soon would be president, and then chairman. "Edgar's er, promotion," Oma called the last, uncomfortable.

Much later, Father and his company got involved in the making of a low-budget local horror movie, in which Father played a scientist interviewed on television. The name of the movie was *Night of the Living Dead.* It was a startling success both in Europe and in the United States. First Mother was angry that he was involved in a horror movie, and then she was angry that he hadn't got a percentage of it.

Not only that, but the Pirates were in the cellar again. They lived in the cellar, like trolls. They hadn't won a pennant since 1927. Nobody could even remember when they won ball games, the bums. They had some hitters, but no pitchers.

On the yellow back wall of our Richland Lane garage, I drew a target in red crayon. The target was a batter's strike zone. The old garage was dark inside; I turned on the bare bulb. Then I walked that famously lonely walk out to the mound, our graveled driveway, and pitched.

I squinted at the strike zone, ignoring the jeers of the batter—oddly, Ralph Kiner. I received no impressions save those inside the long aerial corridor that led to the target. I threw a red-and-blue rubber ball, one of those with a central yellow band. I wound up; I drew back. The target held my eyes. The target set me spinning as the sun from a distance winds the helpless spheres. Entranced and drawn, I swung through the moves and woke up with the ball gone. It felt as if I'd gathered my own body, pointed it carefully, and thrown it down a tunnel bored by my eyes.

I pitched in a blind fever of concentration. I pitched, as I did most things, in order to concentrate. Why do elephants drink? To forget. I loved living at my own edge, as an explorer on a ship presses to the ocean's rim; mind and skin were one joined force curved out and alert, prow and telescope. I pitched, as I did most things, in a rapture.

Now here's the pitch. I followed the ball as if it had been my own head, and watched it hit the painted plastered wall. High and outside; ball one. While I stood still stupefied by the effort of the pitch, while I stood agog, unbreathing, mystical, and unaware, here came the daggone rubber ball again, bouncing out of the garage. And I had to hustle up some snappy fielding, or lose the ball in a downhill thicket next door.

The red, blue, and yellow ball came spinning out to the driveway, and sprang awry on the gravel; if I nabbed it, it was apt to bounce out of my mitt. Sometimes I threw the fielded grounder to first—sidearm—back to the crayon target, which had become the first baseman. Fine, but the moronic first baseman spat it back out again at once, out of the dark garage and bouncing crazed on the gravel; I bolted after it, panting. The pace of this game was always out of control.

So I held the ball now, and waited, and breathed, and fixed on the target till it mesmerized me into motion. In there, strike one. Low, ball two.

Four balls, and they had a man on. Three strikeouts, and you had retired the side. Happily, the opposing batters, apparently paralyzed by admiration, never swung at a good pitch. Unfortunately, though, you had to keep facing them; the retired side resurrected immediately from its ashes, fresh and vigorous,

while you grew delirious—nutsy, that is, from fielding a
bouncing ball every other second and then stilling your heart
and blinking the blood from your eyes so you could concentrate on the pitch.

Amy's friend Tibby had an older brother, named Ricky; he
was younger than I was, but available. We had no laughing
friendship, such as I enjoyed with Pin Ford, but instead a
working relationship: we played a two-handed baseball game.
Tibby and Ricky's family lived secluded at the high dead end
of Richland Lane. Their backyard comprised several kempt
and gardened acres. It was here in the sweet mown grass, here
between the fruit trees and the rhubarb patch, that we passed
long, hot afternoons pitching a baseball. Ricky was a sober,
good-looking boy, very dark; his father was a surgeon.

We each pitched nine innings. The other caught, hunkered
down, and called each pitch a ball or a strike. That was the
essence of it: Catcher called it. Four walks scored a side. Three
outs retired a side, and the catcher's side came on to pitch.

This was practically the majors. You had a team to root for,
a team that both received pitches and dished them out. You
kept score. The pitched ball came back right to you—after a
proper, rhythmical interval. You had a real squatting catcher.
Best, you had a baseball.

The game required the accuracy I was always working on.
It also required honor. If when you were catching you made
some iffy calls, you would be sorry when it was your turn to
pitch. Ricky and I were, in this primitive sense, honorable.
The tag ends of summer—before or after camp, before or after
Lake Erie—had thrown us together for this one activity, this
chance to do some pitching. We shared a catcher's mitt every
inning; we pitched at the catcher's mitt. I threw as always by
imagining my whole body hurled into the target; the rest
followed naturally. I had one pitch, a fast ball. I couldn't
control the curve. When the game was over, we often played
another. Then we thanked each other formally, drank some

hot water from a garden hose, and parted—like, perhaps, boys.

On Tuesday summer evenings I rode my bike a mile down Braddock Avenue to a park where I watched Little League teams play ball. Little League teams did not accept girls, a ruling I looked into for several years in succession. I parked my bike and hung outside the chain-link fence and watched and rooted and got mad and hollered, "Idiot, catch the ball!" "Play's at first!" Maybe some coach would say, "Okay, sweetheart, if you know it all, you go in there." I thought of disguising myself. None of this was funny. I simply wanted to play the game earnestly, on a diamond, until it was over, with eighteen players who knew what they were doing, and an umpire. My parents were sympathetic, if amused, and not eager to make an issue of it.

At school we played softball. No bunting, no stealing. I had settled on second base, a spot Bill Mazeroski would later sanctify: lots of action, lots of talk, and especially a chance to turn the double play. Dumb softball: so much better than no ball at all, I reluctantly grew to love it. As I got older, and the prospect of having anything to do with young Ricky up the street became out of the question, I had to remind myself, with all loyalty and nostalgia, how a baseball, a real baseball, felt.

A baseball weighted your hand just so, and fit it. Its red stitches, its good leather and hardness like skin over bone, seemed to call forth a skill both easy and precise. On the catch—the grounder, the fly, the line drive—you could snag a baseball in your mitt, where it stayed, snap, like a mouse locked in its trap, not like some pumpkin of a softball you merely halted, with a terrible sound like a splat. You could curl your fingers around a baseball, and throw it in a straight line. When you hit it with a bat it cracked—and your heart cracked, too, at the sound. It took a grassy stain nicely, stayed round, smelled good, and lived lashed in your mitt all winter, hibernating.

There was no call for overhand pitches in softball; all my training was useless. I was playing with twenty-five girls, some of whom did not, on the face of it, care overly about the game at hand. I waited out by second and hoped for a play to the plate.

A TORNADO HIT OUR NEIGHBORHOOD one morning. Our neighborhood was not only leafy Richland Lane and its hushed side streets, but also Penn Avenue, from which Richland Lane loftily arose. Old Penn Avenue was a messy, major thoroughfare still cobblestoned in the middle lanes, and full of stoplights and jammed traffic. There were drugstores there, old apartment buildings, and some old mansions. Penn Avenue was the city—tangled and muscular, a broad and snarled fist. The tornado broke all the windows in the envelope factory on Penn Avenue and ripped down mature oaks and maples on Richland Lane and its side streets—trees about which everyone would make, in my view, an unconscionable fuss, not least perhaps because they would lie across the streets for a week.

After the tornado passed I roamed around and found a broken power line. It banged violently by the Penn Avenue curb; it was shooting sparks into the street. I couldn't bring myself to leave the spot.

The power line was loosing a fireball of sparks that melted

the asphalt. It was a thick twisted steel cable usually strung overhead along Penn Avenue; it carried power—4,500 kilovolts of it—from Wilkinsburg ("City of Churches") to major sections of Pittsburgh, to Homewood and Brushton, Shadyside, and Squirrel Hill.

It was melting a pit for itself in the street. The live wire's hundred twisted ends spat a thick sheaf of useless yellow sparks that hissed. The sparks were cooking the asphalt gummy; they were burning a hole. I watched the cable relax and sink into its own pit; I watched the yellow sparks pool and crackle around the cable's torn end and splash out of the pit and over the asphalt in a stream toward the curb and my shoes. My bare shins could feel the heat. I smelled tarry melted asphalt and steel so hot it smoked.

"If you touch that," my father said, needlessly, "you're a goner."

I had gone back to the house to get him so he could see this violent sight, this cable all but thrashing like a cobra and shooting a torrent of sparks.

While the tornado itself was on—while the buckeye trees in our yard were coming apart—Mother had gathered Amy and Molly and held them with her sensibly away from the windows; she urged my father and me to join them. Father had recently returned from his river trip and was ensconced tamed in the household again. And here was a pleasant, once-in-a-lifetime tornado, the funnel of which touched down, in an almost delicate point, like a bolt of lightning, on our very street. He and I raced from window to window and watched; we saw the backyard sycamore smash the back-porch roof; we saw the air roaring and blowing full of sideways-flying objects, and saw the leafy buckeye branches out front blow white and upward like skirts.

"With your taste for natural disaster," Mother said to me later, "you should try to arrange a marriage with the head of the International Red Cross."

*   *   *

Now the torn cable lay near the curb, away from traffic. Its loose power dissipated in the air, a random destructiveness. If you touched it, you would turn into Reddy Kilowatt. Your skin would wiggle up in waves like an electrified cat's in a cartoon; your hair would rise stiff from your head; anyone who touched you by mistake would stick to you wavy-skinned and paralyzed. You would be dead but still standing, the power surging through your body in electrical imitation of life. Passersby would have to knock you away from the current with planks.

Father placed a ring of empty Coke bottles around the hissing power line and went back home to call Duquesne Light. I stayed transfixed. Other neighborhood children showed up, looked at the cable shooting sparks, and wandered away to see the great killed trees. I stood and watched the thick billion bolts swarm in the street. The cable was as full as a waterfall, never depleted; it dug itself a pit in which the yellow sparks spilled like water. I stayed at the busy Penn Avenue curb all day staring, until, late in the afternoon, someone somewhere turned off the juice.

Streetcars ran on Penn Avenue. Streetcars were orange, clangy, beloved things—loud, jerky, and old. They were powerless beasts compelled to travel stupidly with their wheels stuck in the tracks below them. Each streetcar had one central headlight, which looked fixedly down its tracks and nowhere else. The single light advertised to drivers at night that something was coming that couldn't move over. When a streetcar's tracks and wires rounded a corner, the witless streetcar had to follow. Its heavy orange body bulged out and blocked two lanes; any car trapped beside it had to cringe stopped against the curb until it passed.

Sometimes a car parked at the curb blocked a streetcar's route. Then the great beast sounded its mournful bell: it emitted a long-suffering, monotonous bong . . . bong . . . bong

. . . and men and women on the sidewalk shook their heads sympathetically at the motorman inside, the motorman more inferred than seen through the windshield's bright reflections.

Penn Avenue smelled of gasoline, exhaust fumes, trees' sweetness in the spring, and, year round, burnt grit. On the blocks from Lang to Richland Lane were buildings in wild assortment: two drugstores, Henry Clay Frick's mansion with his old daughter somewhere inside, a dark working-class bar called the Evergreen Café, a corner grocery store, the envelope factory, a Westinghouse plant, some old apartment buildings, and a parklike Presbyterian seminary.

You walked on sidewalks whose topography was as intricate as Pittsburgh's, and as hilly. Frost-heaved peaks of cement arose, broke, and, over years, subsided again like Appalachians beside deep pits in which clean grass grew from what looked like black grease. Every long once in a while, someone repaired the sidewalk, to the tune of four or five squares' worth. The sidewalks were like greater Pittsburgh in this, too—cut into so many parts, so many legal divisions, that no one was responsible for all of it, and it all crumbled.

It was your whole body that knew those sidewalks and streets. Your bones ached with them; you tasted their hot dust in your bleeding lip; their gravel worked into your palms and knees and stayed, blue under the new skin that grew over it.

You rode your bike across Penn Avenue with the light: a lane of asphalt, a sunken streetcar track just the width of a thin bike wheel, a few feet of brown cobblestones, another streetcar track, more cobblestones or some cement, more tracks, and another strip of asphalt. The old cobblestones were pale humpy ovals like loaves. When you rode your bike over them, you vibrated all over. A particularly long humpy cobblestone could knock you down in a twinkling if it caught your bike's front wheel. So could the streetcar's tracks, and they often did; your handlebars twisted in your hands and threw you like a wrestler. So you had to pay attention, alas, and could not simply coast along over cobblestones, blissfully vibrating all over. Now the city was replacing all the cobblestones, block by block. The cobblestones had come from Pittsburgh's riverbeds. In the nineteenth century, children had earned pennies by dragging them up from the water and selling them to paving contractors. They had been a great and late improvement on mud.

The streetcars' overhead network of wires made of Penn Avenue a loose-roofed tunnel. The wires cut the sky into rectangles inside which you could compose various views as you walked. Here were a yellow brick apartment top and some flattened fair-weather clouds; here were green sycamore leaves in the foreground, and a faded orange rooftop advertising sign, and a yellow streetlight, and a slab of neutral sky.

Streetcars traveled with their lone trolley sticks pushed up by springs into these overhead wires. A trolley stick carried a trolley wheel; the trolley wheel rolled along the track of hot electric wire overhead as the four wheels rolled along the cold grooved track below. At night, and whenever it rained, the streetcars' trolleys sparked. They shot a radiant fistful of sparks at every crossing of wires. Sometimes a streetcar accidentally "threw the trolley." Bumping over a switch or rounding a bend, the trolley lost the wire and the spring-loaded stick flew up and banged its bare side crazily against the hot wire. Big yellow sparks came crackling into the sky and fell glowing toward the roofs of cars. The motorman had to brake the streetcar, go around to its rear, and haul the wayward, sparking trolley stick down with a rope. This happened so often that there was a coil of rope for that purpose at the streetcar's stern, neat and cleated like a halyard on a mast.

So the big orange streetcars clanged and spat along; they stopped and started, tethered to their wires overhead and trapped in their grooves below. Every day at a hundred intersections they locked horns with cars that blocked their paths—

cars driven by insensible, semiconscious people, people who had just moved to town, teenagers learning to drive, the dread Ohio drivers, people sunk in rapturous conversation.

"Bong bong," bleated the stricken streetcar, "bong," and its passengers tried to lean around to see what was holding it up, and its berserk motorman gestured helplessly, furiously, at the dumb dreaming car—a shrug, a wave, a fist:

> I'm a streetcar!
> What can I do?
> What can I do
> but wait for you jerks
> to figure out that I'm a streetcar!

I tried to kill a streetcar by overturning it.

Pin Ford and I were hiding under a purple beech tree on the lawn of the Presbyterian seminary on Penn Avenue.

Through the beech's low dense branches she and I could make out Penn Avenue's streetcar lanes. It was midafternoon. Now a streetcar was coming toward us. We had been waiting. We had just stuck a stone in the streetcar track. This one seemed like a stone big enough to throw it over. Would the streetcar go over? Did we hope it would go over? We spotted its jiggling trolley stick first, high above the roofs of cars. Then we saw its round orange shoulder, humped like a cobblestone, and its lone simple eye. I pressed a thumb and finger between ribs on both sides of my breastbone, to try to calm myself.

It had started with pennies. A streetcar's wheel could slick a penny and enlarge it to a stripe. What would it do to a stone? It would crunch and crumble a stone. How big a stone? We ran between moving cars and placed ever bigger stones in the streetcar track; we ran back under the beech tree to watch.

This last stone was a coarse gray conglomerate, five inches by two by two. Was it reinforced concrete? Through the low-slung beech boughs we saw the streetcar draw nigh; we covered our lower faces with our hands.

The streetcar hit the stone audibly and rose like a beached

whale. Its big orange body faltered in the air, heaved toward the lane of cars beside it, trembled, and finally fell down on its track and broke the stone. And went on, bumping again only slightly when the rear wheel went over it. Pin Ford and I lay low.

In that instant while the streetcar stopped upraised over its track like an animal bewildered, while it swayed over the cars' lane and hung on its side and its trolley stick dangled askew, I saw it continue its roll; I saw precisely which cars it would fall on, and which dim people silhouetted inside the cars and the streetcar would be the most surprised. I saw, too, in that clear instant, that if the streetcar did derail, I would have to come forward and give myself up to the police, and do time, and all that, for the alternative was living all the rest of life on the lam.

What can we make of the inexpressible joy of children? It is a kind of gratitude, I think—the gratitude of the ten-year-old who wakes to her own energy and the brisk challenge of the world. You thought you knew the place and all its routines, but you see you hadn't known. Whole stacks at the library held books devoted to things you knew nothing about. The boundary of knowledge receded, as you poked about in books, like Lake Erie's rim as you climbed its cliffs. And each area of knowledge disclosed another, and another. Knowledge wasn't a body, or a tree, but instead air, or space, or being—whatever pervaded, whatever never ended and fitted into the smallest cracks and the widest space between stars.

Any way you cut it, colors and shadows flickered from multiple surfaces. Just enough work had already been done on everything—moths, say, or meteorites—to get you started and interested, but not so much there was nothing left to do. Often I wondered: was it being born just now, in this century, in this country? And I thought: no, any time could have been like this, if you had the time and weren't sick; you could, especially if you were a boy, learn and do. There was joy in concentration, and the world afforded an inexhaustible wealth of projects to concentrate on. There was joy in effort, and the world resisted effort to just the right degree, and yielded to it at last. People cut Mount Rushmore into faces; they chipped here and there for years. People slowed the spread of yellow fever; they sprayed the Isthmus of Panama puddle by puddle. Effort alone I loved. Some days I would have been happy to push a pole around a threshing floor like an ox, for the pleasure of moving the heavy stone and watching my knees rise in turn.

I was running down the Penn Avenue sidewalk, revving up for an act of faith. I was conscious and self-conscious. I knew well that people could not fly—as well as anyone knows it—but I also knew the kicker: that, as the books put it, with faith all things are possible.

Just once I wanted a task that required all the joy I had. Day after day I had noticed that if I waited long enough, my strong unexpressed joy would dwindle and dissipate inside me, over many hours, like a fire subsiding, and I would at last calm down. Just this once I wanted to let it rip. Flying rather famously required the extra energy of belief, and this, too, I had in superabundance.

There were boxy yellow thirties apartment buildings on those Penn Avenue blocks, and the Evergreen Café, and Miss Frick's house set back behind a wrought-iron fence. There were some side yards of big houses, some side yards of little houses, some streetcar stops, and a drugstore from which I had once tried to heist a five-pound box of chocolates, a Whitman sampler, confusing "sampler" with "free sample." It was past all this that I ran that late fall afternoon, up old Penn Avenue on the cracking cement sidewalks—past the drugstore and bar, past the old and new apartment buildings and the long dry lawn behind Miss Frick's fence.

I ran the sidewalk full tilt. I waved my arms ever higher and faster; blood balled in my fingertips. I knew I was foolish. I knew I was too old really to believe in this as a child would, out of ignorance; instead I was experimenting as a scientist would, testing both the thing itself and the limits of my own courage in trying it miserably self-conscious in full view of the whole world. You can't test courage cautiously, so I ran hard and waved my arms hard, happy.

Up ahead I saw a business-suited pedestrian. He was coming stiffly toward me down the walk. Who could ever forget this first test, this stranger, this thin young man appalled? I banished the temptation to straighten up and walk right. He flattened himself against a brick wall as I passed flailing—although I had left him plenty of room. He had refused to meet my exultant eye. He looked away, evidently embarrassed. How surprisingly easy it was to ignore him! What I was letting rip, in fact, was my willingness to look foolish, in his eyes and in my own. Having chosen this foolishness, I was a free being. How could the world ever stop me, how could I betray myself, if I was not afraid?

I was flying. My shoulders loosened, my stride opened, my heart banged the base of my throat. I crossed Carnegie and ran up the block waving my arms. I crossed Lexington and ran up the block waving my arms.

A linen-suited woman in her fifties did meet my exultant eye. She looked exultant herself, seeing me from far up the block. Her face was thin and tanned. We converged. Her warm, intelligent glance said she knew what I was doing—not because she herself had been a child but because she herself took a few loose aerial turns around her apartment every night for the hell of it, and by day played along with the rest of the world and took the streetcar. So Teresa of Avila checked her unseemly joy and hung on to the altar rail to hold herself down. The woman's smiling, deep glance seemed to read my own awareness from my face, so we passed on the sidewalk—a beautiful upright woman walking in her tan linen suit, a kid running and flapping her arms—we passed on the sidewalk with a look of accomplices who share a humor just beyond irony. What's a heart for?

*   *   *

I crossed Homewood and ran up the block. The joy multiplied as I ran—I ran never actually quite leaving the ground—and multiplied still as I felt my stride begin to fumble and my knees begin to quiver and stall. The joy multiplied even as I slowed bumping to a walk. I was all but splitting, all but shooting sparks. Blood coursed free inside my lungs and bones, a light-shot stream like air. I couldn't feel the pavement at all.

I was too aware to do this, and had done it anyway. What could touch me now? For what were the people on Penn Avenue to me, or what was I to myself, really, but a witness to any boldness I could muster, or any cowardice if it came to that, any giving up on heaven for the sake of dignity on earth? I had not seen a great deal accomplished in the name of dignity, ever.

ONE SUNDAY AFTERNOON Mother wandered through our kitchen, where Father was making a sandwich and listening to the ball game. The Pirates were playing the New York Giants at Forbes Field. In those days, the Giants had a utility infielder named Wayne Terwilliger. Just as Mother passed through, the radio announcer cried—with undue drama—"Terwilliger bunts one!"

"Terwilliger bunts one?" Mother cried back, stopped short. She turned. "Is that English?"

"The player's name is Terwilliger," Father said. "He bunted."

"That's marvelous," Mother said. " 'Terwilliger bunts one.' No wonder you listen to baseball. 'Terwilliger bunts one.' "

For the next seven or eight years, Mother made this surprising string of syllables her own. Testing a microphone, she repeated, "Terwilliger bunts one"; testing a pen or a typewriter, she wrote it. If, as happened surprisingly often in the course of various improvised gags, she pretended to whisper something else in my ear, she actually whispered, "Terwilliger bunts one." Whenever someone used a French phrase, or a Latin one, she answered solemnly, "Terwilliger bunts one." If Mother had had, like Andrew Carnegie, the opportunity to cook up a motto for a coat of arms, hers would have read simply and tellingly, "Terwilliger bunts one." (Carnegie's was "Death to Privilege.")

She served us with other words and phrases. On a Florida trip, she repeated tremulously, "That . . . is a royal poinciana." I don't remember the tree; I remember the thrill in her voice. She pronounced it carefully, and spelled it. She also liked to say "portulaca."

The drama of the words "Tamiami Trail" stirred her, we learned on the same Florida trip. People built Tampa on one coast, and they built Miami on another. Then—the height of visionary ambition and folly—they piled a slow, tremendous road through the terrible Everglades to connect them. To build the road, men stood sunk in muck to their armpits. They fought off cottonmouth moccasins and six-foot alligators. They slept in boats, wet. They blasted muck with dynamite, cut jungle with machetes; they laid logs, dragged drilling machines, hauled dredges, heaped limestone. The road took fourteen years to build up by the shovelful, a Panama Canal in reverse, and cost hundreds of lives from tropical, mosquito-carried diseases. Then, capping it all, some genius thought of the word Tamiami: they called the road from Tampa to Miami, this very road under our spinning wheels, the Tamiami Trail. Some called it Alligator Alley. Anyone could drive over this road without a thought.

Hearing this, moved, I thought all the suffering of road building was worth it (it wasn't my suffering), now that we had this new thing to hang these new words on—Alligator Alley for those who liked things cute, and, for connoisseurs like Mother, for lovers of the human drama in all its boldness and terror, the Tamiami Trail.

Back home, Mother cut clips from reels of talk, as it were, and played them back at leisure. She noticed that many Pitts-

burghers confuse "leave" and "let." One kind relative bright-
ened our morning by mentioning why she'd brought her son
to visit: "He wanted to come with me, so I left him." Mother
filled in Amy and me on locutions we missed. "I can't do it
on Friday," her pretty sister told a crowded dinner party,
"because Friday's the day I lay in the stores."

(All unconsciously, though, we ourselves used some pure
Pittsburghisms. We said "tele pole," pronounced "telly
pole," for that splintery sidewalk post I loved to climb. We
said "slippy"—the sidewalks are "slippy." We said, "That's all
the farther I could go." And we said, as Pittsburghers do say,
"This glass needs washed," or "The dog needs walked"—a
usage our father eschewed; he knew it was not standard English, nor even comprehensible English, but he never let on.)

"Spell 'poinsettia,'" Mother would throw out at me, smiling with pleasure. "Spell 'sherbet.'" The idea was not to make
us whizzes, but, quite the contrary, to remind us—and I, especially, needed reminding—that we didn't know it all just yet.

"There's a deer standing in the front hall," she told me one
quiet evening in the country.

"Really?"

"No. I just wanted to tell you something once without your
saying, 'I know.'"

Supermarkets in the middle 1950s began luring, or bothering, customers by giving out Top Value Stamps or Green
Stamps. When, shopping with Mother, we got to the head of
the checkout line, the checker, always a young man, asked,
"Save stamps?"

"No," Mother replied genially, week after week, "I build
model airplanes." I believe she originated this line. It took me
years to determine where the joke lay.

Anyone who met her verbal challenges she adored. She had
surgery on one of her eyes. On the operating table, just before
she conked out, she appealed feelingly to the surgeon, saying,
as she had been planning to say for weeks, "Will I be able to

play the piano?" "Not on me," the surgeon said. "You won't pull that old one on me."

It was, indeed, an old one. The surgeon was supposed to answer, "Yes, my dear, brave woman, you will be able to play the piano after this operation," to which Mother intended to reply, "Oh, good, I've always wanted to play the piano." This pat scenario bored her; she loved having it interrupted. It must have galled her that usually her acquaintances were so predictably unalert; it must have galled her that, for the length of her life, she could surprise everyone so continually, so easily, when she had been the same all along. At any rate, she loved anyone who, as she put it, saw it coming, and called her on it.

She regarded the instructions on bureaucratic forms as straight lines. "Do you advocate the overthrow of the United States government by force or violence?" After some thought she wrote, "Force." She regarded children, even babies, as straight men. When Molly learned to crawl, Mother delighted in buying her gowns with drawstrings at the bottom, like Swee'pea's, because, as she explained energetically, you could easily step on the drawstring without the baby's noticing, so that she crawled and crawled and crawled and never got anywhere except into a small ball at the gown's top.

When we children were young, she mothered us tenderly and dependably; as we got older, she resumed her career of anarchism. She collared us into her gags. If she answered the phone on a wrong number, she told the caller, "Just a minute," and dragged the receiver to Amy or me, saying, "Here, take this, your name is Cecile," or, worse, just, "It's for you." You had to think on your feet. But did you want to perform well as Cecile, or did you want to take pity on the wretched caller?

During a family trip to the Highland Park Zoo, Mother and I were alone for a minute. She approached a young couple holding hands on a bench by the seals, and addressed the young man in dripping tones: "Where have you been? Still got those baby-blue eyes; always did slay me. And this"—a swift nod at the dumbstruck young woman, who had removed her hand from the man's—"must be the one you were telling me about. She's not so bad, really, as you used to make out. But listen, you know how I miss you, you know where to reach me, same old place. And there's Ann over there—see how she's grown? See the blue eyes?"

And off she sashayed, taking me firmly by the hand, and leading us around briskly past the monkey house and away. She cocked an ear back, and both of us heard the desperate man begin, in a high-pitched wail, "I swear, I never saw her before in my life. . . ."

On a long, sloping beach by the ocean, she lay stretched out sunning with Father and friends, until the conversation gradually grew tedious, when without forethought she gave a little push with her heel and rolled away. People were stunned. She rolled deadpan and apparently effortlessly, arms and legs extended and tidy, down the beach to the distant water's edge, where she lay at ease just as she had been, but half in the surf, and well out of earshot.

She dearly loved to fluster people by throwing out a game's rules at whim—when she was getting bored, losing in a dull sort of way, and when everybody else was taking it too seriously. If you turned your back, she moved the checkers around on the board. When you got them all straightened out, she denied she'd touched them; the next time you turned your back, she lined them up on the rug or hid them under your chair. In a betting rummy game called Michigan, she routinely played out of turn, or called out a card she didn't hold, or counted backward, simply to amuse herself by causing an uproar and watching the rest of us do double takes and have fits. (Much later, when serious suitors came to call, Mother subjected them to this fast card game as a trial by ordeal; she used it as an intelligence test and a measure of spirit. If the poor man could stay a round without breaking down or running out, he got to marry one of us, if he still wanted to.)

She excelled at bridge, playing fast and boldly, but when the stakes were low and the hands dull, she bid slams for the devilment of it, or raised her opponents' suit to bug them, or showed her hand, or tossed her cards in a handful behind her back in a characteristic swift motion accompanied by a vibrantly innocent look. It drove our stolid father crazy. The hand was over before it began, and the guests were appalled. How do you score it, who deals now, what do you do with a crazy person who is having so much fun? Or they were down seven, and the guests were appalled. "Pam!" "Dammit, Pam!" He groaned. What ails such people? What on earth possesses them? He rubbed his face.

She was an unstoppable force; she never let go. When we moved across town, she persuaded the U.S. Post Office to let her keep her old address—forever—because she'd had stationery printed. I don't know how she did it. Every new post officer worker, over decades, needed to learn that although the Doaks' mail is addressed to here, it is delivered to there.

Mother's energy and intelligence suited her for a greater role in a larger arena—mayor of New York, say—than the one she had. She followed American politics closely; she had been known to vote for Democrats. She saw how things should be run, but she had nothing to run but our household. Even there, small minds bugged her; she was smarter than the people who designed the things she had to use all day for the length of her life.

"Look," she said. "Whoever designed this corkscrew never used one. Why would anyone sell it without trying it out?" So she invented a better one. She showed me a drawing of it. The spirit of American enterprise never faded in Mother. If capitalizing and tooling up had been as interesting as theorizing and thinking up, she would have fired up a new factory every week, and chaired several hundred corporations.

"It grieves me," she would say, "it grieves my heart," that the company that made one superior product packaged it poorly, or took the wrong tack in its advertising. She knew, as she held the thing mournfully in her two hands, that she'd never find another. She was right. We children wholly sympathized, and so did Father; what could she do, what could anyone do, about it? She was Samson in chains. She paced.

She didn't like the taste of stamps so she didn't lick stamps; she licked the corner of the envelope instead. She glued sandpaper to the sides of kitchen drawers, and under kitchen cabinets, so she always had a handy place to strike a match. She designed, and hounded workmen to build against all norms, doubly wide kitchen counters and elevated bathroom sinks. To splint a finger, she stuck it in a light-weight cigar tube. Conversely, to protect a pack of cigarettes, she carried it in a Band-Aid box. She drew plans for an over-the-finger toothbrush for babies, an oven rack that slid up and down, and—the family favorite—Lendalarm. Lendalarm was a beeper you attached to books (or tools) you loaned friends. After ten days, the beeper sounded. Only the rightful owner could silence it.

She repeatedly reminded us of P. T. Barnum's dictum: You could sell anything to anybody if you marketed it right. The adman who thought of making Americans believe they needed underarm deodorant was a visionary. So, too, was the hero who made a success of a new product, Ivory soap. The executives were horrified, Mother told me, that a cake of this stuff floated. Soap wasn't supposed to float. Anyone would be able to tell it was mostly whipped-up air. Then some inspired adman made a leap: Advertise that it floats. Flaunt it. The rest is history.

She respected the rare few who broke through to new ways. "Look," she'd say, "here's an intelligent apron." She called upon us to admire intelligent control knobs and intelligent pan handles, intelligent andirons and picture frames and knife sharpeners. She questioned everything, every pair of scissors, every knitting needle, gardening glove, tape dispenser. Hers was a restless mental vigor that just about ignited the dumb household objects with its force.

*   *   *

Torpid conformity was a kind of sin; it was stupidity itself, the mighty stream against which Mother would never cease to struggle. If you held no minority opinions, or if you failed to risk total ostracism for them daily, the world would be a better place without you.

Always I heard Mother's emotional voice asking Amy and me the same few questions: Is that your own idea? Or somebody else's? *"Giant* is a good movie," I pronounced to the family at dinner. "Oh, really?" Mother warmed to these occasions. She all but rolled up her sleeves. She knew I hadn't seen it. "Is that your considered opinion?"

She herself held many unpopular, even fantastic, positions. She was scathingly sarcastic about the McCarthy hearings while they took place, right on our living-room television; she frantically opposed Father's wait-and-see calm. "We don't know enough about it," he said. "I do," she said. "I know all I need to know."

She asserted, against all opposition, that people who lived in trailer parks were not bad but simply poor, and had as much right to settle on beautiful land, such as rural Ligonier, Pennsylvania, as did the oldest of families in the finest of hidden houses. Therefore, the people who owned trailer parks, and sought zoning changes to permit trailer parks, needed our help. Her profound belief that the country-club pool sweeper was a person, and that the department-store saleslady, the bus driver, telephone operator, and house-painter were people, and even in groups the steelworkers who carried pickets and the Christmas shoppers who clogged intersections were people—this was a conviction common enough in democratic Pittsburgh, but not altogether common among our friends' parents, or even, perhaps, among our parents' friends.

Opposition emboldened Mother, and she would take on anybody on any issue—the chairman of the board, at a cocktail party, on the current strike; she would fly at him in a flurry of passion, as a songbird selflessly attacks a big hawk.

"Eisenhower's going to win," I announced after school. She lowered her magazine and looked me in the eyes: "How do you know?" I was doomed. It was fatal to say, "Everyone says so." We all knew well what happened. "Do you consult this Everyone before you make your decisions? What if Everyone decided to round up all the Jews?" Mother knew there was no danger of cowing me. She simply tried to keep us all awake. And in fact it was always clear to Amy and me, and to Molly when she grew old enough to listen, that if our classmates came to cruelty, just as much as if the neighborhood or the nation came to madness, we were expected to take, and would be each separately capable of taking, a stand.

THE FRENCH AND INDIAN WAR was a war of which I, for one, reading stretched out in the bedroom, couldn't get enough. The names of the places were a litany: Fort Ticonderoga on the Hudson, Fort Vincennes on the Wabash. The names of the people were a litany: the Sieur de Contrecoeur; the Marquis de Montcalm; Major Robert Rogers of the Rangers; the Seneca Chief Half-King.

How witless in comparison were the clumsy wars of Europe: on this open field at nine o'clock sharp, soldiers in heavy armor, dragged from their turnip patches in feudal obedience to Lord So-and-So, met in long ranks the heavily armored men owned or paid for by Lord So-and-So, and defeated them by knocking them over like ninepins. What was at stake? A son's ambition, or an earl's pride.

In the French and Indian War, and the Indian wars, a whole continent was at stake, and it was hard to know who to root for as I read. The Indians were the sentimental favorites, but they were visibly cruel. The French excelled at Indian skills and had the endearing habit of singing in boats. But if they won, we would all speak French, which seemed affected in the woods. The Scotch-Irish settlers and the English army were very uneasy allies, but their cruelties were invisible to me, and their partisans wrote all the books that fell into my hands.

It all seemed to take place right here, here among the blossoming rhododendrons outside the sunporch windows just below our bedroom, here in the Pittsburgh forest that rose again from every vacant lot, every corner of every yard the mower missed, every dusty crack in the sidewalk, every clogged gutter on the roof—an oak tree, a sycamore, a mountain ash, a pine.

For here, on the tip of the point where the three rivers met, the French built Fort Duquesne. It linked French holdings on the Great Lakes to their settlement at New Orleans. It was 1754; the forest was a wilderness. From Fort Duquesne the French set their Indian allies to raiding farflung English-speaking settlements and homesteads. The Indians burned the farms and tortured many farm families. From Fort Duquesne the French marched out and defeated George Washington at nearby Fort Necessity. From Fort Duquesne the French marched out and defeated General Edward Braddock: Indian warriors shot from cover, which offended those British soldiers who had time to notice before they died. It was here in 1758 that General John Forbes established British hegemony over the Mississippi watershed, by driving the French from the point and building Fort Pitt.

Here our own doughty provincials in green hunting shirts fought beside regiments of rangers in buckskins, actual Highlanders in kilts, pro-English Iroquois in warpaint, and British regulars in red jackets. They came marching vividly through the virgin Pittsburgh forest; they trundled up and down the nearby mountain ridges by day and slept at night on their weapons under trees. Pioneer scouts ran ahead of them and behind them; messengers snuck into their few palisaded forts, where periwigged English officers sat and rubbed their foreheads while naked Indians in the treetops outside were setting arrows on fire to burn down the roof.

Best, it was all imaginary. That the French and Indian War took place in this neck of the woods merely enhanced its storied quality, as if that fact had been a particularly pleasing literary touch. This war was part of my own private consciousness, the dreamlike interior murmur of books.

Costumed enormous people, transparent, vivid, and bold as decals, as tall and rippling as people in dreams, shot at each other up and down the primeval woods, race against race. Just as people in myths travel rigidly up to the sky, or are placed there by some great god's fingers, to hold still forever in the midst of their loving or battles as fixed constellations of stars, so the fighting cast of the French and Indian War moved in a colorful body—locked into position in the landscape but still loading muskets or cowering behind the log door or landing canoes on a muddy shore—into books. They were fabulous and morally neutral, like everything in history, like everything in books. They were imagination's playthings: toy soldiers, toy settlers, toy Indians. They were a part of the interior life; they were private; they were my own.

In books these wars played themselves out ceaselessly; the red-warpainted Indian tomahawked the settler woman in calico, and the rangy settler in buckskin spied out the Frenchman in military braid. Whenever I opened the book, the war struck up again, like a record whose music sounded when the needle hit. The skirling of Highlanders' bagpipes came playing again, high and thin over the dry oak ridges. The towheaded pioneer schoolchildren were just blabbing their memorized psalms when from right outside the greased parchment window sounded the wild and fatal whoops of Indian warriors on a raid.

The wild and fatal whoops, the war whoops of the warriors, the red warriors whooping on a raid. It was a delirium. The tongue diddled the brain. Private life, book life, took place where words met imagination without passing through world.

I could dream it all whenever I wanted—and how often I wanted to dream it! Fiercely addicted, I dosed myself again and again with the drug of the dream.

Parents have no idea what the children are up to in their bedrooms: They are reading the same paragraphs over and over in a stupor of violent bloodshed. Their legs are limp with horror. They are reading the same paragraphs over and over, dizzy with gratification as the young lovers find each other in the French fort, as the boy avenges his father, as the sound of muskets in the woods signals the end of the siege. They could not move if the house caught fire. They hate the actual world. The actual world is a kind of tedious plane where dwells, and goes to school, the body, the boring body which houses the eyes to read the books and houses the heart the books enflame. The very boring body seems to require an inordinately big, very boring world to keep it up, a world where you have to spend far too much time, have to *do* time like a prisoner, always looking for a chance to slip away, to escape back home to books, or escape back home to any concentration—fanciful, mental, or physical—where you can lose your self at last. Although I was hungry all the time, I could not bear to hold still and eat; it was too dull a thing to do, and had no appeal either to courage or to imagination. The blinding sway of their inner lives makes children immoral. They find things good insofar as they are thrilling, insofar as they render them ever more feverish and breathless, ever more limp and senseless on the bed.

Throughout these long, wonderful wars, I saw Indian braves behind every tree and parked car. They slunk around, fairly bursting with woodcraft. They led soldiers on miraculous escapes through deep woods and across lakes at night; they paddled their clever canoes noiselessly; they swam underwater without leaving bubbles; they called to each other like owls. They nocked their arrows silently on the brow of the hill and snuck up in their soft moccasins to the camp where the enemy lay sleeping under heavy guard. They shrieked, drew their osage bows, and never missed—all the while communing deeply with birds and deer.

I had been born too late. I would have made a dandy scout, although I was hungry all the time, because I had taught myself, with my friend Pin, to walk in the woods silently: without snapping a twig, which was easy, or stepping on a loud leaf, which was hard. Experience taught me a special, rolling walk for skulking in silence: you step down with your weight on the ball of your foot, and ease it to your heel.

The Indians who captured me would not torture me, but would exclaim at my many abilities, and teach me more, all the while feeding me handsomely. Soon I would talk to animals, become invisible, ride a horse naked and shrieking, shoot things.

I practiced traveling through the woods in Frick Park without leaving footprints. I practiced tracking people and animals, such as the infamous pedigreed dachshunds, by following sign. I knew the mark of Walter Milligan's blunt heel and the mark of Amy's sharp one. I practiced sneaking up on Mother as she repotted a philodendron, Father as he washed the car, saying, as I hoped but doubted the Indians said, "Boo."

At SCHOOL we memorized a poem:

> Where we live and work today
> Indian children used to play—
> All about our native land
> Where the shops and houses stand.

Richland Lane was untrafficked, hushed, planted in great shade trees, and peopled by wonderfully collected children. They were sober, sane, quiet kids, whose older brothers and sisters were away at boarding school or college. Every warm night we played organized games—games that were the sweetest part of those sweet years, that long suspended interval between terror and anger.

On the quiet dead-end side street, among the still brick houses under their old ash trees and oaks, we paced out the ritual evenings. I saw us as if from above, even then, even as I stood in place living out my childhood and knowing it, aware of myself as if from above and behind, skinny and exultant on the street. We are silent, waiting or running, spread out on the pale street like chessmen, stilled as priests, relaxed and know-ing. Someone hits the ball, someone silent far up the street catches it on the bounce; we move aside, clearing a path. Carefully the batter lays down the bat perpendicular to the street. Carefully the hushed player up the street rolls the ball down to the bat. The rolled ball hits the bat and flies up unpredictably; the batter misses his catch; he and the fielder switch positions. Indian Ball.

> And there were no roads at all.
> And the trees were very tall.

Capture the Flag was, essentially, the French and Indian War. The dead-end street (Europe) saw open combat at its fixed border. Brute strength could win. We disdained the street, although of course we had to guard its border. We fought the real war in the backyards (America)—a limitless wilderness of trees, garbage cans, thickets, back porches, and gardens, where no one knew where the two sides' territories ended, and where strategy required bold and original plan-ning, private initiative, sneaky scouting, and courage.

If someone cheated at any game, or incurred the group's wrath in any way, the rest of us gave him, or her, Indian burns: we wrung a bare arm with both hands close together till the skin chafed. Worse—reserved for practically capital crimes—was the dreaded but admired typewriter torture, which we understood to be, in modern guise, an old Indian persuader. One of us straddled the offender, bared his or her breastbone, and lightly tapped fingertips there—very lightly, just where the skin covers the bone most closely. This light tapping does not hurt at all for the first five minutes or so.

We were nice kids who rarely resorted to torture. We played Red Rover, a variation on Prisoners' Base called Beck-ons Wanted, and Crack the Whip. Everything else, and parts of these games, too, smacked of Indians. By day, Pin Ford and I played at being Indians straight out. Her parents were also young, and she was my age, an only child; they lived two doors up. Pin's real name was Barbara. She was tan and blond, sturdy, smooth of skin; she was agreeable and quick to laugh. Her courage and her flair for the visual arts hadn't yet formed. She was content now to stalk the neighborhood and knock over the odd streetcar.

As Indians, Pin and I explored the wooded grounds of the Presbyterian seminary at our backyards. We made bows and arrows: we peeled and straightened deadfall sticks for arrows, and cut, stealthily, green boughs to bend for bows. With string we rigged our mothers' Chesterfield cigarette cartons over our shoulders as quivers. We shot our bows. We threw knives at targets, and played knife-throwing games. We walked as the Indians had walked, stirring no leaves, snapping no twigs. We built an Indian village, Navajo style, under the seminary's low copper beech: we baked clay bricks on slate roofing tiles set on adobe walls around a twiggy fire.

We named the trees. We searched the sky for omens, and inspected the ground for sign.

We came home and found our mothers together in our side yard by the rose garden, tanning on chaise longues. They were both thin and blond. They held silvered cardboard reflectors up to their flung-back chins. Over their closed eyelids they had placed blue eye-shaped plastic cups, joined over the nose.

THE ATTIC BEDROOM where I drew my baseball mitt was a crow's nest, a treehouse, a studio, an office, a forensic laboratory, and a fort. It interested me especially for a totemic brown water stain on a sloping plaster wall. The stain looked like a square-rigged ship heeled over in a storm. I examined this ship for many months. It was a painting, not a drawing; it had no lines, only forms awash, which rose faintly from the plaster and deepened slowly and dramatically as I watched and the seas climbed and the wind rose before anyone could furl the sails. Those distant dashes over the water—were they men sliding overboard? Were they storm petrels flying? I knew a song whose chorus asked, What did the deep sea say?

My detective work centered around the attic, and sometimes included Pin Ford. We filed information on criminal suspects in a shoe box. We got the information by hanging around the Evergreen Café on Penn Avenue and noting suspicious activity.

One dark, rainy afternoon when I was alone, I saw a case of beer inside the trunk of a man's car. If that wasn't suspicious, I didn't know what was. I was lurking just outside the drugstore, where I could see the Evergreen Café clientele without being seen. I memorized the car license number, of course, as anyone would—but my real virtue as a detective was that I could memorize the whole man, inch by inch, by means of sentences, and later reproduce the man in a drawing.

When I came home from the dark rain that afternoon I walked through floor after floor of the lighted house, wetting the golden rugs and muttering, until I got to the attic stairs and the attic itself. There I repaired to a card table under the square-rigged ship. I wrote down the suspect's car's make and license number. I wrote down my stabs at his height and age, and a description of his clothes. Then I turned on the radio, opened a cheap drawing tablet, and relaxed to the business of drawing the man who had stepped out of the Evergreen Café and revealed a case of beer in the trunk of his car.

By accident I drew a sloppy oval that looked like his head. I copied a page of these. Paying attention, I marked off some rough ratios: the crucial intervals between eye sockets, head-top, and chin. Unconsciously again, I let my hand scribble lines for features. I sat up to play back in my head certain memorized sentences: he has a wide mouth; his mouth corners fall directly beneath eyes' outer corners; forehead is round; ears are high, triangular. My dumb hand molded the recurved facial masses and shaded the eye sockets for its own pleasure with slanting parallel lines. I sat enchanted and unwitting in a trance.

> What will the weather be?
> Tell us, Mister Weather Man.

The radio woman enunciated her slow, terrible song. She sounded her notes delicately, as did the idiot xylophone that preceded her. A wind was rising outside. Across the attic room, the blackened windows rattled. I saw their glossed reflections on the pale walls wag. The rain battered the roof over my head, over the waterlogged ship. I heard the bare buckeye boughs hitting the house.

I was drawing the head. I shut my eyes. I could not see the man's face eidetically. That is, I could not reproduce it interiorly, study it, and discover new things, as some few people can look at a page, print it, as it were, in their memories, and read it off later. I could produce stable images only rarely. But like anyone, I could recall and almost see fleet torn fragments of a scene: a raincoat sleeve's wrinkling, a blond head bending, red-lighted rain falling on asphalt, a pesteringly interesting pattern in a cordovan shoe, which rises and floats across that face I want to see. I perceived these sights as scraps that floated like blowing tissue across some hollow interior space, some space at the arching roof of the rib cage, perhaps. I swerved to study them before they slid away.

I hoped that the sentences would nail the blowing scraps down. I hoped that the sentences would store scenes like rolls of film, rolls of film I could simply reel off and watch. But of course, the sentences did not work that way. The sentences suggested scenes to the imagination, which were no sooner repeated than envisioned, and envisioned just as poorly and just as vividly as actual memories. Here was Raggedy Ann, say, an actual memory, with her red-and-white-striped stockings and blunt black feet. And here, say, was a barefoot boy asleep in a car, his cheeks covered thinly with blood. Which was real? The barefoot boy was just as vivid. It was easier to remember a sentence than a sight, and the sentences suggested sights new or skewed. These were dim regions, these submerged caves where waters mingled. On my cheap tablet I was drawing round lips, suns, fish in schools.

Soon someone would call me for dinner. But I would not come, I suddenly realized, and I would not answer the call—ever—for I would have died of starvation. They would find me, having slid off my chair, half under the card table, lying dead on the floor. And so young.

In the blue shoe box on the card table they would find my

priceless files. I had written all my data about today's suspect, drawn his face several times from several angles, and filed it all under his car's license number. When the police needed it, it was ready.

Privately I thought the reference librarian at the Homewood Library was soft in the head. The week before, she had handed me, in broad daylight, the book that contained the key to Morse code. Without a word, she watched me copy it, pocket the paper, and leave.

I knew how to keep a code secret, if she didn't. At home I memorized Morse code promptly, and burned the paper.

I had read the library's collection of popular forensic medicine, its many books about Scotland Yard and the FBI, a dull biography of J. Edgar Hoover, and its Sherlock Holmes. I knew I was not alone in knowing Morse Code. The FBI knew it, Scotland Yard knew it, and every sparks in the navy knew it. I read everything I could get about ham radios. All I needed was a receiver. I could listen in on troop maneuvers, intelligence reports, and disasters at sea. And I could rescue other hams from calamity, to which, as a class, they seemed remarkably prone.

I knew that police artists made composite drawings of criminal suspects. Witnesses to crimes selected, from a varied assortment, a stripe of crown hair, a stripe or two of forehead, a stripe of eyes, and so forth. Police artists—of whose ranks I was an oblate—made a drawing that combined these elements; newspapers published the drawings; someone recognized the suspect and called the police.

When Pin Ford and I were running low on suspects, and had run out of things to communicate in Morse code, I sat at my attic table beside the shoe box file and drew a variety of such stripes. I amused myself by combining them into new faces. So God must sit in heaven, at a card table, fingering a heap of stripes—hairlines, jawlines, brows—and joining them at whim to people a world. I began wondering if the stock of individual faces on earth through all of time is infinite.

My sweetest ambition was to see a drawing of mine on a newspaper's front page: HAS ANYBODY SEEN THIS MAN? I didn't care about reducing crime, any more than Sherlock Holmes did. I rather wished there were more crime, and closer by. What interested me was the schematic likeness, how recognizable it was, and how startlingly few things you needed to strike a resemblance. You needed only a few major proportions in the head. The soft tissues scarcely mattered; they were merely decorations that children drew. What mattered was the framing of the skull.

And so in that faraway attic, among the boughs of buckeye trees, year after year, I drew. I drew formal, sustained studies of my left hand still on the card table, of my baseball mitt, a saddle shoe. I drew from memory the faces of the people I knew, my own family just downstairs in the great house—oh, but I hated these clumsy drawings, these beloved faces so rigid on the page and lacking in tenderness and irony. (Who could analyze a numb skull when all you cared about was a lively caught glance, the pleased rising of Mother's cheek, the soft amused setting of Amy's lip, Father's imagining eye in its socket?) And I drew from memory the faces of people I saw in the streets. I formed sentences about them as I looked at them, and repeated the sentences to myself as I wandered on.

I wanted to notice everything, as Holmes had, and remember it all, as no one had before. Noticing and remembering were the route to Scotland Yard, where I intended to find my niche. They were also, more urgently, the route to the corner yard on Edgerton Avenue, to life in the house we had left and lost.

Hadn't I already forgotten the floor plan of that house where I had lived for seven years? I could see a terrifying oblong of light bend across a room's corner; I could see my mother talking on the phone in the dark stairwell, and Jo Ann

Sheehy skating at night on the iced street, and the broom-closet door opening to reveal—the broom. But who could stitch these ripped remnants together? I could no longer conjure up the face of Walter Milligan, the red-haired Irish boy I had chased up and down a football field—could no longer remember his face because I had neglected to memorize it.

Noticing and remembering everything would trap bright scenes to light and fill the blank and darkening past which was already piling up behind me. The growing size of that blank and ever-darkening past frightened me; it loomed beside me like a hole in the air and battened on scraps of my life I failed to claim. If one day I forgot to notice my life, and be damned grateful for it, the blank cave would suck me up entire.

From now on, I would beat the days into my brain. Every year, every month, I vowed this vow in a different form.

But the new scenes I tried to memorize with the aid of sentences were as elusive and random as the scenes I remembered without effort. They were just as broken, trivial, capsizing, submerged. Instead of a suspect's face I saw red-lighted rain in front of a car's taillight. Instead of the schoolyard recess scene I loved, the dodgeball game I tried to memorize at one moment, and then at another—my friends and I excited and whooping—I saw a coarse cement corner, and the cyclone fence above it, and only a flash of dark green school uniforms below. Instead of my sister Molly just starting to walk I saw the smocking on her blue dress, and her stained palm. These were torn and out-of-focus scenes playing on windblown scraps. They dissolved when I tried to inspect them, or dimmed, or slid dizzyingly away, like a ship's stern yawing down the dark lee slope of a wave.

BUT HE SAID UNTO JESUS, And who is my neighbor?

And Jesus answering said, A certain man went down from Jerusalem to Jericho, and fell among thieves.

And he said unto him, Who is my neighbor?

But a certain Samaritan came where he was.

And went to him, and bound up his wounds, and brought him to an inn, and took care of him.

And he said unto him, Which now, thinkest thou, was neighbor unto him that fell among the thieves?

And he said unto him, Who IS my neighbor?

And Jesus answering said, A certain man went down from Jerusalem to Jericho, and fell among thieves.

Who IS my neighbor?

Then said Jesus unto him, Go, and do thou likewise.

This was my "Terwilliger bunts one." This and similar fragments of Biblical language played in my head like a record on which the needle has stuck, played at the back of my mind and moved at the root of my tongue and sounded deep in my ears without surcease. Who IS my neighbor?

Every July for four years, Amy and I trotted off to a Presbyterian church camp. It was cheap, wholesome, and nearby. There we were happy, loose with other children in cabins under pines. If our parents had known how pious and low church this camp was, they would have yanked us. We memorized Bible chapters, sang rollicking hymns around the clock, held nightly devotions including extemporaneous prayers, and filed out of the woods to chapel twice on Sundays dressed in white shorts. The faith-filled theology there was only half a step out of a tent; you could still smell the sawdust.

We met all sorts of girls at camp. There were a dozen girls from an orphanage, who had never been adopted. Among these I admired an older girl named Liz—a large-framed, bony girl with dry blond curls and high red cheekbones, who wore a wool lumberjack shirt. Every Sunday night, gathered in our bare old rec hall of a chapel, we children could request a favorite hymn if we could recite a Bible verse. Year after year, big Liz returned unadopted to camp and, Sunday after Sunday, requested "No One Ever Cared for Me Like Jesus."

I had a head for religious ideas. They were the first ideas I ever encountered. They made other ideas seem mean.

For what shall it profit a man, if he shall gain the whole world and lose his own soul? And lose his own soul? And lose his own soul? Know ye that the Lord he is God: it is he that hath made us, and not we ourselves; we are his people, and the sheep of his pasture. Arise, and take up thy bed, and walk. And he said unto him, WHO IS MY NEIGHBOR?

Who shall ascend into the hill of the Lord? or who shall stand in his holy place? He that hath clean hands, and a pure heart; who hath not lifted up his soul unto vanity, nor sworn deceitfully.

The earth is the Lord's, and the fulness thereof; the world, and they that dwell therein. The heavens declare the glory of God; and the firmament sheweth his handywork. Verily I say unto you, that one of you shall betray me.

* * *

Every summer we memorized these things at camp. Every Sunday in Pittsburgh we heard these things in Sunday school. Every Thursday we studied these things, and memorized them, too (strictly as literature, they said), at school. I had miles of Bible in memory: some perforce, but most by hap, like the words to songs. There was no corner of my brain where you couldn't find, among the files of clothing labels and heaps of rocks, among the swarms of protozoans and shelves of novels, whole tapes and snarls and reels of Bible. Later, before I left Pittsburgh for college, I would write several poems in deliberate imitation of its sounds, those repeated feminine endings followed by thumps, or those long hard beats followed by softness. Selah.

The Bible's was an unlikely, movie-set world alongside our world. Light-shot and translucent in the pallid Sunday-school watercolors on the walls, stormy and opaque in the dense and staggering texts they read us placidly, sweet-mouthed and earnest, week after week, this world interleaved our waking world like dream.

The adult members of society adverted to the Bible unreasonably often. What arcana! Why did they spread this scandalous document before our eyes? If they had read it, I thought, they would have hid it. They didn't recognize the vivid danger that we would, through repeated exposure, catch a case of its wild opposition to their world. Instead they bade us study great chunks of it, and think about those chunks, and commit them to memory, and ignore them. By dipping us children in the Bible so often, they hoped, I think, to give our lives a serious tint, and to provide us with quaintly magnificent snatches of prayer to produce as charms while, say, being mugged for our cash or jewels.

In Sunday school at the Shadyside Presbyterian Church, the handsome father of rascal Jack from dancing school, himself a vice-president of Jones & Laughlin, whose wife was famous at the country club for her tan, held a birch pointer in his long fingers and shyly tapped the hanging paper map, shyly because he could see we weren't listening. Who would listen to this? Why on earth were we here? There in blue and yellow and green were Galilee, Samaria itself, and Judaea, he said—and I pretended to pay attention as a courtesy—the Sea of Galilee, the river Jordan, and the Dead Sea. I saw on the hanging map the coasts of Judaea by the far side of Jordan, on whose unimaginable shores the pastel Christ had maybe uttered such cruel, stiff, thrilling words: Sell whatsoever thou hast.

James and John, the sons of Zebedee, he made them fishers of men. And he came to the Lake of Gennesaret, and he came to Capernaum. And he withdrew in a boat. And a certain man went down from Jerusalem to Jericho. See it here on the map? Down. He went down, and fell among thieves.

And the swine jumped over the cliff.

And the voice cried, Samuel, Samuel. And the wakened boy Samuel answered, Here am I. And at last he said, Speak.

Hear O Israel, the Lord is one.

And Peter said, I know him not; I know him not; I know him not. And the rich young ruler said, What must I do? And the woman wiped his feet with her hair. And he said, Who touched me?

And he said, Verily, verily, verily, verily; life is not a dream. Let this cup pass from me. If it be thy will, of course, only if it be thy will.

I GOT MY ROCK COLLECTION from our grandparents' paper boy. He handed it to me in three heavy grocery bags; he said he had no time for a rock collection. Amy and I visited Oma and Company every Friday; while Mary cooked dinner, I roamed their solemn neighborhood, where our family would, as it happened, soon live ourselves. The indigenous children kept mum inside their stone houses; the paper boy—having pedaled his thick black bike, plus rocks, up from an Italian neighborhood down the hill—was the only sign of life.

The paper boy got the rock collection from a solitary old man named Downey, who until recently had lived just up the street from my grandparents. Mr. Downey had collected the rocks from all over. He had given them to the paper boy, in the grocery bags, explaining that he knew no one else. Then he had died. The paper boy, who was kind but very busy, did not remember the names of any of the rocks except the stalactites; he recalled, not helpfully, that Mr. Downey had found them in a cave. The stalactites were sorry-looking at their broken ends: sharp, yellow, and hollow, like fallen deciduous teeth.

* * *

Now I had these rocks. They were yellow, green, blue, and
red. Most were the size of half-bricks. One small white wafer
had blue stone stars. Some were knobby, some grainy, some
slick. There was a shining brown mineral the color of shoe
polish; its cubed crystals made a scratchy chunk. There was a
rusty cluster of petrified roses. There was a frozen froth of
platinum bubbles. It was a safe bet all these rocks had names.

From the Homewood Library's children's books I could
learn only the vaguest, overamazed stories of "the earth's
crust," which didn't interest me. What were all these yellow
and blue rocks in my room, and why did I never find any rocks
so various and sharp? From library adult books I got the true
dope, and it was a long story, which involved me in a project
less like bird-watching or stamp collecting than like life in a
forensic laboratory. The books taught me to identify the rocks.
They also lent me a vision of things, and informed me about
a bizarre set of people.

You got Frederick H. Pough's *Field Guide to Rocks and Minerals.* Using this and other books, you identified your rocks
one by one, keying them out as you key out plants with Gray's
Manual, through a series of diagnostic tests.

You determined, for instance, where your rock fit on Mohs'
scale of hardness. Mr. Mohs (Herr Mohs, actually) had devised a series of homespun tests for rock hardness, much as
Mr. Beaufort had dreamed up homespun tests for wind force.
Does smoke rise straight from the chimney? The wind is not
blowing. Is your house falling over? It's blowing force ten.
Number one on Mohs' scale was soft rock, to wit, talc. Can
you crumble it in your fingers? It's soft. What you have there
is talcum powder. Can it scratch a fingernail, a copper penny,
a pane of glass, and a knife blade? It's quartz. You can scratch
quartz with topaz, ruby, and diamond. If it makes your diamond saw clog, it's a meteorite.

You subjected your rocks to scratch tests. You procured a
piece of bathroom tile (always, in the books, hexagonal, such

as you find in old New York bathrooms and nowhere else) and stroked your rock across its unglazed underside. What color was the streak?

Yellow pyrite drew a black streak, black limonite drew a yellow streak, and black hematite drew a red streak. (Some minerals, Pough explained, to my mystification, are "not truly black . . . but only look so.") The streaks were brilliant pigments, richer than crayon strokes, deeper than pastel strokes; they were powdery pure pigments bright as greasepaint. It was a wonder the earth wasn't streaked like a Van Gogh landscape, and all the people streaked like warpath Indians.

You performed other testing marvels on your rocks—at least, the people in the books did. They dripped acid on them; they shone ultraviolet lights on them; they split them, sawed them, and set them on fire (diamond "burns easily"). They smelled and tasted them. Cracked arsenic smells like garlic. Epsomite is bitter, halotrichite tastes like ink, soda niter "tastes cooling." Those ardent mineralogists who licked their chrysocolla specimens found that their tongues got stuck.

During these tests, the rocks behaved with scarcely less vigor than the scientists. Borax "swells into great 'worms' as it melts, and finally shrinks to almost nothing." Other minerals "may send up little horns." Some change color when you heat them, or glow, or melt, burn, dissolve, or turn magnetic. Some fly apart (decrepitate). If you should happen to place a hunk of gummite on film, it will take its own picture.

At the end of all these tests, especially if you knew where you found your rocks, you could learn what you had in the paper bags. Or you could, as I did, read the texts' mineral descriptions a thousand times until you hit on something that sounded plausible. You could also go directly to the answers by studying the labeled rocks for sale at the Carnegie Museum shop.

Eventually I identified the rocks. The petrified roses were barite, probably from Oklahoma. The scratchy brown mineral was bauxite—aluminum ore. The black glass was obsidian; the booklet of transparent sheets was mica; the goldeny iridescent handful of soft crystals was chalcopyrite, an ore of copper, whose annoying name I loved to repeat: chalcopyrite. I had shiny green hornblende, rose quartz, starry moss agate, and dull hornfels, which was a mere rock. (A mineral is a pure inorganic compound; you can express its constituents in a chemical formula. A rock is just a mixture of minerals. Worthless, weedy rock is gangue rock.)

I had glassy drops of perlite called Apache tears, bubbly pyrite (fool's gold), and—a favorite—brick-red cinnabar. I had speckly gneiss rock, a chip of crystal tourmaline like a stick of anise candy, and green malachite in a silky chunk. I had milky turquoise, opalized wood, two sorry stalactites, banded jasper, and a lump of coal.

From the book I learned that there was fine stuff hidden in the earth. In the rock underfoot, in the mountain roadside rock, were sealed pockets lined with crystals. You could break a brown rock and find a vug—a pocket—sharp with amethysts.

In Maine, someone with a hammer had discovered a single feldspar crystal twenty feet across. Other New England outcrops have yielded "sparkling blue beryl crystals 18 to 27 feet long." Copper miners find peacock ore, a bronze mineral locked in rock, which tarnishes at once to "an astonishing royal purple" when it hits the light.

The rock I'd seen in my life looked dull because in all ignorance I'd never thought to knock it open. People have cracked ordinary New England pegmatite—big, coarse granite—and laid bare clusters of red garnets, or topaz crystals, chrysoberyl, spodumene, emerald. They held in their hands crystals that had hung in a hole in the dark for a billion years unseen.

I was all for it. I would lay about me right and left with a hammer, and bash the landscape to bits. I would crack the earth's crust like a piñata and spread to the light the vivid prizes in chunks within. Rock collecting was opening the mountains. It was like diving through my own interior blank blackness to remember the startling pieces of a dream: there was a blue lake, a witch, a lighthouse, a yellow path. It was like poking about in a grimy alley and finding an old, old coin. Nothing was as it seemed. The earth was like a shut eye. Mother's not dead, dear—she's only sleeping. Pry open the thin lid and find a crystalline intelligence inside, a rayed and sidereal beauty. Crystals grew inside rock like arithmetical flowers. They lengthened and spread, adding plane to plane in awed and perfect obedience to an absolute geometry that even the stones—maybe only the stones—understood.

The study of minerals reverted alarmingly to the classification of crystals, which in turn smacked dismayingly of math. I was in this, as it were, for my health. Nothing compelled me to finish reading a sentence that began "The macrodomes become, for obvious reasons, *clinodomes*," or "Remember this: *b*-pinacoid equals the brachypinacoid." Yet even the mumbo-jumbo had its charms. It sounded like Sid Caesar. Pough's *Field Guide to Rocks and Minerals* included a diagram of what looked like an angular inner tube or a corduroy hassock. The caption explained the diagram: "Rutile sixling." Here also was a line drawing of a set of penetration twins, and a meticulous side view of a pinacoid, labeled "Side view of pinacoid." Chrysoberyl, I learned—a blue-green aluminum oxide—has the exuberant-sounding "habit" of trilling.

The awesome story of earth's crust's buckling and shifting unfortunately failed to move me in the slightest. But here was an interesting find. Only a quirk of chemistry prevented the ground's being a heap of broken rubble. I hadn't thought of that. Why isn't it all a heap of broken rubble? For the bedrock fractures and cleaves, notoriously; it uplifts, crumbles, splits, shears, and folds. All this action naturally shatters the crust. But it happens that the abundant element silicon is water soluble at high temperatures. This element heals the scars.

Dissolved silicon seeps everywhere underground and slips into fissures and veins; it fills in, mends, and cements the rubble, over and over, from age to age. It heals all the thick wounds on the continents' skin and under the oceans; it solidifies as it cools, uplifting, and forms pale veins of scarry quartz running through everything; it dominates the granite bedrock on which we build our cities, the granite interior of mountains, and the beds that underlie the plains.

No one has ever found a rock as old as the earth. All the old rock went under. The age of the earth is 4.8 billion years, and of the oldest rock, a Labrador greenstone, a mere 3.8 billion years. The rock we see is mostly a mishmash of scar tissue and recent rubble. If there were no soluble silicon, how many feet thick, or miles thick, I wondered, would the sterile rubble be?

Many of the rocks in my collection were veins of some bright mineral in a matrix of quartz. The round stones I gathered along Lake Erie's shore were striped with bands of white or tinted quartz. The planet was all healed rubble, rubble joined and smoother as if a god had rolled it over in his hands like snow.

People who collected rocks called themselves "rockhounds." In the worst of cases, they called their children "pebble pups." Rockhounds seemed to be wild and obsessive amateurs, my kind of people, who had stepped aside from the rush of things to devote themselves to folly.

A collector would be foolish, one book advised, to sell to a gem dealer a fine crystal of, say, ruby or sapphire, when it was obviously of much more value to the collector uncut—a brilliant stub growing from a rough matrix as it was found, a prize specimen in a beloved collection. One book cautioned me against refining any gold I found—any nuggets, dust, or gold-bearing quartz. For I could own or transport all the raw native gold I wanted, but if I refined it in any way I was "obliged by law" to sell it to a licensed gold dealer or the U.S. mint.

These, then, were books which advised, in detail, how to avoid making money, right here in America. Right here in Pittsburgh were people who dug up the nation's mineral wealth, played with it, stored it behind glass, looked at it, fled in a flat-out sprint from anyone who threatened to buy it for dollars, and ultimately gave it to the paper boy. I applauded this with the uncanny, exultant, spreading sensation you have when you realize that your name is really legion—but I wasn't so persnickety that I wasn't inspired by a 1953 story of two Western collectors. These men found two petrified logs that made their Geiger counters click. Uranium-bearing silicates had replaced the logs' wood. The men sold the petrified logs to the Atomic Energy Commission for $35,000.

Some rockhounds had recently taken up scuba diving. These people dove down into "brawling mountain streams" with tanks on their backs to look for crystals underwater, or to pan for gold. The gold panning was especially good under boulders in rapids.

One book included a photograph of a mild-looking hobbyist in his basement workshop: he sawed chunks of Utah wonderstone into wavy, landscapy-looking slabs suitable for wall hangings. Here was a photograph of rockhounds in the field: Two men on a steep desert hillside delightedly smash a flat rock to bits with two hammers. Far below stands a woman in a dress and sensible shoes, doing nothing. Here is their campsite: a sagging black pyramidal tent pitched on the desert floor. A Studebaker fender nudges the foreground. The very hazards of field collecting tempted me: "tramping for miles over rough country," facing cold, heat, rain, cactus, rough lava, insects, rattlesnakes, scorpions, and glaring alkali flats. Collectors fell over boulders and damaged crystals. Their ballpoint pens ran out of ink. They carried sledgehammers, chains, snakebite kits, Geiger counters, canteens, tarps, maps, three-ton hydraulic jacks, mattocks, gold pans, dynamite (see *The*

Blaster's Handbook, published by Du Pont), cuff-link boxes, gads, sacks, ultraviolet lamps, pry bars, folding chairs, and the inevitable bathroom tiles.

Getting back home alive only aggravated their problems. If you bring home five hundred pounds of rocks from an average collecting trip, what do you do with them? Splay them attractively about the garden, one book suggested lamely. Give them away. Hold yard sales. One collector left five tons of rough rock in his yard when he moved. The books stopped just short of advising collectors how to deal with their wives.

The problem of storage and display were surprising. A roomful of rocks was evidently as volatile as a roomful of baby raccoons. Once you commit yourself to your charges, you scarcely dare take your eyes off them.

If you have some sky-blue chalcanthite on a shelf, or gypsum, or borax, or trona, it will crumble of its own accord to powder. Your crystals of realgar (an orange-red ore of arsenic) will "disintegrate to a dust of orpiment," which in turn will decompose. Your hanksite and soda niter will absorb water from the air and dissolve into little pools. Your proustite and silver ores will tarnish and then decompose. Your orange beryl will fade to pink, your brown topaz will lose all its color, your polished opals will craze. Finally, your brass-yellow marcasite will release sulfuric acid. The acid will eat your labels, your shelves, and eventually your whole collection.

On the other hand, rock collecting had unique rewards. For example, the thinner you sliced your specimens when you sawed them up, the more specimens you had. In this way you could multiply your collection without leaving home.

When you pry open the landscape, you find wonders—gems made of corpses, even, and excrement. In Puget Sound you could find fossil oysters and clams that had turned to agate, called agatized oysters, agatized clams. In Colorado you could find fossil shrimps turned to scarlet and precious carnelian. People have found dinosaur bones turned to jasper.

Petrified wood is abundant in every county of every state, because soluble silicon seeps everywhere. In Southern states you could find petrified leaves and twigs. There are often worm borings in petrified wood, and inside the opalized tunnels you might find gemmy piles of petrified worm excrement. Dinosaur excrement fossilizes, too. Bird and bat guano petrifies into a mineral called taranakite, which a book described as "unctuous to touch."

I wanted to find these things. I also wanted to find wulfenite crystals the color of cranberries, from Chile, and big transparent cubes of Iceland spar. In Durango, Mexico, I might find rosy adamite, tabular orange sulfenite crystals, mimetite in yellow mammillary crusts, or light green pyramids of scorodite. In Paterson, New Jersey, I could find great pearly crystals of phlogopite, or radiating splinters of white pectolite, or stilbite in bundles like cauliflower. People made extensive mineral discoveries in Tsumeb, Southwest Africa, in Haddam, Connecticut, in Westphalia, Germany, and in Westchester County, New York. Every day for the past two hundred years, one book said, someone has stumbled "on a brand-new outcrop that nobody before has explored." "A lifetime of study," another book said stirringly, "would not make you the master of every phase" of mineralogy.

I thought to specialize in interesting names. In Massachusetts and Connecticut, collectors found a mineral called sillimanite, named for a Yale professor. My specialized collection would feature sillimanite, radio opal, yowah nuts, and agaty potch.

Rock collecting is pleasantly simple for a bookish child, for it scarcely matters which rocks you actually have and which you only imagine having. I might as well throw into my future collection some clams that had turned to agate, too, and some carnelian shrimps. Similarly, field trips don't take much gas. You never think, How could I get a jeep? You forget your condition. You do not see yourself as a figure; you see the world.

From what box canyons have you not extricated yourself, hand over hand, hauling your pickax and Geiger counter in your knapsack? Sharp eyes—you spotted that rattlesnake. I knew you would. You could write a book: the fiery raw glare of the alkali flats, how it shrivels your eyes and blinds your brain in two holes like gimlets, whatever gimlets are, and your jeep tracks crumble over it white on white; and how, when you finally got to the hills you held your hot hammer by its wood handle, planted your big-booted feet in the hillside and felt the hot hill rock through your coarse pants on your thighs. And you broke rocks, hit rocks that cracked like ice in your palm, with your buddy beside you, both of you seeing what you could see. Doubloons, maybe, again, or uranium.

There were now 340 rocks in my room. I labeled them. On November evenings alone in my room while it rained, on February nights while snow piled in the buckeye boughs outside my window, when the paper on the Panama Canal was out of the way, and the Latin memorized, and my friends talked to on the phone until there was nothing left of the schoolday to analyze; while Margaret ran water in the kitchen and Mother talked Molly into going to bed and Father poked the fold from his section of the evening paper and Amy sat silent on the floor with her spelling book and played with the bows on Father's shoes, I played at my maple desk with books and rocks.

From stiff index cards I cut tiny squares, an eighth of an inch by an eighth of an inch. Holding the squares with tweezers, I printed numerals on them, never thinking to print the numerals before cutting the paper. In a dizzying meticulous mess I slid the wee numbers against the drippy rubber slope of a mucilage jar, and wiggled them onto flat faces of the rocks. When the glue dried the next day, I dabbed a brushful of varnish over rock and number. I was cataloguing the collection.

As the books advised, I listed by number in a notebook each

specimen's name, date, and locality. "Locality," when it wasn't Mr. Downey's grocery bags, was often the Carnegie Museum shop, where I bought trays of thumbnail minerals glued to cardboard sheets. I soaked the glue from these and labeled them with my own compulsive little numbers. When one day I discovered I had, characteristically, lost the notebook cata- logue, I discovered simultaneously that I didn't need it. I knew them by sight: that favorite dry red cinnabar, those Lake Erie ruby granites and flintstones, Mr. Downey's big chunks of pale oolite, dark wavy serpentine, hornblende, gneiss, tourmaline, Apache tears, all of them.

Often I imagined the solitary Mr. Downey, that invisible man from my grandparents' rarefied street of executives and lawyers. Every few years he had unearthed from the cellar his loose khaki pants and his tight hiking boots. He clambered into a pickup truck concealed in his ivy-grown garage, and took off for Oklahoma, where he scouted the lonesome hills with a hammer. He filled his stout sack with moss agate, chal- copyrite, and petrified roses. For reasons unimaginable, he drove back to hushed old Pittsburgh, pulled into his secret driveway, changed his clothes, and sat for years on end at his library desk to study his rocks. When he felt something inside him pulling him down, he called to him the blackhaired paper boy, who was collecting quarters on his black bike.

Maybe he hadn't died at all. Maybe he'd simply escaped underground. He cracked open Pittsburgh like a geode. Who knew what lay inside the streaked hillsides under the high- porched workers' houses, under the streetcar tracks, under the flat or sloping greens of the country-club golf courses, under the dancing-school building, the trout-stocked streams in the highlands or the dried-out stream under the bridge in Frick Park, under the sled-riding hills, the Ellis School, the stained opened cuts on the boulevard roadsides into town—who knew? He had screwed in wedges here and there, tapped them each once or twice, and laid bare the invisible city: crystal-crusted cavities lined with fire opals and red plume agates, where cobalt bloomed and onyx and jacinth grew sharp. He visited the underground corridors where spinel crystals twinned underfoot, and blue cubes of galena cut his hands, and carnelian nodules hung wet overhead among pale octahedrons of fluorite, among frost agates and moonstones, red jasper, blue lazulite, stubs of garnet, black chert. Of course he hadn't come back. Who would?

AFTER I READ *The Field Book of Ponds and Streams* several times, I longed for a microscope. Everybody needed a microscope. Detectives used microscopes, both for the FBI and at Scotland Yard. Although usually I had to save my tiny allowance for things I wanted, that year for Christmas my parents gave me a microscope kit.

In a dark basement corner, on a white enamel table, I set up the microscope kit. I supplied a chair, a lamp, a batch of jars, a candle, and a pile of library books. The microscope kit supplied a blunt black three-speed microscope, a booklet, a scalpel, a dropper, an ingenious device for cutting thin segments of fragile tissue, a pile of clean slides and cover slips, and a dandy array of corked test tubes.

One of the test tubes contained "hay infusion." Hay infusion was a wee brown chip of grass blade. You added water to it, and after a week it became a jungle in a drop, full of one-celled animals. This did not work for me. All I saw in the microscope after a week was a wet chip of dried grass, much enlarged.

Another test tube contained "diatomaceous earth." This was, I believed, an actual pinch of the white cliffs of Dover. On my palm it was an airy, friable chalk. The booklet said it was composed of the silicaceous bodies of diatoms—one-celled creatures that lived in, as it were, small glass jewelry boxes with fitted lids. Diatoms, I read, come in a variety of transparent geometrical shapes. Broken and dead and dug out of geological deposits, they made chalk, and a fine abrasive used in silver polish and toothpaste. What I saw in the microscope must have been the fine abrasive—grit enlarged. It was years before I saw a recognizable, whole diatom. The kit's diatomaceous earth was a bust.

All that winter I played with the microscope. I prepared slides from things at hand, as the books suggested. I looked at the transparent membrane inside an onion's skin and saw the cells. I looked at a section of cork and saw the cells, and at scrapings from the inside of my cheek, ditto. I looked at my blood and saw not much; I looked at my urine and saw long iridescent crystals, for the drop had dried.

All this was very well, but I wanted to see the wildlife I had read about. I wanted especially to see the famous amoeba, who had eluded me. He was supposed to live in the hay infusion, but I hadn't found him there. He lived outside in warm ponds and streams, too, but I lived in Pittsburgh, and it had been a cold winter.

Finally late that spring I saw an amoeba. The week before, I had gathered puddle water from Frick Park; it had been festering in a jar in the basement. This June night after dinner I figured I had waited long enough. In the basement at my microscope table I spread a scummy drop of Frick Park puddle water on a slide, peeked in, and lo, there was the famous amoeba. He was as blobby and grainy as his picture; I would have known him anywhere.

Before I had watched him at all, I ran upstairs. My parents were still at table, drinking coffee. They, too, could see the famous amoeba. I told them, bursting, that he was all set up, that they should hurry before his water dried. It was the chance of a lifetime.

Father had stretched out his long legs and was tilting back in his chair. Mother sat with her knees crossed, in blue slacks, smoking a Chesterfield. The dessert dishes were still on the table. My sisters were nowhere in evidence. It was a warm evening; the big dining-room windows gave onto blooming rhododendrons.

Mother regarded me warmly. She gave me to understand that she was glad I had found what I had been looking for, but that she and Father were happy to sit with their coffee, and would not be coming down.

She did not say, but I understood at once, that they had their pursuits (coffee?) and I had mine. She did not say, but I began to understand then, that you do what you do out of your private passion for the thing itself.

I had essentially been handed my own life. In subsequent years my parents would praise my drawings and poems, and supply me with books, art supplies, and sports equipment, and listen to my troubles and enthusiasms, and supervise my hours, and discuss and inform, but they would not get involved with my detective work, nor hear about my reading, nor inquire about my homework or term papers or exams, nor visit the salamanders I caught, nor listen to me play the piano, nor attend my field hockey games, nor fuss over my insect collection with me, or my poetry collection or stamp collection or rock collection. My days and nights were my own to plan and fill.

When I left the dining room that evening and started down the dark basement stairs, I had a life. I sat to my wonderful amoeba, and there he was, rolling his grains more slowly now, extending an arc of his edge for a foot and drawing himself along by that foot, and absorbing it again and rolling on. I gave him some more pond water.

I had hit pay dirt. For all I knew, there were paramecia, too, in that pond water, or daphniae, or stentors, or any of the many other creatures I had read about and never seen: volvox, the spherical algal colony; euglena with its one red eye; the elusive, glassy diatom; hydra, rotifers, water bears, worms. Anything was possible. The sky was the limit.

WHAT DOES IT FEEL LIKE to be alive?

Living, you stand under a waterfall. You leave the sleeping shore deliberately; you shed your dusty clothes, pick your barefoot way over the high, slippery rocks, hold your breath, choose your footing, and step into the waterfall. The hard water pelts your skull, bangs in bits on your shoulders and arms. The strong water dashes down beside you and you feel it along your calves and thighs rising roughly back up, up to the roiling surface, full of bubbles that slide up your skin or break on you at full speed. Can you breathe here? Here where the force is greatest and only the strength of your neck holds the river out of your face? Yes, you can breathe even here. You could learn to live like this. And you can, if you concentrate, even look out at the peaceful far bank where maples grow straight and their leaves lean down. For a joke you try to raise your arms. What a racket in your ears, what a scatter-shot pummeling!

It is time pounding at you, time. Knowing you are alive is watching on every side your generation's short time falling away as fast as rivers drop through air, and feeling it hit.

Who turned on the lights? You did, by waking up: you flipped the light switch, started up the wind machine, kicked on the flywheel that spins the years. Can you catch hold of a treetop, or will you fly off the diving planet as she rolls? Can you ride out the big blow on a coconut palm's trunk until you fall asleep again, and the winds let up? You fall asleep again, and you slide in a dream to the palm tree's base; the winds die off, the lights dim, the years slip away as you idle there till you die in your sleep, till death sets you cruising down the Tamiami Trail.

Knowing you are alive is feeling the planet buck under you, rear, kick, and try to throw you; you hang on to the ring. It is riding the planet like a log downstream, whooping. Or, conversely, you step aside from the dreaming fast loud routine and feel time as a stillness about you, and hear the silent air asking in so thin a voice, Have you noticed yet that you will die? Do you remember, remember, remember? Then you feel your life as a weekend, a weekend you cannot extend, a weekend in the country.

O Augenblick verweile.

My friend Judy Schoyer was a thin, messy, shy girl whose thick blond curls lapped over her glasses. Her cheeks, chin, nose, and blue eyes were round; the lenses and frames of her glasses were round, and so were her heavy curls. Her long spine was supple; her legs were long and thin so her knee socks fell down. She did not care if her knee socks fell down. When I first knew her, as my classmate at the Ellis School, she sometimes forgot to comb her hair. She was so shy she tended not to move her head, but only let her eyes rove about. If my mother addressed her, or a teacher, she held her long-legged posture lightly, alert, like a fawn ready to bolt but hoping its camouflage will work a little longer.

Judy's family were members of the oldest, most liberal, and best-educated ranks of Pittsburgh society. They were Unitarians. I visited her Unitarian Sunday school once. There we folded paper to make little geese; it shocked me to the core. One of her linear ancestors, Edward Holyoke, had been president of Harvard University in the eighteenth century, which fact paled locally before the greater one, that her great-grandfather's brother had been one of the founding members of Pittsburgh's Duquesne Club. She was related also to Pittsburgh's own Stephen Foster.

Judy and her family passed some long weekends at a family farmhouse in the country on a little river, the nearest town to which was Paw Paw, West Virginia. When they were going to the farm, they said they were going to Paw Paw. The trip was a four-hour drive from Pittsburgh. Often they invited me along.

There in Paw Paw for the weekend I imagined myself in the distant future remembering myself now, twelve years old with Judy. We stood on the high swinging plank bridge over the river, in early spring, watching the first hatch of small flies hover below us.

The river was a tributary of the distant Potomac—a tributary so stony, level, and shallow that Judy's grandmother regularly drove her old Model A Ford right through it, while we hung out over the running boards to try and get wet. From above the river, from the hanging center of the swinging bridge, we could see the forested hill where the big house stood. There at the big house we would have dinner, and later look at the Gibson girls in the wide, smelly old books in the cavernous living room, only recently and erratically electrified.

And from the high swinging bridge we could see in the other direction the log cabin, many fields away from the big house, where we children stayed alone: Judy and I, and sometimes our friend Margaret, who had a dramatic, somewhat morbid flair and who wrote poetry, and Judy's good-natured younger brother. We cooked pancakes in the cabin's fireplace; we drew water in a bucket from the well outside the door.

By Friday night when we'd carried our duffel and groceries from the black Model A at the foot of the hill, or over the undulating bridge if the river was high, when we children had banged open the heavy log-cabin door, smelled the old logs and wood dust, found matches and lighted the kerosene lanterns, and in the dark outside had drawn ourselves a bucket of sweet water (feeling the rope go slack and hearing the bucket hit, then feeling the rope pull as the bucket tipped and filled), and hunted up wood for a fire, smelled the loamy nighttime forest again, and heard the whippoorwill—by that time on Friday night I was already grieving and mourning, only just unpacking my nightgown, because here it was practically Sunday afternoon and time to go.

"What you kids need," Mrs. Schoyer used to say, "is more exercise."

How exhilarating, how frightening, to ride the tippy Model A over the shallow river to the farm at Paw Paw, to greet again in a new season the swaying bridge, the bare hills, the woods behind the log cabin, the hayloft in the barn—and know I had just so many hours. From the minute I set foot on that land across the river, I started ticking like a timer, fizzing like a fuse.

On Friday night in the log cabin at Paw Paw I watched the wild firelight on Judy's face as she laughed at something her cheerful brother said, laughed shyly even here. When she laughed, her cheeks rose and formed spheres. I loved her spherical cheeks and knocked myself out to make her laugh. I could hardly see her laughing eyes behind her glasses under hanging clumps of dark-blond curls. She was nimble, swaybacked, long-limbed, and languid as a heron, and as abrupt. In Pittsburgh she couldn't catch a ball—nearsighted; she perished of bashfulness at school sports. Here she could climb a tree after a kitten as smoothly as a squirrel could, and run down her nasty kicking pony with authority, and actually hit it, and scoop up running hens with both swift arms. She spoke softly and not often.

Judy treated me with amused tolerance. At school I was, if not a central personage, at least a conspicuous one; and I had boyfriends all along and got invited to the boys' school dances. Nevertheless, Judy put up with me, not I with Judy. She possessed a few qualities that, although they counted for nothing at school, counted, I had to admit, with me. Her goodness was both intrinsic and a held principle. This thin, almost speechless child had moral courage. She intended her own life—starting when she was about ten—to be not only harmless but good. I considered Judy's goodness, like Judy's farm, a nice place to visit. She put up with my fast-talking avoidance of anything that smacked of manual labor. That she was indulging me altogether became gradually clear to both of us—though I pretended I didn't know it, and Judy played along.

On Saturday mornings in Paw Paw we set out through the dewy fields. I could barely lay one foot before the other along the cowpath through the pasture, I was so nostalgic for this scene already, this day just begun, when Judy and I were twelve. With Margaret we boiled and ate blue river mussels; we wrote and staged a spidery melodrama. We tried to ride the wretched untrained pony, which scraped us off under trees. We chopped down a sassafras tree and made a dirty tea; and we started to clean a run-over snake, in order to make an Indian necklace from its delicate spine, but it smelled so bad we quit.

After Saturday-night dinner in the big-house dining room— its windows gave out on the cliffside treetops—Mr. Schoyer told us, in his calm, ironic voice, Victor Hugo's story of a French sailor who was commended for having heroically captured a cannon loose on the warship's deck, and then hanged for having loosed the cannon in the first place. There were usually a dozen or more of us around the table, rapt. When the household needed our help, Mrs. Schoyer made mild, wry suggestions, almost diffidently.

I would have liked going to prison with the Schoyers. My own family I loved with all my heart; the Schoyers fascinated me. They were not sharply witty but steadily wry. In Pittsburgh they invited foreigners to dinner. They went to art galleries, they heard the Pittsburgh Symphony. They weren't tan. Mr. Schoyer, who was a corporation lawyer, had majored in classical history and literature at Harvard. Like my father, he had studied something that had no direct bearing on the clatter of coin. He was always the bemused scholar, mild and democratic, posing us children friendly questions as if Pittsburgh or Paw Paw were Athens and he fully expected to drag from our infant brains the Pythagorean theorem. What do you make of our new President? Your position on capital punishment? Or, conversationally, after I had been branded as a lover of literature, "You recall that speech of Pericles, don't you?" or "Won't you join me in reading 'A Shropshire Lad' or 'Ballad of East and West'?" At Paw Paw the Schoyers did every wholesome thing but sing. None of them could carry a tune.

If there was no moon that night, we children took a flashlight down the steep dirt driveway from the big house and across the silvery pastures to the edge of the woods where the log cabin stood. The log cabin stayed empty, behind an old vine-hung gate, except when we came. In front of the cabin we drew water from the round stone well; under the cabin we put milk and butter in the cold cellar, which was only a space dug in the damp black dirt—dirt against which the butter's wrap looked too thin.

That was the farm at Paw Paw, West Virginia. The farm lay far from the nearest highway, off three miles of dirt road. When at the end of the long darkening journey from Pittsburgh we turned down the dirt road at last, the Schoyers' golden retriever not unreasonably began to cry, and so, unreasonably, invisibly, did I. Some years when the Schoyers asked me to join them I declined miserably, refused in a swivet, because I couldn't tolerate it, I loved the place so.

*   *   *

I knew what I was doing at Paw Paw: I was beginning the lifelong task of tuning my own gauges. I was there to brace myself for leaving. I was having my childhood. But I was haunting it, as well, practically reading it, and preventing it. How much noticing could I permit myself without driving myself round the bend? Too much noticing and I was too self-conscious to live; I trapped and paralyzed myself, and dragged my friends down with me, so we couldn't meet each other's eyes, my own loud awareness damning us both. Too little noticing, though—I would risk much to avoid this—and I would miss the whole show. I would wake on my deathbed and say, What was that?

YOUNG CHILDREN HAVE NO SENSE OF WONDER. They bewilder well, but few things surprise them. All of it is new to young children, after all, and equally gratuitous. Their parents pause at the unnecessary beauty of an ice storm coating the trees; the children look for something to throw. The children who tape colorful fall leaves to the schoolroom windows and walls are humoring the teacher. The busy teacher halts on her walk to school and stoops to pick up fine bright leaves "to show the children"—but it is she, now in her sixties, who is increasingly stunned by the leaves, their brightness all so much trash that litters the gutter.

This year at the Ellis School my sister Amy was in the fifth grade, with Mrs. McVicker. I remembered Mrs. McVicker fondly. Every year she reiterated the familiar (and, without a description of their mechanisms, the sentimental) mysteries that schoolchildren hear so often and so indifferently: that each snowflake is different, that some birds fly long distances, that acorns grow into oaks. Caterpillars turn into butterflies. The stars are large and very far away. She struck herself like a gong with these same mallets every year—a sweet old schoolteacher whom we in our time had loved and tolerated for her innocence.

Now that I was an aging veteran of thirteen or so, I was becoming case-softened myself. Imperceptibly I had shed my indifference. I was getting positively old: the hatching of wet robins in the spring moved me. I saw them from the school library window, as if on an educational film: a robin sprawled on a nest in the oak, and four miserable hatchlings appeared. They peeped. I knew this whole story; who didn't? Nevertheless I took to checking on the robins a few times a day. Their mother rammed worms and bugs down their throats; they grew feathers and began to hop up and down in the nest. Bit by bit they flew away; I saw them from the schoolyard taking test flights under the oak. Glory be, I thought during all those weeks, hallelujah, and never told a soul.

Even my friends began to seem to me marvelous: Judy Schoyer laughing shyly, her round eyes closed, and quick Ellin Hahn, black-haired and ruddy, who bestrode the social world like a Colossus, saying always just the right and funny thing. Where had these diverse people come from, really? I watched little Molly turn from a baby into a child and become not changed so much as ever more herself, kind-hearted, nervous, both witty and humorous: was this true only in retrospect? People's being themselves, year after year, so powerfully and so obliviously—what was it? Why was it so appealing? Personality, like beauty, was a mystery; like beauty, it was useless. These useless things were not, however, flourishes and embellishments to our life here, but that life's center; they were its truest note, the heart of its form, which drew back our thoughts repeatedly.

Somewhere between one book and another a child's passive acceptance had slipped away from me also. I could no longer see the world's array as a backdrop to my private play, a dull, neutral backdrop about which I had learned all I needed to know. I had been chipping at the world idly, and had by accident uncovered vast and labyrinthine further worlds within it. I peered in one day, stepped in the next, and soon wandered in deep over my head. Month after month, year after year, the true and brilliant light, and the complex and multifaceted coloration, of this actual, historical, waking world invigorated me. Its vastness extended everywhere I looked, and precisely where I looked, just as forms grew under my gaze as I drew.

This was the enthusiasm of a child, like that of a field-working scientist, and like that of the artist making a pencil study. One took note; one took notes. The subject of the study was the world's things: things to sort into physical categories, and things to break down into physical structures.

I was not to discover literature and ideas for a few more years. All I had awakened to was the world's wealth of information. I was reading books on drawing, painting, rocks, criminology, birds, moths, beetles, stamps, ponds and streams, medicine. (Somehow I missed those other childhood mainstays, astronomy, coins, and dinosaurs.) How I wished I could find agreeable books on thin air! For everything, I had gathered, was something. And for me, during those few years before I vanished into a blinded rage, everything was interesting.

Nothing could be less apparently interesting, for example, than a certain infuriatingly dull sight I always looked at with hatred. It was raining and Mother was driving us along one of Pittsburgh's clogged narrow highways. I looked out through the rain on the window and saw by the roadside the raw cuts the road builders carved through the rolling rocky hills, carved long dreary decades ago, to lay the road. Blasting bores scarred these banks of sandstone and shale in streaks; gritty rain streamed down their cut faces and dissolved the black soot and coal dust and car exhaust. The car stopped and started. I stared dully through the spotted windshield. Gray rivulets poured down the rock, mile after highway mile, and puddled at the berm where the rock met the winter-killed grass and mud.

This sight slew me in my seat. It was so dull it unstrung me, so I could barely breathe. How could I flee it, the very land-scape, the dull rock, the bleak miles, the dark rain? I slumped under the weight of my own passive helplessness. Sometimes I memorized billboards. I tried traveling with my eyes closed, and that was even worse.

But now I knew that even rock was interesting—at least in theory. Mr. Pough and Herr Mohs could stand here mightily in the rain, singing songs and swinging picks into the rock cuts by the side of the road. Even I could tap some shale just right, rain or shine, and open the rock to bones of fossil fish. There might be trilobites on the hilltops, star sapphires. Right along these wretched rainy roads, Mohs and Pough could have, as the saying went, a field day.

If even rock was interesting, if even this ugliness was worth whole shelves at the library, required sophisticated tools to study, and inspired grown men to crack mountains and saw crystals—then what wasn't?

Everything in the world, every baby, city, tetanus shot, tennis ball, and pebble, was an outcrop of some vast and hitherto concealed vein of knowledge, apparently, that had compelled people's emotions and engaged their minds in the minutest detail without anyone's having done with it. There must be bands of enthusiasts for everything on earth—fanatics who shared a vocabulary, a batch of technical skills and equip-ment, and, perhaps, a vision of some single slice of the beauty and mystery of things, of their complexity, fascination, and unexpectedness. There was no one here but us fanatics: bird-watchers, infielders, detectives, poets, rock collectors, and, I inferred, specialists in things I had not looked into—violin makers, fishermen, Islamic scholars, opera composers, people who studied Bali, vials of air, bats. It seemed to take all these

people working full time to extract the interest from everything and articulate it for the rest of us.

Every least thing I picked up was proving to be the hanging
end of a very long rope.

For the sentimental Mrs. McVicker I had written on assignment a paper on William Gorgas—the doctor in charge of
workers' health during the digging of the Panama Canal. Lik-
ing that, I wrote another, on Walter Reed. The struggle
against yellow fever fired me, and I retained an interest in
medicine, especially epidemiology. So now, a few years later,
on the couch on the sunporch, I was reading Paul de Kruif's
overwrought *Microbe Hunters.*

Old Anton Leeuwenhoek looked through his lenses at a
drop of rainwater and shouted to his daughter, "Come here!
Hurry! There are little animals in this rainwater! . . . They
swim! They play around!" His microscope "showed little
things to him with a fantastic clear enormousness." My microscope was similar. Since I had found the amoeba, I regularly
found little animals. I found them in rainwater. I let a bowl of
rainwater sit by the basement furnace for a week. When I
examined a drop at low power, sure enough, little animals
swam, and played around, with fantastic clear enormousness.

Not only was the roadside rock interesting; even the rainwater that streamed down its cut face was interesting. Mineral
crystals made the rock; lively animals made the rain. Now
when I traveled the grim highways and saw the dull rock
receive the dull rain, and realized there would be nothing else
to look at until we got where we were going, and Mother and
I were all talked out—now when I felt the familiar restless
hatred begin to rise at the stupidity and ugliness of this sight,
I bade myself look directly at some streaky rock cut and said
to myself, thundered to myself, "Think!"

Everywhere, things snagged me. The visible world turned
me curious to books; the books propelled me reeling back to
the world.

At school I saw a searing sight. It turned me to books; it turned me to jelly; it turned me much later, I suppose, into an early version of a runaway, a scapegrace. It was only a freshly hatched Polyphemus moth crippled because its mason jar was too small.

The mason jar sat on the teacher's desk; the big moth emerged inside it. The moth had clawed a hole in its hot cocoon and crawled out, as if agonizingly, over the course of an hour, one leg at a time; we children watched around the desk, transfixed. After it emerged, the wet, mashed thing turned around walking on the green jar's bottom, then painstakingly climbed the twig with which the jar was furnished.

There, at the twig's top, the moth shook its sodden clumps of wings. When it spread those wings—those beautiful wings—blood would fill their veins, and the birth fluids on the wings' frail sheets would harden to make them tough as sails. But the moth could not spread its wide wings at all; the jar was too small. The wings could not fill, so they hardened while they were still crumpled from the cocoon. A smaller moth could have spread its wings to their utmost in that mason jar, but the Polyphemus moth was big. Its gold furred body was almost as big as a mouse. Its brown, yellow, pink, and blue wings would have extended six inches from tip to tip, if there had been no mason jar. It would have been big as a wren.

The teacher let the deformed creature go. We all left the classroom and paraded outside behind the teacher with pomp and circumstance. She bounced the moth from its jar and set it on the school's asphalt driveway. The moth set out walking. It could only heave the golden wrinkly clumps where its wings should have been; it could only crawl down the school driveway on its six frail legs. The moth crawled down the driveway toward the rest of Shadyside, an area of fine houses, expensive apartments, and fashionable shops. It crawled down the driveway because its shriveled wings were glued shut. It crawled down the driveway toward Shadyside, one of several sections of town where people like me were expected to settle after college, renting an apartment until they married one of the boys and bought a house. I watched it go.

I knew that this particular moth, the big walking moth, could not travel more than a few more yards before a bird or a cat began to eat it, or a car ran over it. Nevertheless, it was crawling with what seemed wonderful vigor, as if, I thought at the time, it was still excited from being born. I watched it go till the bell rang and I had to go in. I have told this story before, and may yet tell it again, to lay the moth's ghost, for I still see it crawl down the broad black driveway, and I still see its golden wing clumps heave.

I had not suspected, among other things, that moths came so big. From a school library book I learned there were several such enormous American moths, all wild silk moths which spun cocoons, and all common.

Gene Stratton Porter's old *Moths of the Limberlost* caught my eye; for some years after I read it, it was my favorite book. From one of its queer painted photographs I learned what the Polyphemus moth would have looked like whole: it was an unexpected sort of beauty, brown and wild. It had pink stripes, lavender crescents, yellow ovals—all sorts of odd colors no one would think to combine. Enormous blue eye-spots stared eerily from its hind wings. Coincidentally, it was in the Polyphemus chapter that the book explained how a hatched moth must spread its wings quickly, and fill them with blood slowly, before it can fly.

Gene Stratton Porter had been a vigorous, loving kid who grew up long ago near a swampy wilderness of Indiana, and had worked up a whole memorable childhood out of insects, of all things, which I had never even noticed, and my childhood was half over.

When she was just a tot, she learned how entomologists carry living moths and butterflies without damaging them. She commonly carried a moth or butterfly home from her forest and swamp wanderings by lightly compressing its thorax between thumb and index finger. The insect stops moving but is not hurt; when you let it go, it flies away.

One day, after years of searching, she found a yellow swallowtail. This is not the common tiger swallowtail butterfly, but *Papilio turnus:* "the largest, most beautiful butterfly I had ever seen." She held it carefully in the air, its wings high over the back of her fingers. She wanted to show the fragile, rare creature to her father and then carry it back to precisely where she found it. But she was only a child, and so she came running home with it instead of walking. She tripped, and her fingers pinched through the butterfly's thorax. She broke it to pieces. And that was that. It was like one of Father's bar jokes.

There was a terror connected with moths that attracted and repelled me. I would face down the terror. I continued reading about moths, and branched out to other insects.

I liked the weird horned beetles rumbling along everywhere, even at the country club, whose names were stag, elephant, rhinoceros. They were so big I could hear them walk; their sharp legs scraped along the poolside concrete. I liked the comical true bugs, like the red-and-blue-striped leafhoppers, whose legs looked like yellow plastic; they hopped on roses in the garden at home. At Lake Erie I watched the solitary wasps that hunted along the beach path; they buried their paralyzed caterpillar prey in holes they dug so vigorously the sand flew. I even liked the dull little two-winged insects, the diptera, because this order contained mosquitoes, about several species of which I knew something because they bore interesting diseases. I studied under the microscope our local mosquitoes in various stages—a hairy lot—dipped in a cup from Molly's wading pool.

To collect insects I equipped myself with the usual paraphernalia: glass-headed pins, a net, and a killing jar. It was insects in jars again—but unlike the hapless teacher who put the big moth's cocoon in the little mason jar, I knew, I thought, what I was doing. In the bottom of the killing jar—

formerly a pickle jar—I laid a wad of cotton soaked in cleaning fluid containing carbon tetrachloride, which compound I thrilled myself by calling, offhandedly, "carbon tet." A circle of old door screen prevented the insects' tangling in the cotton. I placed each insect on the screen and quickly tightened the jar lid. Then, as if sensitively, I looked away. After a suitable interval I poured out the dead thing as carefully as I could, and pinned it and its festive, bunting-like row of fluttering labels in a cigar box. My grandfather had saved the cigar boxes, one for each order of insect; they smelled both sharp and sweet, of cedar and leaf tobacco. I pinned the insects in rows, carefully driving the pins through chitinous thoraxes just where the books indicated. Four beetles I collected were so big they had a cigar box to themselves.

Once I returned to my attic bedroom after four weeks at summer camp. There, beside the detective table, under the plaster-stain ship, was the insect collection, a stack of cigar boxes. I checked the boxes. In the big beetles' cigar box I found a rhinoceros beetle crawling on its pin. The pin entered the beetle through that triangle in the thorax between the wing-cover tops; it emerged ventrally above and between the legs. The big black beetle's six legs hung down waving in the air, well above the floor of the cigar box. It crawled and never got anywhere. It must have been pretty dehydrated; the attic was hot. Presumably the beetle's legs had been waving in the air like that in search of a footing for the past four weeks.

I hated insects; that was the fact. I never caught my stamp collection trying to crawl away.

Butterflies die with folded wings. Before they're mounted, butterflies require an elaborate chemical treatment to relax their dead muscles, a bit more every day, so you can spread their brittle wings without shattering them. After a few grueling starts at this relaxing and spreading of dead butterflies, I avoided it. When on rare occasions I killed butterflies, I stuck them away somewhere and forgot about them.

One hot evening I settled on my bed in my summer nightgown with a novel I had looked forward to reading. I lay back, opened the book, and a dead butterfly dropped headfirst on my bare neck. I jumped up, my skin crawling, and it slid down my nightgown. Somehow it stuck to my sweaty skin; when I brushed at it—whooping aloud—it fragmented, and pieces stuck to my hands and rained down on the floor. Most of the dead butterfly, which still looked as if it were demurely praying while falling apart, with folded yellow wings in shreds and a blasted black body, fell out on my foot. I brushed broken antennae and snapped legs from my neck; I wiped a glittering yellow dust of wing scales from my belly, and they stuck to my palm.

I hated insects; that I knew. Fingering insects was touching the rim of nightmare. But you have to study something. I never considered turning away from them just because I was afraid of them.

I liked their invisibility; they did not matter, so they did not exist. People's nervous systems edited out the sight of insects before it reached their brains; my seeing insects let me live alongside human society in a different sensory world, just as insects themselves do. That I collected specimens at the country-club pool pleased me; I did not really mind that my friends turned bilious when I showed them my prizes. I loved the sport of catching butterflies; they took bad hops, like aerial grounders. (I did not know then that the truly athletic, life-loving entomologists study dragonflies, which are fantastically difficult to catch—fast, sharp-eyed, hard to outwit.) Cringing, I taught myself to paralyze butterflies through the net, holding them lightly at the thorax as Gene Stratton Porter had done. I brought them out of the net and let them fly away—lest they fall on me dead later.

How confidently I had overlooked all this—rocks, bugs, rain. What else was I missing?

I opened books like jars. Here between my hands, here between some book's front and back covers, whose corners

poked dents in my palm, was another map to the neighborhood I had explored all my life, and fancied I knew, a map
depicting hitherto invisible landmarks. After I learned to see
those, I looked around for something else. I never knew
where my next revelation was coming from, but I knew it was
coming—some hairpin curve, some stray bit of romance or
information that would turn my life around in a twinkling.

I INTENDED TO LIVE the way the microbe hunters lived. I wanted to work. Hard work on an enormous scale was the microbe hunters' stock-in-trade. They took a few clear, time-consuming steps and solved everything. In those early days of germ theory, large disease-causing organisms, whose cycles traced straightforward patterns, yielded and fell to simple procedures. I would know just what to do. I would seize on the most casual remarks of untutored milkmaids. When an untutored milkmaid remarked to me casually, "Oh, everyone knows you won't get the smallpox if you've had the cowpox," I would perk right up.

Microbe Hunters sent me to a biography of Louis Pasteur. Pasteur's was the most enviable life I had yet encountered. It was his privilege to do things until they were done. He established the germ theory of disease; he demonstrated convincingly that yeasts ferment beer; he discovered how to preserve wine; he isolated the bacillus in a disease of silkworms; he demonstrated the etiology of anthrax and produced a vaccine for it; he halted an epidemic of cholera in fowls and inoculated a boy for hydrophobia. Toward the end of his life, in a rare idle moment, he chanced to read some of his early published papers and exclaimed (someone overheard), "How beautiful! And to think that I did it all!" The tone of this exclamation was, it seemed to me, astonished and modest, for he had genuinely forgotten, moving on.

Pasteur had not used up all the good work. Mother told me again and again about one of her heroes, a doctor working for a federal agency who solved a problem that arose in the late forties. Premature babies, and only premature babies, were turning up blind, in enormous numbers. Why? What do premature babies have in common?

"Look in the incubators!" Mother would holler, and knock the side of her head with the heel of her hand, holler outraged, glaring far behind my head as she was telling me this story, holler, "Look in the incubators!" as if at her wit's end facing a roomful of doctors who wrung their useless hands and accepted this blindness as one of life's tough facts. Mother's hero, like all of Mother's heroes, accepted nothing. She rolled up her sleeves, looked in the incubators, and decided to see what happened if she reduced the oxygen in the incubator air. That worked. Too much oxygen had been blinding them. Now the babies thrived; they got enough oxygen, and they weren't blinded. Hospitals all over the world changed the air mixture for incubators, and prematurity no longer carried a special risk of blindness.

Mother liked this story, and told it to us fairly often. Once she posed it as a challenge to Amy. We were all in the living room, waiting for dinner. "What would you do if you noticed that all over the United States, premature babies were blind?" Without even looking up from her homework, Amy said, "Look in the incubators. Maybe there's something wrong in the incubators." Mother started to whoop for joy before she realized she'd been had.

Problems still yielded to effort. Only a few years ago, to the wide-eyed attention of the world, we had seen the epidemic of poliomyelitis crushed in a twinkling, right here in Pittsburgh.

We had all been caught up in the polio epidemic: the early neighbor boy who wore one tall shoe, to which his despairing father added another two soles every year; the girl in the iron lung reading her schoolbook in an elaborate series of mirrors while a volunteer waited to turn the page; my friend who limped, my friend who rolled everywhere in a wheelchair, my friend whose arm hung down, Mother's friend who walked with crutches. My beloved dressed-up aunt, Mother's sister, had come to visit one day and, while she was saying hello, flung herself on the couch in tears; her son had it. Just a touch, they said, but who could believe it?

When Amy and I had asked, Why do we have to go to bed so early? Why do we have to wash our hands again? we knew Mother would kneel to look us in the eyes and answer in a low, urgent voice, So you do not get polio. We heard polio discussed once or twice a day for several years.

And we had all been caught up in its prevention, in the wild ferment of the early days of the Salk vaccine, the vaccine about which Pittsburgh talked so much, and so joyously, you could probably have heard the crowd noise on the moon.

In 1953, Jonas Salk's Virus Research Laboratory at the University of Pittsburgh had produced a controversial vaccine for polio. The small stories in the Pittsburgh *Press* and the *Post-Gazette* were coming out in *Life* and *Time*. It was too quick, said medical colleagues nationwide: Salk had gone public without first publishing everything in the journals. He rushed out a killed-virus serum without waiting for a safe live-virus one, which would probably be better. Doctors walked out of professional meetings; some quit the foundation that funded the testing. Salk was after personal glory, they said. Salk was after money, they said. Salk was after big prizes.

Salk tested the serum on five thousand Pittsburgh schoolchildren, of whom I was three, because I kept changing ele-

mentary schools. Our parents, like ninety-five percent of all
Pittsburgh parents, signed the consent forms. Did the other
mothers then bend over the desk in relief and sob? I don't
know. But I don't suppose any of them gave much of a damn
what Salk had been after.

When Pasteur died, near a place wonderfully called Saint-
Cloud, he murmured to the devoted assistants who surrounded his bed, *"Il faut travailler."*

Il faut indeed *travailler*— no one who grew up in Pittsburgh
could doubt it. And no one who grew up in Pittsburgh could
doubt that the great work was ongoing. We breathed in optimism—not coal dust—with every breath. What couldn't be
done with good hard *travail?*

The air in Pittsburgh had been dirty; now we could see it
was clean. An enormous, pioneering urban renewal was under
way; the newspapers pictured fantastic plans, airy artists'
watercolors, which we soon saw laid out and built up in steel
and glass downtown. The Republican Richard King Mellon
had approached Pittsburgh's Democratic, Catholic mayor,
David L. Lawrence, and together with a dozen business leaders they were razing the old grim city and building a sparkling
new one; they were washing the very air. The Russians had
shot Sputnik into outer space. In Shippingport, just a few miles
down the Ohio River, people were building a generating
plant that used atomic energy—an idea that seemed completely dreamy, but there it was. A physicist from Bell Laboratories spoke to us at school about lasers; he was about as
wrought up a man as I had ever seen. You could not reasonably believe a word he said, but you could see that he believed
it.

We knew that "Doctor Salk" had spent many years and
many dollars to produce the vaccine. He commonly worked
sixteen-hour days, six days a week. Of course. In other laboratories around the world, other researchers were working just
as hard, as hard as Salk and Pasteur. Hard work bore fruit.

This is what we learned growing up in Pittsburgh, growing up in the United States.

Salk had isolated seventy-four strains of polio virus. It took him three years to verify the proposition that a workable vaccine would need samples of only three of these strains. He grew the virus in tissues cultured from monkey kidneys. The best broth for growing the monkey tissue proved to be Medium Number 199; it contained sixty-two ingredients in careful proportion.

This was life itself: the big task. Nothing exhilarated me more than the idea of a life dedicated to a monumental worthwhile task. Doctor Salk never watched it rain and wished he had never been born. How many shovelfuls of dirt did men move to dig the Panama Canal? Two hundred and forty million cubic yards. It took ten years and twenty-one thousand lives and $336,650,000, but it was possible.

I thought a great deal about the Panama Canal, and always contemplated the same notion: You could take more time, and do it with teaspoons. I saw myself and a few Indian and Caribbean co-workers wielding teaspoons from our kitchen: Towle, Rambling Rose. And our grandchildren, and their grandchildren. Digging the canal across the isthmus at Panama would tear through a good many silver spoons. But it could be done, in theory and therefore in fact. It was like Mount Rushmore, or Grand Coulee Dam. You hacked away at the landscape and made something, or you did not do anything, and just died.

How many filaments had Thomas Edison tried, over how many years, before he found one workable for incandescence? How many days and nights over how many years had Marie Curie labored in a freezing shed to isolate radium? I read a biography of George Washington Carver: so many years on the soybean, the peanut, the sweet potato, the waste from ginning cotton. I read biographies of Abraham Lincoln, Thomas Edison, Daniel Boone.

It was all the same story. You have a great idea and spend grinding years at dull tasks, still charged by your vision. All the people about whom biographies were not written were people who failed to find something that took years to do. People could count the grains of sand. In my own life, as a sideline, and for starters, I would learn all the world's languages.

What if people said it could not be done? So much the better. We grew up with the myth of the French Impressionist painters, and its queer implication that rejection and ridicule guaranteed, or at any rate signaled, a project's worth. When little George Westinghouse at last figured out how to make air brakes, Cornelius Vanderbilt of the New York Central Railroad said to him, "Do you mean to tell me with a straight face that a moving train can be stopped with wind?" "They laughed at Orville," Mother used to say when someone tried to talk her out of a wild scheme, "and they laughed at Wilbur."

I had small experience of the evil hopelessness, pain, starvation, and terror that the world spread about; I had barely seen people's malice and greed. I believed that in civilized countries, torture had ended with the Enlightenment. Of nations' cruel options I knew nothing. My optimism was endless; it grew sky-high within the narrow bounds of my isolationism. Because I was all untried courage, I could not allow that the loss of courage was a real factor to be reckoned in. I put my faith in willpower, that weak notion by which children seek to replace the loving devotion that comes from intimate and dedicated knowledge. I believed that I could resist aging by willpower.

I believed then, too, that I would never harm anyone. I usually believed I would never meet a problem I could not solve. I would overcome any weakness, any despair, any fear. Hadn't I overcome my fear of the ghosty oblong that coursed round my room, simply by thinking it through? Everything was simple. You found good work, learned all about it, and did it.

Questions of how to act were also transparent to reason. Right and wrong were easy to discern: I was right, and Amy was wrong. Many of my classmates stole things, but I did not. Sometimes, in a very tight spot, when at last I noticed I had a moral question on my hands, I asked myself, What would Christ have done? I had picked up this method (very much on the sly—we were not supposed really to believe these things) from Presbyterian Sunday school, from summer camp, or from any of the innumerable righteous orange-bound biographies I read. I had not known it to fail in the two times I had applied it.

As for loss, as for parting, as for bidding farewell, so long, thanks, to love or a land or a time—what did I know of parting, of grieving, mourning, loss? Well, I knew one thing; I had known it all along. I knew it was the kicker. I knew life pulled you in two; you never healed. Mother's emotions ran high, and she suffered sometimes from a web of terrors, because, she said, her father died when she was seven; she still missed him.

My parents played the Cole Porter song "It's All Right with Me." When Ella Fitzgerald sang, "There's someone I'm trying so hard to forget—don't you want to forget someone too?," these facile, breathy lyrics struck me as an unexpectedly true expression of how it felt to be alive. This was experience at its most private and inarticulate: longing and loss. "It's the wrong time, it's the wrong place, though your face is charming, it's the wrong face." I was a thirteen-year-old child; I had no one to miss, had lost no one. Yet I suspect most children feel this way, probably all children feel this way, as adults do; they mourn this absence or loss of someone, and sense that unnamable loss as a hole or hollow moving beside them in the air.

Loss came around with the seasons, blew into the house when you opened the windows, piled up in the bottom desk and dresser drawers, accumulated in the back of closets, heaped in the basement starting by the furnace, and came creeping up the basement stairs. Loss grew as you did, without your consent; your losses mounted beside you like earthworm castings. No willpower could prevent someone's dying. And no willpower could restore someone dead, breathe life into that frame and set it going again in the room with you to meet your eyes. That was the fact of it. The strongest men and women who had ever lived had presumably tried to resist their own deaths, and now they were dead. It was on this fact that all the stirring biographies coincided, concurred, and culminated.

Time itself bent you and cracked you on its wheel. We were getting ready to move again. I knew I could not forever keep riding my bike backward into ever-older neighborhoods to look the ever-older houses in the face. I tried to memorize the layout of this Richland Lane house, but I couldn't force it into my mind while it was still in my bones.

I saw already that I could not in good faith renew the increasingly desperate series of vows by which I had always tried to direct my life. I had vowed to love Walter Milligan forever; now I could recall neither his face nor my feelings, but only this quondam urgent vow. I had vowed to keep exploring Pittsburgh by bicycle no matter how old I got, and planned an especially sweeping tour for my hundredth birthday in 2045. I had vowed to keep hating Amy in order to defy Mother, who kept prophesying I would someday not hate Amy. In short, I always vowed, one way or another, not to change. Not me. I needed the fierceness of vowing because I could scarcely help but notice, visiting the hatchling robins at school every day, that it was mighty unlikely.

As a life's work, I would remember everything—everything, against loss. I would go through life like a plankton net. I would trap and keep every teacher's funny remark, every face on the street, every microscopic alga's sway, every conversation, configuration of leaves, every dream, and every scrap of overhead cloud. Who would remember Molly's infancy if not me? (Unaccountably, I thought that only I had noticed—not Molly, but time itself. No one else, at least, seemed bugged by it. Children may believe that they alone have interior lives.)

Some days I felt an urgent responsibility to each change of light outside the sunporch windows. Who would remember any of it, any of this our time, and the wind thrashing the buckeye limbs outside? Somebody had to do it, somebody had to hang on to the days with teeth and fists, or the whole show had been in vain. That it was impossible never entered my reckoning. For work, for a task, I had never heard the word.

WE WERE MOVING THAT SPRING because our beloved grandfather had died, of a brain tumor. It was the year I got a microscope, and traveled with Judy Schoyer to Paw Paw, watched robins fledge from the school library window, and saw the Polyphemus moth walk toward Shadyside; I was not thirteen. I was expecting to attend an upper-school dance at the boys' school, Shady Side Academy, to which an older boy had invited me, but our grandfather died that day, and our father cried, and the dance was out. I shamed myself by minding that the dance was out.

Our grandfather had been a straitlaced, gentle man, whose mild and tolerant presence had soothed Oma for forty-four years. He doted on Amy and me, from a Scotch-Irish banker's distance; we loved him. For several weeks that spring as he lay in the hospital, the tumor pressed on his brain in such a way that he could say only one word, "Balls." Amy and I watched him move on the bed between sheets; he twisted inside a thin hospital gown. Neither of us had seen him angry before; he was angry now, and shocked. "Balls," he replied to any inquiry, "balls" for hello and "balls" for goodbye. Goodbye it was, and he died.

Oma sadly sold their Pittsburgh house. She and Mary Burinda moved into a pair of penthouse apartments in Shadyside. In the summer, Oma and Mary and Henry lived at Lake Erie. In the fall, they moved back to Pittsburgh and Oma caught opening nights at the Nixon Theater. And for the winter and spring, Oma and Mary moved to Pompano Beach, Florida, where they had an apartment on the water.

Oma sold their house, and we had bought it. A year later we moved from Richland Lane, from the generous house with the glass sunporch under buckeye trees. We moved to Oma's old stone house, another corner house, high on a hilly street where all the houses were old stone, and all their roofs were old slate, and the few children played—if they played at all—inside.

We lived now on a hushed hill packed with little castles. There were only three, dead-end streets. The longest street, winding silently into the very empyrean, was Glen Arden Drive. The McCulloughs lived at one end of it, and the McCradys at the other. Houses rarely changed hands; from here, there was nowhere in town to move to. The next step was a seat at the right hand of God.

In horizontal space, our family now lived near our first house on Edgerton Avenue, near St. Bede's Church. In vertical space, we were quite distant from it. Queerly, an inhumanly long and steep flight of outdoor stairs connected our newest neighborhood to our oldest one. These were the Glen Arden steps. From the top of Glen Arden Drive, between two houses, thirty concrete steps descended a scruffy unbuildable cliff to Dallas Avenue below, across the street from St. Bede's. The steps made a dark old tunnel. They were like the stairway in the poem, the stairway to the sea where down the blind are driven. Their concrete was so rough it ruined your shoes.

Children from below played there; Popsicle wrappers and wrecked plastic toys kept the cliff a mess. People's maids used the steps to connect with Dallas Avenue buses—the maids climbed wearily up the cruel steps in the morning, and wearily down them at night.

The steps landed between and behind two small ordinary Pittsburgh brick houses; a walkway sloped down into the daylight of Dallas Avenue, where buses ran. If I stood on Dallas Avenue waiting for the bus to art class and looked across the street at the corner, by squinting down across the rows of sycamores at St. Bede's I could make out our first house. There it was on the farthest visible corner, painted white again, and there were the Lombardy poplars behind it, next to the alley. Down that now leafy street Jo Ann Sheehy had skated, and I had run from the nuns and run from the man whose windshield we hit with a snowball. There were the maple trees Henry planted when Amy and I were born.

Too old to play on the steps, instead I dreamed about them—how I dreamed about them!—a hundred steep steps dark as a chute. Fuzzy staghorn sumac poked their cold pipe rails. I dreamed about the blackened soil and frozen candy wrappers on the dizzying cliff they spanned. I dreamed the steps let me down in the wrong place. I dreamed the steps swayed underfoot, and rose, and tilted me over the ocean. I dreamed I couldn't find the steps.

That first spring our family walked out together, as we had not done for many years, to see the Memorial Day parade pass down Dallas Avenue. Our neighbors did, too; once a year the pale families emerged from their stone houses and climbed stiffly down the Glen Arden steps to watch the Memorial Day parade.

Now our family was seeing the once familiar parade from the other side of the street. A dozen bands passed, and the brass horns wagged from side to side in time. The kids from the big all-black high school came bopping and tossing batons.

I felt the low drumbeats in my breastbone. More marching bands passed, then shuffling ranks of men, then children, in uniforms. Horses, of all things, walked by or skittered, backing the crowd. Then, to everyone's boredom, open cars drove by; it was over. Loose children on bikes, made with excitement, rode squiggles and loops at the parade's rear, like tails on a kite. We stayed to hear the music wind away up toward the cemetery.

When the parade had passed, the people from the two sides of Dallas Avenue were left looking at each other. There were our former neighbors. Mother crossed over and talked to some of them. There were some of my earliest friends, altered, and my dear old friend Cathy Lindsey, whom I had already met up with again in our big public art classes; we always sat together. Now we waved across Dallas Avenue. The Sheehy women were there: Jo Ann in pink makeup, and her mother listless in a wide housedress, holding some sort of baby. The nice Fahey boys weren't there; they had moved. Father and I saw the polio boy who had worn such a tall shoe; now, miraculously, he had grown almost all the way up and had two equally long, good legs. He never knew us, so we didn't wave.

People were scattering. The Glen Arden families wordlessly climbed back up the thirty cement steps, and burst out like dead souls on another full scene enacted on a higher plane. They looked around strangely from between the two high houses, got their bearings so that the highest circle of Glen Arden Drive seemed like the very horizon, glided to their own houses, and closed their doors again.

Since we had moved, my reading had taken a new turn. Books wandered in and out of my hands, as they had always done, but now most of them had a common theme. This new theme was the source of imagination at its most private—never mentioned, rarely even brought to consciousness. It was, essentially, a time, and a series of places, to which I returned nightly. So also must thousands, or millions, of us who grew up in the 1950s, reading what came to hand. What came to hand in those years were books about the past war: the war in England, France, Belgium, Norway, Italy, Greece; the war in Africa; the war in the Pacific, in Guam, New Guinea, the Philippines; the war, Adolf Hitler, and the camps.

We read Leon Uris's popular novels, *Exodus,* and, better, *Mila 18,* about the Warsaw ghetto. We read Hersey's *The Wall*—again, the Warsaw ghetto. We read *Time* magazine, and *Life,* and *Look.* It was in the air, that there had been these things. We read, above all, and over and over, for we were young, Anne Frank's *The Diary of a Young Girl.* This was where we belonged; here we were at home.

I say "we," but in fact I did not know anyone else who read these things. Perhaps my parents did, for they brought the books home. What were my friends reading? We did not then talk about books; our reading was private, and constant, like the interior life itself. Still, I say, there must have been millions of us. The theaters of war—the lands, the multiple seas, the very corridors of air—and the death camps in Europe, with their lines of starved bald people . . . these, combined, were the settings in which our imaginations were first deeply stirred.

Earlier generations of children, European children, I inferred, had had on their minds heraldry and costumed adventure. They read *The Count of Monte Cristo* and *The Three Musketeers.* They read about King Arthur and Lancelot and Galahad; they read about Robin Hood. I had read some of these things and considered them behind me. It would have been pleasant, I suppose, to close your eyes and imagine yourself in a suit of armor, astride an armored horse, fighting a battle for honor with broadswords on a pennanted plain, or in a copse of trees.

But of what value was honor when, in book after book, the highest prize was a piece of bread? Of what use was a broadsword, or even a longbow, against Hitler's armies which occupied Europe, against Hitler's Luftwaffe, Hitler's Panzers, Hitler's U-boats, or against Hitler's S.S., who banged on the door and led Anne Frank and her family away? We closed our eyes and imagined how we would survive the death camps—maybe with honor and maybe not. We imagined how we would escape the death camps, imagined how we would liberate the death camps. How? We fancied and schemed, but we had read too much, and knew there was no possible way. This was a novel concept: Can't do. We were in for the duration. We closed our eyes and waited for the Allies, but the Allies were detained.

Now and over the next few years, the books appeared and we read them. We read *The Bridge Over the River Kwai, The*

Young Lions. In the background sang a chorus of smarmy librarians:

> The world of books is a child's
> Land of enchantment.
> When you open a book and start reading
> You enter another world—the world
> Of make-believe—where anything can happen.

We read *Thirty Seconds Over Tokyo,* and *To Hell and Back.* We read *The Naked and the Dead, Run Silent, Run Deep,* and *Tales of the South Pacific,* in which American sailors saw native victims of elephantiasis pushing their own enlarged testicles before them in wheelbarrows. We read *The Caine Mutiny, Some Came Running.*

I was a skilled bombardier. I could run a submarine with one hand, and evade torpedoes, depth charges, and mines. I could disembowel a soldier with a bayonet, survive under a tarp in a lifeboat, and parachute behind enemy lines. I could contact the Resistance with my high-school French and eavesdrop on the Germans with my high-school German:

"Du! Kleines Mädchen! Bist du französisches Mädchen oder bist du Amerikanischer spy?"

"Je suis une jeune fille de la belle France, Herr S.S. Officer."

"Prove it!"

"Je suis, tu es, il est, nous sommes, vous êtes, ils sont."

"Very gut. Run along and play."

What were librarians reading these days? One librarian pressed on me a copy of *Look Homeward, Angel.* "How I envy you," she said, "having a chance to read this for the very first time." But it was too late, several years too late.

At last Hitler fell, and scientists working during the war came up with the atomic bomb. We read *On the Beach, A Canticle for Leibowitz;* we read *Hiroshima.* Reading about the bomb was a part of reading about the war: these were actual things and events, large in their effects on millions of people, vivid in their nearness to each man's or woman's death. It was a relief to turn from life to something important.

At school we had air-raid drills. We took the drills seriously; surely Pittsburgh, which had the nation's steel, coke, and aluminum, would be the enemy's first target.

I knew that during the war, our father, who was 4-F because of a collapsing lung, had "watched the skies." We all knew that people still watched the skies. But when the keen-eyed watcher spotted the enemy bomber over Pittsburgh, what, precisely, would be his moves? Surely he could only calculate, just as we in school did, what good it would do him to get under something.

When the air-raid siren sounded, our teachers stopped talking and led us to the school basement. There the gym teachers lined us up against the cement walls and steel lockers, and showed us how to lean in and fold our arms over our heads. Our small school ran from kindergarten through twelfth grade. We had air-raid drills in small batches, four or five grades together, because there was no room for us all against the walls. The teachers had to stand in the middle of the basement rooms: those bright Pittsburgh women who taught Latin, science, and art, and those educated, beautifully mannered European women who taught French, history, and German, who had landed in Pittsburgh at the end of their respective flights from Hitler, and who had baffled us by their common insistence on tidiness, above all, in our written work.

The teachers stood in the middle of the room, not talking to each other. We tucked against the walls and lockers: dozens of clean girls wearing green jumpers, green knee socks, and pink-soled white bucks. We folded our skinny arms over our heads, and raised to the enemy a clatter of gold scarab bracelets and gold bangle bracelets.

If the bomb actually came, should we not let the little kids— the kindergartners like Molly, and the first and second graders—go against the wall? We older ones would stand in the middle with the teachers. The European teachers were almost used to this sort of thing. We would help them keep spirits up; we would sing "Frère Jacques," or play Buzz.

Our house was stone. In the basement was a room furnished with a long wooden bar, tables and chairs, a leather couch, a refrigerator, a sink, an ice maker, a fireplace, a piano, a record player, and a set of drums. After the bomb, we would live, in the manner of Anne Frank and her family, in this basement. It had also a larger set of underground rooms, which held a washer and a dryer, a workbench, and, especially, food: shelves of canned fruits and vegetables, and a chest freezer. Our family could live in the basement for many years, until the radiation outside blew away. Amy and Molly would grow up there. I would teach them all I knew, and entertain them on the piano. Father would build a radiation barrier for the basement's sunken windows. He would teach me to play the drums. Mother would feed us and tend to us. We would grow close.

I had spent the equivalent of years of my life, I thought, in concentration camps, in ghettos, in prison camps, and in lifeboats. I knew how to ration food and water. We would each have four ounces of food a day and eight ounces of water, or maybe only four ounces of water. I knew how to stretch my rations by hoarding food in my shirt, by chewing slowly, by sloshing water around in my mouth and wetting my tongue well before I swallowed. If the water gave out in the taps, we could drink club soda or tonic. We could live on the juice in canned food. I figured the five of us could live many years on the food in the basement—but I was not sure.

One day I asked Mother: How long could we last on the food in the basement? She did not know what I had been reading. How could she have known?

"The food in the basement? In the freezer and on the shelves? Oh, about a week and a half. Two weeks."

She knew, as I knew, that there were legs of lamb in the freezer, turkeys, chickens, pork roasts, shrimp, and steaks. There were pounds of frozen vegetables, quarts of ice cream, dozens of Popsicles. By her reckoning, that wasn't many family dinners: a leg of lamb one night, rice, and vegetables; steak the next night, potatoes, and vegetables.

"Two weeks! We could live much longer than two weeks!"

"There's really not very much food down there. About two weeks' worth."

I let it go. What did I know about feeding a family? On the other hand, I considered that if it came down to it, I would have to take charge.

It was clear that adults, including our parents, approved of children who read books, but it was not at all clear why this was so. Our reading was subversive, and we knew it. Did they think we read to improve our vocabularies? Did they want us to read and not pay the least bit of heed to what we read, as they wanted us to go to Sunday school and ignore what we heard?

I was now believing books more than I believed what I saw and heard. I was reading books about the actual, historical, moral world—in which somehow I felt I was not living.

The French and Indian War had been, for me, a purely literary event. Skilled men in books could survive it. Those who died, an arrow through the heart, thrilled me by their last words. This recent war's survivors, some still shaking, some still in mourning, taught in our classrooms. *"Wir waren aus-gebommt,"* one dear old white-haired Polish lady related in German class, her family was "bombed out," and we laughed, we smart girls, because this was our slang for "drunk." Those who died in this war's books died whether they were skilled or not. Bombs fell on their cities or ships, or they starved in the camps or were gassed or shot, or they stepped on land mines and died surprised, trying to push their intestines back in their abdomens with their fingers and thumbs.

What I sought in books was imagination. It was depth, depth of thought and feeling; some sort of extreme of subject matter; some nearness to death; some call to courage. I myself was getting wild; I wanted wildness, originality, genius, rapture, hope. I wanted strength, not tea parties. What I sought in books was a world whose surfaces, whose people and events and days lived, actually matched the exaltation of the interior life. There you could live.

Those of us who read carried around with us like martyrs a secret knowledge, a secret joy, and a secret hope: There is a life worth living where history is still taking place; there are ideas worth dying for, and circumstances where courage is still prized. This life could be found and joined, like the Resistance. I kept this exhilarating faith alive in myself, concealed under my uniform shirt like an oblate's ribbon; I would not be parted from it.

We who had grown up in the Warsaw ghetto, who had seen all our families gassed in the death chambers, who had shipped before the mast, and hunted sperm whale in Antarctic seas; we who had marched from Moscow to Poland and lost our legs to the cold; we who knew by heart every snag and sandbar on the Mississippi River south of Cairo, and knew by heart Morse code, forty parables and psalms, and lots of Shakespeare; we who had battled Hitler and Hirohito in the North Atlantic, in North Africa, in New Guinea and Burma and Guam, in the air over London, in the Greek and Italian hills; we who had learned to man minesweepers before we learned to walk in high heels—were we going to marry Holden Caulfield's roommate, and buy a house in Point Breeze, and send our children to dancing school?

THE BOYS WERE CHANGING. Those froggy little beasts had elongated and transformed into princes and gods. When it happened, I must have been out of the room. Suddenly here they all were, Richie and Rickie and Dan and all, diverse in their varied splendors, each powerful and mysterious, immense, and possessed of an inexplicable knowledge of arcana.

The boys wandered the neighborhoods now, and showed up at girls' houses, as if by accident. They would let us listen to them talk, and we heard them mention the state legislature, say, or some opinion of Cicero's, or the Battle of the Marne— and those things abruptly became possible topics in society because those magnificent boys had pronounced their names.

Where had they learned all this, or, more pertinently, why had they remembered it? We girls knew precisely the limits of the possible and the thinkable, we thought, and were permanently astonished to learn that we were wrong. Whose idea of sophistication was it, after all, to pay attention in Latin class? It was the boys' idea. Everything was. Everything they thought of was bold and original like that. While we were worried about sending valentines, they were worried about sending troops.

Plus their feet were so big. You could look at the boys' sheer physical volume with uncomprehending astonishment forever. Had the braces on their teeth been restraining their very bones? For look at them. You would never tire of running your wondering eyes over the mystery of their construction, so plain, and the mystery of their bulk, and the mystery of their skin, and even their strange boxy clothes. The boys.

We ran, we fancied, to sweetness, we girls. The boys, as we got to know them, were cynical. They addressed each other out of the corners of their mouths in cryptic staccato phrases, all clever references to that larger world wherein they dwelt and where we longed to go ourselves. If you got to know them, apparently, they would tell you about their teachers at Shady Side Academy—teachers my own father had studied under, but about whom, alas, he could come up with precious little.

We girls chafed, whined, and complained under our parents' strictures. The boys waged open war on their parents. They cursed their fathers, and disobeyed them outright. ("What can they do? Throw me out?") Was this not breathtakingly bold? The boys' pitched battles with their parents were legendary; the punishments they endured melted our hearts.

Each year as we rose through the grades, dancing school met an hour later, until one year it vanished into the darkness, and was replaced by, or transmogrified into, another institution altogether, that of country-club subscription dances.

The engraved invitation came in the mail: The Sewickley Country Club was hosting a subscription dinner dance several weeks thence. Each of several appropriate country clubs, it turned out, gave precisely one such dance a year, at a time that coincided with boarding-school vacations. I knew Sewickley children, having opposed on playing fields their school's ferocious field hockey team. The old village of Sewickley had come to prominence late in the nineteenth century when some families quit their grandparents' mansions on Fifth Avenue and moved in a body to that green and pleasant land. They zoned it to a fare-thee-well and furnished it with a country club, a Presbyterian church, and a little expensive school. Now they were asking us to a dinner dance.

We showed up at our own country club in pale spaghetti-strap dresses and silk shoes, to board a yellow bus in the snow. There we all were: the same boys, the same girls. How did they know? I wondered which of those remote country-club powers, those white-haired sincere men, those golden-haired, long-toothed, ironic women, had met on what firm cloud over western Pennsylvania to apportion and schedule these events among the scattered country clubs, and had pored over what unthinkable list of school children to discuss which schoolchildren should be asked to these dances they held for what reason. If you were part Jewish, would they find you out, like Hitler? How small a part could they detect? What was at the end of all this novitiate—solemn vows?

We dined that night in faraway Sewickley, at long linen-covered tables marked by place cards. Our shrimp cocktails were already at our places. We were like Beauty in the castle of the Beast: that is, I, at least, never laid eyes on the unknown adult or adults who had presumably invited us, designed and ordered the invitations, secured a room and a band, and devised the menu. There were some adults against the walls, all dressed up, who ignored us and whom we ignored.

My dinner partner was a fragile redhead from Sewickley, a Paulie—from St. Paul's School—whose hulking twin sisters had several times mown me down on the hockey field. From him I learned that some girls my age voluntarily played golf. Like many of the boys, he was good-natured, polite, somewhat cowed, and delicately handsome. One was not, however, thank God, required to fall in love at a subscription dance, although it had been known to happen.

We ate chicken breast in velvet sauce on ham. We ate wild rice, tomato aspic, and, as a concession to our being in fact children, hot fudge sundaes or green peppermint parfaits.

During dessert the band straggled in and set up by the freezing French doors to the terrace. The band was an unmatched set of bored men in dark suits and red carnations. The only bands that counted in our book were Lester Lanin's and Eddy Duchin's. These men, as at all subscription dances, were merely locals: a drum, a bass, a piano, a clarinet. Their boredom, and the possible death of their musical ambitions, and the probable complete disregard of everyone with whom they had dealt over this engagement, unless they had had the good fortune to run into my mother, had drained all the expression from their faces. Sometimes, though, on a jitterbug or a Charleston, you could pry a wink out of the drummer.

The band struck up, not surprisingly, "Mountain Greenery." This frenzied sequence of notes had been our cue conditioned since we were ten. We danced.

There were boys here from far away—not only from familiar Fox Chapel and expected Sewickley, but also from Ligonier, that pretty village in the distant mountains where the Mellons lived. There were older boys here, who had already been to deb parties. And there were some very tall boys—some of ours and some of theirs—whose shoulders rose above our heads like those few lone trees which burst through the canopy in a rain forest. Although these big boys' status was as great as their stature, they rarely smiled or relaxed, but instead looked worriedly around over our headtops, frowning, earnest, always at the edge of a wince.

"Isn't he cute?"

In the densely carpeted ladies' rooms we all hurried. We didn't meet each other's eyes in the long mirrors.

"Which?"

"Which what?"

"Which is cute?"

It was always one of the wincing giants who was cute. We ran combs through our hair and pounded back along the labyrinthine club corridors to the dance floor. Yes, very cute.

One blond, sharp-toothed boarding-school boy, a famously witty chess player, was wearing patent-leather pumps. On his feet, that is, where his shoes should be, he was wearing low-slung, dainty, shiny pumps, like ballet practice shoes, with satin bows at the toes—and he carried it off. Thus I learned yet again that more things were possible in the world than I had dreamed. He and a friend had driven a car through the snow to this dance. The friend was a sarcastic boy, narrow-skulled and overbred as a collie, who said he hung around in the Hill District. The Hill District was Pittsburgh's cruelest and coolest black ghetto, where more babies died than anywhere else in the United States. Up on the Hill, he went to whorehouses. Was this not bold, evil, original? Our own boys would never think of that.

I had sat near these two at dinner. They had traveled. From their boarding school they had walked, loose, in the towns of Connecticut, and knew them well enough to dismiss them. I danced with each of them. How light the blond boy's shoulders felt! With what smooth disdain did the blond boy lead me walking beside him four steps before he pulled me in again to him, as easily as if my arm had been the bowline of a boat!

And we were buoyant when we danced, we two, were we not? Had he noticed?

This light-shouldered boy could jitterbug, old style, and would; he was more precious than gold, yea, than much fine gold. We jitterbugged. There was nothing flirtatious about it. It was more an exultant and concentrated collaboration, such as aerialists enjoy—and I hope they enjoy it—when they catch each other twirling in midair. Only the strength in our fingertips kept us alive. If they weakened or slipped, his fingertips or mine, we'd fall spinning backward across the length of the room and out through the glass French doors to the snowy terrace, and if we were any good we'd make sure we fell on the downbeat, snow or no snow. For this was, at last, rock and roll. We danced in front of the band; I wished the music were louder.

The last dance was slow; the lights dimmed. The light-shouldered blond boy moved me over and across the golden dark floor and in and out of his arms. He released me and caught me, slowly, and turned me and spun me, and paused on the odd long note so I had to raise a leg from the hip to keep us afloat, and I held him loosely but surely for the count of four, amazed.

He was bare-handed, as were all the boys at these dances. We retained our white cotton gloves. It was easier now to imagine his warmth, the heel of his naked left hand on my glove. But it still required imagination. The thick cotton stretched flat across the dip of my palm like a trampoline; it repelled the bulge of his hand and held away his heat.

"Keep your back straight," my mother had told me years ago. "Don't let your arm weigh and drag on a boy's shoulder, no matter how tired you are. Dance on the balls of your feet, no matter how tall you are. Chin up."

The drummer stretched in the dark and rubbed the back of his neck. He began packing up, retaining, however, his brushes for "Good Night, Ladies," at whose opening bars we all groaned.

We groaned because we had to part and lacked the words to manage it smoothly. We groaned because we had to ride back through the snow for an hour and a half with our boys on a bus, and we never figured out how to conduct ourselves on this bus. Were we to kiss, or sing camp songs?

"How was it?" my mother asked the next morning. She lowered the Sunday paper she'd been paging through. How was what? I could barely remember. Someone's father had picked us up at our club and driven us another hour home. I didn't get in till after two. Now it was Sunday morning. I was dressed up again and looking for a pair of clean white cotton gloves for church. So was Amy. If there was such a pair, I wanted to find it first.

"How was it?" she asked, and then I remembered and began to understand how it was. It was wonderful, that's how it was. It was absolutely wonderful.

THAT MORNING IN CHURCH after our first subscription dance, we reconvened on the balcony of the Shadyside Presbyterian Church. I sat in the first balcony row, and resisted the impulse to stretch my Charleston-stiff legs on the balcony's carved walnut rail. The blond boy I'd met at the dance was on my mind, and I intended to spend the church hour recalling his every word and gesture, but I couldn't concentrate. Beside me sat my friend Linda. Last night at the dance she had been a laughing, dimpled girl with an advanced sense of the absurd. Now in church she was grave, and didn't acknowledge my remarks.

Near us in the balcony's first row, and behind us, were the boys—the same boys with whom we had traveled on a bus to and from the Sewickley Country Club dance. Below us spread the main pews, filling with adults. Almost everyone in the church was long familiar to me. But this particular Sunday in church bore home to me with force a new notion: that I did not really know any of these people at all. I thought I did—but, being now a teenager, I thought I knew almost everything. Only the strongest evidence could penetrate this illusion, which distorted everything I saw. I knew I approved almost nothing. That is, I liked, I adored, I longed for, everyone on earth, especially India and Africa, and particularly everyone on the streets of Pittsburgh—all those friendly, democratic, openhearted, sensible people—and at Forbes Field, and in all the office buildings, parks, streetcars, churches, and stores, excepting only the people I knew, none of whom was up to snuff.

The church building, where the old Scotch-Irish families assembled weekly, was a Romanesque chunk of rough, carved stone and panes of dark slate. Covered in creeper, long since encrusted into its quietly splendid site, it looked like a Scottish rock in the rain.

Everywhere outside and inside the church and parish hall, sharp carved things rose from the many dim tons of stone. There were grainy crossed keys, pelicans, anchors, a phoenix, ivy vines, sheaves of wheat, queer and leering mammal heads like gargoyles, thistles for Scotland, lizards, scrolls, lions, and shells. It looked as if someone had once in Pittsburgh enjoyed a flight or two of fancy. If your bare hand or arm brushed against one of the stone walls carelessly, the stone would draw blood.

My wool coat sat empty behind me; its satin lining felt cool on the backs of my arms. I hated being here. It looked as if the boys did, too. Their mouths were all open, and their eyelids half down. We were all trapped. At home before church, I had been too rushed to fight about it.

I imagined the holy war each boy had fought with his family this morning, and lost, resulting in his sullen and suited presence in church. I thought of Dan there, ruddy-cheeked, and of wild, sweet Jamie beside him, each flinging his silk tie at his hypocrite father after breakfast, and making a desperate stand in some dark dining room lighted upward by snowlight from the lawns outside—struggling foredoomed to raise the stone and walnut weight of this dead society's dead institutions, battling for liberty, freedom of conscience, and so forth.

The boys, at any rate, slumped. Possibly they were hung over.

While the nave filled we examined, or glared at, the one thing before our eyes: the apse's enormous gold mosaic of Christ. It loomed over the chancel; every pew in the nave and on the balcony looked up at it. It was hard to imagine what long-ago board of trustees had voted for this Romish-looking mosaic, so glittering, with which we had been familiarizing ourselves in a lonely way since infancy, when our eyes could first focus on distance.

Christ stood barefoot, alone and helpless-looking, his palms outcurved at his sides. He was wearing his robes. He wasn't standing on anything, but instead floated loose and upright inside a curved, tiled dome. The balcony's perspective foreshortened the dome's curve, so Christ appeared to drift flattened and clumsy, shriveled but glorious. Barefoot as he was, and with the suggestion of sandstone scarps behind him, he looked rural. Below me along the carpeted marble aisles crept the church's families; the women wore mink and sable stoles. Hushed, they sat and tilted their hatted heads and looked at the rural man. His skies of shattered gold widened over the sanctuary and almost met the square lantern tower, gold-decorated, over the nave.

The mosaic caught the few church lights—lights like tapers in a castle—and spread them dimly, a dusting of gold like pollen, throughout the vast and solemn space. There was nothing you could see well in this rich, Rembrandt darkness—nothing save the minister's shining face and Christ's gold vault—and yet there was no corner, no scratchy lily work, you couldn't see at all.

It was a velvet cord, maroon, with brass fittings, that reserved our ninth-grade balcony section for us. We sat on velvet cushions. Below us, filling the yellow pews with dark furs, were the rest of the families of the church, who seemed to have been planted here in dignity—by a God who could see how hard they worked and how few pleasures they took for themselves—just after the Flood went down. There were Linda's parents and grandparents and one of her great-grandparents. Always, the same old Pittsburgh families ran this church. The men, for whose forefathers streets all over town were named, served as deacons, trustees, and elders. The women served in many ways, and ran the Christmas bazaar.

I knew these men; they were friends and neighbors. I knew what they lived for, I thought. The men wanted to do the right thing, at work and in the community. They wore narrow, tight neckties. Close-mouthed, they met, in volunteer boardrooms and in club locker rooms, the same few comfortable others they had known since kindergarten. Their wives and children, in those days, lived around them on their visits home. Some men found their families bewildering, probably; a man might wonder, wakened by reports of the outstanding misdeeds of this son or that son, how everyone had so failed to understand what he expected. Some of these men held their shoulders and knuckles tight; their laughter was high and embarrassed; they seemed to be looking around for the entrance to some other life. Only some of the doctors, it seemed to me, were conspicuously interested and glad. During conversations, they looked at people calmly, even at their friends' little daughters; their laughter was deep, long, and joyful; they asked questions; and they knew lots of words.

I knew the women better. The women were wise and strong. Even among themselves, they prized gaiety and irony, gaiety and irony come what may. They coped. They sighed, they permitted themselves a remark or two, they lived essentially alone. They reared their children with their own two hands, and did all their own cooking and driving. They had no taste for waste or idleness. They volunteered their considerable energies, wisdom, and ideas at the church or the hospital or the service organization or charity.

Life among these families partook of all the genuine seriousness of life in time. A child's birth was his sole entrée, just as it is to life itself. His birthright was a regiment of families and a phalanx of institutions which would accompany him, solidly but at a distance, through this vale of tears.

Families whose members have been acquainted with each other for as long as anyone remembers grow not close, but respectful. They accumulate dignity by being seen at church every Sunday for the duration of life, despite their troubles and sorrows. They accumulate dignity at club luncheons, dinners, and dances, by gracefully and persistently, with tidy hair and fitted clothes, occupying their slots.

In this world, some grown women went carefully wild from time to time. They appeared at parties in outlandish clothes, hair sticking out, faces painted in freckles. They shrieked, sang, danced, and parodied anything—that is, anything at all outside the tribe—so that nothing, almost, was sacred. These clowns were the best-loved women, and rightly so, for their own sufferings had taught them what dignity was worth, and every few years they reminded the others, and made them laugh till they cried.

My parents didn't go to church. I practically admired them for it. Father would drive by at noon and scoop up Amy and me, saying, "Hop in quick!" so no one would see his weekend khaki pants and loafers.

Now, in unison with the adults in the dimness below, we read responsively, answering the minister. Our voices blended low, so their joined sound rose muffled and roaring, rhythmic, like distant seas, and soaked into the rough stone vaults and plush fittings, and vanished, and rose again:

> The heavens declare the glory of God:
> AND THE FIRMAMENT SHOWETH HIS
>   HANDYWORK.
> Day unto day uttereth speech,
> AND NIGHT UNTO NIGHT SHOWETH
>   KNOWLEDGE.
> There is no speech nor language, where their
>   voice is not heard.

The minister was a florid, dramatic man who commanded a batch of British vowels, for which I blamed him absolutely, not knowing he came from a Canadian farm. His famous radio ministry attracted letters and even contributions from Alaskan lumberjacks and fishermen. The poor saps. What if one of them, a lumberjack, showed up in Pittsburgh wearing a lumberjack shirt and actually tried to enter the church building? Maybe the ushers were really bouncers.

I had got religion at summer camp, and had prayed nightly there and in my bed at home, to God, asking for a grateful heart, and receiving one insofar as I requested it. Inasmuch as I despised everything and everyone about me, of course, it was taken away, and I was left with the blackened heart I had chosen instead. As the years wore on, the intervals between Julys at camp stretched, and filled with country-club evenings, filled with the slang of us girls, our gossip, and our intricately shifting friendships, filled with the sight of the boys whose names themselves were a litany, and with the absorbing study of their nonchalance and gruff ease. All of which I professed, from time to time, when things went poorly, to disdain.

Nothing so inevitably blackened my heart as an obligatory Sunday at the Shadyside Presbyterian Church: the sight of orphan-girl Liz's "Jesus" tricked out in gilt; the minister's Britishy accent; the putative hypocrisy of my parents, who forced me to go, though they did not; the putative hypocrisy of the expensive men and women who did go. I knew enough of the Bible to damn these people to hell, citing chapter and verse. My house shall be called the house of prayer; but ye have made it a den of thieves. Every week I had been getting madder; now I was going to plain quit. One of these days, when I figured out how.

After the responsive reading there was a pause, an expectant hush. It was the first Sunday of the month, I remembered, shocked. Today was Communion. I would have to sit through Communion, with its two species, embarrassment and tedium—and I would be late getting out and Father would have to drive around the block a hundred times. I had successfully avoided Communion for years.

From their pews below rose the ushers and elders—everybody's father and grandfather, from Mellon Bank & Trust et cetera—in tailcoats. They worked the crowd smoothly, as always. When they collected money, I noted, they were especially serene. Collecting money was, after all, what they did during the week; they were used to it. Down each pew an usher thrust a long-handled velvet butterfly net, into the invisible interior of which we each inserted a bare hand to release a crushed, warm dollar bill we'd stored in a white glove's palm.

Now with dignity the ushers and elders hoisted the round sterling silver trays which bore Communion. A loaded juice tray must have weighed ten pounds. From a cunning array of holes in its top layer hung wee, tapered, lead-crystal glasses. Each held one-half ounce of Welch's grape juice.

The seated people would pass the grape-juice trays down the pews. After the grape juice came bread: flat silver salvers bore heaps of soft bread cubes, as if for stuffing a turkey. The elders and ushers spread swiftly and silently over the marble aisles in discreet pairs, some for bread cubes, some for grape juice, communicating by eyebrow only. An unseen organist, behind stone screens, played a muted series of single notes, a restless, breathy strain in a minor key, to kill time.

Soon the ushers reached the balcony where we sat. There our prayers had reached their intensest pitch, so fervent were we in our hopes not to drop the grape-juice tray.

I passed up the Welch's grape juice, I passed up the cubed bread, and sat back against my coat. Was all this not absurd? I glanced at Linda beside me. Apparently it was not. Her hands lay folded in her lap. Both her father and her uncle were elders.

It was not surprising, really, that I alone in this church knew what the barefoot Christ, if there had been such a person, would think about things—grape juice, tailcoats, British vowels, sable stoles. It was not surprising because it was becoming quite usual. After all, I was the intelligentsia around these parts, single-handedly. The intelligentsium. I knew why these people were in church: to display to each other their clothes. These were sophisticated men and women, such as we children were becoming. In church they made business connections; they saw and were seen. The boys, who, like me, were starting to come out for freedom and truth, must be having fits, now that the charade of Communion was in full swing.

I stole a glance at the boys, then looked at them outright, for I had been wrong. The boys, if mine eyes did not deceive me, were praying. Why? The intelligentsia, of course, described itself these days as "agnostic"—a most useful word. Around me, in seeming earnest, the boys prayed their unthinkable private prayers. To whom? It was wrong to watch, but I watched.

On the balcony's first row, to my right, big Dan had pressed his ruddy cheeks into his palms. Beside him, Jamie bent over his knees. Over one eye he had jammed a fist; his other eye was crinkled shut. Another boy, blond Robert, lay stretched over his arms, which clasped the balcony rail. His shoulders were tight; the back of his jacket rose and fell heavily with his breathing. It had been a long time since I'd been to Communion. When had this praying developed?

Dan lowered his hands and leaned back slowly. He opened his eyes, unfocused to the high, empty air before him. Wild Jamie moved his arm; he picked up a fistful of hair from his forehead and held it. His eyes fretted tightly shut; his jaws worked. Robert's head still lay low on his outstretched sleeves; it moved once from side to side and back again. So they struggled on. I finally looked away.

Below the balcony, in the crowded nave, men and women were also concentrating, it seemed. Were they perhaps pretending to pray? All heads were bent; no one moved. I began to doubt my own omniscience. If I bowed my head, too, and shut my eyes, would this be apostasy? No, I'd keep watching the people, in case I'd missed some clue that they were actually doing something else—bidding bridge hands.

For I knew these people, didn't I? I knew their world, which was, in some sense, my world, too, since I could not, outside of books, name another. I knew what they loved: their families, their houses, their country clubs, hard work, the people they knew best, and summer parties with old friends full of laughter. I knew what they hated: labor unions, laziness, spending, wildness, loudness. They didn't buy God. They didn't buy anything if they could help it. And they didn't work on spec.

Nevertheless, a young father below me propped his bowed head on two fists stacked on a raised knee. The ushers and their trays had vanished. The people had taken Communion. No one moved. The organist hushed. All the men's heads were bent—black, white, red, yellow, and brown. The men sat absolutely still. Almost all the women's heads were bent down, too, and some few tilted back. Some hats wagged faintly from side to side. All the people seemed scarcely to breathe.

I was alert enough now to feel, despite myself, some faint, thin stream of spirit braiding forward from the pews. Its flawed and fragile rivulets pooled far beyond me at the altar. I felt, or saw, its frail strands rise to the wide tower ceiling, and mass in the gold mosaic's dome.

The gold tesserae scattered some spirit like light back over the cavernous room, and held some of it, like light, in its deep curve. Christ drifted among floating sandstone ledges and deep, absorbent skies. There was no speech nor language. The people had been praying, praying to God, just as they seemed to be praying. That was the fact. I didn't know what to make of it.

I left Pittsburgh before I had a grain of sense. Who IS my neighbor? I never learned what the strangers around me had known and felt in their lives—those lithe, sarcastic boys in the balcony, those expensive men and women in the pews below—but it was more than I knew, after all.

YEARS BEFORE THIS, on long-ago summer Sundays, before Father went down the Ohio and ended up selling his boat, he used to take me out with him on the water. It was a long drive to the Allegheny River; it was a long wait, collecting insects in the grass among the pebbles on shore, till Father got the old twenty-four-foot cabin cruiser ready to go. But the Allegheny River, once we got out on it, was grand. Its distant shores were mostly wooded on both sides; coal barges, sand barges, and shallow-draft oil tankers floated tied up at a scattering of docks. Father wore tennis shoes on his long feet, and a sun-bleached cotton captain-style hat. He always squinted outside, hat or no hat, because his eyes were such a pale blue; the sun got in them. He was so tall he had to lean under the housetop to man the wheel.

We stopped at islands and swam. There were wooded islands in the river—like Smoky Island at Pittsburgh's point, where Indians had tortured their English and Scotch-Irish captives by night. The Indians had tied the soldiers and settlers to trees, heaped hot coals on their feet, and let their small boys practice archery on them. Indian women heated rifle barrels and ramrods over fires till they glowed, then drove them through prisoners' nostrils or ears. The screams of the tortured settlers on Smoky Island reached French soldiers at Fort Duquesne, who had handed them over to the Indians reluctantly, they said. "Humanity groans at being forced to use such monsters."

Father and I tied up at Nine-Mile Island, upstream from Smoky Island, and I jumped from a high rope-swing into the water, after poor Father told me all about those boaters' children who'd been killed or maimed dropping from this very swing. He could not bear to watch; he shut his eyes. From the tree branch at the top of the ladder I jumped onto the swing; when I let go over the water, momentum shot me forward like a slung stone. I swam up to find the water's surface again, and called to Father onshore, "It's okay now."

Our boat carved through the glossy water. Pittsburgh's summer skies are pale, as they are in many river valleys. The blinding haze spread overhead and glittered up from the river. It was the biggest sky in town.

We rode up in the locks and down in the locks. The locks scared me, for the huge doors that locked out the river leaked, and loud tons of water squirted in, and we sat helpless below the river with nothing to do but wait for the doors to give way. Enormous whirlpools dragged at the boat; we held on to the lock walls, clawed, with a single hand line and a boat hook. Once I dropped the boat hook, a new one with a teak handle, and the whirlpools sucked it down. To where? Where did the whirlpools put the water they took, and where would they put you, all ground up, if you fell in?

Oh, the river was grand. Outside the lock and back on the go, I sang wild songs at the top of my voice out over the roaring boat's stern. We raced under old steel bridges set on stone pilings in the river. How do people build bridges? How did anyone set those pilings, pile those stones, under the water?

Whenever I was on the river, I seemed to be visiting a fascinating place I had forgotten all about, where physical causes had physical effects, and great things got done, slowly, heavily, because people understood materials and forces.

Father on these boat outings answered my questions at length. He explained that people built coffer dams to set bridge pilings in a river. They lowered a kind of big pipe, or tight set of walls, to the bottom, and pumped all the water out of it; then the men could work there. I imagined the men piling and mortaring stones, with the unhurried ease of stone masons; they stood on gasping catfish and stinky silt. They were working under the river, at the bottom of a well of air. Just a few inches away, outside their coffer dam, a complete river of water was sliding downhill from western New York to the Gulf of Mexico. Above the workers' heads, boats and barges went by, their engines probably buzzing the cofferdam walls. What a life. Father said that some drowned in accidents, or got crushed; it was dangerous work. He said, answering my question, that these workers made less money than the men I knew, men I privately considered wholly unskilled. The bridge pilings obsessed me; I thought and thought about the brave men who built them in the rivers. I tried to imagine their families, their lunches, their boots. I tried to imagine what it would feel like to accomplish something so useful as building a bridge. What a queer world was the river, where I admired everything and knew nothing.

Father explained how to make glass from sand. He explained, over and over, because I was usually too frightened to hear right, how the river locks worked; they ran our boat up or down beside the terrible dams. The concrete navigation dams made slick spillways like waterfalls across the river. From upstream it was hard to see the drop's smooth line. Drunks forgot about the dams from time to time, and drove their boats straight over, killing themselves and everyone else on board. How did the drunks feel, while they were up loose in the air at the wheels of their boats for a split second, when they remembered all of a sudden the dam? "Oh yes, the dam." It seemed like a familiar feeling.

On the back of a chart—a real nautical chart, with shoals and soundings, just as in *Life on the Mississippi*—Father drew a diagram of a water system. The diagram made clear something I'd always wondered about: how water got up to the top floors of houses. The water tower was higher than the highest sinks, that was all; through all those labyrinthine pipes, the water sought its own level, seeming to climb up, but really still trickling down. He explained how steam engines worked, and suspension bridges, and pumps.

Father explained so much technology to me that for a long time I confused it with American culture. If pressed, I would have claimed that an American invented the irrigation ditch. Certainly the cofferdam was American, I thought, and the water tower, the highway tunnel—these engineering feats— and everything motorized, and everything electrical, and in short, everything I saw about me newer than fishnets, sail- boats, and spoons.

Technology depended on waterworks. The land of the forty-eight states was an extended and mighty system of con- trolled slopes, a combination Grand Coulee Dam and Niagara Falls. The water fell and the turbines spun and the lights came on, so steel mills could run all night. Then the steel made cars, millions of cars, and workers bought the cars, because Henry Ford in 1910 had come up with the idea of paying them enough to buy things. So the water rolled down the conti- nent—just plain fell—and everyone got rich.

Now, years later, Father had picked Amy and me up after church. When we got out of the car in the garage, we could hear Dixieland, all rambling brasses and drums, coming from the house. We hightailed it inside through the snow on the back walk and kicked off our icy dress shoes. I was in stock- ings. I could eat something, and go to my room. I had my own room now, and when I was home I stayed there and read or sulked.

While we were making sandwiches, though, Father started explaining the world to us once again. I stuck around. There in the kitchen, Father embarked upon an explanation of American economics. I don't know what prompted it. His voice took on urgency; he paced. Money worked like water, he said.

We were all listening, even little Molly. Molly, at four, had an open expression, smooth and quick, and fine blond hair; she was eating on the hoof, like the rest of us, and looking up, a pale face at thigh level, following the conversation. Mother futzed around the kitchen in camel-colored wool slacks; she rarely ate.

Did we know how water got up to our attic bathroom? Money worked the same way, he said, worked the way locks on the river worked, worked the way water flowed down from high water towers into our attic bathroom, the way the Allegheny and the Monongahela flowed into the Ohio, and the Ohio flowed into the Mississippi and out into the Gulf of Mexico at New Orleans. The money, once you got enough of it high enough, would flow by gravitation, all over everybody.

"It doesn't work that way," our mother said. She offered Molly tidbits: a drumstick, a beet slice, cheese. "Remember those shacks we see in Georgia? Those barefoot little children who have to quit school to work in the fields, their poor mothers not able to feed them enough"—we could all hear in her voice that she was beginning to cry—"not even able to keep them dressed?" Molly was looking at her, wide-eyed; she was bent over looking at Molly, wide-eyed.

"They shouldn't have so many kids," Father said. "They must be crazy."

The trouble was, I no longer believed him. It was beginning to strike me that Father, who knew the real world so well, got some of it wrong. Not much; just some.

Part Three

PITTSBURGH WASN'T REALLY ANDREW CARNEGIE'S
TOWN. We just thought it was. Steel wasn't the only major
industry in Pittsburgh. We just had to think to recall the
others.

Andrew Carnegie started out in Pittsburgh as a tiny bobbin
boy, and ended up a tiny millionaire; he was only five feet
three. When he was twenty-four, having scrambled, he became superintendent of the Western Division of the Pennsylvania Railroad. Whenever wrecks blocked the railroad tracks,
Carnegie showed up to supervise. He hopped around the
wrecked freight cars; he ordered the big workmen to lay
tracks around the wrecks or even, quick, to burn the wrecks
to save the schedule. He liked to tell about one such night,
when an enormous, unknowing Irish workman picked him
straight up off the ground and set him aside like a gate, boom-
ing at him, "Get out of the way, you brat of a boy. You're
eternally in the way of the men who are trying to do their
job."

The Carnegies emigrated from Scotland when Andrew was thirteen. A bookish family of Lowland Scots radicals, they championed universal suffrage, and hated privilege and hereditary wealth. "As a child," he recalled, "I could have slain king, duke, or lord, and considered their death a service to the state." When later Edward VII offered him a title, he refused it.

The then fashionable suburb of Homewood, where young Carnegie moved with his mother in 1859, was part of an old estate. The center of life there was the estate house of eighty-year-old Judge William Wilkins and his wife, Mathilda. Wilkins had served in government under three Presidents and returned to Pittsburgh; Mathilda Wilkins was from a prominent family whose members had served in two cabinets. The Civil War was then heating up, and the talk one social evening was of Negroes. Young Carnegie was among the guests. Mrs. Wilkins complained of Negroes' "forwardness." It was disgraceful, she said: Negroes admitted to West Point.

"Oh, Mrs. Wilkins," Carnegie piped up. He was then only in his twenties, but a man of convictions, which he didn't shed when he visited the great house. "There is something even worse than that. I understand that some of them have been admitted to heaven!"

"There was a silence that could be felt," Carnegie recalled. "Then dear Mrs. Wilkins said gravely:

" 'That is a different matter, Mr. Carnegie.' "

Carnegie started making steel. He wrote four books. He preached what he called, American style, the Gospel of Wealth. A man of wealth should give it away for the public good, and not weaken his sons with it. "The man who dies rich, dies disgraced."

In 1901, when he was sixty-six, Carnegie sold the Carnegie Company to J. P. Morgan, for $480 million. His share came to $250 million. Carnegie added this sum to his considerable other wealth—he had to build a special steel room in Hoboken, New Jersey, to house the bulky paper bonds, pesky things—and set about giving it away. He managed to get rid of $350 million of it before he died, in 1919, leaving for himself while he lived, and his family when he died, very much less than a tithe.

Carnegie's top steelmen were share-owning partners—forty of them—most of whom had worked their way up from the blast furnaces, smelters, and rolling mills. When J. P. Morgan bought the company he called U.S. Steel, these forty split the rest of the take, and became instant millionaires. One went to a barber on Penn Avenue for his first shampoo; the barber reported that the washing "brought out two ounces of fine Mesabi ore and a scattering of slag and cinders."

Carnegie gave over $40 million to build 2,509 libraries. All the early libraries had graven over their doors: LET THERE BE LIGHT.

But a steelworker, speaking for many, told an interviewer, "We didn't want him to build a library for us, we would rather have had higher wages." At that time steelworkers worked twelve-hour shifts on floors so hot they had to nail wooden platforms under their shoes. Every two weeks they toiled an inhuman twenty-four-hour shift, and then they got their sole day off. The best housing they could afford was crowded and filthy. Most died in their forties or earlier, from accidents or disease. Workers' lives were almost unbearable in Düsseldorf then, too, and in Lisle, and Birmingham, and Ghent. It was the Gilded Age.

While Carnegie was visiting Scotland in 1892, his man Henry Clay Frick had loosed three hundred hired guns— Pinkertons—on unarmed strikers and their families at the Homestead plant up the river, strikers who subsequently beat the daylights out of Pinkertons with their fists. Frick then called in the entire state militia, eight thousand strong, whose armed occupation of the Homestead plant not only broke the strike but also killed all unions in the steel industry nationwide until 1936.

Pittsburgh's astounding wealth came from iron and steel,

and also from aluminum, glass, coke, electricity, copper, natural gas—and the banking and transportation industries that put up the money and moved the goods. Some of the oldest Scotch-Irish and German families in Pittsburgh did well, too, like the sons of Scotch-Irish Judge Mellon. Andrew Mellon, a banker, invested in aluminum when the industry consisted of a twenty-two-year-old Oberlin College graduate who made it in his family's woodshed. He also invested in coke, iron, steel, and oil. When he was named Secretary of the Treasury, quiet Andrew Mellon was one of three Americans who had ever amassed a billion dollars. (Carnegie's strategy was different; he followed the immortal dictum: "Put all your eggs in the one basket and—*watch that basket.*")

By the turn of the century, Pittsburgh had the highest death rate in the United States. That was the year before Carnegie sold his steel company. Typhoid fever epidemics recurred, because Pittsburgh's council members wouldn't filter the drinking water; they disliked public spending. Besides, a water system would mean a dam, and a dam would yield cheap hydroelectric power, so the power companies would buy less coal; coal-company owners and their bankers didn't want any dams. Pittsburgh epidemics were so bad that boatmen on the Ohio River wouldn't handle Pittsburgh money, for fear of contagion.

While Carnegie was unburdening himself publicly of his millions, many people were moved, understandably, to write him letters. His friend Mark Twain wrote him one such: "You seem to be in prosperity. Could you lend an admirer a dollar & a half to buy a hymn book with? God will bless you. I feel it. I know it. . . . P.S. Don't send the hymn-book, send the money."

Among Andrew Carnegie's benefactions was Pittsburgh's Carnegie Institute, with its school (Carnegie Tech), library, museum of natural history, music hall, and art gallery. "This is my monument," he said. By the time he died, it occupied twenty-five acres.

* * *

It was a great town to grow up in, Pittsburgh. With one thousand other Pittsburgh schoolchildren, I attended free art classes in Carnegie Music Hall every Saturday morning for four years. Every week, seven or eight chosen kids reproduced their last week's drawings in thick chalks at enormous easels on stage in front of the thousand other kids. After class, everyone scattered; I roamed the enormous building.

Under one roof were the music hall, library, art museum, and natural history museum. Late in the afternoon, after the other kids were all gone, I liked to draw hours-long pencil studies of the chilly marble sculptures in the great hall of classical sculpture. I sat on one man's plinth and drew the next man over—until, during the course of one winter, I had worked my way around the great hall. From these sculptures I learned a great deal about the human leg and not much about the neck, which I could hardly see. I ate a basement-cafeteria lunch and wandered the fabulous building. The natural history museum dominated it.

I felt I was most myself here, here in the churchlike dark lighted by painted dioramas in which tiny shaggy buffalo grazed as far as the eye could see on an enormous prairie I could span with my arms. I could lose myself here, here in the cavernous vault with the shadow of a tyrannosaurus skeleton spread looming all over the domed ceiling, the skeleton shadow enlarged the size of the Milky Way, each bone a dark star.

There was a Van de Graaff generator; you could make a bright crack of lightning strike it from a rod. From a vaulted ceiling hung a cracked wooden skiff—the soul boat of Sesostris III, which Carnegie had picked up in Egypt. Upstairs there were stuffed songbirds in drawers, and empty, faded birdskins in drawers, drab as old handkerchiefs. There were the world's insects on pins and needles; their legs hung down, utterly dead. There were big glass cases you could walk around, in which various motionless American Indians made baskets, started fires, embroidered moccasins, painted pots, chipped spearheads, carried papooses, smoked pipes, drew bows, and skinned rabbits, all of them wearing soft and pale doeskin clothing. The Indians looked stern, even the children, and had bright-red skin. I never thought to draw them; they weren't sculptures.

Sometimes I climbed the broad marble stairs to the art gallery. Carnegie's plans for the art gallery had gone somewhat awry—gang agley—because its first curator was a Scotch-Irish Pittsburgher whose rearing had made it painful for him to spend money. He rarely acquired anything that cost over twenty-five dollars, and liked to buy wee drawings, almost any drawings, in bargain batches, "2 for $10" "3 for $20." By my day, things had improved enormously, and the gallery would buy even large Abstract Expressionist canvases if the artists were guaranteed famous enough. Our school hauled us off to the art gallery once a year for the International Exhibition, but I rarely visited it on my Saturdays in the building, except when *Man Walking* was there.

Carnegie set up the International Exhibition in 1896 to bring contemporary art from all over the world each year to the art museum. Artists competed for a prize, and the museum's curators could buy what they liked, if they felt they could afford it, or if they liked any of it. In 1961, Giacometti's sculpture *Man Walking* won the International. I was sixteen. Everything I knew outside the museum was alien to me, then and for the next few years until I left home.

I saw the sculpture: a wiry, thin person, long legs in full stride, thrust his small, mute head forward into the empty air. Six feet tall, bronze. I read about the sculpture every time I opened the paper; I saw its picture; I climbed the marble stairs alone to look at it again and again. To see *Man Walking,* I walked past abstract canvases by Robert Motherwell, Franz Kline, Adolph Gottlieb. . . . I stopped and looked at their paintings. At school I began to draw abstract forms in rectangles and squares. But more often, then and for many years, I drew what I thought of as the perfect person, whose form matched his inner life, and whose name was, Indian style, Man Walking.

I saw a stilled figure in a swirl of invisible motion. I saw a touchy man moving through a still void. Here was the thinker in the world—but there was no world, only the abyss through which he walked. Man Walking was pure consciousness made poignant: a soul without a culture, absolutely alone, without even a time, without people, speech, books, tools, work, or even clothes. He knew he was walking, here. He knew he was feeling himself walk; he knew he was walking fast and thinking slowly, not forming conclusions, not looking for anything. He himself was barely there. He was in spirit and in form a dissected nerve. He looked freshly made of clay by God, visibly pinched by sure fingertips. He looked like Adam depressed, as if there were no world. He looked like Ahasuerus, condemned to wander without hope. His blind gaze faced the vanishing point.

Man Walking was so skinny his inner life was his outer life; it had nowhere else to go. The point where his head met his spine was the point where spirit met matter. The sculptor's soul floated to his fingertips; I met him there, on Man Walking's skin.

I drew Man Walking in his normal stalking pose and, later, dancing with his arms in the air. What if I fell in love with a man, and he took off his shirt, and I saw he was Man Walking, made of bronze, with Giacometti's thumbprints on him? Well then, I would love him more, for I knew him well; I would hold, if he let me, his twisty head.

Week after week, year after year, after art class I walked the vast museum, and lost myself in the arts, or the sciences. Scientists, it seemed to me as I read the labels on display cases (bivalves, univalves; ungulates, lagomorphs), were collectors and sorters, as I had been. They noticed the things that engaged the curious mind: the way the world develops and divides, colony and polyp, population and tissue, ridge and crystal. Artists, for their part, noticed the things that engaged the mind's private and idiosyncratic interior, that area where the life of the senses mingles with the life of the spirit: the shattering of light into color, and the way it shades off round a bend. The humble attention painters gave to the shadow of a stalk, or the reflected sheen under a chin, or the lapping layers of strong strokes, included and extended the scientists' vision of each least thing as unendingly interesting. But artists laid down the vision in the form of beauty bare—Man Walking—radiant and fierce, inexplicable, and without the math.

It all got noticed: the horse's shoulders pumping; sunlight warping the air over a hot field; the way leaves turn color, brightly, cell by cell; and even the splitting, half-resigned and half-astonished feeling you have when you notice you are walking on earth for a while now—set down for a spell—in this particular time for no particular reason, here.

As A CHILD I READ HOPING TO LEARN everything, so I
could be like my father. I hoped to combine my father's grasp
of information and reasoning with my mother's will and vitality. But the books were leading me away. They would propel
me right out of Pittsburgh altogether, so I could fashion a life
among books somewhere else. So the Midwest nourishes us
(Pittsburgh is the Midwest's eastern edge) and presents us
with the spectacle of a land and a people completed and certain. And so we run to our bedrooms and read in a fever, and
love the big hardwood trees outside the windows, and the
terrible Midwest summers, and the terrible Midwest winters,
and the forested river valleys with the blue Appalachian
Mountains to the east of us and the broad great plains to the
west. And so we leave it sorrowfully, having grown strong and
restless by opposing with all our will and mind and muscle its
simple, loving, single will for us: that we stay, that we stay and
find a place among its familiar possibilities. Mother knew we
would go; she encouraged us.

* * *

I had awakened again, awakened from my drawing and reading, from my exhilarating game playing, from my intense collecting and experimenting, and my cheerful friendships, to see on every side of me a furious procession of which I had been entirely unaware. A procession of fast-talking, keen-eyed, high-stepping, well-dressed men and women of all ages had apparently hoisted me, or shanghaied me, some time ago, and were bearing me breathless along I knew not where. This was the startling world in which I found that I had been living all along. Packed into the procession, I pedaled to keep up, but my feet only rarely hit the ground.

The pace of school life quickened, its bounds tightened, and a new kind of girl emerged from the old. The old-style girl was obedient and tidy. The new-style girl was witty and casual. It was a small school, twenty in a class. We all knew who mattered, not only in our class but in the whole school. The teachers knew, too.

In summer we girls commonly greeted each other, after a perfunctory hello, by extending our forearms side by side to compare tans. We were blond, we were tan, our teeth were white and straightened, our legs were brown and depilated, our blue eyes glittered pale in our dark faces; we laughed; we shuffled the cards fast and dealt four hands. It was not for me. I hated it so passionately I thought my shoulders and arms, swinging at the world, would split off from my body like loose spinning blades, and fly wild and slice everyone up. With all my heart, sometimes, I longed for the fabled Lower East Side of Manhattan, for Brooklyn, for the Bronx, where the thoughtful and feeling people in books grew up on porch stoops among seamstress intellectuals. There I belonged if anywhere, there where the book people were—recent Jewish immigrants, everybody deep every livelong minute. I could just see them, sitting there feeling deeply. Here, instead, I saw polished fingernails clicking, rings flashing, gold bangle bracelets banging and ringing together as sixteen-year-old girls like me pushed their cuticles back, as they ran combs through their just-washed, just-cut, just-set hair, as they lighted Marlboros with hard snaps of heavy lighters, and talked about other girls or hair. It never crossed my mind that you can't guess people's lives from their chatter.

This was the known world. Women volunteered, organized the households, and reared the kids; they kept the traditions, and taught by example a dozen kinds of love. Mother polished the brass, wiped the ashtrays, stood barefoot on the couch to hang a picture. Margaret Butler washed the windows, which seemed to yelp. Mother dusted and polished the big philodendrons, tenderly, leaf by leaf, as if she were washing babies' faces. Margaret came sighing down the stairs with an armful of laundry or wastebaskets. Mother inspected the linens for a party; she fetched from a closet the folding felted boards she laid over the table. Margaret turned on the vacuum cleaner again. Mother and Margaret changed the sheets and pillowcases.

Then Margaret left. I had taken by then to following her from room to room, trying to get her to spill the beans about being black; she kept moving. Nothing changed. Mother wiped the stove; she ran the household with her back to it. You heard a staccato in her voice, and saw the firm force of her elbow, as she pressed hard on a dried tan dot of bean soup, and finally took a fingernail to it, while quizzing Amy about a car pool to dancing school, and me about a ride back from a game. No page of any book described housework, and no one mentioned it; it didn't exist. There was no such thing.

A woman at our country club, a prominent figure at our church, whose daughters went to Ellis, never washed her face all summer, to preserve her tan. We rarely saw the pale men at all; they were off pulling down the money on which the whole scene floated. Most men came home exhausted in their gray suits to scantily clad women smelling of Bain de Soleil, and do-nothing tanned kids in Madras shorts.

There was real beauty to the old idea of living and dying where you were born. You could hold a place in a kind of eternity. Your grandparents took you out to dinner Sunday nights at the country club, and you could take your own grand-children there when that time came: more little towheads, as squint-eyed and bony-legged and Scotch-Irish as hillbillies. And those grandchildren, like figures in a reel endlessly un-reeling, would partake of the same timeless, hushed, muffled sensations.

They would join the buffet line on Sunday nights in winter at the country club. I remember: the club lounges before dinner dimly lighted and opulent like the church; the wool rugs absorbing footsteps; the lined damask curtains lapping thickly across tall, leaded-glass windows. The adults drank old-fashioneds. The fresh-haired children subsisted on bour-bon-soaked maraschino cherries, orange slices, and ice cubes. They roved the long club corridors in slippery shoes; they opened closet doors, tried to get outside, laughed so hard they spit their ice cubes, and made sufficient commotion to rouse the adults to dinner. In the big dining room, layers of fine old unstarched linen draped the tables as thickly as hospital beds. Heavy-bottomed glasses sank into the tablecloths soundlessly.

And sempiternal too were the summer dinners at the coun-try club, the sun-shocked people somnambulistic as angels. The children's grandchildren could see it. Space and light multiplied the club rooms; the damask curtains were heaved back; the French doors now gave out onto a flagstone terrace overlooking the swimming pool, near the sixth hole. On the terrace, men and women drank frozen daiquiris, or the un-varying Scotch, and their crystal glasses clicked on the glass tabletops, and then stuck in pools of condensation as if held magnetically, so they had to skid the glasses across the screech-ing tabletops to the edges in order to raise them at all. The cast-iron chair legs, painted white, marked and chipped the old flagstones, and dug up the interstitial grass.

The dressed children on the terrace looked with longing down on the tanned and hilarious children below. The chil-dren below wouldn't leave the pool, although it was seven-thirty; they knew no parent would actually shout at them from the flagstone terrace above. When these poolside children jumped in the water, the children on the terrace above could see their shimmering gray bodies against the blue pool. The water knit a fabric of light over their lively torsos and limbs, a loose gold chain mail. They looked like fish swimming in wide gold nets.

The children above were sunburnt, and their cotton dresses scraped their shoulders. The outsides of their skins felt hot, and the insides felt cold, and they tried to warm one arm with another. In summer, no one drank old-fashioneds, so there was nothing for children to eat till dinner.

This was the world we knew best—this, and Oma's. Oma's world was no likely alternative to ours; Oma had a chauffeur and her chauffeur had to drink from his own glass.

My forays into Oma's world changed. I was working in the summers now. The summer I sold men's bathing suits, I ate lunch alone in a dark bar and played the numbers for a quarter every week, right there in the underworld. I no longer went to the Lake with Amy. But for a few spring vacations after our grandfather died, Amy and I visited Oma and Mary in their apartment in Pompano Beach, Florida.

On my last visit, I was fifteen. Everything I was required to do, such as sit at a table with other people, either bored me to fury or infuriated me to a kind of benumbed lethargy. I was finding it difficult to live—finished with everything I knew and ignorant of anything else. I woke every morning full of hope, and was livid with rage before breakfast, at one thing or another.

Oma and I argued that year, over a word. Because something I was talking about seemed to require it, Oma said the word for padded, upholstered furniture was "overstuffed." I wouldn't hear of it, having never heard of it. "It's not overstuffed; it's stuffed just right." Oma pointed out that it was just barely possible that she knew something on earth that I didn't. I couldn't quite believe her.

In Oma's Pompano Beach apartment, I lounged on the bright print bamboo furniture and looked at the Asian objects she had been collecting all her life: gaudy Chinese cloisonné lamps, lacquered chests, sentimental Japanese porcelain figurines—women in whiteface with cocked heads and pink circles on their cheeks—gold, bossed mirrors, foot-long yellow ashtrays shaped like carp, and a pair of green ceramic long-tailed birds, which took up the breakfast table. It was years before I learned that Asian art was supposed to be delicate.

In Florida, Mary Burinda drove the machine. Oma rode in the front seat; Amy and I sat in back. That year, Oma's current, roseate Cadillac had an extra row of upholstered seats, which folded against the front seat's back—like, but not very like, the extra seats in a cab. An especially long distance stretched between the front seat and the back.

One day, we were driving back from Miami; Oma had been "looking at shoes." (Oma had announced at breakfast, "Today I want to look at shoes," and I repeated the phrase to myself all morning, marveling, to learn what it might feel like to want to look at shoes.)

Without provocation, she broke down, grieving for our grandfather. She rubbed her round face in her hands. Mary, at the wheel, expostulated, shocked, *"Missus* Doak. Oh, Missus *Doak."* She added, "That was two years ago, Missus Doak." This occasioned a fresh outburst, which broke our hearts. I saw Oma's red hair and her lowered head wipe back and forth.

Then she rallied and began defensively, "But you know, he was never cross with me."

"Never once?" someone ventured from the depths of the back seat.

"Well, once. Yes, once." Her voice lightened.

They were driving, she said, on a high mountain road. I saw the back of her round head swivel; she was looking up and away, remembering. The two of them were driving along a dreadful road, she said, a perfectly horrible road, in Tennessee maybe. Her voice grew shrill.

"There was a sheer drop just outside my window, and I thought we were going over. We were going over, I tell you." She was furious at the thought. "And he got very cross with me."

She had never seen him so angry. "He said I could either hush, or get out and walk. Can you imagine!"

She was awed. So was I. We were both awed, that he had dared. It cheered everyone right up.

The bird-watching was fine in the nearby Fort Lauderdale city park. Right in the middle of town, the park was mostly wild forest, with a few clearings and roads. Oma and Mary drove me to the park early every morning, and picked me up at noon. There I saw some of the few smooth-billed anis in the United States. They were black parrot-beaked birds; they hung around the park's dump. The binoculars I wore banged against my skinny rib cage. I filled a notebook with sketches, information, and records. I saw myrtle warblers in the clearings. I saw a coot and a purple gallinule side by side, just as Peterson had painted them in the field guide; they swam in a lagoon under sea grape trees. They seemed, as common birds seem to the delirious beginner, miraculous and rare. (The tizzy that birds excite in the beginner are a property of the beginner, not of the birds; so those who love the tizzy itself must ever keep beginning things.)

Often I was startled to see, through binoculars and flattened by their lenses, glimpsed through the dark subtropical leaves, the white hull of some pleasure cruiser setting out on a Lauderdale canal. Who would go cruising beside houses and lawns, when he could be watching smooth-billed anis? I alone was sane, I thought, in a world of crazy people. Standing in the park's smelly dump, I shrugged.

Afternoons I wandered the blinding beach, swam, and read

about tide pools in Maine; I was reading *The Edge of the Sea*.
On the beach I found skeletons of velella, or by-the-wind-
sailors. From the high apartment windows I looked at the
lifeguards around the pool below, and wondered how I might
meet them. By day, Oma and Mary shopped. Evenings we
went out to dinner. Amy was as desperately bored as I was,
but I wouldn't let her follow me; I addressed her in French.
Everyone knew this was our last Florida trip.

It was on this visit that Oma asked me, when we were alone,
what exactly it was that homosexuals did. She was miffed that
she'd been unable to command this information before now.
She said she'd wondered for many years without knowing who
she could ask.

Amy and I boarded our plane back to Pittsburgh. It would
be softball season at school, and a new baseball season for the
Pirates, whose hopes were resting on a left-handed reliever,
Elroy Face, and on the sober starter, Vernon Law—the Dea-
con—and on the big bat of our right fielder, Roberto Clemente, whom everyone in town adored.

Flying back, looking out over the Blue Ridge, I remembered a game I had seen at Forbes Field the year before:
Clemente had thrown from right field to the plate, as apparently easily as a wheel spins. The ball seemed not to arc at all;
the throw caught the runner from third. You could watch this
man at inning's end lope from right field to the dugout, and
you'd weep—at the way his joints moved, and the ease and
power in his spine.

I was ready for all that, but it was only late March, and
snowing in Pittsburgh when we got off the plane, and dark.
At least we were tan.

WHEN I WAS FIFTEEN, I FELT IT COMING; now I was sixteen, and it hit.

My feet had imperceptibly been set on a new path, a fast path into a long tunnel like those many turnpike tunnels near Pittsburgh, turnpike tunnels whose entrances bear on brass plaques a roll call of those men who died blasting them. I wandered witlessly forward and found myself going down, and saw the light dimming; I adjusted to the slant and dimness, traveled further down, adjusted to greater dimness, and so on. There wasn't a whole lot I could do about it, or about anything. I was going to hell on a handcart, that was all, and I knew it and everyone around me knew it, and there it was.

I was growing and thinning, as if pulled. I was getting angry, as if pushed. I morally disapproved most things in North America, and blamed my innocent parents for them. My feelings deepened and lingered. The swift moods of early childhood—each formed by and suited to its occasion—vanished. Now feelings lasted so long they left stains. They arose from nowhere, like winds or waves, and battered at me or engulfed me.

When I was angry, I felt myself coiled and longing to kill someone or bomb something big. Trying to appease myself, during one winter I whipped my bed every afternoon with my uniform belt. I despised the spectacle I made in my own eyes—whipping the bed with a belt, like a creature demented!—and I often began halfheartedly, but I did it daily after school as a desperate discipline, trying to rid myself and the innocent world of my wildness. It was like trying to beat back the ocean.

Sometimes in class I couldn't stop laughing; things were too funny to be borne. It began then, my surprise that no one else saw what was so funny.

I read some few books with such reverence I didn't close them at the finish, but only moved the pile of pages back to the start, without breathing, and began again. I read one such book, an enormous novel, six times that way—closing the binding between sessions, but not between readings.

On the piano in the basement I played the maniacal "Poet and Peasant Overture" so loudly, for so many hours, night after night, I damaged the piano's keys and strings. When I wasn't playing this crashing overture, I played boogie-woogie, or something else, anything else, in octaves—otherwise, it wasn't loud enough. My fingers were so strong I could do push-ups with them. I played one piece with my fists. I banged on a steel-stringed guitar till I bled, and once on a particularly piercing rock-and-roll downbeat I broke straight through one of Father's snare drums.

I loved my boyfriend so tenderly, I thought I must transmogrify into vapor. It would take spectroscopic analysis to locate my molecules in thin air. No possible way of holding him was close enough. Nothing could cure this bad case of gentleness except, perhaps, violence: maybe if he swung me by the legs and split my skull on a tree? Would that ease this insane wish to kiss too much his eyelids' outer corners and his temples, as if I could love up his brain?

I envied people in books who swooned. For two years I felt myself continuously swooning and continuously unable to swoon; the blood drained from my face and eyes and flooded my heart; my hands emptied, my knees unstrung, I bit at the air for something worth breathing—but I failed to fall, and I couldn't find the way to black out. I had to live on the lip of a waterfall, exhausted.

When I was bored I was first hungry, then nauseated, then furious and weak. "Calm yourself," people had been saying to me all my life. Since early childhood I had tried one thing and then another to calm myself, on those few occasions when I truly wanted to. Eating helped; singing helped. Now sometimes I truly wanted to calm myself. I couldn't lower my shoulders; they seemed to wrap around my ears. I couldn't lower my voice although I could see the people around me flinch. I waved my arm in class till the very teachers wanted to kill me.

I was what they called a live wire. I was shooting out sparks that were digging a pit around me, and I was sinking into that pit. Laughing with Ellin at school recess, or driving around after school with Judy in her jeep, exultant, or dancing with my boyfriend to Louis Armstrong across a polished dining-room floor, I got so excited I looked around wildly for aid; I didn't know where I should go or what I should do with myself. People in books split wood.

When rage or boredom reappeared, each seemed never to have left. Each so filled me with so many years' intolerable accumulation it jammed the space behind my eyes, so I couldn't see. There was no room left even on my surface to live. My rib cage was so taut I couldn't breathe. Every cubic centimeter of atmosphere above my shoulders and head was heaped with last straws. Black hatred clogged my very blood. I couldn't peep, I couldn't wiggle or blink; my blood was too mad to flow.

*   *   *

For as long as I could remember, I had been transparent to myself, unselfconscious, learning, doing, most of every day. Now I was in my own way; I myself was a dark object I could not ignore. I couldn't remember how to forget myself. I didn't want to think about myself, to reckon myself in, to deal with myself every livelong minute on top of everything else—but swerve as I might, I couldn't avoid it. I was a boulder blocking my own path. I was a dog barking between my own ears, a barking dog who wouldn't hush.

So this was adolescence. Is this how the people around me had died on their feet—inevitably, helplessly? Perhaps their own selves eclipsed the sun for so many years the world shriveled around them, and when at last their inescapable orbits had passed through these dark egoistic years it was too late, they had adjusted.

Must I then lose the world forever, that I had so loved? Was it all, the whole bright and various planet, where I had been so ardent about finding myself alive, only a passion peculiar to children, that I would outgrow even against my will?

I QUIT THE CHURCH. I wrote the minister a fierce letter. The assistant minister, kindly Dr. James H. Blackwood, called me for an appointment. My mother happened to take the call.

"Why," she asked, "would he be calling you?" I was in the kitchen after school. Mother was leaning against the pantry door, drying a crystal bowl.

"What, Mama? Oh. Probably," I said, "because I wrote him a letter and quit the church."

"You—what?" She began to slither down the doorway, weak-kneed, like Lucille Ball. I believe her whole life passed before her eyes.

As I climbed the stairs after dinner I heard her moan to Father, "She wrote the minister a letter and quit the church."

"She—what?"

Father knocked on the door of my room. I was the only person in the house with her own room. Father ducked under the doorway, entered, and put his hands in his khakis' pockets. "Hi, Daddy." Actually, it drove me nuts when people came in my room. Mother had come in just last week. My room was getting to be quite the public arena. Pretty soon they'd put it on the streetcar routes. Why not hold the U.S. Open here? I was on the bed, in uniform, trying to read a book. I sat up and folded my hands in my lap.

I knew that Mother had made him come—"She listens to you." He had undoubtedly been trying to read a book, too.

Father looked around, but there wasn't much to see. My rock collection was no longer in evidence. A framed tiger swallowtail, spread and only slightly askew on white cotton, hung on a yellowish wall. On the mirror I'd taped a pencil portrait of Rupert Brooke; he was looking off softly. Balanced on top of the mirror were some yellow-and-black FALLOUT SHELTER signs, big aluminum ones, which Judy had collected as part of her antiwar effort. On the pale maple desk there were, among other books and papers, an orange thesaurus, a blue three-ring binder with a boy's name written all over it in every typeface, a green assignment notebook, and Emerson's *Essays*.

Father began, with some vigor: "What was it you said in this brilliant letter?" He went on: But didn't I see? That people did these things—quietly? Just—quietly? No fuss? No flamboyant gestures. No uncalled-for letters. He was forced to conclude that I was deliberately setting out to humiliate Mother and him.

"And your poor sisters, too!" Mother added feelingly from the hall outside my closed door. She must have been passing at that very moment. Then, immediately, we all heard a hideous shriek ending in a wail; it came from my sisters' bathroom. Had Molly cut off her head? It set us all back a moment—me on the bed, Father standing by my desk, Mother outside the closed door—until we all realized it was Amy, mad at her hair. Like me, she was undergoing a trying period, years long; she, on her part, was mad at her hair. She screeched at it in the mirror; the sound carried all over the house, kitchen, attic, basement, everywhere, and terrified all the rest of us, every time.

The assistant minister of the Shadyside Presbyterian Church, Dr. Blackwood, and I had a cordial meeting in his office. He was an experienced, calm man in a three-piece suit; he had a mustache and wore glasses. After he asked me why I had quit the church, he loaned me four volumes of C. S. Lewis's broadcast talks, for a paper I was writing. Among the volumes proved to be *The Problem of Pain,* which I would find fascinating, not quite serious enough, and too short. I had already written a paper on the Book of Job. The subject scarcely seemed to be closed. If the all-powerful creator directs the world, then why all this suffering? Why did the innocents die in the camps, and why do they starve in the cities and farms? Addressing this question, I found thirty pages written thousands of years ago, and forty pages written in 1955. They offered a choice of fancy language saying, "Forget it," or serenely worded, logical-sounding answers that so strained credibility (pain is God's megaphone) that "Forget it" seemed in comparison a fine answer. I liked, however, C.S. Lewis's effort to defuse the question. The sum of human suffering we needn't worry about: There is plenty of suffering, but no one ever suffers the sum of it.

Dr. Blackwood and I shook hands as I left his office with his books.

"This is rather early of you, to be quitting the church," he said as if to himself, looking off, and went on mildly, almost inaudibly, "I suppose you'll be back soon."

Humph, I thought. Pshaw.

NOW IT WAS MAY. Daylight Saving Time had begun; the colored light of the long evenings fairly split me with joy. White trillium had bloomed and gone on the forested slopes in Fox Chapel. The cliffside and riverside patches of woods all over town showed translucent ovals of yellow or ashy greens; the neighborhood trees on Glen Arden Drive had blossomed in white and red.

Baseball season had begun, a season which recalled but could never match last year's National League pennant and seventh-game World Series victory over the Yankees, when we at school had been so frenzied for so many weeks they finally and wisely opened the doors and let us go. I had walked home from school one day during that series and seen Pittsburgh's Fifth Avenue emptied of cars, as if the world were over.

A year of wild feelings had passed, and more were coming. Without my noticing, the drummer had upped the tempo. Someone must have slipped him a signal when I wasn't looking; he'd speeded things up. The key was higher, too. I had a driver's license. When I drove around in Mother's old Dodge convertible, the whole town smelled good. And I did drive around the whole town. I cruised along the blue rivers and across them on steel bridges, and steered up and down the scented hills. I drove winding into and out of the steep neighborhoods across the Allegheny River, neighborhoods where I tried in vain to determine in what languages the signs on storefronts were written. I drove onto boulevards, highways, beltways, freeways, and the turnpike. I could drive to Guatemala, drive to Alaska. Why, I asked myself, did I drive to—of all spots on earth—our garage? Why home, why school?

Throughout the long, deadly school afternoons, we junior and senior girls took our places in study hall. We sat at desks in a roomful of desks, whether or not we had something to do, until four o'clock.

Now this May afternoon a teacher propped open the study hall's back door. The door gave onto our hockey field and, behind it, Pittsburgh's Nabisco plant, whence, O Lordy, issued the smell of shortbread today; they were baking Lorna Doones. Around me sat forty or fifty girls in green cotton jumpers and spring-uniform white bucks. They rested their chins on the heels of both hands and leaned their cheeks on curled fingers; their propped heads faced the opened pages of *L'Étranger, Hamlet, Vanity Fair.* Some girls leaned back and filed their nails. Some twisted stiff pieces of their hair, to stay not so much awake as alive. Sometimes in health class, when we were younger, we had all been so bored we hooked our armpits over our chairs' backs so we cut off all circulation to one arm, in an effort to kill that arm for something to do, or cause a heart attack, whichever came first. We were, in fact, getting a dandy education. But sometimes we were restless. Weren't there some wars being fought somewhere that I, for one, could join?

I wrote a name on a notebook. I looked at the study-hall ceiling and tried to see that boy's familiar face—light and dark,

bold-eyed, full of feeling—on the inside of my eyelids. Failing
that, I searched for his image down the long speckled tunnel
or corridor I saw with my eyes closed. As if visual memory
were a Marx brothers comedy, I glimpsed swift fragments—a
wry corner of his lip, a pointy knuckle, a cupped temple—
which crossed the corridor so fast I recognized them only as
soon as they vanished. I opened my eyes and wrote his name.
His depth and complexity were apparently infinite. From the
tip of his lively line of patter to the bottom of his heartbroken,
hopeful soul was the longest route I knew, and the best.

The heavy, edible scent of shortbread maddened me in my
seat, made me so helpless with longing my wrists gave out; I
couldn't hold a pen. I looked around constantly to catch someone's eye, anyone's eye.

It was a provocative fact, which I seemed to have discovered, that we students outnumbered our teachers. Must we
then huddle here like sheep? By what right, exactly, did these
few women keep us sitting here in this clean, bare room to no
purpose? Lately I had been trying to enflame my friends with
the implications of our greater numbers. We could pull off a
riot. We could bang on the desks and shout till they let us out.
Then we could go home and wait for dinner. Or we could bear
our teachers off on our shoulders, and—what? Throw them
into the Lorna Doone batter? I got no takers.

I had finished my work long ago. "Works only on what
interests her," the accusation ran—as if, I reflected, obedience
outranked passion, as if sensible people didn't care what they
stuck in their minds. Today as usual no one around me was
ready for action. I took a fresh sheet of paper and copied on
it random lines in French:

> Ô saisons, ô châteaux!
> Is it through these endless nights that you sleep
>   in exile
> Ô million golden birds, ô future vigor?
> Oh, that my keel would split! Oh, that I would
>   go down in the sea!

I had struck upon the French Symbolists, like a canyon of sharp crystals underground, like a long and winding corridor lined with treasure. These poets popped into my ken in an odd way: I found them in a book I had rented from a drugstore. Carnegie and school libraries filled me in. I read Enid Starkie's Rimbaud biography. I saved my allowance for months and bought two paperbound poetry books, the Penguin *Rimbaud,* and a Symbolist anthology in which Paul Valéry declaimed, *"Azure! c'est moi . . ."* I admired Gérard de Nerval. This mad writer kept a lobster as a pet. He walked it on a leash along the sidewalks of Paris, saying, "It doesn't bark, and knows the secrets of the deep."

I loved Rimbaud, who ran away, loved his skinny, furious face with the wild hair and snaky, unseeing eyes pointing in two directions, and his poems' confusion and vagueness, their overwritten longing, their hatred, their sky-shot lyricism, and their oracular fragmentation, which I enhanced for myself by reading and retaining his stuff in crazed bits, mostly from *Le Bateau Ivre,* The Drunken Boat. (The drunken boat tells its own story, a downhill, downstream epic unusually full of words.)

Now in study hall I saw that I had drawn all over this page; I got out another piece of paper. Rimbaud was damned. He said so himself. Where could I meet someone like that? I wrote down another part:

> There is a cathedral that goes down and a lake
>   that goes up.
> There is a troupe of strolling players in costume,
>   glimpsed on the road through the edge of
>   the trees.

I looked up from the new page I had already started to draw all over. Except for my boyfriend, the boys I knew best were out of town. They were older, prep-school and college boys whose boldness, wit, breadth of knowledge, and absence of scruples fascinated me. They cruised the deb party circuit all over Pennsylvania, holding ever-younger girls up to the light like chocolates, to determine how rich their centers might be. I smiled to recall one of these boys: he was so accustomed to the glitter of society, and so sardonic and graceful, that he carried with him at all times, in his jacket pocket, a canister of dance wax. Ordinary boys carried pocket knives for those occasions which occur unexpectedly, and this big, dark-haired boy carried dance wax for the same reason. When the impulse rose, he could simply sprinkle dance wax on any hall or dining-room floor, take a girl in his arms, and whirl her away. I had known these witty, handsome boys for years, and only recently understood that when they were alone, they read books. In public, they were lounge lizards; they drank; they played word games, filling in the blanks desultorily; they cracked wise. These boys would be back in town soon, and my boyfriend and I would join them.

Whose eye could I catch? Everyone in the room was bent over her desk. Ellin Hahn was usually ready to laugh, but now she was working on something. She would call me as soon as we got home. Every day on the phone, I unwittingly asked Ellin some blunt question about the social world around us, and at every question she sighed and said to me, "You still don't get it"—or often, as if addressing a jury of our incredulous peers, "She still doesn't get it!"

Looking at the study-hall ceiling, I dosed myself almost fatally with the oxygen-eating lines of Verlaine's "The long sobs / of the violins / of autumn / wound my heart / with a languor / monotone."

This unsatisfying bit of verse I repeated to myself for ten or fifteen minutes, by the big clock, over and over, clobbering myself with it, the way Molly, when she had been a baby, banged the top of her head on her crib.

> Ô world, ô college, ô dinner . . .
> Ô unthinkable task . . .

Funny how badly I'd turned out. Now I was always in trouble. It felt as if I was doing just as I'd always done—I explored the neighborhood, turning over rocks. The latest rocks were difficult. I'd been in a drag race, of all things, the previous September, and in the subsequent collision, and in the hospital; my parents saw my name in the newspapers, and their own names in the newspapers. Some boys I barely knew had cruised by that hot night and said to a clump of us girls on the sidewalk, "Anybody want to come along for a drag race?" I did, absolutely. I loved fast driving.

It was then, in the days after the drag race, that I noticed the ground spinning beneath me, all bearings lost, and recognized as well that I had been loose like this—detached from all I saw and knowing nothing else—for months, maybe years. I whirled through the air like a bull-roarer spun by a lunatic who'd found his rhythm. The pressure almost split my skin. What else can you risk with all your might but your life? Only a moment ago I was climbing my swing set, holding one cold metal leg between my two legs tight, and feeling a piercing oddness run the length of my gut—the same sensation that plucked me when my tongue touched tarnish on a silver spoon. Only a moment ago I was gluing squares of paper to rocks; I leaned over the bedroom desk. I was drawing my baseball mitt in the attic, under the plaster-stain ship; a pencil study took all Saturday morning. I was capturing the flag, turning the double play, chasing butterflies by the country-club pool. Throughout these many years of childhood, a transparent sphere of timelessness contained all my running and spinning as a glass paperweight holds flying snow. The sphere of this idyll broke; time unrolled before me in a line. I woke up and found myself in juvenile court. I was hanging from crutches; for a few weeks after the drag race, neither knee worked. (No one else got hurt.) In juvenile court, a policeman wet all ten of my fingertips on an ink pad and pressed them, one by one, using his own fingertips, on a form for the files.

*   *   *

Turning to the French is a form of suicide for the American who loves literature—or, as the joke might go, it is at least a cry for help. Now, when I was sixteen, I had turned to the French. I flung myself into poetry as into Niagara Falls. Beauty took away my breath. I twined away; I flew off with my eyes rolled up; I dove down and succumbed. I bought myself a plot in Valéry's marine cemetery, and moved in: cool dirt on my eyes, my brain smooth as a cannonball. It grieves me to report that I tried to see myself as a sobbing fountain, apparently serene, tall and thin among the chill marble monuments of the dead. Rimbaud wrote a lyric that gently described a man sleeping out in the grass; the sleeper made a peaceful picture, until, in the poem's last line, we discover in his right side two red holes. This, and many another literary false note, appealed to me.

I'd been suspended from school for smoking cigarettes. That was a month earlier, in early spring. Both my parents wept. Amy saw them weeping; horrified, she began to cry herself. Molly cried. She was six, missing her front teeth. Like Mother and me, she had pale skin that turned turgid and red when she cried; she looked as if she were dying of wounds. I didn't cry, because, actually, I was an intercontinental ballistic missile, with an atomic warhead; they don't cry.

Why didn't I settle down, straighten out, shape up? I wondered, too. I thought that joy was a childish condition that had forever departed; I had no glimpse then of its return the minute I got to college. I couldn't foresee the pleasure—or the possibility—of shedding sophistication, walking away from rage, and renouncing French poets.

While I was suspended from school, my parents grounded me. During that time, Amy began to visit me in my room.

When she was thirteen, Amy's beauty had grown inconspicuous; she seemed merely pleasant-looking and tidy. Her green uniform jumper fit her neatly; her thick hair was smoothly turned under; her white McMullen collars looked sweet. She had a good eye for the right things; people respected her for it. I think that only we at home knew how spirited she could get. "Oh, no!" she cried when she laughed hard. "Oh, no!" Amy adored our father, rather as we all did, from afar. She liked boys whose eyebrows met over their noses. She liked boys, emphatically; she followed boys with her big eyes, awed.

In my room, Amy listened to me rant; she reported her grade's daily gossip, laughed at my jokes, cried, "Oh, no!" and told me about the book she was reading, Wilkie Collins, *The Woman in White.* I liked people to tell me about the books they were reading. Next year, Amy was going to boarding school in Philadelphia; Mother had no intention of subjecting the family to two adolescent maelstroms whirling at once in the same house.

Late one night, my parents and I sat at the kitchen table; there was a truce. We were all helpless, and tired of fighting. Amy and Molly were asleep.

"What are we going to do with you?"

Mother raised the question. Her voice trembled and rose with emotion. She couldn't sit still; she kept getting up and roaming around the kitchen. Father stuck out his chin and rubbed it with his big hands. I covered my eyes. Mother squeezed white lotion into her hands, over and over. We all smoked; the ashtray was full. Mother walked over to the sink, poured herself some ginger ale, ran both hands through her short blond hair to keep it back, and shook her head.

She sighed and said again, looking up and out of the night-black window, "Dear God, what are we going to do with you?" My heart went out to them. We all seemed to have exhausted our options. They asked me for fresh ideas, but I had none. I racked my brain, but couldn't come up with anything. The U.S. Marines didn't take sixteen-year-old girls.

Outside the study hall that May, a cardinal sang his round-noted song, and a robin sang his burbling song, and I slumped at my desk with my heart pounding, too harried by restlessness to breathe. I collected poems and learned them. I found the British war poets—World War I: Rupert Brooke, Edmund Blunden, Siegfried Sassoon, and especially Wilfred Owen, who wrote bitterly without descending to sarcasm. I found Asian and Middle Eastern poetry in translation—whole heaps of lyrics fierce or limp—which I ripped to fragments for my collection. I wanted beauty bare of import; I liked language in strips like pennants.

Under the spell of Rimbaud I wrote a poem that began with a line from *Une Saison en Enfer*, "Once, if I remember well," and continued, "My flesh did lie confined in hell." It ended, slantingly, to my own admiration, "And in my filth did I lie still." I wrote other poems, luscious ones, in the manner of the Song of Songs. One teacher, Miss Hickman, gave her lunch hour to meet with us about our poems.

It galled me that adults, as a class, approved the writing and memorization of poetry. Wasn't poetry secret and subversive? One sort of poetry was full of beauty and longing; it exhaled, enervated and helpless, like Li Po. Other poems were threats and vows. They inhaled; they poured into me a power I could not spend. The best of these, a mounted Arabic battle cry, I recited to myself by the hour, hoping to trammel the teachers' drone with hoofbeats.

I dosed myself with pure lyricism; I lived drugged on sensation, as I had lived alert on sensation as a little child. I wanted to raise armies, make love to armies, conquer armies. I wanted to swim in the stream of beautiful syllables until I tired. I wanted to bust up the Ellis School with my fists.

One afternoon at Judy Schoyer's house, I saw a white paperback book on a living-room chair: Lucretius, *On the Nature of Things*. Lucretius, said the book's back cover, had flourished in the first century B.C. This book was a prose translation of a long poem in Latin hexameters, the content of which was ancient physics mixed with philosophy. Why was this book in print? Why would anyone read wrong science, the babblings of a poet in a toga—why but from disinterested intellectual curiosity? I regarded the white paperback book as if it had been a meteorite smoldering on the chair's silk upholstery.

It was Judy's father's book. Mr. Schoyer loaned me the book when he was finished with it, and I read it; it was deadly dull. Nevertheless, I admired Judy's lawyer father boundlessly. I could believe in him for months at a time. His recreation proceeded from book to book, and had done so all his life. He had, I recalled, majored in classical history and literature. He wanted to learn the nature of things. He read and memorized poetry. He quizzed us about current events—what is your opinion of our new Supreme Court justice? On the other hand, his mother's family were Holyokes, and he hadn't raised a hand to rescue Judy from having to come out in Salem, Massachusetts. She had already done so, and would not talk about it.

Judy was tall now, high-waisted, graceful, messy still; she smiled forgivingly, smiled ironically, behind her thick glasses. Her limbs were thin as stalks, and her head was round. She spoke softly. She laughed at anything chaotic. Her family took me to the ballet, to the Pittsburgh Symphony, to the Three Rivers Arts Festival; they took me ice skating on a frozen lake in Highland Park, and swimming in Ohiopyle, south of town where the Youghiogheny River widens over flat rock outcrops.

After school, we piled in Judy's jeep. Out of the jeep's open back I liked to poke the long barrel of a popgun, slowly, and aim it at the drivers of the cars behind us, and shoot the cork, which then swung from its string. The drivers put up their hands in mock alarm, or slumped obligingly over their wheels. Pittsburghers were wonderful sports.

All spring long I crawled on my pin. I was reading *General Semantics*—Alfred Korzybski's early stab at linguistics; I'd hit on it by accident, in books with the word "language" in their titles. I read Freud's standard works, which interested me at first, but they denied reason. Denying reason had gotten Rimbaud nowhere. I read without snobbery, excited and alone, wholly free in the indifference of society. I read with the pure, exhilarating greed of readers sixteen, seventeen years old; I felt I was exhuming lost continents and plundering their stores. I knocked open everything in sight—Henry Miller, Helen Keller, Hardy, Updike, and the French. The war novels kept coming out, and so did John O'Hara's. I read popular social criticism with Judy and Ellin—*The Ugly American, The Hidden Persuaders, The Status Seekers.* I thought social and political criticism were interesting, but not nearly so interesting as almost everything else.

Ralph Waldo Emerson, for example, excited me enormously. Emerson was my first crack at Platonism, Platonism as it had come bumping and skidding down the centuries and across the ocean to Concord, Massachusetts. Emerson was a thinker, full time, as Pasteur and Salk were full-time biologists. I wrote a paper on Emerson's notion of the soul—the oversoul, which, if I could banish from my mind the thought of galoshes (one big galosh, in which we have our being), was grand stuff. It was metaphysics at last, poetry with import, philosophy minus the Bible. And Emerson incited to riot, flouting every authority, and requiring each native to cobble up an original relation with the universe. Since rioting seemed to be my specialty, if only by default, Emerson gave me heart.

Enervated, fanatic, filled long past bursting with oxygen I couldn't use, I hunched skinny in the school's green uniform, etiolated, broken, bellicose, starved, over the back-breaking desk. I sighed and sighed but never emptied my lungs. I said to myself, "O breeze of spring, since I dare not know you, / Why part the silk curtains by my bed?" I stuffed my skull with poems' invisible syllables. If unauthorized persons looked at me, I hoped they'd see blank eyes.

On one of these May mornings, the school's headmistress called me in and read aloud my teachers' confidential appraisals. Madame Owens wrote an odd thing. Madame Owens was a sturdy, affectionate, and humorous woman who had lived through two world wars in Paris by eating rats. She had curly black hair, rouged cheeks, and long, sharp teeth. She swathed her enormous body in thin black fabrics; she sat at her desk with her tiny ankles crossed. She chatted with us; she reminisced.

Madame Owens's kind word on my behalf made no sense. The headmistress read it to me in her office. The statement began, unforgettably, "Here, alas, is a child of the twentieth century." The headmistress, Marion Hamilton, was a brilliant and strong woman whom I liked and respected; the school's small-minded trustees would soon run her out of town on a rail. Her black hair flared from her high forehead. She looked up at me significantly, raising an eyebrow, and repeated it: "Here, alas, is a child of the twentieth century."

I didn't know what to make of it. I didn't know what to do about it. You got a lot of individual attention at a private school.

My idea was to stay barely alive, pumping blood and exchanging gases just enough to sustain life—but certainly not enough so that anyone suspected me of sentience, certainly not enough so that I woke up and remembered anything—until the time came when I could go.

> C'est elle, la petite morte, derrière les rosiers . . .
> It is she, the little dead girl, behind the rose bushes . . .
> the child left on the jetty washed out to sea,
> the little farm child following the lane
>   whose forehead touches the sky.

DURING CLASSES ALL MORNING, I drew. Drawing deliberately, as I had learned to do, yielded complex, fresh drawings: the inevitable backs of my friends' heads; their ankles limp at rest over their winter brown oxfords; the way their white shirts' shoulders emerged from their uniform jumpers. I roused myself to these efforts only once or twice a day. I drew Man Walking, too. During the other six or seven hours, when I wasn't fiddling with poetry, I drew at random.

Drawing at random, paying no attention, infuriated me, yet I never stopped. For years as a child I drew faces on the back of my left hand, on the tops of my knees, in my green assignment book, my blue canvas three-ring binder. Later I drew rigid faces on the Latin textbook's mazy printed page, down and across the spaces between lines and words. I drew stretchable cartoons on the wiggly and problematic plane of a book's page edges. Those page edges—pressed slats and slits—could catch and hold your pen the way streetcar tracks caught and held your bike's wheel; they threw you off your curve. But if you overcame this hazard, you could play at stretching and squeezing the Hogarthy face. I drew inside a textbook's illustrations, usually on the bare sky or on the side of a building or cheek. When I was very young, I sometimes drew on my fingernails, and hated myself for it.

I drew at home, too. My lines were hesitant. "You make everything out of hair," Amy complained. It was always faces I drew, faces and bodies, men and women, old and young, mostly women, and many babies. The babies grew as my sister Molly did; they learned to walk.

At Ellis, Molly was in the second grade. The little kids didn't wear uniforms; she wore pretty dresses. I was a forward on the basketball team. Standing around in front of the school, I used to dribble Molly. She bounced hopping under my hand; we both thought it was mighty funny. During class, I drew her hopping in a smocked dress.

If I didn't draw I couldn't bear to listen in class; drawing siphoned off some restlessness. One English teacher, Miss McBride, let me sit in the back of the classroom and paint.

I paid no attention to the drawings. They were manneristic, obsessive, careless grotesques my hand gibbered out like drool. When I did notice them, they repelled me. Mostly these people were monstrous, elongated or compressed. Some were cross-hatched to invisibility, cross-hatched till the paper dissolved into wet lint on the desk. They were swollen of eyelid or lip, megalocephalic, haughty, moribund, manic, and mostly contemplative—lips shut, full-lidded eyes downcast, as serene as I was excited. They wore their ballpoint-pen hair every which way; they wore ill-fitting hats or melting eyeglasses. They wore diapers and ruffled pants, striped ties, brassieres, eye patches, pearls. Some were equipped with hands on which they rested their weary heads or which they waved, shockingly, up at me.

Very often I connected these unwittingly formed people by a pen line leading from the contour of a neck or foot to a drawing of the pen that drew the line and thence to my carefully drawn right hand holding the pen, and my arm and sleeve. I loved bending my thoughts down that pen line and up, that weird trail connecting and separating the conscious and unconscious: the wiggly face half-fashioned, and the sly, full-fashioned, and fashioning hand.

More than once, on family visits far away, or on the streets where I walked to school, or at Forbes Field, I saw a stranger whom I recognized. How well I knew that face, its bee-stung lips, its compressed forehead, its clumsy jaw! And I realized then, with a draining jolt of superstitious dread, that I was seeing in the flesh someone I had once drawn. Someone I had once drawn with a ballpoint pen inside a matchbook, or on an overcrowded page, a scribbled face inside the lines of a photographed woman's skirt. Now here was that face perfectly molded and fleshed in, as private as the drawing and as sad, walking around on a competent body, apparently experienced here, and at home.

Outside the study hall the next fall, the fall of our senior year, the Nabisco plant baked sweet white bread twice a week. If I sharpened a pencil at the back of the room I could smell the baking bread and the cedar shavings from the pencil. I could see the oaks turning brown on the edge of the hockey field, and see the scoured silver sky above shining a secret, true light into everything, into the black cars and red brick apartment buildings of Shadyside glimpsed beyond the trees. Pretty soon all twenty of us—our class—would be leaving. A core of my classmates had been together since kindergarten. I'd been there eight years. We twenty knew by bored heart the very weave of each other's socks. I thought, unfairly, of the Polyphemus moth crawling down the school's driveway. Now we'd go, too.

Back in my seat, I repeated the poem that began, "We grow to the sound of the wind playing his flutes in our hair." The poems I loved were in French, or translated from the Chinese, Portuguese, Arabic, Sanskrit, Greek. I murmured their heart-breaking syllables. I knew almost nothing of the diverse and energetic city I lived in. The poems whispered in my ear the password phrase, and I memorized it behind enemy lines: There is a world. There is another world.

I knew already that I would go to Hollins College in Virginia; our headmistress sent all her problems there, to her alma mater. "For the English department," she told me. William Golding was then writer in residence; before him was Enid Starkie, who wrote the biography of Rimbaud. But, "To smooth off her rough edges," she had told my parents. They repeated the phrase to me, vividly.

I had hopes for my rough edges. I wanted to use them as a can opener, to cut myself a hole in the world's surface, and exit through it. Would I be ground, instead, to a nub? Would they send me home, an ornament to my breed, in a jewelry bag?

I was in no position to comment. We had visited the school; it was beautiful. It was at the foot of Virginia's Great Valley, where the Scotch-Irish had settled in the eighteenth century, following the Alleghenies south.

Epilogue

A DREAM CONSISTS OF LITTLE MORE than its setting, as anyone knows who tells a dream or hears a dream told:

We were squeezing up the stone street of an Old World village.

We were climbing down the gangway of an oceangoing ship, carrying a baby.

We broke through the woods on the crest of a ridge and saw water; we grounded our blunt raft on a charred point of land.

We were lying on boughs of a tree in an alley.

We were dancing in a darkened ballroom, and the curtains were blowing.

The setting of our urgent lives is an intricate maze whose blind corridors we learn one by one—village street, ocean vessel, forested slope—without remembering how or where they connect in space.

You travel, settle, move on, stay put, go. You point your car down the riverside road to the blurred foot of the mountain. The mountain rolls back from the floodplain and hides its own height in its trees. You get out, stand on gravel, and cool your eyes watching the river move south. You lean on the car's hot hood and look up at the old mountain, up the slope of its green western flank. It is September; the golden-rod is out, and the asters. The tattered hardwood leaves darken before they die. The mountain occupies most of the sky. You can see where the route ahead through the woods will cross a fire scar, will vanish behind a slide of shale, and perhaps reemerge there on that piny ridge now visible across the hanging valley—that ridge apparently inaccessible, but with a faint track that fingers its greenish spine. You don't notice starting to walk; the sight of the trail has impelled you along it, as the sight of the earth moves the sun.

Before you the mountain's body curves away backward like a gymnast; the mountain's peak is somewhere south, rolled backward, too, and out of sight. Below you lies the pale and widening river; its far bank is forest now, and hills, and more blue hills behind them, hiding the yellow plain. Overhead and on the mountain's side, clouds collect and part. The clouds soak the ridges; the wayside plants tap water on your legs.

Now: if here while you are walking, or there when you've attained the far ridge and can see the yellow plain and the river shining through it—if you notice unbidden that you are afoot on this particular mountain on this particular day in the company of these particular changing fragments of clouds,—if you pause in your daze to connect your own skull-locked and interior mumble with the skin of your senses and sense, and notice you are living,—then will you not conjure up in imagi-nation a map or a globe and locate this low mountain ridge on it, and find on one western slope the dot which represents you walking here astonished?

You may then wonder where they have gone, those other dim dots that were you: you in the flesh swimming in a swift river, swinging a bat on the first pitch, opening a footlocker with a screwdriver, inking and painting clowns on celluloid, stepping out of a revolving door into the swift crowd on a sidewalk, being kissed and kissing till your brain grew smooth, stepping out of the cold woods into a warm field full of crows, or lying awake in bed aware of your legs and suddenly aware of all of it, that the ceiling above you was under the sky—in what country, what town?

You may wonder, that is, as I sometimes wonder privately, but it doesn't matter. For it is not you or I that is important, neither what sort we might be nor how we came to be each where we are. What is important is anyone's coming awake and discovering a place, finding in full orbit a spinning globe one can lean over, catch, and jump on. What is important is the moment of opening a life and feeling it touch—with an electric hiss and cry—this speckled mineral sphere, our present world.

On your mountain slope now you must take on faith that those apparently discrete dots of you were contiguous: that little earnest dot, so easily amused; that alien, angry adolescent; and this woman with loosening skin on bony hands, hands now fifteen years older than your mother's hands when you pinched their knuckle skin into mountain ridges on an end table. You must take on faith that those severed places cohered, too—the dozens of desks, bedrooms, kitchens, yards, landscapes—if only through the motion and shed molecules of the traveler. You take it on faith that the multiform and variously lighted latitudes and longitudes were part of one world, that you didn't drop chopped from house to house, coast to coast, life to life, but in some once comprehensible way moved there, a city block at a time, a highway mile at a time, a degree of latitude and longitude at a time, carrying a fielder's mitt and the Penguin *Rimbaud* for old time's sake, and a sealed envelope, like a fetish, of untouchable stock certificates someone one hundred years ago gave your grandmother, and a comb. You take it on faith, for the connections are down now, the trail grown over, the highway moved; you can't remember despite all your vowing and memorization, and the way back is lost.

Your very cells have been replaced, and so have most of

your feelings—except for two, two that connect back as far as you can remember. One is the chilling sensation of lowering one foot into a hot bath. The other, which can and does occur at any time, never fails to occur when you lower one foot into a hot bath, and when you feel the chill spread inside your shoulders, shoot down your arms and rise to your lips, and when you remember having felt this sensation from always, from when your mother lifted you down toward the bath and you curled up your legs: it is the dizzying overreal sensation of noticing that you are here. You feel life wipe your face like a big brush.

You may read this in your summer bed while the stars roll westward over your roof as they always do, while the constellation Crazy Swan nosedives over your steaming roof and into the tilled prairie once again. You may read this in your winter chair while Orion vaults over your snowy roof and over the hard continent to dive behind a California wave. "O'Ryan," Father called Orion, "that Irishman." Any two points in time, however distant, meet through the points in between; any two points in our atmosphere touch through the air. So we meet.

I write this at a wide desk in a pine shed as I always do these recent years, in this life I pray will last, while the summer sun closes the sky to Orion and to all the other winter stars over my roof. The young oaks growing just outside my windows wave in the light, so that concentrating, lost in the past, I see the pale leaves wag and think as my blood leaps: Is someone coming?

Is it Mother coming for me, to carry me home? Could it be my own young, my own glorious Mother, coming across the grass for me, the morning light on her skin, to get me and bring me back? Back to where I last knew all I needed, the way to her two strong arms?

And I wake a little more and reason, No, it is the oak leaves in the sun, pale as a face. I am here now, with this my own dear family, up here at this high latitude, out here at the farthest exploratory tip of this my present bewildering age. And still I break up through the skin of awareness a thousand times a day, as dolphins burst through seas, and dive again, and rise, and dive.

I GREW UP IN PITTSBURGH IN THE 1950s, in a house full of comedians, reading books. Possibly because Father had loaded his boat one day and gone down the Ohio River, I confused leaving with living, and vowed that when I got my freedom, I would be the one to do both.

Sometimes after dinner, when my sisters and I were young, Mother could persuade Father to perform Goofus—to "do" Goofus. Goofus, he explained, was an old road-show routine, older than vaudeville, that traveling actors brought to the cities of the young republic, and out into the frontier towns. It was a pantomime, a character, and a song.

Doing Goofus, Father shambled, holding his tall frame unstrung like one of those toy figures whose string collapses when you press the bottoms of their stands. He walked onstage a hayseed, a farm boy, a rube, sticking his neck forward. He sang the syncopated song, dipping his knees mock-idiotically on the beats:

> I was born on a farm down in Ioway,
> Flaming youth who was bound that he'd fly
>   away . . .

Between verses of the song the rube stepped forward and concentrated on some absurdity, like balancing on his finger an imaginary hair plucked from his head. He stiffened the hair with his fingers and, wincing horribly, inserted it into one of his ears. He pushed it through to the other ear till he could grasp it; then he drew it sawing back and forth through his skull with both hands, in one ear and out the other, grinning stupidly in the character of the rube. That was the flaming youth.

"Do you know what you call that?" he asked as he sat back down. The intelligence had come back to his eyes. What? "That," he said. "What you do up there. That is called a 'business.'"

Our father taught us the culture into which we were born. American culture was Dixieland above all, Dixieland pure and simple, and next to Dixieland, jazz. It was the pioneers who went West singing "Bang away my Lulu." When someone died on the Oregon Trail, as someone was always doing, the family scratched a shallow grave right by the trail, because the wagon train couldn't wait. Everyone paced on behind the oxen across the empty desert and some families sang "Bang away my Lulu" that night, and some didn't.

Our culture was the stock-market crash—the biggest and best crash a country ever had. Father explained the mechanics of the crash to young Amy and me, around the dining-room table. He tried to explain why men on Wall Street had jumped from skyscrapers when the stock market crashed: "They lost everything!"—but of course I thought they lost everything only when they jumped. It was the breadlines of the Depression, and the Okies fleeing the Dust Bowl, and the proud men begging on city streets, and families on the move seeking work—dusty women, men in black hats pulled over their eyes, haunted, hungry children: what a mystifying spectacle, this almost universal misery, city families living in cars, farm families eating insects, because—why? Because all the businessmen realized at once, on the same morning, that paper money was only paper. What terrible fools. What did they think it was?

American culture was the World's Fair in Chicago, baseball, the Erie Canal, fancy nightclubs in Harlem, silent movies, summer-stock theater, the California forty-niners, the Alaska gold rush, Henry Ford and his bright idea of paying workers enough to buy cars, P. T. Barnum and his traveling circus, Buffalo Bill Cody and his Wild West Show. It was the Chrysler Building in New York and the Golden Gate Bridge in San Francisco; the *Concord* and the *Merrimack,* the Alamo, the Little Bighorn, Gettysburg, Shiloh, Bull Run, and "Strike the tent."

It was Pittsburgh's legendary Joe Magarac, the mighty Hungarian steelworker, who took off his shirt to reveal his body made of high-grade steel, and who squeezed out steel rail between his knuckles by the ton. It was the brawling rivermen on the Ohio River, the sandhogs who dug Hudson River tunnels, silver miners in Idaho, cowboys in Texas, and the innocent American Indian Jim Thorpe, who had to give all his Olympic gold medals back. It was the men of every race who built the railroads, and the boys of every race who went to war.

Above all, it was the man who wandered unencumbered by family ties: Johnny Appleseed in our own home woods, Daniel Boone in Kentucky, Jim Bridger crossing the Rockies. Father described for us the Yankee peddler, the free trapper, the roaming cowhand, the whalerman, roustabout, gandy dancer, tramp. His heroes, and my heroes, were Raymond Chandler's city detective Marlowe going, as a man must, down these mean streets; Huck Finn lighting out for the territories; and Jack Kerouac on the road.

* * *

Every time we danced, Father brought up Jack Kerouac, *On the Road.*

We did a lot of dancing at our house, fast dancing; everyone in the family was a dancing fool. I always came down from my room to dance. When the music was going, who could resist? I bounced down the stairs to the rhythm and began to whistle a bit, helpless as a marionette whose strings jerk her head and feet.

We danced by the record player in the dining room. For fast dancing, Mother only rarely joined in; perhaps Amy, Molly, and I had made her self-conscious. We waved our arms a lot. I bumped into people, because I liked to close my eyes.

"Turn that record player down!" Mother suggested from the living room. She was embroidering a pillow. Father opened the cabinet and turned the volume down a bit. I opened my eyes.

"Remember that line in *On the Road?*" He addressed me, because between us we had read *On the Road* approximately a million times. Like *Life on the Mississippi,* it was the sort of thing we read. I thought of his blue bookplate: "Books make the man." The bookplate's ship struggled in steep seas, and crowded on too much sail.

I nodded; I knew what he was going to say, because he said it every time we played music; it was always a pleasure. We both reined in our dancing a bit, so we could converse. Sure I remembered that line in *On the Road.*

"Kerouac's in a little bar in Mexico. He says that was the only time he ever got to hear music played loud enough—in that little bar in Mexico. It was in *On the Road.* The only time he ever got to hear the music loud enough. I always remember that."

He laughed, shaking his head; he turned the record player down another notch. If it had ever been at all, it had been a long time since Father had heard the music played loud enough. Maybe he was still imagining it, fondly, some little bar back away somewhere, so small he and the other regulars sat in the middle of the blaring band, or stood snapping their fingers, drinking bourbon, telling jokes between sets. He knew a lot of jokes. Did he think of himself as I thought of him, as the man who had cut out of town and headed, wearing tennis shoes and a blue cap, down the river toward New Orleans?

I was gaining momentum. It was only a matter of months. Downstairs in the basement, I played "Shake, Rattle, and Roll" on the piano. Why not take up the trumpet, why not marry this wonderful boy, write an epic, become a medical missionary to the Amazon as I always intended? What happened to painting, what happened to science? My boyfriend never seemed to sleep. "I can sleep when I'm dead," he said. Was this not grand?

I was approaching escape velocity. What would you do if you had fifteen minutes to live before the bomb went off? Quick: What would you read? I drove up and down the boulevards, up and down the highways, around Frick Park fast, over the flung bridges and up into the springtime hills. My boyfriend and I played lightning chess, ten games an hour. We drove up the Allegheny River into New York and back, and up the Monongahela River into West Virginia and back. In my room I shuffled cards. I wrote poems about the sea. I wrote poems imitating the psalms. I held my pen on the red paper label of the modern jazz record on the turntable, played that side past midnight over and over, and let the pen draw a circle hours thick. In New Orleans—if you could get to New Orleans—would the music be loud enough?

THE
WRITING LIFE

For Bob

THE WRITING LIFE

No one suspects the days to be gods. —EMERSON

Chapter One

Do not hurry; do not rest. —GOETHE

WHEN YOU WRITE, you lay out a line of words. The line of words is a miner's pick, a woodcarver's gouge, a surgeon's probe. You wield it, and it digs a path you follow. Soon you find yourself deep in new territory. Is it a dead end, or have you located the real subject? You will know tomorrow, or this time next year.

You make the path boldly and follow it fearfully. You go where the path leads. At the end of the path, you find a box canyon. You hammer out reports, dispatch bulletins.

The writing has changed, in your hands, and in a twinkling, from an expression of your notions to an epistemological tool. The new place interests you because it is not clear. You attend. In your humility, you lay down the words carefully, watching all the angles. Now the earlier writing looks soft and careless. Process is nothing; erase your tracks. The path is not the work. I hope your tracks have grown over; I hope birds ate the crumbs; I hope you will toss it all and not look back.

The line of words is a hammer. You hammer against the walls of your house. You tap the walls, lightly, everywhere.

After giving many years' attention to these things, you know what to listen for. Some of the walls are bearing walls; they have to stay, or everything will fall down. Other walls can go with impunity; you can hear the difference. Unfortunately, it is often a bearing wall that has to go. It cannot be helped. There is only one solution, which appalls you, but there it is. Knock it out. Duck.

Courage utterly opposes the bold hope that this is such fine stuff the work needs it, or the world. Courage, exhausted, stands on bare reality: this writing weakens the work. You must demolish the work and start over. You can save some of the sentences, like bricks. It will be a miracle if you can save some of the paragraphs, no matter how excellent in themselves or hard-won. You can waste a year worrying about it, or you can get it over with now. (Are you a woman, or a mouse?)

The part you must jettison is not only the best-written part; it is also, oddly, that part which was to have been the very point. It is the original key passage, the passage on which the rest was to hang, and from which you yourself drew the courage to begin. Henry James knew it well, and said it best. In his preface to *The Spoils of Poynton,* he pities the writer, in a comical pair of sentences that rises to a howl: "Which is the work in which he hasn't surrendered, under dire difficulty, the best thing he meant to have kept? In which indeed, before the dreadful *done,* doesn't he ask himself what has become of the thing all for the sweet sake of which it was to proceed to that extremity?"

So it is that a writer writes many books. In each book, he intended several urgent and vivid points, many of which he sacrificed as the book's form hardened. "The youth gets together his materials to build a bridge to the moon," Thoreau noted mournfully, "or perchance a palace or temple on the earth, and at length the middle-aged man concludes to build a wood-shed with them." The writer returns to these materials, these passionate subjects, as to unfinished business, for they are his life's work.

It is the beginning of a work that the writer throws away.

A painting covers its tracks. Painters work from the ground up. The latest version of a painting overlays earlier versions, and obliterates them. Writers, on the other hand, work from left to right. The discardable chapters are on the left. The latest version of a literary work begins somewhere in the work's middle, and hardens toward the end. The earlier version remains lumpishly on the left; the work's beginning greets the reader with the wrong hand. In those early pages and chapters anyone may find bold leaps to nowhere, read the brave beginnings of dropped themes, hear a tone since abandoned, discover blind alleys, track red herrings, and laboriously learn a setting now false.

Several delusions weaken the writer's resolve to throw away work. If he has read his pages too often, those pages will have a necessary quality, the ring of the inevitable, like poetry known by heart; they will perfectly answer their own familiar rhythms. He will retain them. He may retain those pages if they possess some virtues, such as power in themselves, though they lack the cardinal virtue, which is pertinence to, and unity with, the book's thrust. Sometimes the writer leaves his early chapters in place from gratitude; he cannot contemplate them or read them without feeling again the blessed relief that exalted him when the words first appeared—relief that he was writing anything at all. That beginning served to get him where he was going, after all; surely the reader needs it, too, as groundwork. But no.

Every year the aspiring photographer brought a stack of his best prints to an old, honored photographer, seeking his judgment. Every year the old man studied the prints and painstakingly ordered them into two piles, bad and good. Every year the old man moved a certain landscape print into the bad stack. At length he turned to the young man: "You submit this same landscape every year, and every year I put it on the bad stack. Why do you like it so much?" The young photographer said, "Because I had to climb a mountain to get it."

A cabdriver sang his songs to me, in New York. Some we sang together. He had turned the meter off; he drove around midtown, singing. One long song he sang twice; it was the only dull one. I said, You already sang that one; let's sing something else. And he said, "You don't know how long it took me to get that one together."

How many books do we read from which the writer lacked courage to tie off the umbilical cord? How many gifts do we open from which the writer neglected to remove the price tag? Is it pertinent, is it courteous, for us to learn what it cost the writer personally?

You write it all, discovering it at the end of the line of words. The line of words is a fiber optic, flexible as wire; it illumines the path just before its fragile tip. You probe with it, delicate as a worm.

Few sights are so absurd as that of an inchworm leading its dimwit life. Inchworms are the caterpillar larvae of several moths or butterflies. The cabbage looper, for example, is an inchworm. I often see an inchworm: it is a skinny bright green thing, pale and thin as a vein, an inch long, and apparently totally unfit for life in this world. It wears out its days in constant panic.

Every inchworm I have seen was stuck in long grasses. The wretched inchworm hangs from the side of a grassblade and throws its head around from side to side, seeming to wail. What! No further? Its back pair of nubby feet clasps the grass stem; its front three pairs of nubs rear back and flail in the air, apparently in search of a footing. What! No further? What? It searches everywhere in the wide world for the rest of the grass, which is right under its nose. By dumb luck it touches the grass. Its front legs hang on; it lifts and buckles its green

inch, and places its hind legs just behind its front legs. Its body
makes a loop, a bight. All it has to do now is slide its front legs
up the grass stem. Instead it gets lost. It throws up its head and
front legs, flings its upper body out into the void, and panics
again. What! No further? End of world? And so forth, until
it actually reaches the grasshead's tip. By then its wee weight
may be bending the grass toward some other grass plant. Its
davening, apocalyptic prayers sway the grasshead and bump it
into something. I have seen it many times. The blind and
frantic numbskull makes it off one grassblade and onto another one, which it will climb in virtual hysteria for several
hours. Every step brings it to the universe's rim. And now—
What! No further? End of world? Ah, here's ground. What!
No further? Yike!

"Why don't you just jump?" I tell it, disgusted. "Put yourself out of your misery."

I admire those eighteenth-century Hasids who understood
the risk of prayer. Rabbi Uri of Strelisk took sorrowful leave
of his household every morning because he was setting off to
his prayers. He told his family how to dispose of his manuscripts if praying should kill him. A ritual slaughterer, similarly, every morning bade goodbye to his wife and children
and wept as if he would never see them again. His friend asked
him why. Because, he answered, when I begin I call out to the
Lord. Then I pray, "Have mercy on us." Who knows what the
Lord's power will do to me in that moment after I have in-
voked it and before I beg for mercy?

When you are stuck in a book; when you are well into
writing it, and know what comes next, and yet cannot go on;
when every morning for a week or a month you enter its room
and turn your back on it; then the trouble is either of two
things. Either the structure has forked, so the narrative, or the
logic, has developed a hairline fracture that will shortly split
it up the middle—or you are approaching a fatal mistake.

What you had planned will not do. If you pursue your present course, the book will explode or collapse, and you do not know about it yet, quite.

In Bridgeport, Connecticut, one morning in April 1987, a six-story concrete-slab building under construction collapsed, and killed twenty-eight men. Just before it collapsed, a woman across the street leaned from her window and said to a passerby, "That building is starting to shake." "Lady," he said, according to the Hartford *Courant,* "you got rocks in your head."

You notice only this: your worker—your one and only, your prized, coddled, and driven worker—is not going out on that job. Will not budge, not even for you, boss. Has been at it long enough to know when the air smells wrong; can sense a tremor through boot soles. Nonsense, you say; it is perfectly safe. But the worker will not go. Will not even look at the site. Just developed heart trouble. Would rather starve. Sorry.

What do you do? Acknowledge, first, that you cannot do nothing. Lay out the structure you already have, x-ray it for a hairline fracture, find it, and think about it for a week or a year; solve the insoluble problem. Or subject the next part, the part at which the worker balks, to harsh tests. It harbors an unexamined and wrong premise. Something completely necessary is false or fatal. Once you find it, and if you can accept the finding, of course it will mean starting again. This is why many experienced writers urge young men and women to learn a useful trade.

Every morning you climb several flights of stairs, enter your study, open the French doors, and slide your desk and chair out into the middle of the air. The desk and chair float thirty feet from the ground, between the crowns of maple trees. The furniture is in place; you go back for your thermos of coffee. Then, wincing, you step out again through the French doors and sit down on the chair and look over the desktop. You can

see clear to the river from here in winter. You pour yourself
a cup of coffee.

Birds fly under your chair. In spring, when the leaves open
in the maples' crowns, your view stops in the treetops just
beyond the desk; yellow warblers hiss and whisper on the high
twigs, and catch flies. Get to work. Your work is to keep
cranking the flywheel that turns the gears that spin the belt in
the engine of belief that keeps you and your desk in midair.

Putting a book together is interesting and exhilarating. It is
sufficiently difficult and complex that it engages all your intelligence. It is life at its most free. Your freedom as a writer is
not freedom of expression in the sense of wild blurting; you
may not let rip. It is life at its most free, if you are fortunate
enough to be able to try it, because you select your materials,
invent your task, and pace yourself. In the democracies, you
may even write and publish anything you please about any
governments or institutions, even if what you write is demon-
strably false.

The obverse of this freedom, of course, is that your work
is so meaningless, so fully for yourself alone, and so worthless
to the world, that no one except you cares whether you do it
well, or ever. You are free to make several thousand close
judgment calls a day. Your freedom is a by-product of your
days' triviality. A shoe salesman—who is doing others' tasks,
who must answer to two or three bosses, who must do his job
their way, and must put himself in their hands, at their place,
during their hours—is nevertheless working usefully. Further,
if the shoe salesman fails to appear one morning, someone will
notice and miss him. Your manuscript, on which you lavish
such care, has no needs or wishes; it knows you not. Nor does
anyone need your manuscript; everyone needs shoes more.
There are many manuscripts already—worthy ones, most edi-
fying and moving ones, intelligent and powerful ones. If you
believed *Paradise Lost* to be excellent, would you buy it? Why

not shoot yourself, actually, rather than finish one more excellent manuscript on which to gag the world?

To find a honey tree, first catch a bee. Catch a bee when its legs are heavy with pollen; then it is ready for home. It is simple enough to catch a bee on a flower: hold a cup or glass above the bee, and when it flies up, cap the cup with a piece of cardboard. Carry the bee to a nearby open spot—best an elevated one—release it, and watch where it goes. Keep your eyes on it as long as you can see it, and hie you to that last known place. Wait there until you see another bee; catch it, release it, and watch. Bee after bee will lead toward the honey tree, until you see the final bee enter the tree. Thoreau describes this process in his journals. So a book leads its writer.

You may wonder how you start, how you catch the first one. What do you use for bait?

You have no choice. One bad winter in the Arctic, and not too long ago, an Algonquin woman and her baby were left alone after everyone else in their winter camp had starved. Ernest Thompson Seton tells it. The woman walked from the camp where everyone had died, and found at a lake a cache. The cache contained one small fishhook. It was simple to rig a line, but she had no bait, and no hope of bait. The baby cried. She took a knife and cut a strip from her own thigh. She fished with the worm of her own flesh and caught a jackfish; she fed the child and herself. Of course she saved the fish gut for bait. She lived alone at the lake, on fish, until spring, when she walked out again and found people. Seton's informant had seen the scar on her thigh.

It takes years to write a book—between two and ten years. Less is so rare as to be statistically insignificant. One American writer has written a dozen major books over six decades. He wrote one of those books, a perfect novel, in three months. He speaks of it, still, with awe, almost whispering. Who wants to offend the spirit that hands out such books?

Faulkner wrote *As I Lay Dying* in six weeks; he claimed he knocked it off in his spare time from a twelve-hour-a-day job performing manual labor. There are other examples from other continents and centuries, just as albinos, assassins, saints, big people, and little people show up from time to time in large populations. Out of a human population on earth of four and a half billion, perhaps twenty people can write a book in a year. Some people lift cars, too. Some people enter week-long sled-dog races, go over Niagara Falls in barrels, fly planes through the Arc de Triomphe. Some people feel no pain in childbirth. Some people eat cars. There is no call to take human extremes as norms.

Writing a book, full time, takes between two and ten years. The long poem, John Berryman said, takes between five and ten years. Thomas Mann was a prodigy of production. Working full time, he wrote a page a day. That is 365 pages a year, for he did write every day—a good-sized book a year. At a page a day, he was one of the most prolific writers who ever lived. Flaubert wrote steadily, with only the usual, appalling, strains. For twenty-five years he finished a big book every five to seven years. My guess is that full-time writers average a book every five years: seventy-three usable pages a year, or a usable fifth of a page a day. The years that biographers and other nonfiction writers spend amassing and mastering materials are well matched by the years novelists and short-story writers spend fabricating solid worlds that answer to immaterial truths. On plenty of days the writer can write three or four pages, and on plenty of other days he concludes he must throw them away.

Octavio Paz cites the example of "Saint-Pol-Roux, who used to hang the inscription 'The poet is working' from his door while he slept."

The notion that one can write better during one season of the year than another Samuel Johnson labeled, "Imagination

operating upon luxury." Another luxury for an idle imagination is the writer's own feeling about the work. There is neither a proportional relationship, nor an inverse one, between
a writer's estimation of a work in progress and its actual quality. The feeling that the work is magnificent, and the feeling
that it is abominable, are both mosquitoes to be repelled,
ignored, or killed, but not indulged.

The reason to perfect a piece of prose as it progresses—to
secure each sentence before building on it—is that original
writing fashions a form. It unrolls out into nothingness. It
grows cell to cell, bole to bough to twig to leaf; any careful
word may suggest a route, may begin a strand of metaphor or
event out of which much, or all, will develop. Perfecting the
work inch by inch, writing from the first word toward the last,
displays the courage and fear this method induces. The strain,
like Giacometti's penciled search for precision and honesty,
enlivens the work and impels it toward its truest end. A pile
of decent work behind him, no matter how small, fuels the
writer's hope, too; his pride emboldens and impels him. One
Washington writer—Charlie Butts—so prizes momentum,
and so fears self-consciousness, that he writes fiction in a rush
of his own devising. He leaves his house on distracting er-
rands, hurries in the door, and without taking off his coat, sits
at a typewriter and retypes in a blur of speed all of the story
he has written to date. Impetus propels him to add another
sentence or two before he notices he is writing and seizes up.
Then he leaves the house and repeats the process; he runs in
the door and retypes the entire story, hoping to squeeze out
another sentence the way some car engines turn over after the
ignition is off, or the way Warner Bros.' Wile E. Coyote
continues running for several yards beyond the edge of a cliff,
until he notices.

The reason not to perfect a work as it progresses is that,
concomitantly, original work fashions a form the true shape of
which it discovers only as it proceeds, so the early strokes are

useless, however fine their sheen. Only when a paragraph's role in the context of the whole work is clear can the envisioning writer direct its complexity of detail to strengthen the work's ends.

Fiction writers who toss up their arms helplessly because their characters "take over"—powerful rascals, what is a god to do?—refer, I think, to these structural mysteries that seize any serious work, whether or not it possesses fifth-column characters who wreak havoc from within. Sometimes part of a book simply gets up and walks away. The writer cannot force it back in place. It wanders off to die. It is like the astonishing—and common—starfish called the sea star. A sea star is a starfish with many arms; each arm is called a ray. From time to time a sea star breaks itself, and no one knows why. One of the rays twists itself off and walks away. Dr. S. P. Monks describes one species, which lives on rocky Pacific shores: "I am inclined to think that *Phataria . . .* always breaks itself, no matter what may be the impulse. They make breaks when conditions are changed, sometimes within a few hours after being placed in jars. . . . Whatever may be the stimulus, the animal can and does break of itself. . . . The ordinary method is for the main portion of the starfish to remain fixed and passive with the tube feet set on the side of the departing ray, and for this ray to walk slowly away at right angles to the body, to change position, twist, and do all the active labor necessary to the breakage." Marine biologist Ed Ricketts comments on this: "It would seem that in an animal that deliberately pulls itself apart we have the very acme of something or other."

The written word is weak. Many people prefer life to it. Life gets your blood going, and it smells good. Writing is mere writing, literature is mere. It appeals only to the subtlest senses—the imagination's vision, and the imagination's hearing—and the moral sense, and the intellect. This writing that you do, that so thrills you, that so rocks and exhilarates you, as if you were dancing next to the band, is barely audible to anyone else. The reader's ear must adjust down from loud life to the subtle, imaginary sounds of the written word. An ordinary reader picking up a book can't yet hear a thing; it will take half an hour to pick up the writing's modulations, its ups and downs and louds and softs.

An intriguing entomological experiment shows that a male butterfly will ignore a living female butterfly of his own species in favor of a painted cardboard one, if the cardboard one is big. If the cardboard one is bigger than he is, bigger than any female butterfly ever could be. He jumps the piece of cardboard. Over and over again, he jumps the piece of cardboard. Nearby, the real, living female butterfly opens and closes her wings in vain.

Films and television stimulate the body's senses too, in big ways. A nine-foot handsome face, and its three-foot-wide smile, are irresistible. Look at the long legs on that man, as high as a wall, and coming straight toward you. The music builds. The moving, lighted screen fills your brain. You do not like filmed car chases? See if you can turn away. Try not to watch. Even knowing you are manipulated, you are still as helpless as the male butterfly drawn to painted cardboard.

That is the movies. That is their ground. The printed word cannot compete with the movies on their ground, and should not. You can describe beautiful faces, car chases, or valleys full of Indians on horseback until you run out of words, and you will not approach the movies' spectacle. Novels written with film contracts in mind have a faint but unmistakable, and ruinous, odor. I cannot name what, in the text, alerts the reader to suspect the writer of mixed motives; I cannot specify which sentences, in several books, have caused me to read on with increasing dismay, and finally close the books because I smelled a rat. Such books seem uneasy being books; they seem eager to fling off their disguises and jump onto screens.

Why would anyone read a book instead of watching big people move on a screen? Because a book can be literature. It is a subtle thing—a poor thing, but our own. In my view, the more literary the book—the more purely verbal, crafted sentence by sentence, the more imaginative, reasoned, and deep—the more likely people are to read it. The people who read are the people who like literature, after all, whatever that might be. They like, or require, what books alone have. If they want to see films that evening, they will find films. If they do not like to read, they will not. People who read are not too lazy to flip on the television; they prefer books. I cannot imagine a sorrier pursuit than struggling for years to write a book that attempts to appeal to people who do not read in the first place.

You climb a long ladder until you can see over the roof, or over the clouds. You are writing a book. You watch your shod feet step on each round rung, one at a time; you do not hurry and do not rest. Your feet feel the steep ladder's balance; the long muscles in your thighs check its sway. You climb steadily, doing your job in the dark. When you reach the end, there is nothing more to climb. The sun hits you. The bright wideness surprises you; you had forgotten there was an end. You look back at the ladder's two feet on the distant grass, astonished.

The line of words fingers your own heart. It invades arteries, and enters the heart on a flood of breath; it presses the moving rims of thick valves; it palpates the dark muscle strong as horses, feeling for something, it knows not what. A queer picture beds in the muscle like a worm encysted—some film of feeling, some song forgotten, a scene in a dark bedroom, a corner of the woodlot, a terrible dining room, that exalting sidewalk; these fragments are heavy with meaning. The line of words peels them back, dissects them out. Will the bared tissue burn? Do you want to expose these scenes to the light? You may locate them and leave them, or poke the spot hard till the sore bleeds on your finger, and write with that blood. If the sore spot is not fatal, if it does not grow and block something, you can use its power for many years, until the heart resorbs it.

The line of words feels for cracks in the firmament.

The line of words is heading out past Jupiter this morning. Traveling 150 kilometers a second, it makes no sound. The big yellow planet and its white moons spin. The line of words speeds past Jupiter and its cumbrous, dizzying orbit; it looks neither to the right nor to the left. It will be leaving the solar system soon, single-minded, rapt, rushing heaven like a soul. You are in Houston, Texas, watching the monitor. You saw a simulation: the line of words waited still, hushed, pointed with longing. The big yellow planet spun toward it like a pitched ball and passed beside it, low and outside. Jupiter was so large, the arc of its edge at the screen's bottom looked flat. The probe twined on; its wild path passed between white suns small as dots; these stars fell away on either side, like the lights on a tunnel's walls.

Now you watch symbols move on your monitor; you stare at the signals the probe sends back, transmits in your own tongue, numbers. Maybe later you can guess at what they mean—what they might mean about space at the edge of the solar system, or about your instruments. Right now, you are flying. Right now, your job is to hold your breath.

Chapter Two

What if the man could see Beauty Itself, pure,
unalloyed, stripped of mortality and all its
pollution, stains, and vanities, unchanging,
divine, . . . the man becoming, in that communion,
the friend of God, himself immortal; . . . would
that be a life to disregard?   —PLATO

I WRITE THIS in the most recent of my many studies—a pine shed on Cape Cod. The pine lumber is unfinished inside the study; the pines outside are finished trees. I see the pines from my two windows. Nuthatches spiral around their long, coarse trunks. Sometimes in June a feeding colony of mixed warblers flies through the pines; the warblers make a racket that draws me out the door. The warblers drift loosely through the stiff pine branches, and I follow through the thin long grass between the trunks.

The study—sold as a prefabricated toolshed—is eight feet by ten feet. Like a plane's cockpit, it is crammed bulkhead to bulkhead with high-tech equipment. All it needs is an altimeter; I never quite know where I am. There is a computer, a printer, and a photocopying machine. My backless chair, a prie-dieu on which I kneel, slides under the desk; I give it a little kick when I leave. There is an air conditioner, a heater, and an electric kettle. There is a low-tech bookshelf, a shelf of gull and whale bones, and a bed. Under the bed I stow paints—a one-pint can of yellow to touch up the windows' trim, and five or six tubes of artists' oils. The study affords ample room for one. One who is supposed to be writing books. You can read in the space of a coffin, and you can write in the space of a toolshed meant for mowers and spades.

I walk up here from the house every morning. The study and its pines, and the old summer cottages nearby, and the new farm just north of me, rise from an old sand dune high over a creeky salt marsh. From the bright lip of the dune I can see oyster farmers working their beds on the tide flats and sailboats under way in the saltwater bay. After I have warmed myself standing at the crest of the dune, I return under the pines, enter the study, slam the door so the latch catches—and then I cannot see. The green spot in front of my eyes outshines everything in the shade. I lie on the bed and play with a bird bone until I can see it.

Appealing workplaces are to be avoided. One wants a room with no view, so imagination can meet memory in the dark. When I furnished this study seven years ago, I pushed the long desk against a blank wall, so I could not see from either window. Once, fifteen years ago, I wrote in a cinder-block cell over a parking lot. It overlooked a tar-and-gravel roof. This pine shed under trees is not quite so good as the cinder-block study was, but it will do.

"The beginning of wisdom," according to a West African proverb, "is to get you a roof."

It was on summer nights in Roanoke, Virginia, that I wrote the second half of a book, *Pilgrim at Tinker Creek.* (I wrote the first half in the spring, at home.) Ruefully I noted then that I would possibly look back on those times as an idyll. I vowed to remember the difficulties. I have forgotten them now, however, and look back on those times as an idyll.

I slept until noon, as did my husband, who was also writing. I wrote once in the afternoon, and once again after our early dinner and a walk. During those months, I subsisted on that dinner, coffee, Coke, chocolate milk, and Vantage cigarettes.

I worked till midnight, one, or two. When I came home in the middle of the night I was tired; I longed for a tolerant giant, a person as big as a house, to hold me and rock me. In fact, an exhausted daydream—almost a hallucination—of being rocked and soothed sometimes forced itself upon me, and interrupted me even when I was talking or reading.

I had a room—a study carrel—in the Hollins College library, on the second floor. It was this room that overlooked a tar-and-gravel roof. A plate-glass window, beside me on the left, gave out onto the roof, a parking lot, a distant portion of Carvin Creek, some complicated Virginia sky, and a far hilltop where six cows grazed around a ruined foundation under red cedars.

From my desk I kept an eye out. Intriguing people, people I knew, pulled into the parking lot and climbed from their cars. The cows moved on the hilltop. (I drew the cows, for they were made interestingly; they hung in catenary curves from their skeletons, like two-man tents.) On the flat roof just outside the window, sparrows pecked gravel. One of the sparrows lacked a leg; one was missing a foot. If I stood and peered around, I could see a feeder creek run at the edge of a field. In the creek, even from that great distance, I could see muskrats and snapping turtles. If I saw a snapping turtle, I ran downstairs and out of the library to watch it or poke it.

One afternoon I made a pen drawing of the window and the landscape it framed. I drew the window's aluminum frame and steel hardware; I laid in the clouds, and the far hilltop with its ruined foundation and wandering cows. I outlined the parking lot and its tall row of mercury-vapor lights; I drew the cars, and the graveled rooftop foreground.

If I craned my head, I could see a grassy playing field below. One afternoon I peered around at that field and saw a softball game. Since I happened to have my fielder's glove with me in my study, I thought it would be the generous thing to join the game. On the field, I learned there was a music camp on campus for two weeks. The little boys playing softball were musical whizzes. They could not all play ball, but their patter was a treat. "All right, Macdonald," they jeered when one kid came to bat, "that pizzicato won't help you now." It was slightly better than no softball, so I played with them every day, second base, terrified that I would bust a prodigy's fingers on a throw to first or the plate.

I shut the blinds one day for good. I lowered the venetian blinds and flattened the slats. Then, by lamplight, I taped my drawing to the closed blind. There, on the drawing, was the window's view: cows, parking lot, hilltop, and sky. If I wanted a sense of the world, I could look at the stylized outline drawing. If I had possessed the skill, I would have painted, directly on the slats of the lowered blind, in meticulous colors, a *trompe l'oeil* mural view of all that the blinds hid. Instead, I wrote it.

On the Fourth of July, my husband and our friends drove into the city, Roanoke, to see the fireworks. I begged off; I wanted to keep working. I was working hard, although of course it did not seem hard enough at the time—a finished chapter every few weeks. I castigated myself daily for writing too slowly. Even when passages seemed to come easily, as though I were copying from a folio held open by smiling angels, the manuscript revealed the usual signs of struggle— bloodstains, teethmarks, gashes, and burns.

This night, as on most nights, I entered the library at dusk. The building was locked and dark. I had a key. Every night I let myself in, climbed the stairs, found my way between the tall stacks in the dark, located and unlocked my study's door, and turned on the light. I remembered how many stacks I had to hit with my hand in the dark before I turned down the row to my study. Even if I left only to get a drink of water, I felt and counted the stacks with my hand again to find my room. Once, in daylight, I glanced at a book on a stack's corner, a book I presumably touched every night with my hand. The book was *The World I Live In,* by Helen Keller. I read it at once: it surprised me by its strong and original prose.

When I flicked on my carrel light, there it all was: the bare room with yellow cinder-block walls; the big, flattened venetian blind and my drawing taped to it; two or three quotations taped up on index cards; and on a far table some ever-changing books, the fielder's mitt, and a yellow bag of chocolate-covered peanuts. There was the long, blond desk and its chair, and on the desk a dozen different-colored pens, some big index cards in careful, splayed piles, and my messy yellow legal pads. As soon as I saw that desktop, I remembered the task: the chapter, its problems, its phrases, its points.

This night I was concentrating on the chapter. The horizon of my consciousness was the contracted circle of yellow light inside my study—the lone lamp in the enormous, dark library. I leaned over the desk. I worked by hand. I doodled deliriously in the legal-pad margins. I fiddled with the index cards. I reread a sentence maybe a hundred times, and if I kept it I changed it seven or eight times, often substantially.

Now a June bug was knocking at my window. I was wrestling inside a sentence. I must have heard it a dozen times before it registered—before I noticed that I had been hearing a bug knock for half an hour. It made a hollow, bonking sound. Some people call the same fumbling, heavy insects "May beetles." It must have been attracted to my light—what little came between the slats of the blind. I dislike June bugs. Back to work. Knock again, knock again, and finally, to learn what monster of a fat, brown June bug could fly up to a second story and thump so insistently at my window as though it wanted admittance—at last, unthinkingly, I parted the venetian blind slats with my fingers, to look out.

And there were the fireworks, far away. It was the Fourth of July. I had forgotten. They were red and yellow, blue and green and white; they blossomed high in the black sky many miles away. The fireworks seemed as distant as the stars, but I could hear the late banging their bursting made. The sound, those bangs so muffled and out of sync, accompanied at random the silent, far sprays of color widening and raining down. It was the Fourth of July, and I had forgotten all of wide space and all of historical time. I opened the blinds a crack like eyelids, and it all came exploding in on me at once—oh yes, the world.

I have been looking into schedules. Even when we read physics, we inquire of each least particle, What then shall I do this morning? How we spend our days is, of course, how we spend our lives. What we do with this hour, and that one, is what we are doing. A schedule defends from chaos and whim. It is a net for catching days. It is a scaffolding on which a worker can stand and labor with both hands at sections of time. A schedule is a mock-up of reason and order—willed, faked, and so brought into being; it is a peace and a haven set into the wreck of time; it is a lifeboat on which you find yourself, decades later, still living. Each day is the same, so you remember the series afterward as a blurred and powerful pattern.

The most appealing daily schedule I know is that of a turn-of-the-century Danish aristocrat. He got up at four and set out on foot to hunt black grouse, wood grouse, woodcock, and snipe. At eleven he met his friends, who had also been out hunting alone all morning. They converged "at one of these babbling brooks," he wrote. He outlined the rest of his schedule. "Take a quick dip, relax with a schnapps and a sandwich, stretch out, have a smoke, take a nap or just rest, and then sit around and chat until three. Then I hunt some more until sundown, bathe again, put on white tie and tails to keep up appearances, eat a huge dinner, smoke a cigar and sleep like a log until the sun comes up again to redden the eastern sky. This is living. . . . Could it be more perfect?"

There is no shortage of good days. It is good lives that are hard to come by. A life of good days lived in the senses is not enough. The life of sensation is the life of greed; it requires more and more. The life of the spirit requires less and less; time is ample and its passage sweet. Who would call a day spent reading a good day? But a life spent reading—that is a good life. A day that closely resembles every other day of the past ten or twenty years does not suggest itself as a good one. But who would not call Pasteur's life a good one, or Thomas Mann's?

Wallace Stevens in his forties, living in Hartford, Connecticut, hewed to a productive routine. He rose at six, read for two hours, and walked another hour—three miles—to work. He dictated poems to his secretary. He ate no lunch; at noon he walked for another hour, often to an art gallery. He walked home from work—another hour. After dinner he retired to his study; he went to bed at nine. On Sundays, he walked in the park. I don't know what he did on Saturdays. Perhaps he exchanged a few words with his wife, who posed for the Liberty dime. (One would rather read these people, or lead their lives, than be their wives. When the Danish aristocrat Wilhelm Dinesen shot birds all day, drank schnapps, napped, and dressed for dinner, he and his wife had three children under three. The middle one was Karen.)

Like Stevens, Osip Mandelstam composed poetry on the hoof. So did Dante. Nietzsche, like Emerson, took two long walks a day. "When my creative energy flowed most freely, my muscular activity was always greatest. . . . I might often have been seen dancing; I used to walk through the hills for seven or eight hours on end without a hint of fatigue; I slept well, laughed a good deal—I was perfectly vigorous and patient." On the other hand, A. E. Housman, almost predictably, maintained, "I have seldom written poetry unless I was rather out of health." This makes sense too, because writing a book, you can be too well for your own good.

Jack London claimed to write twenty hours a day. Before he undertook to write, he obtained the University of California course list and all the syllabi; he spent a year reading the textbooks in philosophy and literature. In subsequent years, once he had a book of his own under way, he set his alarm to wake him after four hours' sleep. Often he slept through the alarm, so, by his own account, he rigged it to drop a weight on his head. I cannot say I believe this, though a novel like *The Sea-Wolf* is strong evidence that some sort of weight fell on his head with some sort of frequency—but you wouldn't think a man would claim credit for it. London maintained that every writer needed a technique, experience, and a philosophical position. Perhaps the position need not be an airtight one; London himself felt comfortable with a weird amalgam of Karl Marx and Herbert Spencer (Marks & Sparks).

My working the graveyard shift in Virginia affected the book. It was a nature book full of sunsets; it wholly lacked dawns, and even mornings.

I was reading, among other things, Hasidism. If you stay awake one hundred nights, you get the vision of Elijah—the same revelation, earthquake and all. I was not eager for it, although it seemed to be just around the corner. I preferred this: "Rebbe Shmelke of Nickolsburg, it was told, never really heard his teacher, the Maggid of Mezritch, finish a thought because as soon as the latter would say 'and the Lord spoke,' Shmelke would begin shouting in wonderment, 'The Lord spoke, the Lord spoke,' and continue shouting until he had to be carried from the room."

The second floor of the library, where I worked every night, housed the rare-book room. It was a wide, carpeted, well-furnished room. On an end table, as if for decoration, stood a wooden chess set.

One night, stuck on an intractable problem in the writing, I wandered the dark library seeking distraction. I flicked on the lights in the rare-book room and looked at some of the books. I saw the chess set and moved white's king's pawn. I turned off the light and wandered back to my carrel.

A few nights later, I glanced into the rare-book room, and walked in, for black's queen's pawn had moved. I moved out my knight.

Every day, my unseen opponent moved. I moved. I never

saw anyone anywhere near the rare-book room. The college was not in session; almost no one was around. Late at night I heard the night watchmen clank around downstairs in the dark. The watchmen never came upstairs. There was no one upstairs but me.

When the chess game was ten days old, I entered the rare-book room to find black's pieces coming toward me on the carpet. They seemed to be marching, in rows of two. I put them back as they had been, and made my move. The next day, the pieces were all pied on the board. I put them back as they had been. The next day, black had moved, rather brilliantly.

Late one night, while all this had been going on, and while the library was dark and locked as it had been all summer, and I had accustomed myself to the eeriness of it, I left my carrel to cross the darkness and get a drink of water. I saw a strange chunk of light on the floor between stacks. Passing the stacks, I saw the light spread across the hall. I held my breath. The light was coming from the rare-book room; the door was open.

I approached quietly, and looked in the room from an angle. There, at the chess table, stood a baby. The baby had blond curls and was wearing only a diaper.

I paused, considering that I had been playing a reasonable game of chess for two weeks with a naked baby. After a while I could make out the sound of voices; I moved closer to the doorway and peered in. There was the young head librarian and his wife, sitting on chairs. I pieced together the rest of it. The librarian stopped by to pick something up. Naturally, he had a key. The couple happened to have the baby along. The baby, just learning to walk, had cruised from the chairs to the table. The baby was holding on to the table, not studying the chess pieces' positions. I greeted the family and played with the baby until they left.

I never did learn who or what was playing chess with me.

The game went on until my lunatic opponent scrambled the board so violently the game was over.

During that time, I let all the houseplants die. After the book was finished I noticed them; the plants hung completely black dead in their pots in the bay window. For I had not only let them die, I had not moved them. During that time, I told all my out-of-town friends they could not visit for a while.

"I understand you're married," a man said to me at a formal lunch in New York my publisher had arranged. "How do you have time to write a book?"

Sir?

"Well," he said, "you have to have a garden, for instance. You have to entertain." And I thought he was foolish, this man in his seventies, who had no idea what you must do. But the fanaticism of my twenties shocks me now. As I feared it would.

Chapter Three

Another day, another dollar;
fourteen hours on snowshoes and wish I had pie.
—FROM A MAINE TRAPPER'S DIARY

ONCE, in order to finish a book I was writing and yet not
live in the same room with it, I begged a cabin to use as a
study. I finished the book there, wrote some other things, and
learned to split wood. All this was on a remote and sparsely
populated island on Haro Strait, where I moved when I left
Virginia. The island was in northern Puget Sound, Washington State, across the water from Canadian islands.

The cabin was a single small room near the water. Its walls
were shrunken planks, not insulated; in January, February,
and March, it was cold. There were two small metal beds in
the room, two cupboards, some shelves over a little counter,
a wood stove, and a table under a window, where I wrote. The
window looked out on a bit of sandflat overgrown with thick,
varicolored mosses; there were a few small firs where the
sandflat met the cobble beach; and there was the water: Puget
Sound, and all the sky over it and all the other wild islands in
the distance under the sky. It was very grand. But you get used
to it. I don't much care where I work. I don't notice things.
The door used to blow open and startle me witless. I did,
however, notice the cold.

I tried to heat the cabin with the wood stove and a kerosene heater, but I never was warm. I used to work wearing a wool cap, long wool tights, sweaters, a down jacket, and a scarf. I was too lazy to stick a damper in the wood stove chimney; I kept putting off the task for a warm day. Thoreau said that his firewood warmed him twice—because he labored to cut his own. Mine froze me twice, for the same reason. After I learned to split wood, in a manner I am shortly to relate—after I learned to split wood, I stepped out into the brute northeaster and split just enough alder to last me through working hours, which was not enough splitting to warm me. Then I came in and kindled a fire in the stove, all the heat of which vanished up the chimney.

At first, in the good old days, I did not know how to split wood. I set a chunk of alder on the chopping block and harassed it, at enormous exertion, into tiny wedges that flew all over the sandflat and lost themselves. What I did was less like splitting wood than chipping flints. After a few whacks my alder chunk still stood serene and unmoved, its base untouched, its tip a thorn. And then I actually tried to turn the sorry thing over and balance it on its wee head while I tried to chop its feet off before it fell over. God save us.

All this was a very warm process. I removed my down jacket, my wool hat and scarf. Alas, those early wood-splitting days, when I truly warmed myself, didn't last long. I lost the knack.

I did not know it at the time, but during those first weeks when I attacked my wood every morning, I was collecting a crowd—or what passed on the island for a crowd. At the sound of my ax, Doe and Bob—real islanders, proper, wood-splitting islanders—paused in their activities and mustered, unseen, across the sandflat, under the firs. They were watching me (oh, the idleness) try to split wood. It must have been a largely silent comedy. Later, when they confessed, and I railed at them, Bob said innocently that the single remark he had ever permitted himself had been, "I love to watch Annie split wood."

One night, while all this had been going on, I had a dream in which I was given to understand, by the powers that be, how to split wood. You aim, said the dream—of course!—at the chopping block. It is true. You aim at the chopping block, not at the wood; then you split the wood, instead of chipping it. You cannot do the job cleanly unless you treat the wood as the transparent means to an end, by aiming past it. But then, alas, you easily split your day's wood in a few minutes, in the freezing cold, without working up any heat; then you utterly forfeit your only chance of getting warm.

The knack of splitting wood was the only useful thing I had ever learned from any dream, and my attitude toward the powers that be was not entirely grateful. The island comedy was over; everybody had to go back to work; and I never did get warm.

Much has been written about the life of the mind. I find the phrase itself markedly dreamy. The mind of the writer does indeed do something before it dies, and so does its owner, but I would be hard put to call it living.

It should surprise no one that the life of the writer—such as it is—is colorless to the point of sensory deprivation. Many writers do little else but sit in small rooms recalling the real world. This explains why so many books describe the author's childhood. A writer's childhood may well have been the occasion of his only firsthand experience. Writers read literary biography, and surround themselves with other writers, deliberately to enforce in themselves the ludicrous notion that a reasonable option for occupying yourself on the planet until your life span plays itself out is sitting in a small room for the duration, in the company of pieces of paper.

Inside the small room, the writer is deeply preoccupied with things hitherto undreamed of. He finds himself inventing wholly new techniques in the service of his art.

Once, for instance, I had an office in the halls of a university English department, which was of course deserted nights and weekends. There I began writing a terrifically abstract book of literary and aesthetic theory. The kindly secretaries gave me a key to the faculty lounge so I could boil water for coffee at odd hours. The faculty lounge was around the corner and out of my earshot; it had a sink, a single stove burner, and a teakettle. The first night I used this arrangement I forgot all about the water I was boiling and scorched the kettle. It smelled terrible, and I confessed the next day. The secretaries said they would give me another chance.

It was an interesting kettle. Life is so interesting. It was a whistling kettle, but the secretaries did not want it to whistle, so they jammed the circular, perforated lid of an old percolator in its mouth. This aluminum lid became a hot item in the teeth of all that steam, so someone had devised a method of removing it with a springy wooden clothespin. Perhaps that same someone had carried the clothespin to the office for that purpose. Pretty soon people simply left the clothespin clamped on the aluminum percolator lid, which in turn jutted from the kettle's mouth. That is how things were when I got there.

After I burned the kettle, I had to discover a method to remind myself that I had water boiling on the stove in the faculty lounge, so I stuck the clothespin on my finger. It was, as it happened, a strong clothespin, and I had to move it every twenty seconds. This action, and the pain, kept me in the real world until the water actually boiled. This was the theory, and it worked. So that is how I wrote those nights, wrote a book about high holy art: moving a clothespin up and down my increasingly reddened little finger. Why people want to be writers I will never know, unless it is that their lives lack a material footing.

The materiality of the writer's life cannot be exaggerated. If you like metaphysics, throw pots. How fondly I recall thinking, in the old days, that to write you needed paper, pen, and a lap. How appalled I was to discover that, in order to write so much as a sonnet, you need a warehouse. You can easily get so confused writing a thirty-page chapter that in order to make an outline for the second draft, you have to rent a hall. I have often "written" with the mechanical aid of a twenty-foot conference table. You lay your pages along the table's edge and pace out the work. You walk along the rows; you weed bits, move bits, and dig out bits, bent over the rows with full hands like a gardener. After a couple of hours, you have taken an exceedingly dull nine-mile hike. You go home and soak your feet.

Remarkably material also is the writer's attempt to control his own energies so he can work. He must be sufficiently excited to rouse himself to the task at hand, and not so excited he cannot sit down to it. He must have faith sufficient to impel and renew the work, yet not so much faith he fancies he is writing well when he is not.

For writing a first draft requires from the writer a peculiar internal state which ordinary life does not induce. If you were a Zulu warrior banging on your shield with your spear for a couple of hours along with a hundred other Zulu warriors, you might be able to prepare yourself to write. If you were an Aztec maiden who knew months in advance that on a certain morning the priests were going to throw you into a hot volcano, and if you spent those months undergoing a series of purification rituals and drinking dubious liquids, you might, when the time came, be ready to write. But how, if you are neither Zulu warrior nor Aztec maiden, do you prepare yourself, all alone, to enter an extraordinary state on an ordinary morning?

How set yourself spinning? Where is an edge—a dangerous edge—and where is the trail to the edge and the strength to climb it?

*   *   *

Once I wrote a favorite, difficult book, a true account of three consecutive days on an island on the northwest coast. I began the book on one island and wrote most of it on another island; it took a long time. Much of it I wrote as poetry. Its two subjects were the relation of eternity to time and the problem of suffering innocents. The prose—once I decided to print it as prose—was so intense and accented, and the world it described was so charged with meaning, that the very thought of writing a word or two further made me tired. How could I add a sentence, or a paragraph, every day to this work I myself could barely understand? Its tone was fierce and exhilarated. Every time I looked at its part of the room, I got sleepy. I could not just pick up my shovel and walk to the mine. I could not add a word until I was ready, or that word would enfeeble or puncture the work.

On a ship near a coast, I had once seen a heavy-bodied moth panting. The moth stood on the ship's rail beside me and faced the water. It was a sphinx moth, a thick diurnal moth with tiny wings; people often mistake sphinx moths for hummingbirds. In order for them to fly at all, they must supercharge their flight muscles with oxygen. A resting state will not suffice. Beside me on the rail, the sphinx moth raced its engines for takeoff like a jet on a runway. I could see its brown body vibrate and its red-and-black wings tremble. I left its side to fetch drawing paper from my cabin. When I returned, it was still revving up.

Maybe I scared it. After trembling so violently that it seemed it must blow apart, the moth took flight. Its wings blurred, like a hummingbird's. It flew a few yards out over the water before it began losing altitude. It was going down. Its wings buzzed; it gained height and lost, gained and lost, and always lost more than it gained, until its heavy body dragged in the water, and it drowned before my eyes without a splash.

During some of the long, empty months at work on the book, I was living in a one-room log cabin on an empty beach. I had not yet borrowed the freezing cabin up the beach to use as a study; I did not yet know how foolish it was to plan days of solitary confinement, days in which my only activity was walking four or five feet from the bed to the desk. My husband wrote his book in another cabin; he worked much longer hours than I could. When my husband left after breakfast, I looked around the one-room cabin and out at the water and strip of beach. Nothing changed but the tides. Sometimes the empty beach was wide, and sometimes it was narrow. I could see it all from the bed, even on the darkest nights. The bed faced the beach and the water, and so did the desk; so did the table, and so did the sink. The whole house was a ship's rail. I turned to the work. This book interested me more passionately than any other. The task was to change intellectual passion to physical energy and some sort of narrative mastery, from a standing start.

"Bring on the lions!" I cried.

But there were no lions. I spent every day in the company of one dog and one cat whose every gesture emphasized that this was a day throughout whose duration intelligent creatures intended to sleep. I would have to crank myself up.

To crank myself up I stood on a jack and ran myself up. I tightened myself like a bolt. I inserted myself in a vise-clamp and wound the handle till the pressure built. I drank coffee in titrated doses. It was a tricky business, requiring the finely tuned judgment of a skilled anesthesiologist. There was a tiny range within which coffee was effective, short of which it was useless, and beyond which, fatal.

I pointed myself. I walked to the water. I played the hateful recorder, washed dishes, drank coffee, stood on a beach log, watched bird. That was the first part; it could take all morning, or all month. Only the coffee counted, and I knew it. It was boiled Colombian coffee: raw grounds brought just to boiling in cold water and stirred. Now I smoked a cigarette or two and read what I wrote yesterday. What I wrote yesterday needed to be slowed down. I inserted words in one sentence and hazarded a new sentence. At once I noticed that I was writ-ing—which, as the novelist Frederick Buechner noted, called for a break, if not a full-scale celebration.

On break, I usually read Conrad Aiken's poetry aloud. It was pure sound unencumbered by sense. If I ever caught a poem's sense by accident, I could never use that poem again. I often read the Senlin poems, and "Sea Holly." Some days I read part of any poetry anthology's index of first lines. The parallels sounded strong and suggestive. They could set me off, perhaps.

This morning, as on so many mornings, I lacked sufficient fuel for liftoff. I looked at the legal pad pages again. A new section must be begun in the book, and a place found to put it. I wrote four or five sentences on a gamble, smoked more to stimulate the brain or stop the heart, whichever came first, and reheated a fourth mug of coffee. After the first boiling, the grounds sink to the coffeepot's bottom. When you reheat it, you call it refried coffee. I already felt like the empty kettle on a hot burner, the thin kettle whose water had boiled away. The top of my stomach felt bruised or burned—was this how mus-tard gas tasted? I drank the fourth mug without looking at it, any more than you look at the needle in a doctor's hand.

Now, alas, I had cranked too far. I could no longer play the recorder; I would need a bugle. I would break a piano. What could I do around the cabin? There was no wood to split. There was something I needed to fix with a hacksaw, but I rejected the work as too fine. Why not adopt a baby, design a curriculum, go sailing?

The dog opened one eye, cocked it at me, and rolled it up before her lids closed. People should not feed moralistic ani-mals. If they're so holy, where are their books? I was starving, but eating was out of the question. Nausea might temper this energy, but eating would kill it.

I read it again. Reading, I drew all over it. This was usual. Now my drawings tightened and darkened; I pressed them into the paper. They were digging through the paper and into the desk. Where next? I knew where next. It was within my possibilities. If only I could concentrate. I must quit. I was too young to be living at a desk. Many fine people were out there living, people whose consciences permitted them to sleep at night despite their not having written a decent sentence that day, or ever.

Let's dance. I could not draw the lamp any more; it was too little. I walked out on the beach unseeing and fell back in the door, sick, dead, dying. I heated a bowl of soup which I ate blinded by coffee and nicotine, unremembering. I returned to the papers and enclosed a paragraph in parentheses; it meant that tomorrow I would delete the few sentences I wrote today. Too many days of this, I thought, too many days of this.

I do not so much write a book as sit up with it, as with a dying friend. During visiting hours, I enter its room with dread and sympathy for its many disorders. I hold its hand and hope it will get better.

This tender relationship can change in a twinkling. If you skip a visit or two, a work in progress will turn on you.

A work in progress quickly becomes feral. It reverts to a wild state overnight. It is barely domesticated, a mustang on which you one day fastened a halter, but which now you cannot catch. It is a lion you cage in your study. As the work grows, it gets harder to control; it is a lion growing in strength. You must visit it every day and reassert your mastery over it. If you skip a day, you are, quite rightly, afraid to open the door to its room. You enter its room with bravura, holding a chair at the thing and shouting, "Simba!"

Living thus—with your lion tamer's chair, your ax, your conference table, and your clothespin—you may excite in your fellow man not curiosity but profound indifference. It is not my experience that society hates and fears the writer, or that society adulates the writer. Instead my experience is the common one, that society places the writer so far beyond the pale that society does not regard the writer at all.

Whenever an encounter between a writer of good will and a regular person of good will happens to touch on the subject of writing, each person discovers, dismayed, that good will is of no earthly use. The conversation cannot proceed. From such chastening encounters I have always learned far more than I intended.

Once, for example, I learned from a conversation with a neighbor that I had been living as it were in a fool's paragraph.

This neighbor, who crewed on a ferryboat, was one of the world's good, sane people. He was the local sheriff. He was an emergency medical technician, a volunteer fireman, a husband and father, and an unequaled contributor of witty remarks into the window of each car that rolled on and off the ferry. May his tribe increase.

One rainy day, this member of the real world gave me a ride home. I invited him in for a minute, and somehow all hell broke loose.

Politely, he asked me about my writing. Foolishly, not dreaming I was about to set my own world tumbling down about my ears, I said I hated to write. I said I would rather do anything else. He was amazed. He said, "That's like a guy who works in a factory all day, and hates it." Then I was amazed, for so it was. It was *just* like that. Why did I do it? I had never inquired. How had I let it creep up on me? Why wasn't I running a ferryboat, like sane people?

I hid my amazement as well as I could from both of us, and said that actually I avoided writing, and mostly what I did by way of work was fool around, and that for example that morning I had been breaking my brain trying to explain Whitehead to my journal. Why, he wanted to know, was I doing that? Again I stopped completely short; I could not imagine why on earth I was doing that. Why was I doing that?

But I rallied and mustered and said that the idea was to learn things; that you learn a thing and then as a matter of course you learn the next thing, and the next thing. . . . As I spoke he nodded precisely in the way that one nods at the utterances of the deranged. ". . . And then," I finished brightly, "you die!"

At this we exchanged a mutual and enormous smile. Still nodding and smiling in perfect agreement, we ended the visit and walked to the door.

A week later I had a visit so instructive that when it was over, and I had fully absorbed its lesson, I considered never opening my door again. This was a visit from children.

During the week after the ferryman's visit, I asked myself where my life had gone wrong. I was too far removed from the world. My work was too obscure, too symbolic, too intellectual. It was not available to people. Recently I had published a complex narrative essay about a moth's flying into a candle, which no one had understood but a Yale critic, and he had understood it exactly. I myself was trained as a critic. I was a critic writing for critics: was this what I had in mind?

One day, full of such thoughts, I tried to work and failed. After eight hours of watching helplessly while my own inane, manneristic doodles overstepped their margins and covered the pages I was supposed to be writing, I gave up. I decided to hate myself, to make popcorn and read. I had just sunk into the couch, the bowl of popcorn beside me, when I heard footsteps outside. It was two little neighborhood boys, Brad and Brian, who were seven and six. "Smells good in here," Brian said. So we ate the bowl of popcorn on the floor and talked. They played the harmonica; they played the recorder; they played the ukulele.

Then Brian got up and stood by my desk, on which there happened to be a pen drawing of a burning candle.

Brian said, "Is that the candle the moth flew into?"

I looked at him: WHAT?

He said, and I quote exactly, "Is that the candle the moth flew into, and his abdomen got stuck, and his head caught fire?"

WHAT? I said. WHAT? These little blue-jeaned kids were in the first grade. They came up to my pockets. Brad, on the floor, piped up, "I liked that story." Why, if I was sincere in anything, did it seem to console me to repeat to myself, "Oh well, he's older"?

Later, before they left, Brian made certain I understood that whatever sphere of discourse I fancied I shared with any interlocutor, I was wrong. Brian said (admiringly, I thought), "Did you *write* that story?" I started to answer, when he continued, "Or did you type it?"

Here is a fairly sober version of what happens in the small room between the writer and the work itself. It is similar to what happens between a painter and the canvas.

First you shape the vision of what the projected work of art will be. The vision, I stress, is no marvelous thing: it is the work's intellectual structure and aesthetic surface. It is a chip of mind, a pleasing intellectual object. It is a vision of the work, not of the world. It is a glowing thing, a blurred thing of beauty. Its structure is at once luminous and translucent; you can see the world through it. After you receive the initial charge of this imaginary object, you add to it at once several aspects, and incubate it most gingerly as it grows into itself.

Many aspects of the work are still uncertain, of course; you know that. You know that if you proceed you will change things and learn things, that the form will grow under your hands and develop new and richer lights. But that change will not alter the vision or its deep structures; it will only enrich it. You know that, and you are right.

But you are wrong if you think that in the actual writing, or in the actual painting, you are filling in the vision. You cannot fill in the vision. You cannot even bring the vision to light. You are wrong if you think that you can in any way take the vision and tame it to the page. The page is jealous and tyrannical; the page is made of time and matter; the page always wins. The vision is not so much destroyed, exactly, as it is, by the time you have finished, forgotten. It has been replaced by this changeling, this bastard, this opaque lightless chunky ruinous work.

Here is how it happens. The vision is, *sub specie aeternitatis,* a set of mental relationships, a coherent series of formal possibilities. In the actual rooms of time, however, it is a page or two of legal paper filled with words and questions; it is a terrible diagram, a few books' names in a margin, an ambiguous doodle, a corner folded down in a library book. These are memos from the thinking brain to witless hope.

Nevertheless, ignoring the provisional and pathetic nature of these scraps, and bearing the vision itself in mind—having it before your sights like the very Grail—you begin to scratch out the first faint marks on the canvas, on the page. You begin the work proper. Now you have gone and done it. Now the thing is no longer a vision: it is paper.

Words lead to other words and down the garden path. You adjust the paints' values and hues not to the world, not to the vision, but to the rest of the paint. The materials are stubborn and rigid; push is always coming to shove. You can fly—you can fly higher than you thought possible—but you can never get off the page. After every passage another passage follows, more sentences, more everything on drearily down. Time and materials hound the work; the vision recedes ever farther into the dim realms.

And so you continue the work, and finish it. Probably by now you have been forced to toss the most essential part of the vision. But this is a concern for mere nostalgia now: for before your eyes, and stealing your heart, is this fighting and frail finished product, entirely opaque. You can see nothing through it. It is only itself, a series of well-known passages, some colored paint. Its relationship to the vision that impelled it is the relationship between any energy and any work, anything unchanging to anything temporal.

The work is not the vision itself, certainly. It is not the vision filled in, as if it had been a coloring book. It is not the vision reproduced in time; that were impossible. It is rather a simulacrum and a replacement. It is a golem. You try—you try every time—to reproduce the vision, to let your light so shine before men. But you can only come along with your bushel and hide it.

Who will teach me to write? a reader wanted to know.

The page, the page, that eternal blankness, the blankness of eternity which you cover slowly, affirming time's scrawl as a right and your daring as necessity; the page, which you cover woodenly, ruining it, but asserting your freedom and power to act, acknowledging that you ruin everything you touch but touching it nevertheless, because acting is better than being here in mere opacity; the page, which you cover slowly with the crabbed thread of your gut; the page in the purity of its possibilities; the page of your death, against which you pit such flawed excellences as you can muster with all your life's strength: that page will teach you to write.

There is another way of saying this. Aim for the chopping block. If you aim for the wood, you will have nothing. Aim past the wood, aim through the wood; aim for the chopping block.

Chapter Four

*To be buried in lava and not turn a hair, it is
then a man shows what stuff he is made of.*
—BECKETT, *Malone Dies*

WHAT IS THIS WRITING LIFE? I was living alone in a house
once, and had set up a study on the first floor. A portable green
Smith-Corona typewriter sat on the table against the wall. I
made the mistake of leaving the room.

I was upstairs when I felt the first tremor. The floor wagged
under my feet—what was that?—and the picture frames on the
wall stirred. The house shook and made noise. There was a
pause; I found my face in the dresser mirror, deadpan. When
the floor began again to sway, I walked downstairs, thinking
I had better get down while the stairway held.

I saw at once that the typewriter was erupting. The old
green Smith-Corona typewriter on the table was exploding
with fire and ash. Showers of sparks shot out of its caldera—the
dark hollow in which the keys lie. Smoke and cinders poured
out, noises exploded and spattered, black dense smoke rose
up, and a wild, deep fire lighted the whole thing. It shot
sparks.

I pulled down the curtains. When I leaned over the typewriter, sparks burnt round holes in my shirt, and fire singed

a sleeve. I dragged the rug away from the sparks. In the kitchen I filled a bucket with water and returned to the erupting typewriter. The typewriter did not seem to be flying apart, only erupting. On my face and hands I felt the heat from the caldera. The yellow fire made a fast, roaring noise. The typewriter itself made a rumbling, grinding noise; the table pitched. Nothing seemed to require my bucket of water. The table surface was ruined, of course, but not aflame. After twenty minutes or so, the eruption subsided.

That night I heard more rumblings—weak ones, ever farther apart. The next day I cleaned the typewriter, table, floor, wall, and ceiling. I threw away the burnt shirt. The following day I cleaned the typewriter again—a film of lampblack still coated the caldera—and then it was over. I have had no trouble with it since. Of course, now I know it can happen.

Chapter Five

*One cannot be too scrupulous, too sincere, too
submissive before nature . . . but one ought to be more
or less master of one's model.* —CEZANNE

PEOPLE LOVE PRETTY MUCH the same things best. A
writer looking for subjects inquires not after what he loves
best, but after what he alone loves at all. Strange seizures beset
us. Frank Conroy loves his yo-yo tricks, Emily Dickinson her
slant of light; Richard Selzer loves the glistening peritoneum,
Faulkner the muddy bottom of a little girl's drawers visible
when she's up a pear tree. "Each student of the ferns," I read,
"will have his own list of plants that for some reason or another stir his emotions."

Why do you never find anything written about that idiosyncratic thought you advert to, about your fascination with
something no one else understands? Because it is up to you.
There is something you find interesting, for a reason hard to
explain. It is hard to explain because you have never read it
on any page; there you begin. You were made and set here
to give voice to this, your own astonishment. "The most de-
manding part of living a lifetime as an artist is the strict discipline of forcing oneself to work steadfastly along the nerve of
one's own most intimate sensitivity." Anne Truitt, the sculp-

tor, said this. Thoreau said it another way: know your own bone. "Pursue, keep up with, circle round and round your life. . . . Know your own bone: gnaw at it, bury it, unearth it, and gnaw at it still."

Write as if you were dying. At the same time, assume you write for an audience consisting solely of terminal patients. That is, after all, the case. What would you begin writing if you knew you would die soon? What could you say to a dying person that would not enrage by its triviality?

Write about winter in the summer. Describe Norway as Ibsen did, from a desk in Italy; describe Dublin as James Joyce did, from a desk in Paris. Willa Cather wrote her prairie novels in New York City; Mark Twain wrote *Huckleberry Finn* in Hartford, Connecticut. Recently, scholars learned that Walt Whitman rarely left his room.

The writer studies literature, not the world. He lives in the world; he cannot miss it. If he has ever bought a hamburger, or taken a commercial airplane flight, he spares his readers a report of his experience. He is careful of what he reads, for that is what he will write. He is careful of what he learns, because that is what he will know.

The writer knows his field—what has been done, what could be done, the limits—the way a tennis player knows the court. And like that expert, he, too, plays the edges. That is where the exhilaration is. He hits up the line. In writing, he can push the edges. Beyond this limit, here, the reader must recoil. Reason balks, poetry snaps; some madness enters, or strain. Now, courageously and carefully, can he enlarge it, can he nudge the bounds? And enclose what wild power?

The body of literature, with its limits and edges, exists outside some people and inside others. Only after the writer lets literature shape her can she perhaps shape literature. In working-class France, when an apprentice got hurt, or when he got tired, the experienced workers said, "It is the trade entering his body." The art must enter the body, too. A

painter cannot use paint like glue or screws to fasten down the
world. The tubes of paint are like fingers; they work only if,
inside the painter, the neural pathways are wide and clear to
the brain. Cell by cell, molecule by molecule, atom by atom,
part of the brain changes physical shape to accommodate and
fit paint.

You adapt yourself, Paul Klee said, to the contents of the
paintbox. Adapting yourself to the contents of the paintbox,
he said, is more important than nature and its study. The
painter, in other words, does not fit the paints to the world.
He most certainly does not fit the world to himself. He fits
himself to the paint. The self is the servant who bears the
paintbox and its inherited contents. Klee called this insight,
quite rightly, "an altogether revolutionary new discovery."

A well-known writer got collared by a university student
who asked, "Do you think I could be a writer?"

"Well," the writer said, "I don't know. . . . Do you like
sentences?"

The writer could see the student's amazement. Sentences?
Do I like sentences? I am twenty years old and do I like
sentences? If he had liked sentences, of course, he could
begin, like a joyful painter I knew. I asked him how he came
to be a painter. He said, "I liked the smell of the paint."

Hemingway studied, as models, the novels of Knut Hamsun
and Ivan Turgenev. Isaac Bashevis Singer, as it happened, also
chose Hamsun and Turgenev as models. Ralph Ellison studied
Hemingway and Gertrude Stein. Thoreau loved Homer;
Eudora Welty loved Chekhov. Faulkner described his debt to
Sherwood Anderson and Joyce; E. M. Forster, his debt to Jane
Austen and Proust. By contrast, if you ask a twenty-one-year-
old poet whose poetry he likes, he might say, unblushing,
"Nobody's." In his youth, he has not yet understood that
poets like poetry, and novelists like novels; he himself likes
only the role, the thought of himself in a hat. Rembrandt and

Shakespeare, Tolstoy and Gauguin, possessed, I believe, powerful hearts, not powerful wills. They loved the range of materials they used. The work's possibilities excited them; the field's complexities fired their imaginations. The caring suggested the tasks; the tasks suggested the schedules. They learned their fields and then loved them. They worked, respectfully, out of their love and knowledge, and they produced complex bodies of work that endure. Then, and only then, the world flapped at them some sort of hat, which, if they were still living, they ignored as well as they could, to keep at their tasks.

It makes more sense to write one big book—a novel or nonfiction narrative—than to write many stories or essays. Into a long, ambitious project you can fit or pour all you possess and learn. A project that takes five years will accumulate those years' inventions and richnesses. Much of those years' reading will feed the work. Further, writing sentences is difficult whatever their subject. It is no less difficult to write sentences in a recipe than sentences in *Moby-Dick.* So you might as well write *Moby-Dick.* Similarly, since every original work requires a unique form, it is more prudent to struggle with the outcome of only one form—that of a long work—than to struggle with the many forms of a collection. Each chapter of a prolonged narrative is problematic too, of course, and the writer undergoes trials as the structure collapses and coheres by turns—but at least the labor is not all on spec. The chapter already has a context: a tone, setting, characters. The work is already off the ground. You must carry the reader along, but you need not, after the first chapters, bear him aloft while performing a series of tricky introductions.

Writing every book, the writer must solve two problems: Can it be done? and, Can I do it? Every book has an intrinsic impossibility, which its writer discovers as soon as his first excitement dwindles. The problem is structural; it is insoluble;

it is why no one can ever write this book. Complex stories, essays, and poems have this problem, too—the prohibitive structural defect the writer wishes he had never noticed. He writes it in spite of that. He finds ways to minimize the difficulty; he strengthens other virtues; he cantilevers the whole narrative out into thin air, and it holds. And if it can be done, then he can do it, and only he. For there is nothing in the material for this book that suggests to anyone but him alone its possibilities for meaning and feeling.

Why are we reading, if not in hope of beauty laid bare, life heightened and its deepest mystery probed? Can the writer isolate and vivify all in experience that most deeply engages our intellects and our hearts? Can the writer renew our hope for literary forms? Why are we reading if not in hope that the writer will magnify and dramatize our days, will illuminate and inspire us with wisdom, courage, and the possibility of meaningfulness, and will press upon our minds the deepest mysteries, so we may feel again their majesty and power? What do we ever know that is higher than that power which, from time to time, seizes our lives, and reveals us startlingly to ourselves as creatures set down here bewildered? Why does death so catch us by surprise, and why love? We still and always want waking. We should amass half dressed in long lines like tribesmen and shake gourds at each other, to wake up; instead we watch television and miss the show.

And if we are reading for these things, why would anyone read books with advertising slogans and brand names in them? Why would anyone write such books? Commercial intrusion has overrun and crushed, like the last glaciation, a humane landscape. The new landscape and its climate put metaphysics on the run. Must writers collaborate? Well, in fact, the novel as a form has only rarely been metaphysical; it usually presents society. The novel often aims to fasten down the spirit of its time, to make a heightened simulacrum of our recognizable world in order to present it shaped and analyzed. This has never seemed to me worth doing, but it is certainly one thing literature has always done. (Any writer draws idiosyncratic boundaries in the field.) Writers attracted to metaphysics can simply ignore the commercial blare, as if it were a radio, or use historical settings, or flee to nonfiction or poetry. Writers might even, with their eyes wide open, redeem the commercial claptrap from within the novel, using it not just as a quick, cheap, and perfunctory background but—as Updike did in *Rabbit Is Rich*—as part of the world subject to a broad and sanctifying vision.

The sensation of writing a book is the sensation of spinning, blinded by love and daring. It is the sensation of rearing and peering from the bent tip of a grass blade, looking for a route. At its absurd worst, it feels like what mad Jacob Boehme, the German mystic, described in his first book. He was writing, incoherently as usual, about the source of evil. The passage will serve as well for the source of books.

"The whole Deity has in its innermost or beginning Birth, in the Pith or Kernel, a very tart, terrible *Sharpness,* in which the astringent Quality is very horrible, tart, hard, dark and cold Attraction or Drawing together, like *Winter,* when there is a fierce, bitter cold Frost, when Water is frozen into Ice, and besides is very intolerable."

If you can dissect out the very intolerable, tart, hard, terribly sharp Pith or Kernel, and begin writing the book compressed therein, the sensation changes. Now it feels like alligator wrestling, at the level of the sentence.

This is your life. You are a Seminole alligator wrestler. Half naked, with your two bare hands, you hold and fight a sentence's head while its tail tries to knock you over. Several years ago in Florida, an alligator wrestler lost. He was grappling with an alligator in a lagoon in front of a paying crowd. The crowd watched the young Indian and the alligator twist belly to belly in and out of the water; after one plunge, they failed to rise. A young writer named Lorne Ladner described it.

Bubbles came up on the water. Then blood came up, and the water stilled. As the minutes elapsed, the people in the crowd exchanged glances; silent, helpless, they quit the stands. It took the Indians a week to find the man's remains.

At its best, the sensation of writing is that of any unmerited grace. It is handed to you, but only if you look for it. You search, you break your heart, your back, your brain, and then—and only then—it is handed to you. From the corner of your eye you see motion. Something is moving through the air and headed your way. It is a parcel bound in ribbons and bows; it has two white wings. It flies directly at you; you can read your name on it. If it were a baseball, you would hit it out of the park. It is that one pitch in a thousand you see in slow motion; its wings beat slowly as a hawk's.

One line of a poem, the poet said—only one line, but thank God for that one line—drops from the ceiling. Thornton Wilder cited this unnamed writer of sonnets: one line of a sonnet falls from the ceiling, and you tap in the others around it with a jeweler's hammer. Nobody whispers it in your ear. It is like something you memorized once and forgot. Now it comes back and rips away your breath. You find and finger a phrase at a time; you lay it down cautiously, as if with tongs, and wait suspended until the next one finds you: Ah yes, then this; and yes, praise be, then this.

Einstein likened the generation of a new idea to a chicken's laying an egg: *"Kieks— auf einmal ist es da."* Cheep—and all at once there it is. Of course, Einstein was not above playing to the crowd.

One January day, working alone in that freezing borrowed cabin I used for a study on Puget Sound—heated not at all by the alder I chopped every morning—I wrote one of the final passages of a short, difficult book. It was a wildish passage in which the narrator, I, came upon the baptism of Christ in the water of the bay in front of the house. There was a northeaster on—as I wrote. The stormy salt water I saw from the cabin

window looked dark as ink. The parallel rows of breakers
made lively, broken lines, closely spaced row on row, moving
fast and pulling the eyes; they reproduced the sensation of
reading exactly, but without reading's sense. Mostly I shut my
eyes. I have never been in so trancelike a state, and in fact I
dislike, as romantic, the suggestion that any writer works in
any peculiar state. I sat motionless with my eyes shut, like a
Greek funerary marble.

The writing was simple yet graceless; it surprised me. It was
arrhythmical, nonvisual, clunky. It was halting, as if there were
no use trying to invoke beauty or power. It was plain and ugly,
urgent, like child's talk. "He led him into the water," it said,
without antecedents. It read like a translation from the *Gallic
Wars.*

Once when I opened my eyes the page seemed bright. The
windows were steamed and the sun had gone behind the firs
on the bluff. I must have had my eyes closed long. I had been
repeating to myself, for hours, like a song, "It is the grave of
Jesus, where he lay." From Wallace Stevens' poem, "Sunday
Morning." It was three o'clock then; I heated some soup. By
the time I left, I was scarcely alive. The way home was along
the beach. The beach was bright and distinct. The storm still
blew. I was light, dizzy, barely there. I remembered some
legendary lamas, who wear chains to keep from floating away.
Walking itself seemed to be a stunt; I could not tell whether
I was walking fast or slowly. My thighs felt as if they had been
reamed.

And I have remembered it often, later, waking up in that
cabin to windows steamed blue and the sun gone around the
island; remembered putting down those queer, stark sentences half blind on yellow paper; remembered walking ensor-
cerized, tethered, down the gray cobble beach like an aisle.
Evelyn Underhill describes another life, and a better one, in
words that recall to me that day, and many another day, at this
queer task: "He goes because he must, as Galahad went to-

wards the Grail: knowing that for those who can live it, this alone is life."

Push it. Examine all things intensely and relentlessly. Probe and search each object in a piece of art. Do not leave it, do not course over it, as if it were understood, but instead follow it down until you see it in the mystery of its own specificity and strength. Giacometti's drawings and paintings show his bewilderment and persistence. If he had not acknowledged his bewilderment, he would not have persisted. A twentieth-century master of drawing, Rico Lebrun, taught that "the draftsman must aggress; only by persistent assault will the live image capitulate and give up its secret to an unrelenting line." Who but an artist fierce to know—not fierce to seem to know— would suppose that a live image possessed a secret? The artist is willing to give all his or her strength and life to probing with blunt instruments those same secrets no one can describe in any way but with those instruments' faint tracks.

Admire the world for never ending on you—as you would admire an opponent, without taking your eyes from him, or walking away.

One of the few things I know about writing is this: spend it all, shoot it, play it, lose it, all, right away, every time. Do not hoard what seems good for a later place in the book, or for another book; give it, give it all, give it now. The impulse to save something good for a better place later is the signal to spend it now. Something more will arise for later, something better. These things fill from behind, from beneath, like well water. Similarly, the impulse to keep to yourself what you have learned is not only shameful, it is destructive. Anything you do not give freely and abundantly becomes lost to you. You open your safe and find ashes.

After Michelangelo died, someone found in his studio a piece of paper on which he had written a note to his apprentice, in the handwriting of his old age: "Draw, Antonio, draw, Antonio, draw and do not waste time."

Chapter Six

*If this life be not a real fight, in which
something is eternally gained for the universe
by success, it is no better than a game of private
theatricals from which one may withdraw at will.
But it* feels *like a real fight.* —WILLIAM JAMES

THAT ISLAND on Haro Strait haunts me. The few people
there, unconnected to the mainland—lacking ferryboat, electrical cables, and telephone cables—lived lonesome and half
mad out in the wind and current like petrels. They had stuck
their necks out. In summer they slept in open sleep shacks on
the beach. The island lay on the northern edge of the forty-
eight states, and on the western edge of the forty-eight states,
and was fantastically difficult of access. Once you had gone so
far, you might as well test the limits, like an artist playing the
edges, and all but sleep in the waves. With my husband, I
moved there every summer; we spent a winter there, too. Our
cabin on the beach faced west, toward some distant Canadian
islands, and Japan.

The waters there were cold and deep; fierce tides ripped in
and out twice a day. The San Juan Islands aggravated tidal
currents—they made narrow channels through which enormous volumes of water streamed fast. If an ordinary tide
flowed up the beach and caught an oar or a life vest, it swept
it northward on the island faster than you could chase it walk-

ing alongside; you had to run. The incoming tide ran north; the outgoing tide drained south.

Paul Glenn was a painter, a strong-armed, soft-faced, big blond man in his fifties; every summer he lived down the beach. He was a friend of the family. One summer morning I visited him, and asked about his painting. We sat at his kitchen table.

His recent easel painting, and his study of abstract expressionist Mark Tobey's canvases, and his new interest in certain Asian subjects, his understanding of texture in two dimensions, and possibly the mistiness of the Pacific Northwest and its fabulous, busy skies—something, I do not know what, had gotten him experimenting with dipping papers into vats of water on which pools of colored oil floated. He had such papers drying on the kitchen counters. Some of them looked like a book's marbled endpapers, or fine wallpaper—merely decorative. Some others were complex and subtle surfaces, suggestive and powerful. Paul Glenn was learning which techniques of dripping the colors on the water, and which techniques of drawing the paper up through the colors, yielded the interesting results. He had been working at it for six months. How he was going to use the papers was another matter, and the crucial one: he could cut them into collage material, he could fold them into sculpture, he could paint over them and into them. He was following the work wherever it led.

The next summer, we returned to the island. Paul Glenn had spent the winter there. I visited him in his house on the beach in late June. He was tan of face already, and perfectly sane—witty and forceful, if a bit soft of voice.

I asked Paul how his work was going.

"You couldn't have known Ferrar Burn," he said. We were sitting at the round table by the kitchen window. There were white shells on the windowsill, and black beach stones. "He died twenty years ago. He was a joyful man, and a calm and determined one. He brought his family out here—June Burn, who wrote books and newspaper columns, and two little boys, you know North and Bob—out here to this island, where there's nothing but what you can find on the beach or grow."

Evidently Paul did not want to talk about how his work was going. Fair enough.

"Ferrar was striking: he had that same pale, thin skin his sons have, and their black eyes and hair. He and June built that cedar shack up on Fishery Point. It was her study. Their house was near the woods—nice timbers."

Paul knew I knew all this, except what Ferrar looked like. Paul's hair had grown long; he kept moving pale strands of it behind his ears. I was fresh from the mainland, a little too bright and quick. He laughed openly at what he could easily see was my impatience; we had been tolerant friends for a few years.

"One evening," he went on, "Ferrar saw a log floating out in the channel. It looked yellow, like Alaska cedar; he hoped it was Alaska cedar. He rowed out to get it."

Everyone on the island scavenged the valuable logs, for building. If the logs did not wash up on the beach, it took a motorboat to get them in; they were heavy in the water.

"It was high tide, slack. Ferrar saw the log, launched his little skiff at Fishery Point, and rowed out in the channel. Sure enough, it was that beautiful Alaska cedar, that pale yellow wood—just a short log, about eight feet, or he never would have tried it without a motor. I guess he thought he could row it in while the tide was still slack.

"He tied onto the log"—such logs often have a big iron staple hammered into one end—"and started rowing back home with it. He had about twenty feet of line on it. He started rowing home, and the tide caught him."

From Paul's window, I could look north up the beach and see Fishery Point. One of Ferrar's sons still used that old rowboat—a little eight-foot pram, now painted yellow and blue. Paul's blue eyes caught mine again.

"The tide started going out, and it caught that log and dragged it south. Ferrar kept rowing back north toward his house. The tide pulled him south down the strait here"—Paul indicated the long sweep of salt water in front of his house— "from one end to the other. Ferrar kept rowing toward Fishery Point. He might as well have tied onto a whale. He was rowing to the north and moving fast to the south. He traveled stern first. He wanted to be going home, so toward home he kept pulling. When the sun set, at about nine o'clock, he'd swept south the length of this beach, rowing north all the way. When the moon rose a few hours later—he told us—he saw he'd swept south past the island altogether and out into the channel between here and Stuart Island. He had been rowing through those dark hours. He continued to row away from Stuart Island and continued to see it get closer.

"Then he felt the tide go slack, and then he felt it coming in again. The current had reversed.

"Ferrar kept rowing in the half moonlight. The tide poured in from the south. He kept rowing north for home—only now the log was with him. He and his log were both floating on the current, and the current was bearing them up and carrying them like platters. It started getting light at about three o'clock, and he rowed back past this island's southern tip. The sun came up, and he rowed all the length of this beach. The tide brought him back on home. His wife, June, saw him coming; she'd been curious about him all night."

Paul had a wide, loose smile. He shifted in his chair. He raised his coffee cup, as if to say, Cheers.

"He pulled up on his own beach. They got the log rolled beyond the tideline. I saw him a few days later. Everybody knew he'd been carried out almost to Stuart Island, trying to bring in a log. Everybody knew he just kept rowing in the same direction. I asked him about it. He said he had a little backache. I didn't see the palms of his hands."

Paul looked into his empty coffee cup, pleased, and then looked through the window, still smiling. I started to carry my coffee cup to the sink, but he motioned me down. He wasn't finished.

"So that's how my work is going," he said.
What?
"You asked how my work is going," he said. "That's how it's going. The current's got me. Feels like I'm about in the middle of the channel now. I just keep at it. I just keep hoping the tide will turn and bring me in."

Anthropologist Godfrey Lienhardt describes the animistic understanding of the Dinka tribe in the Sudan. A Dinka believes his own memories and daydreams to be external to himself, as external as the hills, and quick with substance. A man who had been imprisoned in Khartoum named his infant daughter Khartoum in order to placate Khartoum, which seized him from time to time vividly. He believed that as he walked about his village, Khartoum itself, the city with its prison, overwhelmed him with the force of its presence.

So that island haunts me. I was not in prison there, but instead loosed on the shore of vastness. As I walk about this enclosed bay on Cape Cod, or as I scroll down a computer file to a blank screen, then from time to time the skies part ahead of my path, or the luminous photons on the screen revert to infinite randomness, and I balk again on the brink. The irrational haunts the metaphysical. The opposites meet in the looping sky above appearances, or in the dark alley behind appearances, where danger and power duel in a blur.

There was no continental shelf; the island beach dropped to the deep and sandless ocean floor. The water was so cold throughout the year that a man overboard died in ten minutes. Once I saw two twenty-four-man war canoes race across a passage. Forty-eight bare-chested Lummi Indians paddled them, singing. Once I saw phosphorescent seas in a winter storm in front of the cabin; in the black night black seas broke in wild lines to the horizon and spilled green foam that glowed when the wind's pitch rose, so I wept on the shore in fear.

I lived on the beach with one foot in fatal salt water and one foot on a billion grains of sand. The brink of the infinite there was too like writing's solitude. Each sentence hung over an abyssal ocean or sky which held all possibilities, as well as the possibility of nothing. In June and July, the twilight lingered till dawn. Our latitude was north of Nova Scotia; the sun never dropped low enough below the horizon to achieve what is called astronomical night. The wide days split life open like an ax. When I sketched or painted the island shore, even with the most literal intentions, the work twined into the infinite again and dissolved, or the infinite assaulted the page again and required me to represent it. My pen piled the page with changing clouds, multiple suns, circles, spirals, and rays. I used the pages at night to light fires.

"I have been doing some skying," Constable wrote a friend. I have been doing some scrolling, here and elsewhere, scrolling up and down beaches and blank monitor screens scrying for signs: dipping pens into ink, dipping papers into vats of color, dipping paddles into seas, and bearing God knows where. The green line of photons forms words at the shore of darkness. Darkness empties behind the screen in an illimitable cone. Shall we go rowing again, we who believe we may indeed row off the edge and fall? Shall we launch again into the deep and row up the skies?

Chapter Seven

It's easy, after all, not to be a writer. Most people aren't writers, and very little harm comes to them.
—JULIAN BARNES, *Flaubert's Parrot*

DAVE RAHM lived in Bellingham, Washington, north of Seattle. Bellingham, a harbor town, lies between the San Juan Islands in Haro Strait and the alpine North Cascade Mountains. I lived there between stints on the island. Dave Rahm was a stunt pilot, the air's own genius.

In 1975, with a newcomer's willingness to try anything once, I attended the Bellingham Air Show. The Bellingham airport was a wide clearing in a forest of tall Douglas firs; its runways suited small planes. It was June. People wearing blue or tan zipped jackets stood loosely on the concrete walkways and runways outside the coffee shop. At that latitude in June, you stayed outside because you could, even most of the night, if you could think up something to do. The sky did not darken until ten o'clock or so, and it never got very dark. Your life parted and opened in the sunlight. You tossed your dark winter routines, thought up mad projects, and improvised everything from hour to hour. Being a stunt pilot seemed the most reasonable thing in the world; you could wave your arms in the air all day and all night, and sleep next winter.

*   *   *

I saw from the ground a dozen stunt pilots; the air show
scheduled them one after the other, for an hour of aerobatics.
Each pilot took up his or her plane and performed a batch of
tricks. They were precise and impressive. They flew upside
down, and straightened out; they did barrel rolls, and straightened out; they drilled through dives and spins, and landed
gently on a far runway.

For the end of the day, separated from all other performances of every sort, the air show director had scheduled a
program titled "DAVE RAHM." The leaflet said that Rahm was
a geologist who taught at Western Washington University. He
had flown for King Hussein in Jordan. A tall man in the crowd
told me Hussein had seen Rahm fly on a visit the king made
to the United States; he had invited him to Jordan to perform
at ceremonies. Hussein was a pilot, too. "Hussein thought he
was the greatest thing in the world."

Idly, paying scant attention, I saw a medium-sized, rugged
man dressed in brown leather, all begoggled, climb in a black
biplane's open cockpit. The plane was a Bücker Jungman,
built in the thirties. I saw a tall, dark-haired woman seize a
propeller tip at the plane's nose and yank it down till the
engine caught. He was off; he climbed high over the airport
in his biplane, very high until he was barely visible as a mote,
and then seemed to fall down the air, diving headlong, and
streaming beauty in spirals behind him.

The black plane dropped spinning, and flattened out spinning the other way; it began to carve the air into forms that
built wildly and musically on each other and never ended.
Reluctantly, I started paying attention. Rahm drew high above
the world an inexhaustibly glorious line; it piled over our
heads in loops and arabesques. It was like a Saul Steinberg
fantasy; the plane was the pen. Like Steinberg's contracting
and billowing pen line, the line Rahm spun moved to form
new, punning shapes from the edges of the old. Like a Klee
line, it smattered the sky with landscapes and systems.

* * *

The air show announcer hushed. He had been squawking all day, and now he quit. The crowd stilled. Even the children watched dumbstruck as the slow, black biplane buzzed its way around the air. Rahm made beauty with his whole body; it was pure pattern, and you could watch it happen. The plane moved every way a line can move, and it controlled three dimensions, so the line carved massive and subtle slits in the air like sculptures. The plane looped the loop, seeming to arch its back like a gymnast; it stalled, dropped, and spun out of it climbing; it spiraled and knifed west on one side's wings and back east on another; it turned cartwheels, which must be physically impossible; it played with its own line like a cat with yarn. How did the pilot know where in the air he was? If he got lost, the ground would swat him.

Rahm did everything his plane could do: tailspins, four-point rolls, flat spins, figure 8's, snap rolls, and hammerheads. He did pirouettes on the plane's tail. The other pilots could do these stunts, too, skillfully, one at a time. But Rahm used the plane inexhaustibly, like a brush marking thin air.

His was pure energy and naked spirit. I have thought about it for years. Rahm's line unrolled in time. Like music, it split the bulging rim of the future along its seam. It pried out the present. We watchers waited for the split-second curve of beauty in the present to reveal itself. The human pilot, Dave Rahm, worked in the cockpit right at the plane's nose; his very body tore into the future for us and reeled it down upon us like a curling peel.

Like any fine artist, he controlled the tension of the audience's longing. You desired, unwittingly, a certain kind of roll or climb, or a return to a certain portion of the air, and he fulfilled your hope slantingly, like a poet, or evaded it until you thought you would burst, and then fulfilled it surprisingly, so you gasped and cried out.

The oddest, most exhilarating and exhausting thing was this: he never quit. The music had no periods, no rests or

endings; the poetry's beautiful sentence never ended; the line
had no finish; the sculptured forms piled overhead, one into
another without surcease. Who could breathe, in a world
where rhythm itself had no periods?

It had taken me several minutes to understand what an
extraordinary thing I was seeing. Rahm kept all that embel-
lished space in mind at once. For another twenty minutes I
watched the beauty unroll and grow more fantastic and unlikely before my eyes. Now Rahm brought the plane down
slidingly, and just in time, for I thought I would snap from the
effort to compass and remember the line's long intelligence;
I could not add another curve. He brought the plane down on
a far runway. After a pause, I saw him step out, an ordinary
man, and make his way back to the terminal.

The show was over. It was late. Just as I turned from the
runway, something caught my eye and made me laugh. It was
a swallow, a blue-green swallow, having its own air show,
apparently inspired by Rahm. The swallow climbed high over
the runway, held its wings oddly, tipped them, and rolled
down the air in loops. The inspired swallow. I always want to
paint, too, after I see the Rembrandts. The blue-green swallow
tumbled precisely, and caught itself and flew up again as if
excited, and looped down again, the way swallows do, but
tensely, holding its body carefully still. It was a stunt swallow.

I went home and thought about Rahm's performance that
night, and the next day, and the next.

I had thought I knew my way around beauty a little bit. I
knew I had devoted a good part of my life to it, memorizing
poetry and focusing my attention on complexity of rhythm in
particular, on force, movement, repetition, and surprise, in
both poetry and prose. Now I had stood among dandelions
between two asphalt runways in Bellingham, Washington, and
begun learning about beauty. Even the Boston Museum of
Fine Arts was never more inspiriting than this small northwest-

ern airport on this time-killing Sunday afternoon in June. Nothing on earth is more gladdening than knowing we must roll up our sleeves and move back the boundaries of the humanly possible once more.

Later I flew with Dave Rahm; he took me up. A generous geographer, Dick Smith, at Western Washington University, arranged it, and came along. Rahm and Dick Smith were colleagues at the university. In geology, Rahm had published two books and many articles. Rahm was handsome in a dull sort of way, blunt-featured, wide-jawed, wind-burned, keen-eyed, and taciturn. As anyone would expect. He was forty. He wanted to show me the Cascade Mountains; these enormous peaks, only fifty miles from the coast, rise over nine thousand feet; they are heavily glaciated. Whatcom County has more glaciers than the lower forty-eight states combined; the Cascades make the Rocky Mountains look like hills. Mount Baker is volcanic, like most Cascade peaks. That year, Mount Baker was acting up. Even from my house at the shore I could see, early in the morning on clear days, volcanic vapor rise near its peak. Often the vapor made a cloud which swelled all morning and hid the snows. Every day the newspapers reported on Baker's activity: would it blow? (A few years later, Mount St. Helens did blow.)

Rahm was not flying his trick biplane that day, but a faster, enclosed plane, a single-engine Cessna. We flew from a bumpy grass airstrip near my house, out over the coast and inland. There was coastal plain down there, but we could not see it for clouds. We were over the clouds at five hundred feet and inside them too, heading for an abrupt line of peaks we could not see. I gave up on everything, the way you do in airplanes; it was out of my hands. Every once in a while Rahm saw a peephole in the clouds and buzzed over for a look. "That's Larsen's pea farm," he said, or "That's Nooksack Road," and he changed our course with a heave.

When we got to the mountains, he slid us along Mount Baker's flanks sideways.

Our plane swiped at the mountain with a roar. I glimpsed a windshield view of dirty snow traveling fast. Our shaking, swooping belly seemed to graze the snow. The wings shuddered; we peeled away and the mountain fell back and the engines whined. We felt flung, because we were in fact flung; parts of our faces and internal organs trailed pressingly behind on the curves. We came back for another pass at the mountain, and another. We dove at the snow headlong like suicides; we jerked up, down, or away at the last second, so late we left our hearts, stomachs, and lungs behind. If I forced myself to hold my heavy head up against the g's, and to raise my eyelids, heavy as barbells, and to notice what I saw, I could see the wrinkled green crevasses cracking the glaciers' snow.

Pitching snow filled all the windows, and shapes of dark rock. I had no notion which way was up. Everything was black or gray or white except the fatal crevasses; everything made noise and shook. I felt my face smashed sideways and saw rushing abstractions of snow in the windshield. Patches of cloud obscured the snow fleetingly. We straightened out, turned, and dashed at the mountainside for another pass, which we made, apparently, on our ear, an inch or two away from the slope. Icefalls and cornices jumbled and fell away. If a commercial plane's black box, such as the FAA painstakingly recovers from crash sites, could store videotapes as well as pilots' last words, some videotapes would look like this: a mountainside coming up at the windows from all directions, ice and snow and rock filling the screen up close and screaming by.

Rahm was just being polite. His geographer colleague wanted to see the fissure on Mount Baker from which steam escaped. Everybody in Bellingham wanted to see that sooty fissure, as did every geologist in the country; no one on earth could fly so close to it as Rahm. He knew the mountain by familiar love and feel, like a face; he knew what the plane could do and what he dared to do.

When Mount Baker inexplicably let us go, he jammed us into cloud again and soon tilted. "The Sisters!" someone shouted, and I saw the windshield fill with red rock. This mountain looked infernal, a drear and sheer plane of lifeless rock. It was red and sharp; its gritty blades cut through the clouds at random. The mountain was quiet. It was in shade. Careening, we made sideways passes at these brittle peaks too steep for snow. Their rock was full of iron, somebody shouted at me then or later; the iron had rusted, so they were red. Later, when I was back on the ground, I recalled that, from a distance, the two jagged peaks called the Twin Sisters looked translucent against the sky; they were sharp, tapered, and fragile as arrowheads.

I talked to Rahm. He was flying us out to the islands now. The islands were fifty or sixty miles away. Like many other people, I had picked Bellingham, Washington, by looking at an atlas. It was clear from the atlas that you could row in the salt water and see snow-covered mountains; you could scale a glaciated mountainside with an ice ax in August, skirting green crevasses two hundred feet deep, and look out on the islands in the sea. Now, in the air, the clouds had risen over us; dark forms lay on the glinting water. There was almost no color to the day, just blackened green and some yellow. I knew the islands were forested in dark Douglas firs the size of skyscrapers. Bald eagles scavenged on the beaches; robins the size of herring gulls sang in the clearings. We made our way out to the islands through the layer of air between the curving planet and its held, thick clouds.

"When I started trying to figure out what I was going to do with my life, I decided to become an expert on mountains. It wasn't much to be, it wasn't everything, but it was something. I was going to know everything about mountains from every point of view. So I started out in geography." Geography proved too pedestrian for Rahm, too concerned with "how many bushels of wheat an acre." So he ended up in geology. Smith had told me that geology departments throughout the country used Rahm's photographic slides—close-ups of geologic features from the air.

"I used to climb mountains. But you know, you can get a better feel for a mountain's power flying around it, flying all around it, than you can from climbing it tied to its side like a flea."

He talked about his flying performances. He thought of the air as a line, he said. "This end of the line, that end of the line—like a rope." He improvised. "I get a rhythm going and stick with it." While he was performing in a show, he paid attention, he said, to the lighting. He didn't play against the sun. That was all he said about what he did.

In aerobatic maneuvers, pilots pull about seven positive g's on some stunts and six negative g's on others. Some gyrations push; others pull. Pilots alternate the pressures carefully, so they do not gray out or black out.

Later I learned that some stunt pilots tune up by wearing gravity boots. These are boots made to hook over a doorway; wearing them, you hang in the doorway upside-down. It must startle a pilot's children, to run into their father or mother in the course of their home wanderings—the parent hanging wide-eyed upside-down in the doorway like a bat.

We were landing; here was the airstrip on Stuart Island—that island to which Ferrar Burn was dragged by the tide. We put down, climbed out of the plane, and walked. We wandered a dirt track through fields to a lee shore where yellow sandstone ledges slid into the sea. The salt chuck, people there called salt water. The sun came out. I caught a snake in the salt chuck; the snake, eighteen inches long, was swimming in the green shallows.

I had a survivor's elation. Rahm had found Mount Baker in the clouds before Mount Baker found the plane. He had wiped it with the fast plane like a cloth and we had lived.

When we took off from Stuart Island and gained altitude, I asked if we could turn over—could we do a barrel roll? The plane was making a lot of noise, and Dick Smith did not hear any of this, I learned later. "Why not?" Rahm said, and added surprisingly, "It won't hurt the plane." Without ado he leaned on the wheel and the wing went down and we went somersaulting over it. We upended with a roar. We stuck to the plane's sides like flung paint. All the blood in my body bulged on my face; it piled between my skull and skin. Vaguely I could see the chrome sea twirling over Rahm's head like a baton, and the dark islands sliding down the skies like rain.

The g's slammed me into my seat like thugs and pinned me while my heart pounded and the plane turned over slowly and compacted each organ in turn. My eyeballs were newly spherical and full of heartbeats. I seemed to hear a crescendo; the wing rolled shuddering down the last ninety degrees and settled on the flat. There were the islands, admirably below us, and the clouds, admirably above. When I could breathe, I asked if we could do it again, and we did. He rolled the other way. The brilliant line of the sea slid up the side window bearing its heavy islands. Through the shriek of my blood and the plane's shakes I glimpsed the line of the sea over the windshield, thin as a spear. How in performance did Rahm keep track while his brain blurred and blood roared in his ears without ceasing? Every performance was a tour de force and a show of will, a *machtspruch.* I had seen the other stunt pilots straighten out after a trick or two; their blood could drop back and the planet simmer down. An Olympic gymnast, at peak form, strings out a line of spins ten stunts long across a mat, and is hard put to keep his footing at the end. Rahm endured much greater pressure on his faster spins using the plane's power, and he could spin in three dimensions and keep twirling till he ran out of sky room or luck.

When we straightened out, and had flown straightforwardly for ten minutes toward home, Dick Smith, clearing his throat, brought himself to speak. "What was that we did out there?"

"The barrel rolls?" Rahm said. "They were barrel rolls."
He said nothing else. I looked at the back of his head; I could
see the serious line of his cheek and jaw. He was in shirt-
sleeves, tanned, strong-wristed. I could not imagine loving
him under any circumstance; he was alien to me, unfazed. He
looked like G.I. Joe. He flew with that matter-of-fact, bored
gesture pilots use. They click overhead switches and turn dials
as if only their magnificent strength makes such dullness en-
durable. The half circle of wheel in their big hands looks like
a toy they plan to crush in a minute; the wiggly stick the wheel
mounts seems barely attached.

A crop-duster pilot in Wyoming told me the life expectancy
of a crop-duster pilot is five years. They fly too low. They hit
buildings and power lines. They have no space to fly out of
trouble, and no space to recover from a stall. We were in
Cody, Wyoming, out on the North Fork of the Shoshone
River. The crop duster had wakened me that morning flying
over the ranch house and clearing my bedroom roof by half
an inch. I saw the bolts on the wheel assembly a few feet from
my face. He was spraying with pesticide the plain old grass.
Over breakfast I asked him how long he had been dusting
crops. "Four years," he said, and the figure stalled in the air
between us for a moment. "You know you're going to die at
it someday," he added. "We all know it. We accept that; it's
part of it." I think now that, since the crop duster was in his
twenties, he accepted only that he had to say such stuff; privately he counted on skewing the curve.

I suppose Rahm knew the fact, too. I do not know how he
felt about it. "It's worth it," said the early French aviator
Mermoz. He was Antoine de Saint-Exupéry's friend. "It's
worth the final smashup."

Rahm smashed up in front of King Hussein, in Jordan,
during a performance. The plane spun down and never came
out of it; it nosedived into the ground and exploded. He
bought the farm. I was living then with my husband out on

that remote island in the San Juans, cut off from everything. Battery radios picked up the Canadian Broadcasting Company out of Toronto, half a continent away; island people would, in theory, learn if the United States blew up, but not much else. There were no newspapers. One friend got the Sunday *New York Times* by mailboat on the following Friday. He saved it until Sunday and had a party, every week; we all read the Sunday *Times* and no one mentioned that it was last week's.

One day, Paul Glenn's brother flew out from Bellingham to visit; he had a seaplane. He landed in the water in front of the cabin and tied up to our mooring. He came in for coffee, and he gave out news of this and that, and—Say, did we know that stunt pilot Dave Rahm had cracked up? In Jordan, during a performance: he never came out of a dive. He just dove right down into the ground, and his wife was there watching. "I saw it on CBS News last night." And then—with a sudden sharp look at my filling eyes—"What, did you know him?" But no, I did not know him. He took me up once. Several years ago. I admired his flying. I had thought that danger was the safest thing in the world, if you went about it right.

Later I found a newspaper. Rahm was living in Jordan that year; King Hussein invited him to train the aerobatics team, the Royal Jordanian Falcons. He was also visiting professor of geology at the University of Jordan. In Amman that day he had been flying a Pitt Special, a plane he knew well. Katy Rahm, his wife of six months, was sitting beside Hussein in the viewing stands, with her daughter. Rahm died performing a Lomcevak combined with a tail slide and hammerhead. In a Lomcevak, the pilot brings the plane up on a slant and pirouettes. I had seen Rahm do this: the falling plane twirled slowly like a leaf. Like a ballerina, the plane seemed to hold its head back stiff in concentration at the music's slow, painful beauty. It was one of Rahm's favorite routines. Next the pilot flies straight up, stalls the plane, and slides down the air on his tail. He brings the nose down—the hammerhead—kicks the engine, and finishes with a low loop.

It is a dangerous maneuver at any altitude, and Rahm was doing it low. He hit the ground on the loop; the tail slide had left him no height. When Rahm went down, King Hussein dashed to the burning plane to pull him out, but he was already dead.

A few months after the air show, and a month after I had flown with Rahm, I was working at my desk near Bellingham, where I lived, when I heard a sound so odd it finally penetrated my concentration. It was the buzz of an airplane, but it rose and fell musically, and it never quit; the plane never flew out of earshot. I walked out on the porch and looked up: it was Rahm in the black and gold biplane, looping all over the air. I had been wondering about his performance flight: could it really have been so beautiful? It was, for here it was again. The little plane twisted all over the air like a vine. It trailed a line like a very long mathematical proof you could follow only so far, and then it lost you in its complexity. I saw Rahm flying high over the Douglas firs, and out over the water, and back over farms. The air was a fluid, and Rahm was an eel.

It was as if Mozart could move his body through his notes, and you could walk out on the porch, look up, and see him in periwig and breeches, flying around in the sky. You could hear the music as he dove through it; it streamed after him like a contrail.

I lost myself; standing on the firm porch, I lost my direction and reeled. My neck and spine rose and turned, so I followed the plane's line kinesthetically. In his open-cockpit, black plane, Rahm demonstrated curved space. He slid down ramps of air, he vaulted and wheeled. He piled loops in heaps and praised height. He unrolled the scroll of the air, extended it, and bent it into Möbius strips; he furled line in a thousand new ways, as if he were inventing a script and writing it in one infinitely recurring utterance until I thought the bounds of beauty must break.

From inside, the looping plane had sounded tinny, like a

kazoo. Outside, the buzz rose and fell to the Doppler effect as the plane looped near or away. Rahm cleaved the sky like a prow and tossed out time left and right in his wake. He performed for forty minutes; then he headed the plane, as small as a wasp, back to the airport inland. Later I learned Rahm often practiced àcrobatic flights over this shore. His idea was that if he lost control and was going to go down, he could ditch in the salt chuck, where no one else would get hurt.

If I had not turned two barrel rolls in an airplane, I might have fancied Rahm felt good up there, and playful. Maybe Jackson Pollock felt a sort of playfulness, in addition to the artist's usual deliberate and intelligent care. In my limited experience, painting, unlike writing, pleases the senses while you do it, and more while you do it than after it is done. Drawing lines with an airplane, unfortunately, tortures the senses. Jet bomber pilots black out. I knew Rahm felt as if his brain were bursting his eardrums, felt that if he let his jaws close as tight as centrifugal force pressed them, he would bite through his lungs.

"All virtue is a form of acting," Yeats said. Rahm deliberately turned himself into a figure. Sitting invisible at the controls of a distant airplane, he became the agent and the instrument of art and invention. He did not tell me how he felt, when we spoke of his performance flying; he told me instead that he paid attention to how his plane and its line looked to the audience against the lighted sky. If he had noticed how he felt, he could not have done the work. Robed in his airplane, he was as featureless as a priest. He was lost in his figural aspect like an actor or a king. Of his flying, he had said only, "I get a rhythm and stick with it." In its reticence, this statement reminded me of Veronese's "Given a large canvas, I enhanced it as I saw fit." But Veronese was ironic, and Rahm was not; he was literal as an astronaut; the machine gave him tongue.

When Rahm flew, he sat down in the middle of art, and

strapped himself in. He spun it all around him. He could not see it himself. If he never saw it on film, he never saw it at all—as if Beethoven could not hear his final symphonies not because he was deaf, but because he was inside the paper on which he wrote. Rahm must have felt it happen, that fusion of vision and metal, motion and idea. I think of this man as a figure, a college professor with a Ph.D. upside down in the loud band of beauty. What are we here for? *Propter chorum,* the monks say: for the sake of the choir.

"Purity does not lie in separation from but in deeper penetration into the universe," Teilhard de Chardin wrote. It is hard to imagine a deeper penetration into the universe than Rahm's last dive in his plane, or than his inexpressible wordless selfless line's inscribing the air and dissolving. Any other art may be permanent. I cannot recall one Rahm sequence. He improvised. If Christo wraps a building or dyes a harbor, we join his poignant and fierce awareness that the work will be gone in days. Rahm's plane shed a ribbon in space, a ribbon whose end unraveled in memory while its beginning unfurled as surprise. He may have acknowledged that what he did could be called art, but it would have been, I think, only in the common misusage, which holds art to be the last extreme of skill. Rahm rode the point of the line to the possible; he discovered it and wound it down to show. He made his dazzling probe on the run. "The world is filled, and filled with the Absolute," Teilhard de Chardin wrote. "To see this is to be made free."